Jon Sobrino

JESUS THE LIBERATOR

A Historical-Theological Reading
of Jesus of Nazareth

Translated from the Spanish by
Paul Burns and Francis McDonagh

ORBIS BOOKS

Maryknoll, New York 10545

The Catholic Foreign Mission Society of America (Maryknoll) recruits and trains people for overseas missionary service. Through Orbis Books, Maryknoll aims to foster the international dialogue that is essential to mission. The books published, however, reflect the opinions of their authors and are not meant to represent the official position of the society.

First published in this translation in Great Britain 1994 by Burns & Oates, Wellwood, North Farm Road, Tunbridge Wells, Kent TN2 3DR and in the United States of America 1993 by Orbis Books, Maryknoll, New York 10545

Published originally in Spain by Editorial Trotta, S.A., Madrid, under the title *Jesucristo liberador. Lectura historica-teológica de Jesús de-Nazaret* in 1991

Original edition © Copyright Editora Vozes Ltda and Editorial Trotta, S.A., 1991

English translation © Orbis Books, 1993

Typeset in Great Britain, printed in the United States of America

ORBIS ISBN 0-88344-930-7

This book is dedicated to the memory of
Ignacio Ellacuría, Segundo Montes, Ignacio Martín Baró,
Juan Ramón Moreno, Amando López, Joaquín López y López,
Julia Elba Ramos and Celina Ramos

Contents

PART III
THE CROSS OF JESUS

Abbreviations and Short Forms

ECA   *Estudios Centroamericanos.* San Salvador.

GS   *Gaudium et spes.* Vatican II, Pastoral Constitution on the Church in the Modern World. Translations are from Walter Abbott, ed., *The Documents of Vatican II.* Piscataway, N.J.: America Press, 1966 and London—Dublin: Geoffrey Chapman, 1966.

Medellín   Second General Conference of Latin American Bishops, held in Medellín, Colombia, in 1968. Translations of the final documents are in *The Church in the Present-day Transformation of of Latin America.* Washington, D.C.: USCC, 1970.

OCD   F.L. Cross, ed., *The Oxford Dictionary of the Christian Church.* London—New York—Toronto: OUP, 1957.

PL   *Patrologiae Cursus Completus, Series Latina.* Ed. J. P. Migne. Paris, 1844-55

Puebla   Third General Conference of Latin American Bishops, held in Puebla, Mexico, in 1979. Translation of the final document in J. Eagleson and P. Scharper eds, *Puebla and Beyond.* Maryknoll, N.Y.: Orbis, 1980; also in *Puebla.* Slough: St Paul, London: CIIR, 1980.

RLT   *Revista Latinoamericana de Teología.* San Salvador.

ST   St Thomas Aquinas, *Summa Theologiae.*

UR   *Unitatis redintegratio.* Vatican II, Decree on Ecumenism. In Abbott, *Documents of Vatican II.*

Introduction

Why Another Book of Christology?

1. Foreword by Way of Confession

This book seeks to present the Christ who is Jesus of Nazareth, and so I have called it "Jesus the liberator." This choice of title was not easy, however, since writing from Latin America and specifically from El Salvador, we tend to speak of "Jesus Christ crucified." Faith points ineluctably to the first title; history forcefully reminds us of the second. Nevertheless it is a fact that the return to Jesus of Nazareth has been the means of retrieving, historically too, a new image of Christ and that this has developed a fruitful faith for believers, for the church and for the processes of liberation. Therefore, this book is written in the midst of crucifixion, but definitely in the hope of liberation.

Liberation and crucifixion provide the basic tension for Christian faith and also the basic objective tension in christology on this continent. Here I prefer to concentrate on the tensions inherent in the mere fact of trying to write a christology. So, by way of personal confession, I wish to start with some questions that faced me as I began to write this book. Is it possible to write a christology? And, more importantly, is it a useful thing to do? Do we need one? These questions are not purely rhetorical, even if they may look it. At the least they should indicate that this book has not been written as an intellectual exercise, nor as a routine one, and they should also serve as a warning against the tendency to trivialize the object of christology, Jesus Christ. So let us tackle these questions.

Of course it is *possible* to write a christology, since many have been written over the centuries and still are being written. But in our days, theology is being overtaken by a feeling of professional impotence in the face of innumerable writings of every sort about Jesus Christ. It is practically impossible to keep track of everything written from exegetic, dogmatic and systematic disciplines on Jesus Christ,[1] to take account of the new christologies being produced in other parts of the Third World, Asia and Africa,[2] and those being rewritten from a woman's standpoint.[3] And it is quite impossible to take account of all the existential

1

christologies at work in the faith and religious practice of peoples, whether in liberating practice, popular religious expression, the infinitely varied religious expression of charismatic movements and sects, the "syncretist" expression of the indigenous Latin American peoples....[4] And yet all these christologies, learned and popular, should in principle be taken into account. José Ignacio González Faus is therefore right to begin his own christology with the confession: "Through my most grevious fault. For the brazenness and audacity of daring to write a christology."[5]

The difficulty is not only technical, however; it goes deeper than this. It stems from the very "object" of christology, Jesus Christ, whom we proclaim in faith as the real, true and unsurpassable manifestation of the mystery of God and the mystery of human beings. To face up to something that is really "mystery" is not easy, to formulate it and conceptualize it is even harder, to do so adequately is impossible. Faith gives this unfathomable mystery a name, "Jesus Christ," but christology cannot exhaust this—I trust it never will—and should not give the impression of knowing too much about Jesus Christ, which will only turn out later to be the most obvious form of not knowing.

And let it not be thought that writing about a "liberator" Christ—a more historical one, therefore—diminishes the difficulty. It is true that the term "liberation" describes realities that are not at all mysterious, but clear and necessary: the end of oppression and crucifixion, the life and dignity of the poor and of all.... But this same word "liberation" also points to a utopia—"integral" liberation in the true sense, though one little used by the magisterium—that of the Kingdom of God coming to be a reality and human beings coming to be simply human. This is why in Latin America we have devised the happy and necessary expression *"mysterium" liberationis.*[6] Nor must one forget that this liberation is brought about in the midst of and in the teeth of the presence of an evil so omnipresent, aberrant and enslaving, that it has to be called by its traditional name, *"mysterium" iniquitatis.*

Christology, then, is up against a mystery. This does not mean that its object is obscure or enigmatic, as if Christ could not be the object of knowledge and reflection. But it does mean that in this object there is as it were an "excess" of luminosity in the presence of an "excess" of historical darkness, and that it therefore always surpasses knowledge. The fact that Jesus Christ is a mystery always imposes a reserve on all christology, which is why Leonardo Boff starts his book on Jesus Christ with this quote from Bonhoeffer: "Speaking of Christ means being silent."[7] So reflecting on the possibility of christology always means taking account of what is impossible in christology, and therefore of the need to partner words with silence, truth with provisionality.

In the second place, I do believe that christology is *useful*, that it can present Christ in a manner beneficial to the faith of believers, to the life of the church and to the configuration of history, but again, without rushing in. Above all, we need to remember that christologies are "transitory compositions that use contingent conceptual instruments",[8] that is, that they are by their nature conceptually limited.

But beyond this limitation, christology can be useful to good ends, but can also be used to bad ends, which should not surprise us, since, being made by human beings, it is also subject to sinfulness and manipulation. We should not forget that historically there have been heretical christologies, which have truncated the total truth of Christ, and, worse, there have been objectively harmful christologies, which have put forward a different Christ and even one objectively contrary to Jesus of Nazareth. Let us remember that this continent has been subjected to centuries of inhuman and anti-Christian oppression, without christology giving any sign of having noticed this and certainly without it providing any prophetic denunciation in the name of Jesus Christ.

In this way christology, even in its orthodox forms, can become a mechanism to prevent faith from guiding the faithful to reproduce the reality of Jesus in their own lives and to build the Kingdom of God, proclaimed by Jesus, in history. This is why Juan Luis Segundo, using a deliberately shocking expression, set out to write an "anti-christology," "a speaking about Jesus that opens a way to seeing him as witness to a still more human and liberated life."[9] Christology therefore has to put an end to the apparent innocence of supposing that the mere fact of writing about Jesus means that what is said is first useful and then used correctly.

It should not be surprising for theologians to set out their own limitations in christology; a minimum of honesty should force them to ask if they are going to bring their own limitations to it, and what these are, what dangers might be produced—even when they set out to write a christology on the so holy and true theme of "the liberating Jesus Christ." All theologians bring their own limitations, and even their own sinfulness. We can only hope that christology will be useful, without forgetting that it can be useless, and even harmful.

Christology is, finally, *necessary*, since human beings are always affected, astonished or challenged by important realities, and this forces them to think. Christians, furthermore, are explicitly told to give reasons for the hope that they have (1 Pet. 3:15). And in Latin America, as we shall see, christology is a necessity for historical reasons: we need to present a Christ who, as a minimum, is the ally of liberation, not of oppression. But none of this can silence the question of what is most necessary and whether and how christology relates to this.

If I may be allowed a personal comment, I have often thought, on seeing the proliferation of books on Christ—including my own—that if we Christians could put into practice a modest percentage of what is said in any normal work of christology, the world would change radically—and the world is not changing radically. This, of course, is not just the fault of christology. But it does make one think that in certain quarters there might be a sort of avidity and curiosity to see "what the latest book of christology has to say," and that christologies thereby become market products or views put about in the Athenian market-place, from which we can all pick and choose at whim, compare them, discuss them, defend them or attack them . . . while everything stays exactly the same in reality.

We sincerely believe that the new Latin American christology has tried to serve "the one thing necessary," but there is still a fear of what J. L. Sicre denounced in his book on the prophets of Israel happening: "The best way of avoiding the word of God is to study the word of God."[10]

So, before starting a christology and before Jesus passes through the filter of concept and loses his freshness, it is good and necessary to allow oneself to be affected and challenged by the gospel. It is true that without the reasoning supplied by christology, reading the gospel can and usually does degenerate into dangerous fundamentalism, and this provides the need for christology. But we must be careful not to end up as enlightened christologues and illiterates of the gospel, of overcoming "fundamentalism" while losing sight of the "fundamentals," what the whole world understands (or should understand) without too many explanations: Jesus' option for the poor, his mercy and justice, his confrontation with the powerful, his persecution and death resulting from all this, his revindicating resurrection. And above all, that it is this Jesus we have to follow.

All I have said so far undoubdtedly contains a lot of rhetoric, but it is not all rhetoric. And so at least one important conclusion can be drawn from it: the modesty of christology. This modesty is imposed on it objectively—something that has escaped the exaggerated "christocentrism" of Western theology—by Christ himself who, in John's theology, tends to withdraw in favour of the Spirit.[11] But I am referring here to the modest frame of mind that should inform all christology. If Pascal is right in stating that without Jesus Christ we do not know who God is or who human beings are, nor what life is and what death is, then the modesty required is clearly not fictitious. It is still less so if we add that without Jesus Christ we cannot fully know what liberation is or what oppression is, nor who the God of life is and what the idols of death are. Christology certainly needs a maximum of intellectual strictness and energy, but it also needs a chastity of the intelligence. It needs to immerse itself in the mystery of Christ, but without touching him, so to speak, without trying to get hold of him.

2. The Reason for this Christology

Having said all that, I obviously need to give some reason for producing a new book of christology. I think there are two types of reason, one more contextual, having to do with the relevance of christology to the present situation, the other more specific, having to do with its permanent character.

Of the contextual reasons, the first is ethical in nature. In Latin America, Jesus is still an important reality; he is present to the masses, unlike in Africa and Asia, and he is still actively present, unlike in Europe and the First World in general. This presence is differentiated, naturally, but whether it is as a reality of faith or as a historical personage or as a socio-cultural symbol, it is there. And not only is it there, but it is used, in very varied ways, to defend one type or another of human, social and even political venture. All this to different degrees, of course, but it still seems to me accurate to state that in a still culturally and socially Christian continent all are concerned to have Jesus Christ on their side, or at least not to seem to have him against them. In this situation, given that Jesus Christ is in fact used, it is the responsibility of christology to show his true face, so that he may be used well, so that Jesus Christ may be at the service of the *mysterium liberationis* and against the *mysterium iniquitatis*.

The second reason is ecclesial. Changes in the church, whether in the direction of renovation, conservation or restoration, always seek to justify themselves by a certain image of Christ. Even when many normative church documents on its own nature exist, the intuition—correct in itself—persists that beyond such documents the final criterion of truth has to be sought in Christ. Therefore, in the present church situation of internal divisions and conflicts, all sides appeal to Christ. So it is important to put forward the truest possible image of Christ, and, where the building of the church is concerned, to put forward the image that will best serve it in its formation as church of the poor, as it calls itself in its own documents.

Of the specific reasons, the first is set out by Jesus himself. To grasp him in faith we have to let him ask: "And you, who do you say that I am?" (Mark 8:29). An answer, then, is not optional, and if it is a reflective and conceptualized answer, it is already, in some sense, christology. And if Christ is grasped in his "universal significative intention,"[12] then, furthermore, there has to be not just a christology, but a history of christologies in order to deal tangentially in history with its subject matter.

In Latin America, being questioned like this has another, existentially more radical expression. Both Christ and the continent are today crucified. And their crosses do not just make one think and change one's manner of thinking, they *force* one to think. The relatively pacific "who do you say that I am?" becomes a pressing question in the mouth of the crucified Christ and of the crucified people. "Suffering precedes thinking," said Feuerbach, but the suffering of the cross also forcibly produces thinking. If the situation of crucified peoples—and of Christ in them— does not force us to think, one can ask what will, or what other thinking can be more necessary and urgent than this.

The second specific reason also stems directly from the reality of Christ. To grasp him in faith we have to understand him as *eu-aggelion*, good news, the appearance of the goodness of God (Tit. 3:4). This means that Christ, if grasped as such, produces joy and gratitude, and no joy and gratitude remain dumb for ever. In many places in Latin America, unlike in other parts of the world, Christ is grasped as good news too, not just as crucified. So Christians talk of Christ with gratitude, and out of gratitude they talk of Christ. And the same happens in christology.

In words devoid of cheap spirituality but full of spiritual strength and intellectual precision, Leonardo Boff states that "the true theologian can speak only from Jesus, that is, moved by his reality experienced in faith and love."[13] What I should like to add is that this experience not only enables us, but forces us to speak. Christology is also done out of gratitude and love.

We have to speak, on the one hand, out of the pain produced by seeing Christ made the object of hijacks and distortions, so that we must go out and do battle and give ourselves up for him, in an attempt to make it harder for people to say of him the terrible words used of God in the scriptures: "because of you his name is blasphemed among the nations." And, on the other hand, we have to speak of Christ out of the joy he produces: "We give thanks to you, Father, for your Son Jesus."

3. Purpose, Content and Basic Orientation of this Book

Explaining the reasoning behind this work already hints at its purpose, but let me spell it out. The *purpose* of this christology is to put forward the truth of Christ from the standpoint of liberation, and this means that it follows the lines I have set out some years ago.[14] In this sense, this christology does not claim to offer a totally original viewpoint, although it does go deeper into central issues of oppression and liberation. The reason for this stress is that liberation is correlative to oppression, and this, in the shape of unjust poverty—to which must be added ethnic, cultural, sexual and other oppressions[15]—not only has not disappeared but has generally increased. To the reader who feels disapppointed by the prospect of "more of the same," I can only say that on this continent we still have "the same" oppression, and that this is on the increase, as the statistics show.

This fact is basic, and I have to insist on it because in some quarters the theology of liberation is spoken of as though it were a passing fashion and one that has already given all it had to give. But whether the specific products of the theology of liberation satisfy or not is one thing, and whether the reality of oppression is a passing fashion is quite another. Most regrettably, it certainly is not. And this, at the very least, should be borne in mind by those who state that this theology is a "contextual" theology. The context, certainly, is what goes on requiring more, not less, liberation, what goes on requiring a christology of liberation.[16]

The *content* of this christology is Jesus Christ in his totality. In this volume, after some methodological chapters, I make a historical-theological reading of the Christ who is Jesus of Nazareth, and in a second, forthcoming volume I shall examine the history of christologies and of faith in Jesus of Nazareth proclaimed as the Christ after his resurrection.

In this volume, I set out the life of Jesus in relation to three central dimensions of his life: his service to the *Kingdom of God*, his relationship to *God-the-Father* and his death on the cross. Throughout this, I endeavour to stress the liberative, and so good-news, dimension of both Jesus' *mission* and his *person*. Jesus' mission is good news (the Kingdom, God's mediation) and it is also good news that it is this very Jesus of Nazareth (God's mediator) who carries it out.[17]. From this point of view, this christology seeks to give emphasis and primacy to the flesh of Jesus and to encourage us, as the author of the Letter to the Hebrews says, to keep "our eyes fixed on Jesus" (Heb. 12:2).

The second volume will deal with the final reality of Jesus proclaimed as the Christ after the resurrection and confessed as true God and true man in dogma. This will be done out of plain believing and ecclesial fidelity, but also because, as González Faus says, christological dogma offers "a structuring category of reality."[18] If Christ is like this, then reality too can be understood as the presence of transcendence in history,[19] each with the proper identity and autonomy, without mixture or separation, by which I mean without the reductionisms that empoverish both, to which human beings are so prone. That reality should be thus is, I hold, a good thing, and accepting that it is thus is also liberating.

Let me add for the sake of clarity that presenting the content of Christ from a liberationist standpoint is, undoubtedly, a methodological choice, but it is not an arbitrary choice, nor is there any reason why it should be a manipulative choice. I shall analyze this in Part I, but for the moment let me simply say this: it is not theoretically manipulative, since there is ample biblical evidence for seeing the person and mission of Christ as primarily liberative, and let us not forget that both New Testament and patristic christologies were made from a salvationist stand-point; nor is it empirically manipulative, since experience shows that approaching Jesus Christ from liberation is generally—though there are always exceptions— more of a help than a hindrance to grasping and confessing his totality; and finally it is not manipulative because christological reflections that start from the liberative aspect do not usually reduce the totality of Christ, but, on the contrary, rediscover dimensions of him absent from other christologies. In this sense, it is not right to affirm that the theology (and christology) of liberation is a "genitive" theology, concerned solely with being "of liberation." This is certainly its main concern, but this leads it to concern itself with the whole of theology and, in this case, of christology.

Finally, a word on the *orientation* of this christology. The "modesty" I mentioned earlier has its counterpart in the way christology can become mystagogy: that is, an introduction to the mystery. More specifically, this means that christology can show a way—that of Jesus—in which human beings can meet the mystery, call it "Father," as Jesus did, and name this Jesus as the Christ. Christology needs to and must draw out the powers of human intelligence, but also other human powers. Its approach has to be rigorously intellectual—even doctrinal, some would add— but its deepest essence lies in being something "spiritual";[20] in that it should help persons and communities to meet Christ, to follow the cause of Jesus, to live as new men and women and to conform this world to the heart of God.

4. A Christology from El Salvador, a Crucified People Living in Hope

To close this long introduction, I should say that the process of writing this book has been a slow one, owing to the situation in El Salvador. To put it simply, there has not been much time to read and research all that I should have liked and should have done. This book has been written in the middle of war, of threats, of conflict and persecution, producing innumerable emergencies requiring an immediate response, and therefore innumerable interruptions to the work schedule. The murder-martyrdom of my brother Jesuits, of Julia Elba and Celina Ramos, left my heart frozen and virtually empty. But this is not the whole, or even the major significance of this book being written in El Salvador.

The reality of this country has made me think a lot, and has also helped me to think about Jesus Christ. This is why I began this introduction by asking about the most appropriate title: Jesus liberator or crucified. In any case, so much tragedy and so much hope, so much sin and so much grace provide a powerful hermeneutical backdrop for understanding Christ and give the gospel the taste of reality.

The gospel's finest and most original phrases—often taken for granted in christologies—resound here with real power, as something real. It is a fact that there are crucified peoples, "flogged Christs," and this gives a better understanding of Christ, the Suffering Servant of Yahweh, hidden among the poor. It is a fact that there are innumerable martyrs who have given their lives out of love and who are still present and active, and this helps us understand the martyr Jesus who was raised from among the dead. It is a fact that my brethren, the four U.S. missionaries and so many others are good news for the poor of this world, and this helps us understand Jesus and his God as good news. It is a fact that "in Monsignor Romero, God passed through El Salvador," as Ignacio Ellacuría said, and this helps us understand that in Jesus, God passed through this world.

So many witnesses and martyrs, so many Christian men and women who are like Jesus, who make one think about Jesus and put one in mind of him. With his usual flair, Karl Rahner said that being human is "a defective mode of being Christ." The "defective" puts us in the realm of hope, but that there should really be "modes of being Christ" is a cause for thanksgiving, in one's personal life above all, but also in the theoretical task of trying to write a christology.

The challenge posed by the situation of El Salvador does not render christology superfluous, but makes it all the more necessary to put all one's intellect into elaborating a christology that will help the resurrection of the Salvadorean people. But I also honestly believe—although the only argument I can put forward is the vulnerable one of reality—that this reality itself clarifies what divinity is and what humanity is, and the Christ who brings the two together.

In the final analysis, this book does no more than—from Jesus—raise the reality I have been experiencing into a theological concept, reflect on a christological faith I find as a living faith, and no more than present Christ, the great witness to God, from the sources in theology, of course, but also from the cloud of witnesses who shed light on the witness by definition. Because of this, despite everything, this book has been written in hope and joy. The crucified Jesus Christ, so omnipresent, is really good news, is truly a liberator Jesus Christ.

PART I

THE METHOD OF LATIN AMERICAN CHRISTOLOGY

Chapter 1

A New Image and a New Faith in Christ

In Latin America, faith in Christ succeeded in surviving through the centuries without special christological discussions, and it could be said that there was no specifically Latin American christology.[1] It is true that at its beginnings there was very powerful meditation on the presence of Christ in the oppressed Indians, which objectively pointed towards a christology of the "body of Christ." Guamán Poma, for example, said, "By faith we know clearly that where there is a poor person there is Jesus Christ himself,"[2] and Bartolomé de las Casas declared, "In the Indies I leave Jesus Christ, our God, being whipped and afflicted, and buffeted and crucified, not once but thousands of times, as often as the Spaniards assault and destroy those people."[3] But this original christological insight did not thrive,[4] and what became the tradition was a christology based on the dogmatic formulas, in which—however well they were known and understood—what was stressed was the divinity of Christ rather than his real and lived humanity.

However, if there were no Latin American christologies until a few years ago, there were certainly images of Christ. On the one hand, there was the image corresponding to the official christology, an abstract image that gave no value to what was central in Jesus of Nazareth. On the other hand, there was the image that stressed the suffering of Jesus on the cross with which the poor identified, and with which they associated their own specific suffering—massive, cruel, imposed and unjust—which has accompanied them from the moment Christ was first preached to them until today.

From the beginning the defeated Indians who accepted Christ did so in a particular way. They did not adopt him in a syncretistic way, but, of the Christ brought by the conquerors they adopted precisely what made them most like him: a Christ who had himself been annihilated and conquered. In this suffering Christ they recognized themselves, and from him they learned patience and resignation to enable them to survive with a minimum of feeling on the cross that was laid on them.[5] What popular religion did down through the centuries, consciously or

11

unconsciously, was to reinterpret the divinity of Christ (and the closeness to God of the Virgin and the saints) as a symbol of the ultimate redoubt of power in the face of its impotence, but what it really sought was consolation in its desolation. Until today the Christ of the poor masses of Latin America is the suffering Christ, with the result that Holy Week is the most important religious occasion of the year, and within that Good Friday, and within that the laying of Christ in the tomb.

1. "Christ the Liberator": the New Image and New Faith of the Oppressed

The image of Christ and the inflicting of suffering have been connected in Latin America from the beginning, and continue to be so. Nevertheless, something new and surprising happened some years ago. The traditional suffering Christ came to be seen, not just as a symbol of suffering to be identified with, but also and especially as a symbol of protest against that suffering and, above all, as a symbol of liberation. "Today in the faith experience of many Christians in Latin America," Leonardo Boff wrote in 1974, "Jesus is seen and loved as the Liberator."[6] This is something new and, after centuries of a one-sided image of Christ, really surprising.

The fact that this new image of Christ exists is what we may call the most important christological fact in Latin America, a real "sign of the times," however widespread it may be, a point I shall come back to. The truth of this image will need to be established, but, starting from the other end, I shall begin by describing it to introduce the topic, since, as something real, it is what will inspire my presentation of Christ.

As a general justification of this choice, let me say that this image better conveys the relevance of Christ for a continent of oppression because it is "liberating," and better recovers the identity of Christ—without losing his totality—because it directs us to "Jesus of Nazareth." And in this historic coincidence of relevance and identity, Latin American christology differs from others, produced in the First World, whose underlying problem is precisely to unify the two. Walter Kasper's words at the beginning of his christology speak volumes: "If the Church worries about identity, it risks a loss of relevance; if, on the other hand, it struggles for relevance, it may forfeit its identity."[7] Latin American christology, in contrast, offers a new real image that unifies both. Let us look at the essentials of this image.

(a) Christ is seen, and this and other terms are used to describe him, above all as *liberator*, with the power to liberate from the various types of slavery that afflict the poor of this continent, to give direction to this liberation and to inspire believers to be its active agents. From this point of view, this image is essentially soteriological for the present, but it also has a New Testament origin in a very precise sense: it retrieves the Jesus of Nazareth sent "to bring good news to the poor [and] to proclaim release to the captives" (Luke 4:18). From this central fact it revalues the whole life, action and destiny of Jesus in such a way that Christ the liberator—without any implication of ignoring the totality of Christ—is, first and foremost, Jesus of Nazareth, the so-called *historical Jesus*.

(b) Corresponding to this new image is *a new way of living faith* in Christ. Many Christians today believe—existentially—in a way that is different and even contrary to their former way, have undergone a radical conversion in their mode of belief and have borne witness to it by an impressive commitment that includes sacrificing their lives. Many Christians have been murdered in Latin America, but not just any Christians, rather those who act consistently in accordance with the new image of Christ the liberator. This fact of generalized martyrdom is the best proof that there really is a new image of Christ, one more faithful to the Christ who is Jesus. Faith in Christ means, first and foremost, *following Jesus.*

(c) This Christ and this faith also provoke *conflict.* Jesus is *for* some, the oppressed, and *against* others, the oppressors. The poor proclaim him as the true Christ, while their oppressors warn against him, attack him, or at the very least seek to introduce other, alienating images of Christ.[8] Following Jesus essentially involves conflict because it means reproducing a way of acting in favour of one group of people and against another, and this gives rise to attacks and persecution. All this is well known and I will come back to it later. What must be added here to avoid oversimplification is that this new image also provokes conflict among the poor because, while all of them seek the same salvation, that is, to deal with the essentials of life with a minimum of efficiency and dignity,[9] christological images of salvation that are anti-liberation keep appearing, such as those associated with spiritualist movements and sects, "Jesus saves" or "Glory to the Lord." This is understandable because in socio-economic situations as tragic today as they were in the past, except that they are enduring and even worsening after the failure of so many hopes for liberation, there is nothing left for many poor people except to cling—albeit in very different outward forms—to the core of the old image, a Christ from whom alone salvation is to be expected, but a salvation that in the last resort is only transcendental, because it seems impossible to attain in history.[10]

Also, one should not exaggerate the quantitative spread of the new image and the new faith, when both are under constant attack from opposed understandings of religion and not sufficiently supported by the institutional church, and so I need to give some explanation for beginning with this image and this faith. First of all, the quantitative argument is not decisive for christology,[11] though it is extremely important for pastoral work. What must be appreciated is the qualitative dimension, and that is impressive. After five centuries an image of Christ has appeared that is different from and existentially contrary to the traditional one. This image has spread sufficiently widely throughout the Latin American continent and, most important of all, has been accepted with surprising universality—unlike the fate of other images of Christ in other places—by educated Christians and the masses, by bishops and lay people, by Latin Americans and those in solidarity with them in other parts of the world. This image and this faith are holding their own despite their intrinsic difficulty and the trials they have had to undergo. And finally, they continue to be the image and the faith that are absolutely necessary—from the point of view of the gospel—in the current situation of the continent.

Whatever may be the scale and the future of the two phenomena, the fact in itself deserves due recognition. It is, and still remains today, the fundamental christological fact of Latin America.[12] Whatever its future, the Christ behind this image and this faith is today something real; it is the Christ whom churches and peoples most need (relevance), and the one most like Jesus (identity). It is therefore also the Christ of whom most account should be taken in the development of a christology.

2. The New Image of Christ as a Break with Alienating Images

This image of Christ the liberator ought not to be new, since it is substantially the image of Jesus in the Gospels, as is admitted in a sense even by the two Vatican Instructions on liberation theology. "The Gospel of Jesus Christ is a message of liberty and a force for liberation."[13] "The gospel . . . is, by its very nature, a message of freedom and liberation."[14] But this has not been the case, and the consequences are well-known and objectively scandalous. Latin America, a massively Christian continent, has experienced appalling oppression without faith in Christ raising any questions about this or the image of Christ encouraging a suspicion that something was very wrong on the continent. From that point of view, the new image of Christ expresses at least that suspicion, and at a deeper level signifies the abolition of that scandalous situation. If for no other reason than this, the new image would have done immense good.

Why this scandal occurred in the past can be explained by various reasons, of course. For the moment I shall concentrate on the more specifically christological ones: that is, how traditional christologies made possible and even encouraged an image of Christ that could be used by the powerful and in such a way that the poor had no alternative but to cling to the one-sided suffering image. I shall analyze them also because this is not just past history; these images are reviving and being encouraged in various ways now.

The basic mechanism that produced the scandalous situation outlined above consisted, schematically, of the following steps: forget and reduce Jesus of Nazareth, so distort Christ and frequently turn him into his opposite. To put it bluntly, Christ was presented in such a way that believers, in order to be such, had no reason to resemble Jesus or follow and carry out Jesus' mission in support of the oppressed. What God had joined together—the bearer of the messianic hopes and the liberation of the oppressed—was put asunder and even into opposition through an image of Christ without Jesus.

Without being anachronistic, we now need to analyze what was the objective responsibility—whatever the subjective intention—of the procedure adopted by christologies in this scandalous situation. I say "procedure" because the issue is not the content of this or that christology, but something more important, an attitude widespread until a few years ago in which Christ in himself was approached with not even a suspicion, at least consciously, that the ways used to present him were those that suited the powerful and the oppressors. Let us look systematically at the fundamental structures of this distortion of Christ.

(a) An "Abstract" Christ

Christologies usually offered an image of Christ as a sublime abstraction. "Sublimity" as essential to an object of faith is obvious, but the "abstraction" is extremely dangerous. This abstraction is possible because the sublime title "Christ" is an adjective which only receives its specific value from the specificity of the noun, Jesus of Nazareth. If Jesus is forgotten, then it becomes possible to fill the adjective with whatever suits at the time, without checking whether Jesus was like that or not, or whether this means leaving the world sunk in its wretchedness or not; or worse still, without asking if this image legitimates the tragedy of the world or brings liberation from it.

What I called possible very often really happened. The abstract Christ was fleshed out, sometimes with the aid of something good in itself, sometimes with something extremely dangerous. In both cases, however, the consequences for the poor were disastrous.

As an example of the first type, I shall mention the image of *Christ as love*. This asserts something true, obviously, but as long as there is no statement, in terms of Jesus, of what this love consists, what its forms and priorities are, the love remains abstract; it may include, but also exclude or even reject, fundamental forms of Jesus' love, such as justice and loving partiality for the poor. For centuries, the "charitable" or purely "assistentialist" Christ made us ignore or even reject Jesus the prophet of justice. The consequence of this serious reduction was advantage for a minority and a neglect of justice for the majority.

As an example of the second type, I shall mention the image of *Christ as power*. It is completely understandable that popular religion should seek a power in Christ, but traditionally Christ as power has been (and continues to be) the image desired above all by the powerful. To obtain it they have to understand power in precisely the opposite way to that in which Jesus understood it, power that is above and because it is above is sanctioned by God. The "powerful" Christ and the "almighty" Lord who are above made us ignore and reject Jesus, whose power is service and whose place is below, in the power of truth and love. They made it seem right that the place of power has to be above, because above is where Christ is. The consequences are to reinforce the sinful tendency to understand power in terms of effectiveness, as imposition sliding into oppression and so to justify, in Christ's name, all sorts of authoritarianism and despotism in state and church.

(b) Christ the "Reconciler"

This is another example of sublime abstraction, and I am mentioning it explicitly because of its impact on the glaring conflicts in Latin American society.

It is a fundamental truth that Christ is the reconciliation of human and divine, as the conciliar statements say, the "recapitulation of everything," in the beautiful words of Irenaeus. But these statements are dangerous if made without sufficient dialectic. In theoretical terms, it is dangerous to pass off as an adequate historical statement what is essentially a limiting, eschatological statement. Historically, it is dangerous to profess faith in Christ the reconciler without having Jesus of Nazareth firmly in mind, and it is dangerous, when remembering him, to present a peaceable Jesus with no prophetic condemnation, a Jesus who proclaimed beatitudes for the poor (who, moreover, were usually not taken to be real poor people) and no curses on the rich, a Jesus who loves everyone, but without specifying the different forms this love takes, defending the poor and issuing a radical call on their oppressors to be converted.

Traditional soteriology, too, has contributed to this naive and too readily reconciling vision of Christ by interpreting his cross as the transcendental reconciliation of God with human beings but outside the context of the historical conflict caused by historical human sins. Paradoxically, the cross has been used as a symbol for the greatest of conflicts and the greatest of sins on the cosmic and transcendental plane, but not to reflect the most serious conflicts and the historical sins that led Jesus to the cross and that today lead the crucified peoples there.

The practical consequences of this have been to produce an image of Christ devoid of the real conflict of history and Jesus' stand on it, which has encouraged quietist or ultra-pacifist ideologies and support for anything going by the name "law and order."

(c) An "Absolutely Absolute" Christ

This criticism may seem shocking, since it is obvious that, for Christian faith, Christ is an absolute, and it may also seem unjust, since the faith itself—and christologies usually advert to this—has always presented Christ essentially "in relation" to the Father and Spirit within the Trinity.

Nevertheless the statement must be criticized if it leads us to ignore Jesus' constitutive historical relatedness to the Kingdom of God and the God of the Kingdom. For this reason, Jesus' transcendent trinitarian relatedness has to be supplemented by his historical relatedness: the fact that Jesus did not exist for himself, but had a reference point in the Kingdom of God and the God of the Kingdom, a Kingdom which, even after the resurrection, is attributed to the Father, until he is all in all (1 Cor. 15:28). I shall analyze this historical relatedness in detail later, but I want to say here that this reminder is important because of the consequences drawn from an "absolutely absolute" image of Christ, that is, when Christ the mediator is made absolute and there is no sense of his constitutive relatedness to what is mediated, the Kingdom of God.

One consequence is to make possible a personalist reduction of the faith, which has led, again, to an abandoning of the historical world to its wretchedness. This is the image of Christ as the ultimate "thou," in relation to whom Christian faith is decided and reaches its highest expression. The ideal of being for Christ, loving Christ is, obviously, a good thing, but if there is a move from this to loving Christ "alone," and to regarding this as the only thing that really matters, it becomes something dangerous, as is shown by the history of the life of perfection and the religious life, since in the name of the highest love for the "mediator" it is possible to undervalue love for one's brothers and sisters and the oppressed—paradoxically, the love Christ demanded on earth for building the "mediation," the Kingdom.

The other consequence is to provide a religious symbol to legitimize historical absolutes that, obviously, are not absolute: particular socio-political structures, Christendom and its modern successors, the church itself. For the powers of this world, in state and church, it is important to insinuate into the minds of their subjects the idea that the absolutely absolute already exists in the "mediator," so that they can pass themselves off as "mediators" who can demand absolute submission, when the only thing that is absolutely absolute is the mystery of God.[15]

Abstraction without specificity, reconciliation without conflict, absoluteness without relation, these are the grave dangers of the traditional image of Christ, which christologies can encourage, consciously or unconsciously. In the crude form in which I have described it here, few would accept that their christology was affected by the critique, but some have clearly been in the past and, in a more sophisticated form, above all by omission, some continue to be today. At all events, we are left with their consequences: centuries of faith in Christ have not been able to respond to the distress of the continent, nor even to suspect that there was something scandalous in the coexistence of unjust poverty and Christian faith.

From this point of view, the new image of Christ the liberator is not only an unexpected and welcome novelty, but also an unmasking and abandonment of the un-Christian or anti-Christian aspects of the earlier images; this also explains why the new image has provoked so much conflict on our continent. What is regarded in terms of faith as extremely positive, the abandonment of alienating images, is regarded by the powerful as extremely dangerous, a challenge to those images.

3. The Image of Christ at Medellín and Puebla

What was said in the last section should be enough to secure acceptance of the new image of Christ, but it has also been sanctioned, in its essential features, by the Latin American church and now forms part of "our church tradition," constituted by Medellín and Puebla.[16] I now want to analyze the most novel features of this image, those which it would be most useful for theoretical christology to consider.

(a) The Image of Christ at Medellín

Medellín did not produce any document about Christ—any more than Vatican II did—nor did it offer any outline of christology in the strict sense; that is why I use the term "image" rather than "christology."

(i) *Salvation as "liberation."* Medellín approaches the figure of Christ from a concern with salvation. In this it is not doing anything new, but at crucial points it expresses this in terms of liberation, which goes beyond the traditional terms of "salvation" or "redemption":

> It is the same God who, in the fullness of time, sends his Son so that, having been made flesh, he might come to free all human beings from all the servitudes to

which they had been condemned by sin, ignorance, hunger, poverty and oppression: in a word, by the injustice and hatred which have their origin in human selfishness ("Justice," 3).

This text is not analytic, and various questions could be asked about it. What is the hierarchy of the servitudes and liberations, and the relationship between them? How does Christ bring about this liberation? Nevertheless the text is novel and above all programmatic: (1) It states that Christ came to bring freedom from a *variety of evils*, moral, physical and social, and in so doing effectively pulls back the concept of salvation more toward the activity of Jesus of Nazareth (welcoming sinners, miracles, condemnations) rather than associating it with the later (reductive) universalization of salvation as redemption from sins. (2) It states that these evils, all of them, are forms of servitude: that is, they represent personal and social situations of oppression and, therefore, Christ's work cannot be understood only as beneficent, but has to be understood formally as *liberation*; this, of course, recovers the original etymological meaning of the term "redemption," in Latin *redemptio*, restoration by means of payment of the slave's freedom, and in Hebrew *gaal*, "recovery by God of what is his and has been stolen, orphans, widows. . . ."

(ii) The "principle of partiality": the poor and poverty . Medellín professes the divinity and humanity of Christ, but introduces into them the principle of partiality, the poor and poverty:

> Christ our saviour not only loved the poor, but also, "being rich, became poor," lived in poverty, centered his mission on the proclamation to the poor of their liberation and founded his Church as a sign of this poverty among human beings ("Poverty of the Church," 7).

This text invites questions about who the poor are and what poverty is, but its overall significance is unmistakable. It introduces into all the dimensions of Christ's being his relationship with the poor and with poverty. The transcendent happening that occurred in the incarnation is described as "becoming poor," metaphorical language, of course, but stressing by its repetition how far the divine has descended, to the human level and within the human level to poverty. Christ's historical life, his mission and his purpose, are described clearly in terms of poverty and his option for the poor.

However correct the (implicit) exegesis of the biblical texts, these statements have programmatic value in introducing into our understanding of Christ what I am calling the principle of partiality. This is extremely important for christology because christology has usually been based on the principle of impartiality: Christ is universally "human" and brings salvation to "all" human beings and to all "equally," although in fact this universality is only apparent and in itself presupposes a view—not formulated from the position of the poor—of divinity, humanity and salvation.

(iii) The hermeneutical principles: hope and practice. Medellín mentions the presence of Christ in current history and ventures to list the signs of this:

> Christ, actively present in our history, foreshadows his eschatological action not only in the impatient human longing for total redemption, but also in those victories which, like signs of what is to come, human beings achieve through activity carried out in love ("Introduction," 5).[17]

The text refers to *Gaudium et spes* 38, but spells it out forcefully in relation to Latin America. In its wording it mentions the "longings" and the "victories" in the context of the longed-for transformation of the continent, while *Gaudium et spes* is content with more general statements, the encouragement Christ gives to "those noble longings . . . by which the human family strives to make its life more human and to render the whole earth submissive to this goal."

The most important thing about this text, however, is that, while it does not say specifically in what form Christ is present in these longings and victories, it says that he is present in them and that he has to be discovered in them, which means that these phenomena become, for christology at least, hermeneutical settings for understanding Christ. And since "longings" refers to hope and "victories" to action, both things can (and must) be interpreted as (logically prior) conditions for the possibility of understanding Christ. In other words, unless we participate in the impatient longing for total redemption and unless we participate in the transforming victories, we shall not adequately grasp the presence of Christ in history.

(iv) The presence of Christ in the oppressed. This topic, which has not usually been dealt with by christology, but has been relegated to spirituality, is taken up again by Medellín. Its premise is that Christ can and must be found today in history, but not where human beings would like to meet him, but where he is, even if this place is scandalous.

Medellín gives this problem first a traditional answer: Christ is present today in the liturgy ("Liturgy," 2) and in the faith communities that bear witness to him ("Lay Movements," 12). But it adds as something new, if indirectly, his presence among the oppressed:

> Where unjust social, political, economic and cultural inequalities are found, there is a rejection of the gift of the Lord's peace, even a rejection of the Lord himself ("Peace," 14).

The text speaks directly of historical situations of injustice, and says of them that they are a rejection of the Lord. Its limitation lies in its failure to identify the victims of injustice as a positive presence of Christ, although it alludes to this in mentioning Matthew 25 in the references. The advantage is in the dynamic language: People can be "rejected" only if they are really present, and if they are present they can also be encountered, as Puebla was to say magisterially.

(b) Puebla's Christological Reflection

Unlike Medellín, Puebla wrote a chapter entitled, "The Truth about Jesus Christ, the Savior We Proclaim" (170-219), prompted by a concern to defend orthodoxy from the real or imagined dangers of the first Latin American christologies, a fear expressed by John Paul II in his opening address.[18] It is undeniable that underlying the document there is a concern with orthodoxy and that there is no longer the assurance and boldness of Medellín's reflections.

However, this worry was unable to stifle the existing liberationist imagery and christology, as a number of texts show. The fundamental reason for this—apart from the interest of a number of bishops and theologians—lay in the surrounding situation: the Medellín image prevailed because it was more faithful to the gospel and more Latin American. As a result, despite its apparent monolithic character and its doctrinal purpose, in the Puebla document various christological images and statements coexist and, curiously, the richest and most novel appear in the chapter, "A Preferential Option for the Poor," not in the chapter on christology.

As compared with Medellín, Puebla insists more on the doctrinal approach, with a top-down history of salvation and christology (182-219). It reaffirms the incarnation and fullness of Christ, and does so to avoid a double danger (real, possible or imagined) said to be present in Latin American christologies: the reduction of the totality of Christ to his humanity, and the reduction of that humanity to a Christ who was "a politician, a leader, a revolutionary or a simple prophet" (178). But this attitude and these statements do not exhaust what Puebla had to say, nor are they what has had most influence subsequently.

First, Puebla recognizes and give thanks for the fact—"we have cause for joy"— that there is in the People of God "a search for the ever new face of Christ, who is the answer to their legitimate yearning for integral liberation" (173). It thereby reaffirms the legitimacy and need for a "new" image, despite centuries of evangelization, and that an essential feature of this new image is that it should be "liberating," and praises Medellín for having encouraged this.

Second, Puebla mentions many features of Jesus of Nazareth—of the "historical Jesus"—which, one assumes, are what will fill out the new and desired image of Christ. On the one hand, in general, it avoids any deep analysis of the features of Jesus that historically provoked conflict—there is merely a comment that "his presence unmasks the evil one" (191)—but, on the other hand, it lists others of great importance: his proclamation of the Kingdom; the beatitudes (though referenced only to Matthew's version, not Luke's) and the Sermon on the Mount as the new law of the Kingdom; the call to follow him, Jesus' inner life, including his openness to rejection by human beings and to temptation; his surrender to death as Yahweh's suffering servant and his resurrection (190-5). In other chapters it also stresses other features of the historical Jesus: his poverty (1141), his example as the good shepherd (681) and his liberating character (1183, 1194).

Finally, Puebla deals with the problem of the presence of Christ now in history and of access to him, and does so in really vigorous and rigorous formulations that, in my opinion, have no parallel in other church documents of the time. It restates the traditional formulas: Christ is present in his church, principally in holy scripture, in the proclamation of the word, in those who gather in his name and in the person of their pastors. And it concludes, "With particular tenderness he chose to identify himself with those who are poorest and weakest" (196).

There is no reason to analyze these words as technical language, careful in all its details, but it is important to note that, depending on the places of Christ's presence that are mentioned, the text changes tone. Of the exalted Christ it says that he "lives" in the midst of us, that he "is present" in the church spaces. But when it mentions his presence in the poor, the language becomes more vigorous. It speaks of Christ's "identification" with them and of "particular tenderness" toward them. There can thus be no doubt that, in speaking of Christ's presence now in history, Puebla gives priority to his presence in the poor.

The aspects of Christ revealed by the poor with whom Christ identifies are not analyzed in the chapter on christology, though they are in the chapter on the preferential option for the poor. This makes two main points. First, that the poor are those to whom Christ's mission is primarily directed, simply because they are poor, "whatever may be the moral or personal situation in which they find themselves" (1142), and that the evangelization of the poor is the sign and proof *par excellence* of Jesus' mission (1142). In this way the essential correlation between the poor and Jesus' mission is reaffirmed.

This statement is Puebla's way of introducing the principle of partiality in Christ. The primary correlation is not between Jesus (and God) and human beings in general, but between Jesus (and God) and the poor of this world, through which, subsequently, the universal correlation can be established. The important conclusion for christology is that to know Jesus it is indeed necessary to get to know the poor.

The second point is that the poor are a sort of sacrament of the presence of Christ. Puebla does not use this language, but it does effectively and dynamically imply it: the poor possess for the church (and, we might add, for all) an "evangelizing potential." "For the poor challenge the church constantly, summoning it to conversion; and many of the poor incarnate in their lives the evangelical values of solidarity, service, simplicity and openness to accepting the gift of God" (1147).

The poor, then, are a quasi-sacrament in two fundamental dimensions of Jesus' mission. In the first place, they call us to conversion, since their very condition, like that of Jesus crucified, is the greatest possible challenge that can be offered to Christians and human beings in general, and in this sense the poor exercise a primary prophetic ministry in their role as victims. And second, they offer realities and values like those that Jesus offered, and in this sense are bearers of a gospel, exercising a primary evangelization.

Whatever examples Puebla uses to illustrate the "evangelizing potential" of the poor, the most important thing is that it formulated the concept. The poor are those to whom Jesus' mission is primarily directed; this is a supremely important and novel idea. In addition, however, they make present Jesus the prophet and evangelizer. They are his dynamic sacrament.

4. The Consequences for Christology

I began my discussion with something really happening today in history, the new image of Christ and the new faith in Christ, and this is not the usual procedure. Other christologies usually start with texts from the past about Christ, and when they consider the present they do so more to show the difficulties it presents for faith in Christ than to show its possibilities. I began in this way, however, because I think the reality of this image and this faith, with their emphasis on liberation and on the presence of Christ now in our history, is a sign of the times.

This leaves reflection with various tasks. As far as content is concerned, christology must establish, from its sources, that Christ is truly a liberator, and in what way. This leads to an analysis of the life and fate of Jesus, which occupies the bulk of this book. As regards method, we have to determine the current *locus* in which christology can and must be done, in accordance with this sign of the times (chapter 2), and we have to justify the decision to begin with the historical Jesus (chapter 3).

Chapter 2

The Ecclesial and Social Setting of Christology

The new image and the new faith have not appeared everywhere, but in particular places. Liberation christology, too, has not appeared everywhere, but, as a matter of fact, in the places where the new image and the new faith have developed. This shows that there is a correlation between christology and actual faith, but also shows that not all places are the same for the development of christology, but that there is something in the place where it is done that points it, or can point it, in a particular direction. This is what I want to consider in this chapter.

1. The Issue of the "Setting" of Christology

In dealing with its object, Jesus Christ, christology has to take account of two fundamental things. The first and more obvious is the data the *past* has given us about Christ, that is, *texts* in which revelation has been expressed. The second, which receives less attention, is the *reality* of Christ in the *present*, that is, his presence now in history, which is the correlative of real faith in Christ.

On this view, the ideal setting for doing christology would be the one where the sources for the past can best be understood and where the presence of Christ and the reality of faith in him can best be grasped.

(a) The Setting of Theology and the Sources of Revelation

Christology's specific sources are God's revelation, embodied in texts from the past, the New Testament in particular and its authoritative interpretation by the magisterium. It might seem, therefore, that the "setting," or *locus*, of christology was not very important, since there are sources for christology that predate any settings, or that the setting would not be crucial and would function at the most as a pastoral demand to apply to a particular situation the universal truth already expressed for all time in the deposit of faith. From this point of view, an analysis of the setting of theology, in the sense of a real place here and now, would not seem to be something crucial.

But things are not that simple. We might ask why "freedom" has been rediscovered in progressive christologies as essential to the gospel, while these christologies have not rediscovered "liberation." And we might ask why Latin American christology has discovered "liberation," which was more or less absent from christologies for centuries,[1] if, according to the two Vatican Instructions, liberation too is "essential" to the gospel message.

The basic reason is not that Latin America has better technical resources for analyzing the "sources" of revelation, but lies in the situation of Latin America. The first Instruction itself implies this, noting that the aspiration for liberation appears strongly "above all in peoples who know the burden of poverty and among the deprived social strata" (I, 1). In Ignacio Ellacuría's words, "The typical place where it appears is among the poor and dispossessed, and not among the rich who dispossess, who tend not to see and even to obscure justice and the need for liberation."[2]

This may seem obvious, but it is crucial: people begin to talk about liberation where oppression is blatant. Not only this: it is in this setting and not in any other that liberation becomes a theological *datum* in the strict sense and as such is rediscovered in revelation. "A sign of the times," in the strict sense—which I shall explain later—was what Ellacuría called it.[3]

To this important example we could add other fundamental theological rediscoveries made in the context of the Latin American situation: the partiality of God and Christ, the reality of the anti-Kingdom against which the Kingdom must be preached, or revaluations of elements included in christology but not taken very seriously: the following of Jesus, the beatitudes, the presence of Christ in the poor. What I want to stress now, however, is the fact that there are "settings" in which important elements in the "sources" of revelation, which had been buried, are rediscovered. If this is true, it is impossible to make an adequate distinction between the "setting" and "source" of revelation, or to accept the need for a "setting" for pastoral reasons only. That is why Ellacuría said:

> The distinction is not strict, still less exclusive, since in a way the setting is the source inasmuch as it enables the source to yield one thing or another, so that, thanks to the setting and by virtue of it, particular contents become relevant and really present. If this distinction is accepted, it would be a mistake to think that direct contact (even if in faith and lived in prayer) with the sources would suffice to enable one to see in them and extract from them what is most adequate for what theological reflection has to construct.[4]

The conclusion as it affects christology is that one setting is not the same as another for grasping what the New Testament writings in general and the Gospels in particular say about Jesus. Both the image of Christ the liberator and the alienating images analyzed previously have been based on readings of the texts of revelation, and the fundamental reason for the different readings was the place from which they were made.

(b) The Setting of Theology and the Signs of the Times

If the setting of christology is important to enable it to read its sources, it is even more important, by definition, if we take seriously the (possible) presence of Christ in current events. I want to say in advance that it is a fundamental truth for *faith* that Christ is Lord of history and, more specifically, that he makes himself present in it through a body. This, a fundamental truth for faith, ought to be fundamental also, in principle, for christology, although I do not think it has been. The result is that christology has to repeat, in accordance with its sources, *that* Christ is present in history today, but does not feel obliged to ask *what element* of Christ is present and *in what*, or to incorporate this present Christ into its procedure.

This presence, undoubtedly, can only take the form of signs, but christology should admit at least the possibility that in these signs Christ becomes present. If this possibility were not accepted in advance, and the reality of these signs, if they really exist, were not incorporated into christological method, christology would turn into mere reinterpretation, updated certainly, but working on the past, into an exposition, in terms of the present, of the New Testament christologies or into a commentary on later reinterpretations of it. This means, in my view, that it would fall into a sort of "christological deism," as though Christ had been present and active at the origin of the faith, but had later lost interest in history or his presence could not be detected.

The very fact of seeing the importance of the presence here and now of Christ and, in general, of God is in itself a great novelty. Vatican II, moreover, made it central by mentioning the "signs of the times." In the council, recognizing these signs was declared to be essential for determining the mission of the church, but in my opinion it ought to be central for christology also. Let us therefore see what the signs of the times mean, and explain it, since there are different understandings of them.

At the council the expression "signs of the times" had two meanings. On the one hand, it had a *historical-pastoral* meaning: the signs of the times are "events which characterize a period" (GS 4), and which are something new as compared with other signs in the past. They are, then, particular historical phenomena, and the purpose of recognizing them, examining them, is directly pastoral: the church needs to identify them if its mission—"to rescue and not to sit in judgment, to serve and not to be served," as it is defined in the closing lines of GS 3—is to be carried out in a relevant way.

On the other hand, "signs of the times" had a *historical-theologal* meaning. The signs are "happenings, needs and desires . . . authentic signs of God's presence and purpose" (GS 11).[5] This statement, like the previous one, mentions historical phenomena, but adds—and this is its crucial importance—that God's presence or purpose has to be discerned in them. History is seen here, not just in its changing and dense novelty, but in its sacramental dimension, in its ability to manifest God in the present.

Doctrinally, the (possible) existence of the signs of the times is now clear, and in general christologies accept it as doctrine. However, the problem is whether they really identify these signs of the times not only in their historical-pastoral sense, which they usually do, but primarily in the historical-theologal sense, which is infrequent, and whether, having identified them, they integrate them into their approach. In my opinion this does not often happen,[6] but it does occur in Latin American theology,[7] following the procedure of Medellín and Puebla.

The identification of the signs of the times in Latin America is also carried out in christology, which is what I am most concerned to stress here. We are told that Christ is present in history and where and how he is present. To concentrate on a supremely important example, the presence of Christ now in the oppressed majorities is affirmed and proclaimed, and in the process the insight of Guamán Poma and Bartolomé de las Casas is retrieved, and weight is given—unusually— to the principle that christology is also the christology of the "body" of Christ. In Ignacio Ellacuría's theological words, "This crucified people is the historical continuation of the suffering servant of Yahweh."[8] In the pastoral words of Archbishop Romero to peasants terrified after a massacre, "You are the image of the pierced God."[9] These statements can be discussed theoretically,[10] but what I want to emphasize here is that Latin American christology does mention the presence of Christ in the present situation, discovers it in the signs of the times, which it understands in the historical-theologal sense:

> Among the many signs always appearing, some striking, some barely percep-
> tible, at any moment there is always one which is primary, in the light of which
> the others have to be identified and interpreted. This sign is always the people
> crucified in history.[11]

To raise the situation of the Latin American poor to that of "Yahweh's suffering servant" or the "pierced God" is to understand them as historical-theologal signs of the times.

This understanding of the signs of the times as historical-theologal is of course a delicate matter. Because of this Latin American christology checks them against and discerns them in the light of revelation. However, discernment itself is a creative act that does not derive mechanically from a pure reading of revelation. If the question is asked once more why Latin American christology feels the urgency and has the audacity to identify these signs of the times and is not content with a doctrine about them, the ultimate—unprovable—reason is that it is in the place from where they can be discerned.

(c) The Setting of Theology and Actual Faith

If, *per impossibile*, there was, in fact, no real faith in Christ in history, Christ would cease to be Christ. This formal statement, which some may find audacious, means that it is important for christology not only to analyze the texts about Christ and take account of his presence now in history, but also to discern and analyze real faith in Christ. The theoretical premise is the correlation between *fides quae*, the content of what is believed, that is, the reality of Jesus Christ, and *fides qua*, the act of believing in this content. It is not that faith creates its object, which is why we always have to go back to the New Testament in order to see if the act of faith corresponds to the reality of Christ, but it is nevertheless true that there is a correlation between the act of believing and what is believed,[12] in such a way that the one refers to the other and therefore "it is perfectly legitimate for a christology to start from our relationship with Jesus Christ."[13]

Analysis of actual faith in Christ is thus important a priori for christology, but I want to insist now that this is also the lesson of Latin American experience. Not only believers' "image" of Christ, but their act of faith, their response to and correspondence in the reality of their lives with this image, helps christology to penetrate the reality of Christ and understand the texts about him.

If this faith is ultimate in character, this means that it is responding to an ultimate reality and so, whether or not the divinity of Christ is mentioned, the radical quality of the act of faith is a statement that Christ is really an ultimate. And the lived content of the act of faith also throws light on aspects of Christ. For example, discipleship in practice is an introduction to the Jesus we follow, real martyrdom is an introduction to Jesus the martyr. Consequently, in analyzing the reality of Christ, Latin American christology has put emphasis on one Jesus and not another, with specific features different from those of other christologies (partiality for the poor, his practice of denouncing and unmasking idols, a person merciful and faithful to the last . . .).

And if we ask why Latin American christology, unlike others, takes seriously the correlation between *fides quae* and *fides qua*, why it does as a matter of fact what Rahner describes as possible and legitimate, the reason again is the place where it is done.

(d) The Setting of Theology as a Real Situation

We have seen that the setting of christology is important in enabling it to make adequate use of its sources, past and present. Nonetheless I have not yet offered a formal definition of this setting or said what its material reality is. In my view, this is where the fundamental option must come. For some christologies the setting of theology is basically texts,[14] although they have to be read in a physical place and take into account the new demands of the situation, the signs of the times in the historical-pastoral sense. For Latin American christology the setting of theology is first and foremost something real, a particular historical situation in which God and Christ are believed to be continuing to make themselves present; this is therefore a theologal setting rather than a theological setting, a setting from which the texts of the past can be re-read more adequately.

The "setting" of christology is not, therefore, a direct categorial *ubi*, a particular place in geographical or spatial terms (universities, seminaries, base communities, bishops' offices . . .) although it has to be in one or several of them, and each of them offers advantages and disadvantages,[15] and ideally the specific positive characteristic of each should be present in all of them. But "setting" here means first and foremost a *quid*, a substantial situation in which christology offers itself, allows itself to be affected, questioned and enlightened.

To decide what this real place is, let us apply to christology the graphic words of José Miranda: "The question is not whether someone is seeking God or not, but whether he is seeking him where God himself said that he is."[16] The setting does not invent the content, but away from this setting it will be difficult to find him and to read adequately the texts about him. Going to this setting, remaining in it and allowing oneself to be affected by it, is essential to christology.

Latin American christology—and specifically as christology—identifies its setting, in the sense of a real situation, as the poor of this world, and this situation is what must be present in and permeate any particular setting in which christology is done. In order to justify this choice, christology can invoke a priori the correlation between Jesus and the poor and his presence in them, as it appears in the New Testament, but it also has the a posteriori conviction that it obtains a wider and sharper view of everything from the perspective of the situation of the poor. It believes that the "entry of the poor on to the stage of history" is the most important fact (Gustavo Gutiérrez), a "sign of the times," the presence of God and his Christ.

In the last resort it is impossible to give a conclusive proof for this conviction, and the hermeneutical circle is always in operation: we see the choice of this setting as demanded by revelation, but this demand is felt only once one is in the setting.[17] The type of justification is the same as in the justification of faith in revelation, the honest conviction that from this setting Christ "makes a difference" for faith and christology,[18] becomes relevant and at the same time discloses his identity.

Identifying a setting is, then, essential for christology. Throughout history there have been various settings, but today in Latin America this setting is identified as the world of the poor because they "constitute the supreme, scandalous prophetic and apocalyptic presence of the Christian God."[19] And if this is the case, christology faces, to put it very simply, the question asked by the oppressed negroes in the United States, "Were you there when they crucified my Lord?" Latin American christology has a very dialectical *Sitz im Leben* or life-context. It is a *Sitz im Leben und im Tode*, a place of life, certainly, as we shall see later, but also a place of death, the crucified people.

2. The Ecclesial Setting: the Church of the Poor

In Latin American christology the situation of the poor doubles as an ecclesial setting (something christologies in general take into account) and a social setting (taken into account much less). It is impossible to make a real distinction between the two, but I shall do so for ease of analysis.[20]

(a) The General Ecclesiality of Christology

The church is a real setting for christology because the texts about Christ are preserved and transmitted in the church, and the church interprets them authoritatively to preserve their fundamental truth. This does not mean that the church is the only home of these texts since, by definition, Jesus Christ is not the exclusive property of the church, but that of humanity, and as a matter of fact there are non-Christians who draw inspiration from these texts and even say to us Christians, "Give us back Jesus." However, there can be no doubt that the church is the place, in practice and by right, where these texts are transmitted.

This, though fundamental, is not the most fundamental aspect of the church as a real setting for christology, since here we are still on the level of what we may call *secondary ecclesiality*, that is, of the church defined as an institution, in this case as guardian of the deposit of faith and ultimate guarantor of truth. All this, however, presupposes something prior, which I call *primary ecclesiality*: the community's act of faith in Christ and the presentation of Christ in history in his dimension as head of a body that is the church.

By "primary ecclesiality" I mean that the ecclesial substance is embodied in the church, that in it real faith, hope and charity are put into practice; in christological terms, discipleship of Christ is enacted. In doing and being this, the church becomes a sacrament in relation to Christ and ultimately becomes his body in history. "The historical bodiliness of the church implies that the reality and the action of Jesus Christ is 'fleshed out' in it so that the church may perform an 'incorporation' of Jesus Christ in the reality of history."[21] First and foremost, in this sense, the church is the setting of christology because it is the setting of faith in Christ and of the embodiment of Christ and, therefore—subsequently, from a logical point of view—it is also a setting because it guards and preserves the texts about Christ, but not vice versa.

Another aspect of primary ecclesiality is that the enactment of faith and the embodiment of Christ should be communal. Faith in Christ is essentially a community faith and not the sum of individual faiths, and this has been true since the resurrection of Christ, which did not simply produce individual faiths, but called into being a community and brought about a situation in which faith had communality as an essential dimension. This means primarily that we carry one another in the faith, give our own faith and receive it, so that, formally, it is the community that believes in Christ. Christology is ecclesial, therefore, not only because individuals believe *within* a community called the church, but because it is a feature of the act of believing that it depends on the faith of others.[22]

Moreover, faith has to be communal because the church is a reality in process. It is essential to the church to be on pilgrimage, a description Vatican II legitimized in the term "people of God," and this pilgrimage includes the action of rethinking its faith throughout history, learning to learn. And this, as J. L. Segundo has shown, can only be done in community: "The very fact that God reveals something with meaning presupposes not only an individual searching, but a community, a people committed to this attempt to learn to learn, and thereby seeking the truth."[23] By this criterion christology is primarily ecclesial because it is carried out within a community with real faith, which makes Christ present, and within a community-in-process, which is the primary agent in reformulating its faith, learning to express and formulate it so that it constantly reveals more of itself.

(b) Particularized through the Church of the Poor

This real community faith and this embodiment of Christ are the primary ecclesial realities, and in Latin American christology they are brought into relation with the poor. When church and poor are brought into an essential relationship, then we get the church of the poor,[24] and this church becomes the ecclesial setting for Latin American christology. Let us examine it.

First, the faith of the church of the poor takes the form first and foremost of liberating activity, discipleship of Jesus, which resembles Jesus in his option for the poor, in his condemnations and in his historical destiny. So the church of the poor has martyrs on a massive scale and, more importantly, they are murdered like Jesus and for the same reasons that brought about Jesus' death. The enactment of the faith of the church of the poor essentially includes, naturally, "confession," but in it faith more often takes the form of "invocation": by being of such a type and acting in such a way people confess the truth of the Christ in whom they believe.[25] This being and acting like Jesus that characterizes the church of the poor is what christology needs to pay attention to in order to get to know Jesus better.

Second, the church of the poor attaches importance to the communal nature of faith, but not merely or mainly for the obvious reasons Walter Kasper lists, following the "theory of institutionalization," to overcome the limitations of the individual in the cognitive domain, to protect fundamental truths from the whims of individual subjectivity or a particular generation of leaders.[26] In the church of the poor the need for a communal faith has different roots.

Just because they are poor, the poor make a difference to the faith of those who are not poor, so that in the church there cannot be mere addition of individual faiths, but complementarity—put more precisely, solidarity—a mutual carrying of one another in faith, allowing oneself to be given faith by the poor and offering them one's own faith. Then, and at the level of content, since the poor are those to whom Jesus' mission was primarily directed, they ask the fundamental questions of faith and do so with power to move and activate the whole community in the process of "learning to learn" what Christ is. Because they are God's preferred, and because of the difference between their faith and the faith of the non-poor, the poor, within the faith community, question christological faith and give it its fundamental direction.

In the church of the poor, finally, Christ becomes present, and this church is his body in history. It is not his body automatically, but insofar as it offers Christ the liberating hope and action and the suffering that can make him present as risen and as crucified. Christology isolates this central fact, not arbitrarily or through pure textual analysis, of Paul or Matthew 25, but because theologians find themselves confronted, like Bartolomé de las Casas, with an atrocious suffering that forces them back to Matthew 25 and, at a more abstract level, to the Pauline texts.

It is tragic that Christ's presence now on our continent should be so overwhelmingly in the mode of crucifixion, though he is present also in the mode of resurrection. This crucifixion, however, because it is impossible to hide, is also beneficial because it forces christology to recognize that a body of Christ really exists in history, and to take it into account in its own activity.

This church of the poor, then, is the ecclesial setting for christology because it is a world shaped by the poor. But I want to say that, even on the level of secondary ecclesiality, the church of the poor has brought forth new things from the "deposit" of faith, and at Medellín and Puebla it reformulated the reality of Christ from the point of view of the poor.

3. The Social-Theologal Setting: the World of the Poor

The ecclesial setting is the real setting for christology within a wider social context, the world of the poor. This is its social-theologal setting.[27] And it needs to be said that if the setting, in its ecclesial dimension, has an influence primarily on the *content* of christology—the question "Who is Jesus Christ?"—the setting in its social dimension has its main influence on the method of christology: "How do we approach Jesus Christ?"

First and foremost, the social setting is a reminder that "theologians do not live in the clouds. . . . No christology is or can be neutral. . . . Christology takes shape within the context of a particular moment in history; it is produced under certain specific modes of material, intellectual, cultural and ecclesial production, and is articulated in terms of certain concrete interests that are not always consciously adverted to."[28] The social setting shapes christology and does so by action or omission that is, consciously or unconsciously, partisan. Liberation christology is at least conscious of this, and has the honesty to recognize it: its thinking is done from the world of the poor and is done to liberate them.

This social world that shapes theologians' thought patterns also shapes them as believers, not just as intellectuals. And if this statement is surprising, let us remember that the social world is nothing other than God's creation—a fact which should not be forgotten by those who accuse theology of turning itself into, reducing itself to, sociology. And let us remember that trying to discover what this world is like is trying to discover what God's creation is like. This is why I talk of a social-*theologal* setting. We should not forget that real faith carries on, is questioned or grows primarily in this real world. In simple terms, believing in Christ is something done, in the last resort, in the real world; its most difficult challenges come from the real world and it is accepted in confrontation with the real world. A particular church situation may encourage or discourage acceptance of Christ, but acceptance that Christ is the revelation of the divine and the human, or rejection of this claim, is something that takes place in the real world and is encouraged or discouraged by this. The social setting is thus the most crucial to faith, the most crucial in shaping the thought pattern of christology, and what requires and encourages the epistemological break.[29] Having said this, I want to analyze how the world of the poor not only influences, but also positively makes possible and encourages this christological thinking.

(a) The World of the Poor: a Situation that gives Food for Thought

It is well known but needs repeating: the historical and social situation of Latin America is marked by unjust, cruel and overwhelming poverty. Medellín began its declaration as follows: "There are in existence many studies of the Latin American people. The poverty that marginalizes large masses of human beings is described in all of these studies. This poverty, as a collective fact, is an injustice which cries out to heaven" ("Justice," 1). Eleven years later Puebla used these words: "So we brand the situation of inhuman poverty in which millions of Latin Americans live as the most devastating and humiliating kind of scourge" (29). The same message is repeated by John Paul II's *Sollicitudo rei socialis*, and socio-economic studies still indicate a growth of poverty.[30]

This fundamental datum is what gives food for thought, what most gives food for thought and what must give a basic orientation to christological thinking. Twenty years ago Hugo Assmann put it like this:

> If the state of domination and dependence in which two-thirds of humanity live, with an annual toll of thirty million dead from starvation and malnutrition, does not become the starting point for *any* Christian theology today, even in the affluent and powerful countries, then theology will be unable to give any historical context or content to its basic themes.[31]

If we do not take this fact of death seriously, theology will be accused of complicity and irrelevance: "Its questions will lack reality and not relate to real men and women."[32] However, the positive aspect is that it requires theology to do real thinking, not just to go through the motions, and to think from a particular point of view, one that promotes the lives of the poor and combats the death that turns them into victims. And if this brings charges of reductionism or dabbling in sociology, let us remember that we are talking about God's *creation*. Threatened life, "this little thing which is God's greatest gift," as Archbishop Romero used to say, is what we have to defend, is what sets our minds working and about which we cannot be neutral. The current European debate about modernity and post-modernity becomes at this point absolutely unintelligible and scandalous: we can opt out of many things, but we cannot opt out of the deaths of the poor.

This is also what stimulates christological thinking and gives it a basic direction: to think about Christ from the perspective of the fact of real life and death, to relate him to the basic needs of the poor,[33] to present Christ as the word of life in the presence of anti-life, as someone who came to bring life, life to the full. And this is what has happened. From this encounter with life and death christology has rescued what is essential about Jesus as the proclamation of a Kingdom of life for the poor which defies the anti-Kingdom of death. From the social position of the poor, this is no small gain. And this social position is also a theologal position.

(b) The World of the Poor: a Situation that gives Power for Thought

The world of the poor is not just a summons to thought; it also offers thought an epistemological advantage: a light that illuminates its subject matter. We are now talking about the light rather than the subject matter, and saying that in the world of the poor there is a light that enables the intellect to see objects that are hard to see without this light. The light is not what we see, but what makes it possible to see. In technical language, the poor give us specific objects to see (*medium in quo*), but they act primarily as a *medium quo* "when they become light, which is not what our gaze directly falls on, but what enables us to see what we are looking for."[34]

To accept that there is light in the world of the poor, and a light that cannot be found in other places, is in the last resort a choice—although one can argue for this in advance on the basis of the transcendental relationship between God and the poor—which acts as a "pre-understanding" of christology.[35] What I want to emphasize, however, is that the so-called option for the poor is more than a pastoral option; it is an all-embracing option to grasp the whole view, but to see it consciously from one position. This does not mean reducing the whole to one of its parts, but we hope—and in this sense the option is also a "wager"—that from the point of view of the poor we will see more and see more clearly than from any other position.

For christology this means using the light of the poor to penetrate better the totality of Christ, and let us remember that christological thinking as such is also obliged to do this by virtue of its specific object. It is said of the Servant of Yahweh that God has set him up as the light of the nations. Pauline theology says that the *crucified* Christ is wisdom, and John's theology says that we must fix our eyes on this man who was *crucified*. If these expressions are not understood as purely rhetorical, they are saying that there is something in this crucified man that gives our intellect a light it does not obtain in other places. This is exactly what I am trying to say about the world of the poor, and I might add that this is why it is so surprising that "Christian" christologies, which are confronted of necessity with a crucified man and have to admit that in him there is a "revelation" of God, are not able to integrate into their method, or even to understand, the option for the poor.

(c) The World of the Poor: a Situation that teaches Thought

I want to say finally that the world of the poor makes the understanding function, or enables it to function, in a particular way that is important for christological thinking.

In the first place, in the world of the poor it is easier for the understanding to transcend the *hybris* active in all human activity, including the primal act of learning the truth, something Paul complains of (Rom. 1:18). Christology also must seek out the place that, of its nature, though not automatically, makes it easier for it to come to know the truth without manipulating it and to hold fast to it. From this point of view, the most appropriate world in which to come to know the truth and avoid manipulating it is the world of the poor. If the poor of this world do not lead us at least to suspect that even christological understanding can be under the influence of *hybris*, nothing will. To enable us to understand sinfulness itself acting within christology—and why shouldn't it be?—nothing more effective has been invented to this day, from Paul to Ignatius Loyola, than coming face to face with a real crucified person. And the same thing continues to happen today when we come face to face with the crucified people: they are the best safeguard against the danger that theology will become ideology. This truth has to be stressed, because the opposite claim is so often made: when theology takes the poor seriously it is usually branded as ideological, while when it ignores them it is usually regarded as a genuine exercise of theological thinking.

Second, the world of the poor is the place that requires and encourages a particular attitude necessary if thinking is to correspond to the object of christology: that it should be done with mercy toward the victims and as good news to those who live in difficult situations.[36] If the world of the poor has any message, by definition it is that effective mercy comes before all else, and must permeate all human and Christian activity, and so also theology. That is why the situation of the poor requires and enables theology to change its existing self-understanding and see itself first and foremost as an *intellectus amoris*, not in opposition to, but distinct from, *intellectus fidei*. More specifically, it has to see itself as *intellectus misericordiae, iustitiae, liberationis*.[37] In this sense, just as liberation theology defines itself as "the theory of an ecclesial and historical praxis,"[38] christology must understand itself primarily as a *Christopraxis*, not to cancel the *logos*, but so that the *logos* may illuminate the truth of Christ in terms of Christ's own desires that liberation should become a reality.

The world of the poor is, then, I believe, what makes theological understanding reflect on its own operation and ask not only if its *product* is liberating or oppressive, but also if its *mode of operation* favours liberation or oppression. When Ignacio Ellacuría offered a philosophical justification for the method of liberation theology, he said that the formal structure of understanding consists in facing real things, and that this act of facing things has a noetic, ethical and practical dimension:

> This act of facing real things in their reality has a threefold dimension: *getting a grip on reality*, which implies being in the reality of things—and not merely facing the idea of things or in touch with their meaning—a "real" being in the reality of things, which in its active nature of being is the complete opposite of a thing-like, inert way of being and implies being among them through their material, active mediations; *taking on the burden of reality*, an expression that indicates the fundamentally ethical character of understanding which was not given to us so that we could evade our real commitments, but to take upon ourselves what things really are and what they demand; *taking responsibility for reality*, an expression that indicates the practical nature of understanding, which only fulfils its function, including that of knowing reality and understanding meaning, when it takes responsibility for real activity.[39]

One might well ask whether this way of envisaging the functioning of understanding could have been formulated in another place.[40] No doubt one influence here is Zubiri's philosophy, but in my view Ellacuría discovered it and definitely took it further from the standpoint of the world of the poor and in commitment to the poor.[41]

What this way of envisaging understanding means for christological thinking, for "knowing" Christ, is the following: it means "getting a grip on the reality of Christ," for which the most effective way is to go back to the historical reality of Jesus of Nazareth; it means "taking on the burden of Christ's reality," that is, readiness to listen to and respond to his real moral demands and persist in that; it means "taking responsibility for Christ's reality," that is, making him productive in a real liberating praxis that makes its cause real.

4. Conclusion: from the Poor to Jesus of Nazareth

In this chapter I have tried to stress the importance of the setting in which christology is done and define it as adequately as possible. For Latin American christology, this place is the situation of the poor, which is ultimately an option whose justification is to be found only within the hermeneutical circle: from the standpoint of the poor we think we come to know Christ better, and it is this better-known Christ, we think, who points us to where the poor are.

The importance of this specific setting for christology is twofold. On the one hand, it performs an epistemological break in the method of approaching and coming to know Jesus Christ:[42] knowing Christ is, in the last resort, following Christ. On the other hand, from this setting and with this method of understanding, christology finds itself looking towards the Christ who is Jesus of Nazareth. "The liberation christology elaborated from the standpoint of Latin America stresses the historical Jesus over the Christ of faith," says Leonardo Boff after analyzing the social setting of christology.[43]

In the next chapter I shall analyze the precise significance of the historical Jesus in Latin American christology, but let me repeat that the ultimate reason for this—though there are others—and what distinguishes it from other christologies' reasons for going back to Jesus is the ecclesial and social setting of this christology: in the world of poverty the poor and Jesus of Nazareth converge and point to each other.

Chapter 3

The "Historical Jesus," The Starting Point for Christology

Starting to write a christology in itself presupposes, in a sense, the theologian's faith in the whole reality of Jesus Christ of which he or she seeks to give an account. Assuming this, however, one still has to face the methodological problem: where does one start in giving an account of this whole?

The question is difficult since faith tells us that Jesus Christ claims a universal meaning for himself: "All things have been created through him and for him. He himself is before all things, and in him all things hold together" (Col. 1:16-7; cf Eph. 1:10). Nor is there any single starting point or one unequivocally required by the New Testament for approaching this whole. There is also some risk involved, since the starting-point chosen, even if the choice is made solely for methodological reasons, will usually produce different, and sometimes dangerous, results.

Though difficult and risky, the choice, however, has to be made, because although the whole reality of Jesus may and, in my opinion, must be present in some form from the beginning in the theologian's mind, the whole as such cannot be the starting point. What we have to find, then, is the starting point that seems most appropriate as an introduction to it.

Let me say from the beginning that I have chosen as my starting point the reality of Jesus of Nazareth, his life, his mission and his fate, what is usually called the "historical Jesus." This is what I shall analyze in this chapter, but before that I shall explain the fundamental reasons for my choice in the light of the serious difficulties it raises in relation to faith itself.

1. The Relationship between Jesus and Christ

(a) Jesus as the Way to Christ

Jesus Christ is a whole that, to put it for now in a simplified way, consists of a historical element (Jesus) and a transcendental element (Christ), and the most characteristic feature of faith as such is the acceptance of the transcendental element: that this Jesus is more than Jesus, that he is *the* Christ. This acceptance is faith, which presupposes that Christ and recognition of him are a gift of God, and that there is nothing that can force God to be like this or force us to recognize God mechanically as this.   This faith element is recognized methodologically in christology in the expression "christology from above" or "descending christology," in terms of which the origin of christology—and not just of faith—is said to be above, in the analysis of the reality of Jesus as Christ.

There is here a central truth that any christology has to accept. The divine purpose was that God should become a human being, and this cannot be concluded from any analysis. Given this, however, we cannot ignore two basic facts that make it possible and, in my opinion, very convenient, to start methodologically with the historical Jesus.

(i) God's descent into history cannot be understood in its pure abstract formality, simply by accepting the great miracle and gift of this descent, but only when we examine what it really consists of. This reality is Jesus of Nazareth. In other words, it is not a matter simply of accepting in faith the miracle and the gift of God's having become a human being, but it is crucial to explain the detail of this process. This explanation alone indicates the fact, of course, but in addition it alone shows the meaning of the fact, God's real approach to human beings to save, sharing their condition even to the extremity of the cross.

This divine miracle is nothing other than the real Jesus of Nazareth. Because of this, faith in Christ must be directed, also and essentially, from the outset to the underside of history, which in christology is indicated methodologically by the term "christology from below" or "ascending christology."

In other words, the fact that a miracle and gift of God exists is faith, and no christology can demonstrate it because it comes from above. However, the *nature* of this miracle and gift is something to be discovered, is to be found here below and therefore christology, accepting from the outset the totality of Jesus Christ, may also start from this point.

(ii) We also have to be aware of the epistemological status of faith-statements. As such they are transcendental statements, and thus limit-statements, not directly accessible to human understanding. Calling them limit-statements does not mean that the things they talk about are meaningless, but it does mean that to have any knowledge of them, to be able to conceptualize and formulate them with a minimum of meaning, requires prior experience of historical realities, so that the ability to formulate and conceptualize these limit-realities presupposes a process that has to be gone through and only at the end of which will it be possible to maintain (or reject) such limit-statements.[1]

This occurs in everyday life with phenomena such as love, freedom and life itself. And it occurs with theological phenomena. The statements that Jesus is Christ, that he is the expression of what is truly divine and truly human, are limit-statements, which, of their nature, require a process of understanding. That is not to say that undergoing this process automatically guarantees ultimate acceptance in faith of these limit-statements, but without this prior process what is confessed in faith would not have any describable meaning. Therefore in scripture transcendental limit-statements come preceded by historical statements. For example, in the canticle of Moses, God is referred to as essentially a liberator (a limit-statement), but this profession of faith comes preceded by the fact of the liberation from Egypt, attributed (in faith) to God. The fact of the liberation from Egypt—however historical it may be in all details—is something that can be known by reason, even if attributing it to God is a matter of faith. However, as regards the point that concerns us here, to make a meaningful limit-statement that God is a liberator, there must exist a prior phenomenon, liberation from Egypt.

The same happens with faith in Christ. To be able to confess meaningfully that Jesus is Christ, it is necessary to know Jesus, to know and analyze data about him which—though there is no obligation about this, since this leap is exclusively a matter of faith—enable a person to take the leap of faith and say, "Jesus *is* Christ."

This is clear from the formation of the first faith in Christ: the first believers were faced with many historical facts of Jesus' life and with the experience of the resurrection. And as a result of these experiences they started to think about who this Jesus was, until they eventually confessed him as Christ. This is true for the present as well, though not in the same way. In a sense, believers now have available to them the result of this process accomplished previously by others, faith in Christ. But it would be an illusion to think that here and now we can have direct access to the end of the process without going through (in life, of course, but also in thought) the stages that led to its formulation. This process began with Jesus of Nazareth. The logical process of christology is, therefore, chronological. Jesus can be understood as the way to Christ.

(b) Jesus as a Safeguard for Christ

The New Testament speaks of Jesus after his resurrection as the risen Lord, and when it speaks about Jesus of Nazareth it is already doing so in terms of faith that this Jesus is Christ. In other words, the New Testament has no interest in presenting Jesus of Nazareth in his factual historical reality. In this sense there is no "jesusology" in it, but always, even when it speaks about Jesus of Nazareth, "christology."

This fundamental truth means that objections are raised against the expression "historical Jesus" for implying that the Gospels were interested in a factual historical Jesus, when in fact they are believing, theologized accounts of Jesus. Neither in practice nor formally are they interested in presenting the factual history and historicity of Jesus. Accordingly, as a systematic term to refer to Jesus of Nazareth, other, more vague terms have been proposed, such as "the earthly Jesus" and others that convey with greater precision the way the phenomenon of Jesus appears in the Gospels, "the historicized Jesus."

Later I shall analyze what I mean by the "historical Jesus," but now I just want to note a central and significant fact: even after faith in Christ, the New Testament goes back to Jesus, and has to go back to Jesus, precisely to safeguard true faith in Christ.

(i) It is a historical fact that, in its origins, the main difficulty for faith in Christ lay not in affirming his transcendence, but in affirming his specific human reality. Paul had to warn the Corinthians that "No one speaking by the Spirit of God ever says 'Let Jesus be cursed!'" (1 Cor. 12:3), which indicates that some Christians, while maintaining faith in Christ, had gone so far as to make the scandalous statement, "Jesus be cursed."   Gnosticism and docetism—the ways the New Testament world had of denying Jesus' flesh—may have been "the most serious crisis [the church] had ever had to sustain."[2]

This is a scandalous and extremely important fact, which has to be thoroughly analyzed. Its possibility arises from the very make-up of the name "Jesus-Christ." "Christ" is an adjective, "anointed," which expresses the relevance of the person anointed, while "Jesus" is a noun, which denotes the specific unrepeatability of a person. Of course we human beings, even believers, *can* introduce into the adjective what is not in the noun and, even worse, we can even introduce into the adjective something contrary to the noun. In simple language, we can confess a Christ who does not resemble Jesus, even a Christ who is at odds with Jesus. What we need to add is that the possibility of manipulating the noun through the adjective becomes a reality, as we saw in the last chapter, and it is not accidental, but rooted in the *hybris* and sinfulness of human beings. Not only can we manipulate Jesus in the name of Christ; we *do*.

(ii) This *hybris* and sinfulness may also be present in christology, since there is nothing in this as a human activity that removes it from the human condition in general, and they are present in it in a specific form. In my opinion, the possibility exists because christological analysis has to distinguish between Jesus and Christ, and the action of this specific *hybris* and sinfulness consists in deciding in advance what Christ is independently of what Jesus was. In this way assumptions are made about concepts that, if we start from Jesus, we cannot make: what it is to be God and what it is to be human. Undoubtedly, some prior concepts have to be used, but in christology these prior concepts ought to function more like nominal definitions which, as it were, break the hermeneutical circle rather than like real definitions that tell us something about Christ. Instead, the movement must be in the opposite direction, and if this is not so, *hybris* and sinfulness are acting in christology.

This means that christology too, as a human activity, has to undergo a specific conversion: it cannot presume to verify the truth of Christ by what we think we already know in advance, but must maintain an openness to receiving from Jesus definitions of the divine and the human. Like any conversion, this one has a high price, since our sinfulness is expressed in refusing to receive the truth.   In christology, however, this has a particularly high price, because in allowing ourselves to receive the truth we encounter the fact that in the divine and the human there exists an unthinkable and scandalous novelty, as we shall see in the course of this book. It is therefore understandable that specifically christological defence mechanisms should appear, and the most extreme of them is to affirm Christ in order not to encounter Jesus. Thus, paradoxical though it may appear, the highest christological affirmation about Christ may subtly become an alibi for not recognizing—and following—Jesus. However, if this conversion were not to take place in christological practice, Christ would cease to appear as a revelation in the strict sense, which would be scandalous for a *Christian* christology.

(iii) The most effective methodological procedure to prevent *hybris* and sinfulness from becoming real in faith and christology, is to see Christ, initially, through Jesus and not the other way round. Although it may seem a play on words, everything is decided by the choice to give methodological priority to one of these statements: "Jesus is Christ," or "Christ? He's Jesus." I believe that the New Testament bluntly says the second,[3] and that this is what makes the new faith new. It decided to say this, as we shall see later in detail, precisely in order to safeguard what it was really concerned about, true faith in Christ.

For these two fundamental reasons—that Jesus is the best way to Christ and his best protection—I choose the "historical Jesus" as my starting point. But before analyzing what I mean by the "historical Jesus" as the starting point for this christology, I want to describe and evaluate other starting points, which will make clearer what is unique about the starting point of Latin American christology.

2. The Different Starting Points of Christology

(a) Conciliar Dogmatic Definitions

In traditional Catholic theology it has been customary to start with the dogmatic formulation of the Council of Chalcedon. This formula, which affirms the divinity of the person of Christ in two natures, divine and human, without mixture and without division, is a fundamental statement that any christology should not only respect but also value highly for the radical way in which it expresses the ultimate mystery of Christ and the ultimate structure of reality. As a starting point, however, it is inadequate because, in addition to the obvious pastoral difficulty of understanding today the terms of the formula, "person," "nature," "*hypostasis*," and the like, there are others relating to form and content.

From a formal point of view, it is commonplace today that dogmatic formulas cannot go further or say more than what scripture states. They may say it in a different way, but they cannot say anything new. They may have the advantage of expressing better and defending the truth of the faith in the conceptual categories and language of a later age (that of the first centuries of the church, for example, under Hellenistic cultural influence), but they cannot be a starting point because of necessity they presuppose something prior, scripture. Without understanding and analysis of scripture, dogmatic formulas remain dumb. In other words, they are limit-statements, a finishing post rather than a starting point, which presuppose a process, as we saw earlier. Dogma, then, is not only chronologically but also logically posterior to scripture.

In addition to these formal difficulties, however, there are more serious difficulties with regard to content. In the first place, the formula asserts in very radical terms that Christ is truly God and truly human, but does not stress, though it may assume, that being God and being human are what was seen in Jesus. It thus gives the impression that Jesus sanctions what we already know, what it is to be God and to be human, and that therefore we can predicate both of Christ. In this case, however, Christ would not be, strictly speaking, the revelation but the confirmation—albeit unexpected—of what we previously knew about the divine and the human. Of course, he would reveal the relationship that exists between the divine and the human, the subsistence of both, without mixture or distinction, in one divine person, but there would be no need for him to reveal what God is and what being human is.

Second, it also gives the impression that dogmatic formulas reconstruct the reality of Christ, as it were, by addition, adding little by little all the attributes of divinity and humanity.[4] In this way the reality of Jesus was gradually reconstructed, as though in a laboratory, so that nothing was left out that at the time was thought of as characteristic of divinity and, above all, of humanity: body, soul, will.... Asserting all this was extremely important in the presence of those who denied it, but it sanctioned an essentialist understanding of Christ's reality.

Consequently, third, dogmatic formulas suffer from this essentialist vision, which comes from Greek thought, with the result that Christ's human nature is not presented as the history of Jesus and the manifestation of the divine nature is understood more as an epiphany of the divinity than as the action of God in history.

And finally, although the salvific intention of the formula is clear, it offers the condition of possibility that Christ may be salvation—the divine sharing in the human to save the human—rather than the specific salvation and liberation that Jesus came to bring, and in terms of which we shall have to understand in a Christian way the universalization of Christ's salvation, but not the other way round.

(b) Biblical-Dogmatic Statements

As a corrective to the use of formal definitions, an attempt was made to construct a biblical starting point, but as yet not from the historical account of Jesus in the New Testament, but from the titles that proclaim his unique reality. I call this approach biblical-dogmatic because, while biblical, it has a similar structure to that based on conciliar dogmatic statements, in that it deals with limit-statements. For example, it focuses on the unique reality of Jesus through honorific titles (Messiah, Son of Man, Lord, Word) or through a theological account of the great events of his life (the resurrection, transfiguration, baptism, virgin birth, pre-existence...).

Unlike the previous approach, this one has a number of advantages, above all pastorally, because the language is apparently more intelligible and its Jewish background to a large extent points us back to the specific form in which the revelation of God in Jesus was historically expressed. These advantages, however, are only apparent.

Both the titles and the presentation of the events of Jesus' life have been reworked theologically and therefore presuppose a datum on which this theological work has been done, Jesus of Nazareth. They are, in other words, limit-statements like the previous ones. Familiarity may make us think that we understand better what we are talking about if we call Christ "Lord" or "Son of God" than if we call him "a divine person in two natures," but the underlying problem is the same, since before studying Jesus as he really was we do not know what we are saying when we call him "Lord" or "Son of God."

In addition, the New Testament does not offer one, but a number of biblical-dogmatic christologies. There is a christology of the Lordship of Christ, another of the Son, another of the Logos, and so forth. The problem is not that there is this plurality of christologies, which is in fact a good thing, but that it forces us to find a core which will help us to organize all of them. We can try to use one of the titles, but then we face the danger of undervaluing others, as has happened with the titles "servant," "lamb that was slain" and the like. We cannot get round this difficulty entirely by appealing to the historical Jesus because there are also different historical traditions about him, but as a methodological principle it is better to begin with the historical data that produced the variety of christologies.

(c) The Kerygma

This position goes back to M. Kähler, who, disappointed with the vain attempt to reconstruct the biography of Jesus, asserted in a famous lecture in 1892 that "The real Christ is the Christ as preached." It was from this point that the distinction between the "historical Jesus" and the "Christ of faith" began to be made. In terms of this distinction, what faith (and christology) are concerned with is not the life of Jesus of Nazareth, which is anyway impossible to reconstruct, but the preaching of the *kerygma* of Christ crucified and risen.

Bultmann is the theologian who most successfully drew out the consequences of this position. For christology, the life of Jesus cannot be the starting point because, firstly, the historical sources are inadequate and, as a matter of principle, faith has nothing to do with what Jesus did and said in his earthly life, but is essentially about what God is doing and saying when the *kerygma* is preached. Christ's reality is made present when his death and resurrection are preached, and those who hear this feel the unavoidable need to decide to live, either by faith, in an authentic existence that accepts the meaning of life from God, or by unbelief, in an inauthentic existence, shutting themselves up in their own egos and so making it impossible for themselves to live a human existence.

This position—corrected by the post-Bultmannians, who do not share the historical scepticism and the view that history is unnecessary for faith—has an important positive aspect. It brings christology back to a real event in the present, the preaching of the *kerygma*, and so introduces the here and now—something occurring in history—into christology. Nevertheless, the limitations are serious. Apart from the limitations of the underlying existentialist and individualist philosophy, the greatest difficulty is that the *kerygma* as such contains nothing specific to guarantee the authenticity or inauthenticity of existence, except the general statement that authenticity is ex-centricity, in the sense of living by the strength and for the sake of something or someone not oneself. The question is: who is the God or neighbour by whose strength and for whose sake we can live authentically, and what in particular do we have to do to live authentically? Formally, there is no answer to these questions in this type of christology.

(d) The Experience of the Presence of Christ Now in Worship

To say that Christ continues to be present now in history is an extremely important statement, not only for faith, but also for christology, as we have already seen. But to say that this presence can be experienced in worship in such a way that we come to know the reality of Jesus of Nazareth is manifest exaggeration. Nevertheless, this is what W. Künneth claimed: "Given that Jesus, in his risen nature, manifests himself effectively in faith, and that faith is sure that Jesus, the Lord, is alive, faith as a result knows the historical existence of Jesus of Nazareth."[5] Apart from being obviously exaggerated, this starting point is open to the clear danger I have already exposed, of a faith that, from the community in Corinth to modern charismatic and spiritualizing movements, derives its justification from Christian worship. The presence of Christ here and now, while it might give guarantees of the existence of Jesus, usually ignores his specific reality and may come into conflict with it. Structurally speaking, it is difficult to start from this position and subsequently reach the total reality of Christ, which includes Jesus as he was in life.

(e) The Resurrection of Christ

The resurrection of Christ as the starting point for christology has the New Testament apparently in its favour. Chronologically, both faith and christology occur, in the strict sense, after and as a result of it. Nevertheless, the resurrection of Christ presents a serious methodological difficulty if we are to convert it into a starting point, analogous to that posed by the dogmatic and New Testament formulas.

For faith the resurrection of Christ is not, like the formulas, a pure concept, but a real event, though on the other hand a limit-reality, which cannot today be known directly, but only from a particular standpoint. Christ's resurrection is today an object of knowledge, but it is at the same time an object of hope and of practice. However, this hope and this practice are not elements of an anthropology already formed before Jesus of Nazareth; rather, they are a hope and practice that need Jesus and, more specifically, need discipleship of Jesus. Therefore, although the resurrection is a gift inasmuch as it is a real event, to be understood it needs something prior to itself, as we shall see later when we analyze the hermeneutics of the resurrection.

The resurrection of Christ was necessary for faith in Christ to appear, and it is therefore a necessary condition for any christology. However, it is not a useful starting point, since until we are clear about who was raised (Jesus of Nazareth), why he was raised (so that God's justice might be made manifest against a world of injustice), how we gain access to the risen one (in the end, through discipleship of Jesus), the resurrection does not necessarily lead to the true Christ.

(f) Jesus' Teaching

Lastly I shall mention the tendency of the European liberal theology of the eighteenth and nineteenth centuries to present Jesus as the teacher and model of universal religion because of his knowledge of God (Friedrich Schleiermacher), or as an exemplary human being, the ideal of the bourgeoisie of the last century (Adolf Harnack). In these christologies, Jesus' teaching is decisive and in this sense this is ultimately a retrieval of something of the historical Jesus.

The limitations, however, are clear. Jesus of Nazareth not only put forward doctrines, but performed works and had a historical fate. More important, Jesus' teachings are not the confirmation of the religious substance of the universal human being, let alone the confirmation of the bourgeois ideal of the human being, but a critique of these. The "historical Jesus," presented in this way, has nothing eschatological or critical about him. He might be a version of the complete human being so many people dream about, but he would not be the revelation of the new human being, who only by being new—through crisis—succeeds in being authentic.

3. The Return to Jesus of Nazareth

There are, then, starting points in christology that are not the historical Jesus. This does not mean that a number of them do not, subsequently, take Jesus into account, nor does it mean, of course, that what is said in them cannot be important for christology. In criticizing them, I have only sought to show their limitations, and also their danger when used as starting points. The real reason, as I have insisted, is the grave danger of forgetting Jesus of Nazareth and the difficulty of really retrieving him if he is not already present in the starting point.

In present-day christologies, however, there has been an important and quite widespread movement that requires analysis: a return to Jesus of Nazareth and an attempt to make him, albeit in different ways, central in reflection. Latin American christology is part of this movement, though in a special way.

(a) European Christologies

In the orbit of Vatican II the so-called progressive christologies recognized that it was necessary to retrieve Jesus of Nazareth for obvious, if ignored, reasons of Christian identity, and for reasons of social and pastoral relevance. In order to describe briefly what was a long process, let us recall the huge speculative undertaking of Karl Rahner (for the moment it is not necessary to discuss his method) to restore to Christ his true humanity and so avoid the painful sensation that—in addition to being contrary to the New Testament and even to dogma—Christ was a myth that was hard to accept in a world in a process of secularization. Rahner never tired of stressing the "true humanity" of Christ and of rejecting an understanding of the incarnation as a chance visit by God to this world disguised as a human being.[6]

However, in addition to this, Rahner insisted on thinking of the humanity of Jesus "sacramentally": Christ is really human, and his specific humanity is the exegesis of the transcendent God, his sacrament among us.[7] Jesus' flesh is the tangible manifestation of God in and for this world and the visible way to reach the mystery of God. Apart from this humanity of Jesus, it is futile to look for the place from which to understand Christ and carry out faith in God. Phraseology that today has a familiar ring then embodied a new truth: when Jesus welcomes sinners, it is God himself who is welcoming them; when Jesus shows love to human beings, it is God himself who is loving them.... And, vice versa, we know that God welcomes and loves through the action of Jesus. And it should be said that this reflection of Rahner's was not just purely academic, but necessary to overcome the profound crisis of believers presented with a transcendence without history and a Christ without Jesus.[8]

The return to the historical Jesus took its course. From emphasis on the "true humanity" of Christ it advanced—as did Rahner himself—to "Jesus of Nazareth."[9] This further step is more than a change of language and is what, formally speaking, provided the basis for the present-day christologies that make Jesus central. And by making "Jesus of Nazareth" central instead of the former "humanity of Christ," christological methodology had to be rethought in the following fundamental aspects.

As far as its contents are concerned, and using a shorthand for now, christology had to end what I called earlier the "absolute absolutization of Christ" when it discovered the double relatedness of Jesus: not only his relatedness within the Trinity, but also his essential historical relatedness to the Kingdom of God and the God of the Kingdom.[10] It also came to see Jesus' essential relatedness to the communities that confessed him as Christ, which made it equally impossible to understand Christ adequately without them.[11] Seeing this double historical relatedness is vitally important if we are not again to divide christology into distinct topics in the manner of the old treatises, instead of defining it in terms of what Jesus was related to. If we do the latter, his relationship within the Trinity to the Father and the Spirit is brought into history through his relationship with the Kingdom of God and the communities sustained by the Spirit.

As regards hermeneutics, existentialist hermeneutics (Bultmann)—easier and indeed required if one's starting-point is the Christ of faith—has in general been replaced by the hermeneutics of praxis, liberation, and so on: and this not only in virtue of the demands of the current historical situation or because of possible demands of a particular philosophical approach, but in virtue of the very object we seek to understand, Jesus of Nazareth. He indeed—and not an abstract, though true, "human nature"—calls for a praxis if we are to have an adequate relationship with him: discipleship.

As regards the interpretation of dogmatic formulas, in the strict sense or in the sense of biblical-dogmatic formulas, they turn into points of arrival rather than of departure, since only in terms of Jesus can their content be understood.

(b) Latin American Christologies

The work done in christology in Latin America in the last twenty years can be seen as formally part of this process of returning to the historical Jesus, though with differences in motivation and in the understanding of the historical dimension of Jesus.

In 1973, in the middle of the obvious convulsions in the church, Hugo Assmann raised the question why christology had not suffered a crisis, when the situation of Latin America clearly demanded a new christology. What it demanded, specifically was the following:

> On the one hand there is the vague, general christology *ad usum omnium* [a reference to the classical christologies previously described], unrelated to any particular situation, and on the other, particular embodiments designed to fit a particular ideological purpose at a particular moment. Somewhere between the two there is a legitimate need for a historically mediating christology relevant to the basic problems of a given historical situation.[12]

Though he does not explicitly mention the historical Jesus, he does indirectly refer to him when he rejects abstract theological slogans such as "'the presence of the risen Christ in the world,' 'Christ the alpha and omega,'... which can be used in a mainly 'epiphanic' sense."[13]

Gustavo Gutiérrez, too, then at the beginning of his career, showed his dissatisfaction with a presentation of Christ that causes this impression of unreality, and added: "To approach the man Jesus of Nazareth, in whom God was made flesh, to penetrate, not only in his teaching but also in his life, what it is that gives his word an immediate, concrete context, is an increasingly urgent task."[14] Leonardo Boff, while not dealing with this issue explicitly in his first book about Jesus Christ, in fact adopts the perspective of the historical Jesus, both in the structuring and in the fundamental material he presents.[15]

The writer who was most intellectually radical in arguing the need for and the importance of a return to the historical Jesus was Ignacio Ellacuría. His fundamental historical interest—"salvation history entails salvation in history"[16]—led him to demand a new, "historically framed" reading of the "different christologies of the New Testament."[17] The purpose is the following:

> Our new christology must give the history of the flesh-and-blood Jesus its full weight as revelation. Today it would be absolutely ridiculous to try to fashion

a christology in which the historical realization of Jesus' life did not play a decisive role. The "mysteries of Jesus' life," which once were treated peripherally as part of ascetics, must be given their full import—provided, of course, that we explore exegetically and historically what the life of Jesus really was.[18]

In epistemological terms, "We have to move on to a historical *logos*, without which every other *logos* is merely speculative and idealist."[19] In theological terms, "The historical life of Jesus is the fullest revelation of the Christian God."[20]

The original insight of the theology of liberation is thus very clear: "We must go back to Jesus." Without his specific historicity, Christ becomes an icon.[21] José Miranda proclaimed this in the form of a manifesto, citing the fundamental reason for returning to Jesus:

> No authority can make everything permitted—justice and exploitation are not that hard to detect—and Christ died to make it clear that not everything is permitted. But not just any Christ. The Christ who is totally irrecoverable for conformity and opportunism is the historical Jesus.[22]

Right from those beginnings of liberation theology, the insight has been maintained, clarified and made productive.[23] Leonardo Boff, in a later work, says it with total clarity: "The liberation christology elaborated from the standpoint of Latin America stresses the historical Jesus over the Christ of faith."[24]

The fact is undeniable. In Latin America there has been an attempt to produce the necessary mediating christology that Hugo Assmann asked for, and this is the christology that begins with Jesus of Nazareth. And the original insight continues in force: "The point is not to let the mystery of Jesus be used to maintain injustice."[25]

4. The Systematic Significance of the "Historical Jesus"

The expression "the historical Jesus" was coined to make a distinction between this Jesus and the "Christ of faith," and for a very specific reason. The "Christ of faith" was to be made the central object of faith and christology and the "Jesus of history" abandoned because of the impossibility of obtaining knowledge about him and because of his irrelevance to faith. Nevertheless, apart from the context in which these issues—now largely settled—arose, we need to analyze what christologies mean by the historical dimension of Jesus of Nazareth, and for what purpose they use the term.

(a) The Meaning of "the Historical Dimension of Jesus" in European Christologies

Let us look first at what European christologies say in order to understand better, by contrast, what Latin American christology says about the historical Jesus.

(i) In the nineteenth century there was an attempt at a biographical approach to Jesus in the so-called "lives of Jesus," an undertaking declared an impossible illusion by Albert Schweitzer, Albert Loisy, and Johann Weiss, and whose epitaph was written by Adolf Harnack in the title of his doctoral thesis, *Vita Iesu scribi nequit,* "The life of Jesus cannot be written." Latin American christology, for its part, makes no pretence at reviving this mission impossible, and is not even directly interested in rescuing—though it accepts them if they turn up—actual words or actions of Jesus, the so-called *ipsissima verba* or *ipsissima facta Iesu.* Above all, it is not motivated by the same fundamental reasons as the original movement to write the life of Jesus, namely, to support "the struggle against the tyranny of dogma."[26] In other words, it is not specifically interested in rejecting knowledge based solely on the authority, in this case ecclesial or dogmatic, questioned by the Enlightenment, searching instead for knowledge based on historical rationality.[27]

(ii) The post-Bultmannians returned to Jesus to prevent the *kerygma* about Christ dissolving into thin air.[28] Obviously, Latin American christology is interested in anchoring the *kerygma* on Jesus of Nazareth, but its main interest is not in finding a solution to the problems raised by the New Testament, but in how to relate the Christ preached in the *kerygma* to the Christ who preaches, that is Jesus of Nazareth.

(iii) In Wolfhart Pannenberg's christology the crucial point is finding in the historical Jesus something essentially anticipatory (proleptic), in the sense that in his very being the historical Jesus points to his own end, the resurrection, which alone will make clear who he is.[29] While this is an important consideration, Latin American christology—while it shares the positive results of this approach—does not value the return to Jesus for this reason. That is, it does not formally concentrate its understanding of the "historical" in what is essentially "open to the future," which is what really concerns Pannenberg if he is to find a basis for his christology without having to appeal to any type of authority.

(iv) Other current christologies stress the importance of the historical Jesus if Christ is to be presented as something unrepeatable and unique, and faith in Christ thereby protected from manipulation by anthropology or sociology and retain its unrepeatable originality. While this is important, Latin American christology's concern is not specifically "to preserve a real and actual unique memory, and to represent it here and now."[30]

(v) Finally, various christologies go back to the historical Jesus to give faith in Christ existential meaning, and to go beyond an understanding of Christ as an "'atemporal' model of true humanity."[31] The attitude Schillebeeckx quotes: "I believe in Jesus as that definitive reality which gives final point and purpose to my life,"[32] is also true for Latin American christology, but on condition of not introducing into the starting point the reduction of what Jesus means for "my" life and of not understanding this primarily in terms of the need for a purely personal meaning for the individual.

Undoubtedly, Latin American christology can and indeed must incorporate various of the meanings of the historical Jesus described above, except the naively biographical quest. It must also take account of them as a corrective to the possible dangers arising from its own starting-point. However, as a whole, it does not share—once more, as part of its methodology—two of the premises operating in these christologies. In passing judgment on them now, I do not want to fall into the anachronism of expecting the pioneers of this movement to have dealt with issues of more recent origin or ignore the sound pastoral concern of these christologies in trying to give answers to the questions thrown up by their secularized environments. Nonetheless, I have to analyze these premises in order to distinguish them from those of Latin American christology.

The *first premise* has to do with Christ's identity, namely that we have to go back to the historical Jesus to understand who he really was and to be intellectually convinced that he is not a myth, which means taking seriously and answering the problem raised by historical criticism. The *second* has to do with Christ's relevance, and asserts that we have to go back to Jesus because his specific reality is a more effective underpinning of a questioned meaning of life than an abstract Christ. And, indeed, in a secularized world it is more reasonable to look for meaning in Jesus' real life than in something presented as a myth.

These approaches are understandable, and even good, but from the point of view of Latin American christology I want to make two critical remarks.

The first is that to approach Jesus historically and not mythically does not necessarily mean that there has been a basic change in what it means to "know" Christ, because it is possible to remain at the level of knowing "about him" but without reflecting on what it means to know this object of knowledge called Christ and what are the conditions of such knowledge. Commenting on the "messianic secret," Jesus' refusal in Mark's Gospel to be proclaimed as the Messiah, J. L. Segundo says, "What we know with most certainty about Jesus is that he actively fled from being *defined* (from being told *what* he was) by people before they understood what values he represented in his statements and actions."[33] The implication, it seems to me, is that knowing Jesus means, first and foremost, being attracted by him to follow him.

The second remark is that if we look for meaning in a historical Jesus, and no longer in a mythical Christ, we have not necessarily abandoned a personalistic and individualistic quest for salvation. It is understandable and legitimate that the threatened self should look for salvation, but this should not happen through undervaluing or relegating to second place the urgent need to save real life from its distress. This approach, moreover, could make Jesus correlative to egocentric individual salvation, which easily becomes egoistical. And since Jesus did not describe things in these terms, discovering the historical Jesus becomes in the end irrelevant even for the individual.

In my opinion, what is happening is that the problem and the solution are both still being dictated by the first Enlightenment, which sought to free individuals from myths and authorities, but which had the individual as its heart, while there is no influence of the second Enlightenment, which, first and foremost, seeks to free real life from its distress, and sees the liberation of the individual as having meaning within this aim.[34] In short, when the christologies described above go back to the historical Jesus they are still under the influence of first Enlightenment suspicion that faith is mythical and authoritarian. In these terms the task is to discover how individuals can reasonably believe and how they can, as individuals, find meaning in this faith.

In Latin America, the approach is different, since the main, immediate problem is not the meaning of life for the individual, but the non-meaning of the tragedy of life and society, within which personal life acquires meaning or non-meaning. From this point of view, the greatest task for faith is not the *demythologization* of Christ, as in progressive theologies, but the *depacification* of Christ, that he should not leave us in peace with the distress of the world, and, of course, his *deidolization*, that people should not be able to oppress the world in his name.

This is what makes "going back to Jesus" different in Latin America from in Europe, and it is in these terms that González Faus formulated it:

> In Europe the historical Jesus is an object of investigation, whereas in Latin America he is a criterion of discipleship. In Europe study of the historical Jesus seeks to establish the possibilities and the reasonableness of the act of believing or not believing. In Latin America the appeal to the historical Jesus seeks to confront people with the dilemma of being converted or not.[35]

What has been said so far is a generalized account of what might be called progressive European theology in the orbit of Vatican II. In this, however, there are also, increasingly, new expressions of what it means to go back to the historical Jesus and the reason for going back to him. It is well known that Jürgen Moltmann and J. B. Metz insist on a Jesus who demands first of all that we follow him in a praxis. Schillebeeckx admits that the Latin American insight has to be incorporated into christology.[36] González Faus, in the last revision of his christology, asserts, on the one hand, that it is not enough "to follow the Jesus of whom history says that he lived in Palestine and died on a cross," but stresses, on the other hand, that without this, pure faith in the risen one, "lacking a criterion of verification, threatens to turn into 'an idolatry camouflaged with Christian words'."[37]

(b) The Meaning of "the Historical Dimension of Jesus" in Latin American Christology

The purpose of going back to the historical Jesus in Latin American christology has been made clear. Let us now examine what we mean in systematic terms in our christology by the "historical Jesus" and what constitutes his positive value as a starting point for it.

(i) The most "historical" aspect of Jesus: practice with spirit. By "historical Jesus" we mean the life of Jesus of Nazareth, his words and actions, his activity and his praxis, his attitudes and his spirit, his fate on the cross (and the resurrection). In other words, and expressed systematically, the history of Jesus.

Since this history is made up of many elements, we have to ask which of them is the "most historical," which is the best introduction to the whole reality of Jesus and best organizes the various elements of this whole. This is what I am going to try to do in this section in a systematic way, insisting that it is a methodological and theoretical reconstruction and that in real existential faith the reconstruction is done in a personal way and is therefore impossible to deduce and not programmable in advance.

(a) My thesis is that the most historical aspect of the historical Jesus is his practice and the spirit with which he carried it out. By "practice" I mean the whole range of activities Jesus used to act on social reality and transform it in the specific direction of the Kingdom of God. The "historical" is thus primarily what sets history in motion,[38] and this practice of Jesus', which in his day set history in motion, is what has come down to our time as a history set in motion to be continued.

The historical dimension of Jesus does not mean, therefore, from a formal point of view what is simply datable in space and time, but what is handed down to us as a trust for us to pass on in our turn. This implies treating the texts of the New Testament in general and the Gospel texts in particular as narratives published to keep alive through history a reality started off by Jesus. This reality, after the resurrection, is responsible for passing on faith in Christ, but in terms of Jesus' own intention its original task was to pass on his practice,[39] in Jesus' own words, discipleship, considered primarily as a continuation of his practice. In this way, the community of perspectives required by hermeneutics is achieved in the continuance of Jesus' practice, which is necessary, though by no means sufficient, to understand the historical Jesus who initiated it.

(b) This in no way nullifies the concern of progressive christologies to look for the meaning of our own lives in the historical Jesus. Practice and meaning are primal aspects of humanity that can neither be ignored, without destroying what is human, or placed in opposition, since they are on different levels. The search for meaning is primal, inherent in any human achievement or destiny, and therefore is present both in Jesus' own practice and in that of his followers.

What I want to stress here is that the search for meaning is also present within a practice and in addition, in my view, it is present within a practice more powerfully than in other places. Questions about meaning certainly do not disappear, but become more urgent in a practice like Jesus': Is hope wiser than resignation? Is love more humanizing than egoism, giving one's life than keeping it for oneself? Do utopias really attract and produce positive effects or are they ultimately escapism? Is the mystery of God ultimate happiness or nonsense?

Practice may also bring to light the most specifically Christian element in fashioning the meaning of life, grace. Practice may be accompanied by human *hybris* and so degenerate into Promethean pride, but it can also be the place where we most deeply experience grace, the sense that we have been given "new" hands to do good.

Beginning for methodological reasons with Jesus' practice does not mean ignoring or slighting the inevitable issue of meaning with which progressive christologies approach Jesus. On the contrary, I believe that the opposite is true: continuing Jesus' practice is what sets off the quest for meaning and, what, with reference to Jesus, solves it or can solve it.

(c) I said that the most historical aspect of Jesus is his practice, and added, the spirit with which he engaged in it and with which he imbued it: honesty toward the real world, partiality for the "little ones," deep-seated mercy, faithfulness to the mystery of God.... This mercy is, in part, a tendency of Jesus, what was given to him in advance, so to say, but is also intimately related with his practice.

On the one hand, this spirit was defined and so became real, through a practice, because it was within that practice, and not in his pure inwardness, that Jesus was challenged and empowered. On the other hand, this spirit was not merely the necessary accompaniment of Jesus' practice, but shaped it, gave it a direction and even empowered it to be historically effective.

I believe that to add the spirit of Jesus to his practice is a relative novelty demanded by Latin American experience, since, far from being opposites, the two things can complement each other in a very positive way, and the process of their complementing each other helps us not to fall either into pure spiritualism or into pure activism.[40]

(d) Identifying the most historical aspect of Jesus as his practice with spirit is, at root, a choice, although there are philosophical arguments to support it. The test of this choice in the last resort is whether when followed through it is a better way into the complete reality of Jesus. Nevertheless, though a choice, it is also plausible in relation to Latin America.

It is not being naive to agree with Leonardo Boff when he says that Latin America offers "a structural similarity between the situations in Jesus' day and those in our own time. In other words, it sees objective oppression and dependence lived out subjectively as contrary to God's historical design."[41] This makes the historical Jesus the most reasonable starting point. However, of the reasons Boff gives for this view, which is what I want to concentrate on here, one is paramount:

> The historical Jesus sheds clear light on the chief elements of christological faith, i.e., following his life and his cause in one's own life. It is in this following that the truth of Jesus surfaces; and it is truth insofar as it enables people to transform this sinful world into the Kingdom of God.[42]

I therefore believe that it is possible, and more adequate, to begin methodologically with Jesus' "practice with spirit," not in the reductive sense, in order to stop there, but for its mystagogical potential to take us into the totality of Jesus better than any other of his attributes.

(ii) From the practice of Jesus to the "person" of Jesus. This formulation might be open to the objection that the "person" of Jesus disappears into his practice, with

the result that we end up reproducing, on a different level, a serious error: just as Christ was reduced to an idea—something against which personalist christology rightly fought—now we are reducing him to a symbol for a style of action. The objection is serious, but it does not do justice to the facts.

(a) First and foremost, in the reality of faith as it is lived, the majority of Latin American Christians who follow the practice of Jesus—though there are always exceptions—do not abandon their faith in the person of Jesus. Very often quite the opposite happens: following the practice of Jesus leads them to a deeper faith in Jesus and, when they encounter crises of faith, it may even be this that is able to reconcile them with Jesus. But this occurs also in christological theory.

One way of answering the objection is to say that the practice we are talking about is not an unspecified practice, but has specific elements, a specific direction and a specific spirit accepted in principle because they are Jesus'. Latin American theology insists on the one hand that what is happening is a following of Jesus and not an imitation, and that for this reason mediations are absolutely necessary, and J. L. Segundo repeats that what revelation offers us is "learning to learn." Nevertheless, at the same time we go back to the practice of Jesus on the premise that this practice contains an essential element of *norma normans, non normata*, an absolute principle, not derived from anything else. What that essential element is, is what we have to analyze, but the premise is clear: we have to go back to Jesus' practice, *because* it is Jesus'.

The essential content of this practice is the liberation of the oppressed, its approach is to come down to their level and take on oneself the sin which is destroying them, its goal is the Kingdom of God, imbued with the spirit of the beatitudes. All this, however, in principle may be present in one way or another in other current formulations of what liberating practice should be, though not necessarily. But if they are accepted *because* this is what Jesus' practice was like, then Jesus' "person," as of right, is retrieved.

In this sense, Latin American christology does not stop at Jesus' practice, as suggested by some materialist readings of the Gospel narratives,[43] but goes on to his person. Or, to paraphrase Willi Marxsen's famous slogan—*Die Sache Jesu geht weiter:* "Jesus' cause," or "the Jesus thing", goes on—Latin American christology wants Jesus' cause really to go on, but it is equally interested in the "Jesus" whose cause is to be advanced. This is both because it is interested in the whole Jesus and because, in order for Jesus' cause to go forward, it is very important to retrieve the "person" of Jesus.

(b) With this clarification, I think that Jesus' practice is what gives us the best chance of understanding and organizing all the elements that make him up: the events of his life, his teaching, his inner attitudes, his fate and his most intimate dimension, his person. I shall analyze this later in detail, but I want to look at it now in outline.

There can be no doubt that through Jesus' practice we understand better what he meant by Kingdom of God and anti-Kingdom, this his practice explains better than anything else his historical destiny on the cross and that it also helps us to understand his transcendent destiny, once we accept it in faith, his resurrection as God's justice to him. And his practice is also what enables us to sense the inner dimension of his person, his hope, his faith, his relationship with God. This is not to say that we can mechanically deduce from an analysis of his practice the sort of personal experience he had of God, and in some cases—for example, the novelty of Jesus' calling God "Father"—if there were no independent data, it would be difficult to deduce them from his practice. But the data we have are illuminated and enhanced by his practice, and the practice makes them coherent. In a word, I think that we have better access to the inner life of Jesus (his mind in history) from his outward practice (his making of history) than vice versa.

To explain this point, it is perhaps worth while turning the argument on its head. Christologies that take as their methodological starting point the "person" of Jesus, his inner attitudes, his relationship with the Father, have more difficulty in retrieving, and retrieve in less radical form, central data of the Gospel narratives: the Kingdom of God, partiality toward the poor, prophetic activity that provoked conflict, discipleship, the cross as a historical fate.... In contrast, those that begin with, and make central, the practice of the Kingdom of God give weight to all these events and do not neglect—have no reason to neglect—the personal dimension of Jesus, and enhance it through the rest. In a word, again, christologies usually find it easier to take seriously the "Father" as Jesus' ultimate personal correlative if they have taken seriously the "God of the Kingdom," than vice versa.

(iii) From the historical Jesus to the total Christ. Through the presentation of the historical Jesus and of the most historical aspects of Jesus, Latin American christology seeks personal access to Jesus. It does this, not by presenting primarily items of knowledge about him so that people can decide what to do and how to relate to the Jesus discovered in this way, but by presenting his practice so that it can be recreated and so give access to Jesus.

Gaining access to Jesus always implies some type of discontinuity, but the presupposition implicit in framing the question at all is that this access is possible only, in the last resort, through some form of continuity between Jesus and those who know him, and this continuity has to be seen in terms of the greatest density of reality, which in my view is practice with spirit. In these terms, gaining access to Jesus is not, in the first place, a matter of knowing about him, or producing a hermeneutic that preserves the distance between Jesus and us and makes knowledge of Jesus possible. It is, in the last resort, a matter of affinity and connaturality, beginning with what is most real in Jesus.

This way of gaining access to the historical Jesus is also logically the most adequate way of gaining access to the Christ of faith. The very act of re-enacting as an ultimate value the practice of Jesus and his history, because they are Jesus'— and all the more if one commits one's very life to this—involves an acceptance of an ultimate authority in Jesus, and doing this is a declaration that he is something really fundamental; it is already a declaration, albeit implicit, that he is the Christ, even if later this confession has to be made explicit.

Of course, in declaring Jesus to be Christ there is a discontinuity, a leap of faith that cannot be mechanically compelled by anything, not even by the continuity expressed in discipleship. Nevertheless this continuity is necessary for the discontinuity of faith to be Christian and not arbitrary, for us to know what Christ we are believing or ceasing to believe in. In faith we confess Christ as the risen Lord and Son by antonomasia (discontinuity), but it is essential to faith to confess him also as the firstborn from the dead with many brothers and sisters, and as the elder brother (continuity).

To follow the practice of Jesus with his spirit is an ethical demand of the historical Jesus himself, but it is also an epistemological principle. I said earlier that knowledge of a limit-phenomenon requires knowledge of objective prior historical phenomena, and now I am saying that the personal exercise of faith in this limit-phenomenon requires some prior subjective affinity in experience. In the case of faith in Christ, the prior objective phenomenon necessary is the phenomenon of the historical Jesus and the prior subjective experience is being his disciple.

To put it negatively, outside discipleship we cannot have sufficient affinity with the object of faith to know what we are talking about when we confess Jesus as the Christ. Put positively, through the affinity produced by discipleship it can be meaningful to proclaim Jesus as Christ, as the revelation of true divinity and true humanity. In the language of the New Testament, it is God's plan that we should become "children in the Son," but if this is his plan it is possible and, if it is possible, then by becoming sons and daughters we attain affinity with the Son and can come to know him.

(iv) Discipleship as mystagogia. In this section I have argued, essentially, that by starting from the historical Jesus and the most historical aspect of Jesus, Latin American christology seeks to be christology in the strict sense. On the level of method—although the real faith of believers and of theologians includes from the beginning some sort of overall faith in Christ—it considers that the logical path of christology is basically chronological. This appears in the following form in the New Testament: (a) the mission of Jesus in the service of the Kingdom, that is, his practice and the demand to engage in it, (b) the mystery of Jesus' identity and (c) the confession of his unrepeatable and saving reality, faith in Christ.

Twenty centuries later we have inherited what one might call the completed process of christology. As a result the *real* starting point is always, in one way, overall faith in Christ, but the *methodological* starting point continues to be the historical Jesus. This is, objectively, the best *mystagogia* toward the Christ of faith, and the affinity we obtain in the practice of discipleship is, subjectively, the best *mystagogia* for gaining access to Jesus and so to Christ.

5. The Return to Jesus in the New Testament

Latin American christology returns to Jesus of Nazareth and discipleship of Jesus, and this has occurred regularly every time Christian faith has faced a serious identity crisis. Francis of Assisi, a radical advocate of renewal, had no intention of being original, but merely tried to return to "following the doctrine and the footsteps of Christ." *Repetitor Christi*, he was called by Leonardo Boff.[44] Ignatius of Loyola, in the second week of his spiritual exercises, prays only for "inner knowledge of the Lord to love him more and follow him." Dietrich Bonhoeffer notes programmatically that "'Follow me' are Jesus' first and last words to Peter."[45] In existential language what is talked about here is following Jesus, but it is the most radical form of going back to Jesus.[46] What I want to stress is that this return to Jesus, and for this reason, had already begun in the New Testament.

(a) The New Testament Writings (except the Gospels)

The New Testament writings offer a variety of christologies, but first and foremost "they are mystagogical works which seek to affect directly and deeply the faith and life of their readers."[47] In other words, even when faith in Christ and more or less developed christologies already exist, the Christian communities are still turning back to Christ. The Gospels do this, but "the space that other New Testament documents devote to Jesus is also considerable, and has attracted less attention."[48] We must pay great attention to this fact in itself, since it shows that retrieving Jesus does not depend on this or that tendency, but seems to have been an objective necessity of Christian life from the beginning. Let us examine this.

The *Letter to the Hebrews* insists that Jesus is already glorified,[49] is the Christ. Nevertheless it repeatedly mentions "Jesus"—ten times and always in relation to suffering, blood, the cross and death—although the name "Jesus" is not interchangeable with "Christ." Referring to this Jesus, it gives important descriptive details. He came from the tribe of Judah (7:14), started the preaching of salvation (2:3), had hearers who passed on his preaching (2:3), was faithful and obedient to God (3:2; 10:5-9), and learned obedience through suffering (2:10; 5:8); he had opponents (12:3), was tempted without falling into sin (2:18; 4:15), offered up prayers and supplications to God with loud cries and tears (5:7-10), died on the cross (12:2) outside the city (12:12), ascended and was raised to the right hand of God (8:1; 13:20; 10:12), and there is a conviction that he will return (9:28; cf. 10:25). In addition, the letter presents Jesus as not only human, but also as a brother like his brothers and sisters in all things (2:17), except sin (4:15). And it sums up his true humanity in his compassion toward the weak and his fidelity to God (2:17).

What is happening here is a retrieving of Jesus. The author "places him before the astonished eyes of the reader with realistic and, up to a point, scandalous features."[50] The important thing is to know why. Jesus is important because his solidarity with his brothers and sisters is what guarantees salvation in the present, despite the community's longing for a salvation originating on high, an "angelic" salvation.[51] He is important also because his priesthood—in which the victim is Jesus himself—is the only efficacious priesthood, for a community upset at the absence of a Christian liturgy comparable with that of the Old Testament. And he is important because from him—"eyes fixed on him"—Christians can learn fortitude in the persecution the community is undergoing.

In *1 Peter*, which is more pastoral in intent, we see a community in a moment of persecution, and to face it the author appeals to Jesus, not only as a model, but also as someone who can inspire the attitudes needed to face suffering. "Christ suffered in the flesh" (4:1). "Rejoice insofar as you are sharing Christ's sufferings" (4:13). "Here, 'to suffer like Jesus' means 'to suffer with Jesus.'"[52]   This also explains why the christology of the letter recalls the Suffering Servant of Yahweh rather than the Lord of the cosmos.

1 John undertakes an unequivocal retrieval of Jesus in the face of the twin dangers of Gnosticism and Docetism.[53] To counter this temptation, the letter relates confession of Jesus to the explicit confession of "Jesus": the person who denies that Jesus is the Messiah is a liar, and the believer is the person who asserts that the Messiah is Jesus. The letter stresses this by adding that he "has come in the flesh" (4:2, 5, 6), and presenting Jesus as the model to be imitated. Christians should behave like him (2:6), abide in him (2:27; cf. 3:23), purify themselves like him (3:3), exercise justice like him (3:7), be in the world like him (4:17). Finally, the summary of Christian existence is presented in the formula "doing as Jesus did," in the last resort, love of one's sisters and brothers. The relationship with the risen Christ is, at its deepest level, being like Jesus, in such a way that "believing"—in the sense of performing the act of faith, not just in the acceptance of doctrinal truths—consists in "doing works" (3:17; cf 1:6).

There is usually more debate about whether there is retrieval of Jesus in the *letters of Paul*, since the core of his christology is the risen Lord and he does not make a detailed theological evaluation of the life of Jesus. Moreover, in the famous text 2 Corinthians 5:16 he states that "even though we once knew Christ from a human point of view, we no longer know him in that way." But things are not that simple.

In the first place, there can be no doubt that Paul presents Jesus in solidarity with human beings and that his whole soteriology depends on this, and that in describing this solidarity he in fact goes back to Jesus. His human condition is described in the phrase "born of a woman" (Gal. 4:5), but with those characteristics which, in different language, depict the life of Jesus: born under the law, made a slave, made into sin. These statements have parallels in the real life of Jesus, since they express and explain his death on the cross. And this cross, central to Paul's theology, is nothing if not historical. In systematic language, the insistence that the risen Lord is none other than the man who was crucified is the fundamental Pauline form of retrieving Jesus.

Second, however, this retrieval of Jesus can be better understood if Pauline theology is considered as an exegesis of Paul's own public and personal life.[54] We should note especially that Paul stresses aspects that define Jesus in terms of the most intimate aspects of his human nature: his faith (Rom. 3:23), not pleasing himself (Rom. 15:3), his warm welcome (Rom. 15:7), his profound weakness (2

Cor. 13:3-4), his acceptance of the human condition (Phil. 2: 6-8). In this context, the expressions "'life of Jesus' (especially in 2 Cor. 4:7-11) and 'death of Jesus' (*passim*) are not so much specific references as a way of living and accepting death."[55]

The question thus becomes whether and how Jesus' life is present in Paul's life. In a sort of declaration of principle, Paul asserts that "To live is Christ" and "Christ lives in me." When he goes into the detail of these statements, Paul describes himself as Christ's slave, says he bears in his flesh the sufferings and agony of Christ, his whole life is a life of service and sacrifice. In the letter to the Galatians, against the law, he says in so many words that we have to obey the law of Christ, which means reproducing the life of Christ in love and giving one's life. "To live is Christ" means living like Christ: having the mind of Christ (1 Cor. 2:16), the compassion of Christ (Phil. 1:18), the inner attitude of Christ (Phil. 2:3-4), the goodness and mercy of Christ (2 Cor. 10:1), the love of Christ (Gal 2:20), the self-giving of Christ (Gal. 2:20). This is nothing other than living like Christ.

Paul, then, carries out a retrieval of Jesus, primarily existentially and sometimes, though not often, with specific references to the life of Jesus. However, at one central point in his theology his approach is polemical, and so totally clear. The Corinthians are enthusiastic about the risen Christ, and Paul reminds them of the cross of Jesus. Faced with the grave danger that the true faith in Christ may be distorted and suppressed, Paul can find no better response than to go back to Jesus, and to the most historical aspect of Jesus, the cross. In conclusion, "We have to say that Pauline christology would become a real mystery without Jesus of Nazareth. It is not because of the intrinsic reference in Paul to Jesus of Nazareth."[56]

The conclusion of this argument is extremely important. The New Testament testifies that there is a return to Jesus even *after* faith in Christ and christologies developed around the risen Christ. Retrieval takes place in various ways, and in a different form from that in the Gospels, something that, far from reducing the importance of the fact, increases it, since it shows that from various viewpoints, with different tendencies and interests, the communities converge in the need to return to Jesus. There is a retrieval of Jesus, and the Gospels are not the only way of carrying it out.

The most important point, however, is that the retrieval is dynamic and saving, not merely a matter of adding items of knowledge about Jesus so that they coexist with the Christ believed in in faith. It is, above all, a retrieval that is necessary every time deeper questions arise about the communities' identity. In order to answer them, they have to go back to Jesus: (a) to obtain knowledge of and to exercise Christian identity: being a Christian is, in the last resort, being like Jesus; (b) in order to defend this identity against the fundamental danger that the risen one may be manipulated: the risen one is the one who was crucified, and no other; (c) in order to maintain fortitude and hope in times of tribulation and persecution: eyes fixed on Christ.

(b) The Gospels

The Gospels are not the only way of retrieving Jesus, as we have seen, but they retrieve him in a way quite distinct from others, one which, in my view, is unsurpassable. This is not because they go back to the history of Jesus, but because of the way they do so. It is well known that the Gospels were written by believers for believers and that therefore they should not be expected to tell the life of Jesus, but to give a theological interpretation of his life. It is also well known that they were written by and for believers in the communities, and therefore we must expect, not just one, but several theological interpretations, and so we must think in terms of different christologies in the Gospels.

(i) At the time when the Gospels were written, professions of faith, hymns and incipient christologies already existed. Faith in Jesus as the Christ was already secure, and in the confession that Jesus was the Christ Christians expressed their assurance of salvation, and concentrated on this in the first stage of the faith. Nevertheless this faith was not enough, and they went back to Jesus as a matter of principle, precisely to maintain the authenticity of that faith and protect it against degeneration. Thus, referring to Mark's Gospel, Eduard Schweizer comments, "The most remarkable thing is that it was written at all."[57] Put simply, the first Christians had already realized that pure faith in Christ was not enough to meet the fundamental crises of identities faced by the communities. In triumphalist communities (such as Mark's) or those wrestling with the Jewish Law (such as Matthew's), or those with tensions between rich and poor (such as Luke's), it was not enough to confess Christ; it was necessary to refer back to Jesus, and to the reality of Jesus.

(ii) The Gospels do not just go back to Jesus, but do so in a particular way, by telling the story of his life and fate. It will be said, and rightly, that their account is not biography, but theology, and that in writing a history of Jesus they produce a theology of Jesus. But it is no less true to say that in order to produce a theology of Jesus they write a history of Jesus, and this is their essential contribution. Let us look at the essentials of this history.

The Gospel narratives produce polemical histories of Jesus, but not only because they mention the polemics in which Jesus himself was involved during his life, but because the Gospels make the passion of Jesus their core, in such a way that it has been said that "the Gospels are a passion narrative with a long prologue" (M. Kähler). The passion of Jesus is a tragedy in itself, however much later theologizing found a saving dimension in it, and it remains a scandal even after the resurrection. The fact that the Gospels give it such crucial importance is, in itself, polemical, and shocks us into asking who the Christ we believe in really is, and what faith and salvation are.

All the Gospel narratives make Jesus the central character. However different the communities may be, they all go back to Jesus and go back, essentially, to the same Jesus since, even with the obvious differences between some and others, they all converge in presenting the fundamental structure of Jesus' life: the beginning and development of his mission, the confrontation with the powerful, persecution and death. In this way the retrieval of Jesus carried out by the communities offers the possibility of following Jesus. Every community and every Gospel adds its own features to the life of Jesus, but they offer the essentials of Jesus, to avoid complaints of misrepresentation, we might say, and to be reproduced.

The narratives are in the last resort gospel, that is, good news, *eu-aggelion*. The term is prior to the four Gospels, and is used by Paul to proclaim the saving truth of the death and resurrection of Christ. What the "Gospels" add is that to tell the story of Jesus' life is in itself good news, first because the good news is the core of Jesus' message to the poor, and secondly because it is good news that Jesus was as he was.

This, I believe, is the specific characteristic of the retrieval of Jesus carried out by the Gospels: if we wish to know about the true Christ we believe in, and live truly in accordance with this Christ, nothing can replace an account of the history of Jesus. Those who come to the Gospels in search of factual information about Jesus insist that the Gospels do not in any way offer the history of Jesus, but are just as much theologized texts as any other New Testament writings. But the question remains why the earlier theological constructions in hymns and professions of faith did not suffice. The Gospels' reply goes in two directions: it is true that it is impossible to write a history of Jesus without producing a theology about him, but it is also true—and this is the specific contribution of the Gospels—that it is impossible to produce a theology about Jesus without writing a history of him. Presenting the history of Jesus, however theologized, is the best way of giving truth and substance to believers' faith and encouragement to their lives. And this is, in my view, the permanent value of the specific way of going back to Jesus that the Gospels offer.

6. Latin American Christology as "Gospel" Christology

This is in fact the method of Latin American christology, to do theology about Jesus by writing a history of him. This explains why the christology produced in Latin America has tended to take the form of narrative christology, more in the style of the Gospels than of the other New Testament writings, though this does not mean that there is no systematic treatment of Christ.

(a) Critical Use of the "Historical Jesus"

In this approach Latin American christology faces the question that is usually the one other christologies tackle first, but that I have left till last in this discussion: What can we really know about Jesus of Nazareth? If we could really not know anything about him, or only insignificant things, the claim to produce a christology based on the historical Jesus would be futile. Christology would become at most a christomythology, which might have an interest for what the myth symbolized, but would radically invalidate a claim that is essential to the Christian faith, that God's saving approach to this world in Jesus of Nazareth is real and historical. Let us, then, see what Latin American christology says about what we might call the "historical facts" of Jesus.

First of all, it does not ignore the issue. It does not ignore it in practice because it accepts the reservations imposed by historical criticism, nor in principle, because it accepts that works belonging to the genre "Gospel" are accounts of faith, as literary criticism shows and as the end of John's Gospel proclaims: "These [signs] are written so that you may come to believe that Jesus is the Messiah" (20:31). In other words, it knows that it is not possible to gain adequate access to the "historical" Jesus, but only to a "historical version" of Jesus. Nonetheless, it does not share the scepticism of previous periods, and think it is impossible to know anything about Jesus, but it accepts some fundamental data, which allow us access to the basic structure of Jesus' life, about which there seems today to be a consensus.

This basic consensus about the historical facts might be summarized as follows.[58] On the level of *facts* we have Jesus' baptism by John, the initial successes (and perhaps also some conflicts) of his preaching, the choosing and sending out of some followers to preach, increasing threats and persecution, and the passion and death on the cross. On the level of *conduct*, we have activity involving miracles and exorcisms, preaching in parables, critical attitudes to the Law and the Temple, the call to conversion, discipleship and faith in God. On the level of *words*, there are two authentic *words* of Jesus, "kingdom" and "*Abba*," and the sayings that justified his condemnation.

Latin American systematic christology has not distinguished itself in the area of historical criticism, or in the development of criteria for the historicity of the Gospels, but in fact some of the criteria of historicity already developed by others are in use.[59] To illustrate this in the analysis of the term "Kingdom of God," the criteria of historicity are: (a) that it appears in all the strata of the synoptic traditions, and (b) that it reappears in the Gospels even if it does not appear as a central element in other New Testament writings, and (c) that it makes Jesus' fate appropriate.

What Latin American christology adds *a priori* to these criteria is the *a posteriori* conviction of the historical plausibility that "things were like that." Jesus' life, seen from its historical end, seems historically very plausible. This conviction is due to the "structural similarity" of situations. We know that in our own day there are thousands of people whose deaths are like Jesus' and the causes of whose deaths—as alleged by their executioners—are similar to the cause alleged against Jesus. These lives that today lead to this type of death have essentially the same structure as that claimed for the life of Jesus: proclamation of the Kingdom to the poor, defence of the oppressed and confrontation with their oppressors, the proclamation of the God of life and the condemnation of idols.

In purely logical terms, it is impossible to rule out the hypothesis that the story of Jesus' life could have been the product of the communities' imagination or sheer self-interest. That it may have been partly this is plausible, and even necessary, but that it should be totally and essentially so is very implausible.

In support of this conviction, Latin American christology can call on the argument of "reality." Seen in terms of the reality of Latin America, if Jesus "died like that," it is very plausible to assert that "he lived like that." It is not a logical conclusion, but it is used to show the internal historical coherence of the Gospel narratives of Jesus' life, seen in terms of events today. In other words, the subjective pre-understanding (*Vorverständnis*) with which we approach the Gospel narratives here and now, shaped and forced by the objectivity of what happens day by day, makes the substantial historicity of these narratives plausible and appropriate.

(b) Christology as "Gospel"

I have said that the method of Latin American christology is inspired by that of the Gospels, and I have also said that it has nothing original to offer when the Gospels are analyzed as "sources of knowledge" about Jesus. Nevertheless it does offer something original when the Gospels are analyzed specifically as "gospel." This means: (a) that Jesus is seen as good news and (b) that he is seen as good news by and for the communities.

As regards the first point, Latin American christology does indeed share the same historical conviction that underlies the writing, publication and proclamation of the "gospels," namely that there is good news to be told. This news is true for faith, and it is critical and demanding, but it is above all good. In this conviction, Latin American christology stands apart from others, not for any merits of its own, but because this is how Jesus is understood—at least still today—in Latin America. For whatever reasons, in other places Christ is no longer automatically understood as good news, and it is the difficult and valuable task of christologies precisely to win back for Jesus his dimension of being "good news," when it is not easy to win acceptance for his dimension of "truth." However, in Latin America Christ continues to be good news, as we have seen in analyzing his new image.

Giving priority to the Gospels in Latin American christology does not mean, therefore, merely starting with historicized accounts of Jesus in order to obtain information about him, but also, and very fundamentally, to reassert decisively his dimension of good news. Latin American christology analyzes the specific content of this good news, but insists that, whatever method of analysis is used, it should not remove, but reinforce, what is central in the Gospel narratives, that it is good news.

As regards the second point, Latin American christology reproduces, *mutatis mutandis*, the approach of the christologies of the first communities. Precisely because it does not seek directly to analyze Christ-in-himself, but in his quality as good news, a reference to real communities is essential.

From this point of view, the fact that there are four Gospels and behind them an infinity of little gospels, far from making christology's task more difficult, shows it how to proceed. Christology is developed when a community is placed in contact with Jesus and/or memories of him. It is the community that remembers, and so selects certain things in Jesus. And this is what Latin American christology also seeks to do.

On the one hand, study of the Gospel texts has already sent this christology in a particular direction, but on the other hand the creation of the historical figure of Jesus has been taking place on the basis of the communities' "memory," no longer "proximate" memories but "remote" memories already turned into history by the first communities. It is the communities who first grasp (and sing) "the great good news, liberation." It is from this real understanding of Jesus today that more technical christology produces new christological titles, such as "Jesus Christ the Liberator," as legitimate in principle as those of the New Testament (Lord, Logos...) or those of modern christologies: "the absolute bearer of salvation" (Karl Rahner), or "Christ, the omega point of evolution" (Teilhard de Chardin).

In this way of proceeding there is no manipulation of Christ, or, at least, not necessarily. The very fact that both the first communities and those of today continue to go back to Jesus, continue to insist that the good news is what he brings and what he is, let Jesus make demands on them, declare him the *norma normans* of liberation and the way to work for it, shows that there is no manipulation. What there is, both now and in the past, is a circularity between a Jesus who is for the communities and communities who take Jesus as their reference.

This in no way removes the need—indeed, it creates it—for theological analysis (and, on another level, the magisterium) to continue to make sure that this circularity is as correct as possible. However, in spite of everything, christology can only develop by taking into account two poles, Jesus and the communities. It therefore has to be essentially contextual christology, although it also has to incorporate universal dogmatic statements. But it is one thing to incorporate the generic universal in terms of the reality of the communities so that it may become a real universal, and another to start from the generic universal as though it was already established for ever, and subsequently apply it to the communities. In my opinion the method implied by the Gospels is the first rather than the second.

There are two important lessons that Latin American christology learns from the Gospels. The first is that we cannot turn the figure of Jesus into theology without turning him into history and telling the story of his life and fate. Without this, faith has no history. The second is that we cannot turn Jesus into history without turning him into theology as good news and so an essential reference for the communities. Without this, history has no faith.

This mutual relationship of doing theology by writing history and writing history by doing theology is what Latin American christology tries to introduce into its own method in order to be faithful to its object, Jesus Christ, who has been given to it in gospels: the life of Jesus is *gospel* and gospel is the *life* of Jesus.

This is what I shall analyze in later chapters. I shall do so by organizing Jesus' life around three fundamental and historically established data: (a) his relationship with the Kingdom of God, (b) his relationship with God the Father, and (c) his death on the cross.

PART II

THE MISSION AND FAITH OF JESUS

Chapter 4

Jesus and the Kingdom of God

The first thing that strikes one in beginning to analyze the reality of Jesus of Nazareth is that he did not make himself the focus of his preaching and mission. Jesus knew himself, lived and worked from something and for something distinct from himself. This fact, which can be deduced from faith if one accepts that Jesus was truly a human being and behaved in a manner appropriate to a creature, emerges incontrovertibly from the Gospels. Jesus' life was an outward-directed one, directed to something very different from himself.

In the Gospels this something central in Jesus' life is expressed by two terms: "Kingdom of God" and "Father." Of both, the first thing to say is that they are authentic words of Jesus. The second is that they are all-embracing, since by "Kingdom of God" Jesus expresses the whole of reality and of what is to be done, and by "Father" Jesus expresses the personal reality that gives final meaning to his life, that in which he rests and what in turn does not allow him to rest. Finally, "Kingdom of God" and "Father" are systematically important realities for theology, giving it a basis on which better to organize and grade Jesus' multiple external activities, to conjecture his inner being and, undoubtedly, to explain his historical fate of dying on the cross.

Both realities, Kingdom and Father, though distinct and not simply inter-changeable, complement one another, and so "the Kingdom explains God's being *abba* and the Fatherhood of God provides a basis for and explanation of the Kingdom."[1] In making an analysis, however, one has to choose to begin with one or the other, and here I begin with Jesus' relationship to the Kingdom, because this is how the Gospels begin, because they give a lot of information on it, and because, I think, one can approach Jesus' overall reality better by starting from his external activities on behalf of the Kingdom and moving from there to his inner relationship with God, than one can by working the other way round.

1. The Final Reality for Jesus: the Kingdom of God

Both Mark and Matthew present the start of Jesus' public ministry in these words:

"... Jesus came to Galilee, proclaiming the good news from God, and saying, 'The time is fulfilled and the Kingdom of God has come near; repent, and believe in the good news" (Mark 1:14-15; Matt. 4:17). In Luke the start of his public life takes place in the synagogue at Nazareth with the proclamation of the good news to the poor and the liberation of the oppressed (Luke 4:18), but Jesus himself relates the good news to the Kingdom: "I must proclaim the good news of the kingdom of God to the other cities also; for I was sent for this purpose" (4:43, cf. 8:1). The Q source sums up Jesus' mission programmatically in terms of good news to the poor (see Matt. 11:2-5; Luke 7:18-22), which is equivalent to the good news of the Kingdom.

The Synoptics make this initial presentation of Jesus from the standpoint of the Kingdom with the clear intention of putting forward a programmatic summary of his mission. Because of this, because of the high number of times the expression appears in the Synoptics, nearly always put into Jesus' mouth, and because it appears in very varied contexts in his preaching (parables, apocalyptic discourses, exhortations, ethical demands, prayer), there can be no doubt of the historical and theological centrality of the Kingdom of God for Jesus himself. Said from what is denied, "Jesus proclaims the Kingdom of God and not himself."[2] Said from what is affirmed, "the central theme of Jesus' preaching was the true sovereignty of God."[3]

It is clear, then, that the final reality for Jesus was not himself,[4] but neither was it the purely ahistorical transcendence suggested by "Kingdom of heaven,"[5] and of course it was not the church.[6] But if this is clear and generally accepted today, we still need to make explicit what has until now remained implicit: not only did Jesus not preach himself, but the final reality for him was not simply "God" but "the Kingdom of God." There is of course no debate about the fact that Jesus preached and spoke of God as Father, and that this Father was his final personal reference, whom he also offered to others—all of which will be examined in the next chapter. What I want to stress here is that for Jesus even "God" is seen within a wider reality: "the Kingdom of God."

This means that Jesus expresses final reality in a dual unity or in a unified duality. In the final reality there is always God and something that is not God. And therefore we have to speak of God *and* of the Kingdom; or, in other words, we have to speak of God *and* of a will carried out by God, of God *and* of the people of God, and so on. For Jesus, therefore, final reality has a transcendent dimension and a historical dimension. The latter depends on the former and what the "Kingdom" might be depends on what "God" might be (so, for example, the coming of the Kingdom is presented differently by John the Baptist and by Jesus, because they had different understandings of God); inversely, though, understanding of God will depend on what the Kingdom is seen to be. What needs to be stressed is that, for Jesus, God is not a reality that could be not linked to history, or history to God, but the relationship of God to history is essential to God.

The reason for this conception of God held by Jesus is known and has its roots deep in the Old Testament; it still needs to be re-emphasized. God never appears as a God-in-himself, but as a God for history, and, therefore, as the God-of-a-people. "I will be your God and you shall be my people" is Israel's confession of faith. In this, an essentially relational God is proclaimed, who *reveals himself* and who *is* in relation to a people. However different the traditions of God in the Old Testament may be, they have this in common: that God is a God-*of*, a God-*for*, a God-*in*, *never a God-in-himself*. So, in Exodus, God is the one who listens to the cry of the people in order to set them free and form them into a nation and make them God's people. In the prophetic traditions, God is the one who defends the oppressed, denouncing oppressors and proclaiming a new covenant with God's people. In the apocalyptic traditions, God is the one who will re-form his people and the whole of creation eschatologically. In the wisdom traditions, God still appears as provident, and in reflections on his silence, it is an active and speaking silence; it is not the mere absence of God from history, but a silence that makes itself felt. On the basis of these traditions, Jesus, too, understands final reality as a dual unity, a God who gives himself to history or a history that comes to be according to God.[7] This dual unity, which is final reality, is what is formally meant by the expression "Kingdom of God" and is what Jesus preached.

Nevertheless, we are faced with a paradox here. Jesus often speaks of the Kingdom of God, but never says what it actually is. "Jesus never tells us expressly *what* this Kingdom of God is. All he says is *that* it is at hand."[8] Not even in the so-called parables of the Kingdom does Jesus define what the Kingdom might be; though he stresses its novelty, its demands, its scandal..., he never defines it, "he never clarifies the concept of 'God's sovereignty' as such."[9]

It has to be said that we should not be surprised on principle by Jesus' non-definition of what the Kingdom of God is. In another context and using different language, the Synoptics state that the day of the Kingdom is not known by Jesus himself, but only by God (Mark 13:32); that is, that knowledge of the final reality, of the Kingdom, belongs to God alone. If Jesus had defined it, he would have gone beyond his own historicity and his appearance on earth would not have been in human form. From this we should not conclude, needless to say, that Jesus knew nothing about the Kingdom or that this was just an empty phrase for him. What we can deduce is the need for a method for verifying what Jesus thought about the Kingdom of God. I am going to put forward three ways by which this verification might proceed.

The first way, and the one most commonly used in theology,[10] is what can be called the *notional way*, which examines the notion Jesus had of the Kingdom by comparing it with earlier notions in Israel. It starts from Jesus' historical conscious-ness, dependent in this, as in so many other things, on the Old Testament. In this sense, it shows that Jesus did not proclaim anything absolutely new to his listeners, but that what was new with him was his concentration on the already familiar theme of the Kingdom of God. "The essentially traditional expectation of the coming Kingdom of God was changed into the one decisive perspective."[11] It is also notable that Jesus used the terminology of the Kingdom, whereas "the terms which in the biblical and Judaic tradition usually denoted salvation are absent from or very rare in Jesus' preaching."[12]

A second way, rarely used in theology, is what might be called the *way of the addressee*, and Jesus' addressees were, as we shall see, the poor. If Jesus' proclamation shows a correlation between the Kingdom and his audience, then the latter can tell us something about the former; this applies more if the Kingdom of God is presented not only as a *truth*, but as *good news*, since then the addressees will intrinsically clarify what is "good" in the news.[13]

A third way is the *way of the practice* of Jesus—understanding practice in the broad sense of his words and actions—on the basis that what Jesus said and did was in the service of proclaiming the Kingdom. As Edward Schillebeeckx says, "its specific content stems from the whole of Jesus' activity."[14] This methodological choice is sometimes imposed by Jesus himself when he relates his activity specifically to the Kingdom, in casting out demons, for example. It is also possible since many of Jesus' activities effectively express signs of what was understood by the Kingdom of God, as in his meals. And it is at least probable on the basis that Jesus' preaching and activities were intrinsically related.

These methodological reflections on how to establish what the Kingdom of God meant for Jesus are not mere abstractions. Modern theology, even its progressive wings, generally uses what I have called the notional way, sometimes adding the way of practice, but generally ignores the way of the addressee, on which liberation theology insists. And the resulting conclusions are very different.

2. The Notional Way: the Hoped-for Utopia in the Midst of the Sufferings of History

I propose to start by analyzing briefly the notions of the Kingdom of God in the Old Testament, those most current at the time of Jesus and the new elements Jesus brought to these notions.

(a) The Kingdom of God in the Old Testament

The expression "Kingdom of God" (*malkuta Jahvewh, basiliea tou theou*) is a late apocalyptic formulation,[16] but associating Yahweh with kingship is common in the Old Testament, above all in the Psalms and liturgy. This terminology is not original or specific to Israel, but existed throughout the ancient Near East. What Israel did—as it did with other aspects of the surrounding religions—was to historicize the notion of God-king, in accordance with its fundamental belief that Yahweh intervenes in history. "When Israel became integrated into the institution, originally foreign to it, of monarchy, it also took over its symbols to express its belonging to the God who saved it and made it his."[17]

This kingship of Yahweh—his capacity for intervening in history—was presented with differing emphases and dimensions throughout the history of Israel. So in the time of Moses, Yahweh's leadership was stressed, and at the time of the Judges, his exclusivity. During the monarchy—not without serious theological conflicts—the kingship of Yahweh was made compatible with that of the king of Israel, who was adopted by Yahweh. It was not till after the failure of the monarchy, through the national catastrophes of exile, captivity and occupation by foreign powers, that a clearer idea emerged of what the hoped-for reign of God was: a future as a kingdom of justice for Israel as a people within the boundaries of Israel. Apocalyptic universalized this expectation, extending it even to the bounds of the cosmos; it also, thanks to its historical pessimism, eschatologized it: that is, made the appearance of the reign of God coincide with the end of time, when the definitive renovation of all reality and the resurrection of the dead will take place, since this world as it is cannot receive God.

So confession of the kingship of Yahweh is basic to Israel and runs right through its history; it is another way of saying that God acts in history and takes Israel's side. But we need to be clear about what was formally understood by this kingship if we are to avoid the misunderstandings that the term "kingdom" can produce today. "The Kingdom of God" is not a geo-political entity (although it expresses the hope of a particular people) in the sense that medieval Christendom, for example, understood it, so that the church was for practical purposes taken as being the geographical confines that separated it from the infidels. Nor is it directly a "cultic-ascendent" entity, meaning for example that Israel recognized Yahweh alone as its king, though Israel undoubtedly did so in its liturgy in response to Yahweh.[18]

The Kingdom of God has two essential connotations: (1) that God rules in his acts, (2) that it exists in order to transform a bad and unjust historical-social reality into a different good and just one. So the term "reign" of God is actually more appropriate than "kingdom" of God. As the psalm says: "for he is coming to judge the earth. He will judge the world with righteousness, and the peoples with his truth" (Ps. 96:13). So God's "reign" is then the positive action through which God transforms reality and God's "Kingdom" is what comes to pass in this world when God truly reigns: a history, a society, a people transformed according to the will of God. And the first thing to note about it is that "the main characteristic of this Kingdom is that God carries out the royal idea of justice."[19] The Kingdom of God is, then, a highly positive reality, good news, but also a reality highly critical of the bad and unjust present.

There are three aspects of this reign of God awaited by Israel that are vital if we are to understand it properly and avoid distorting it. The first is its real incidence on human history, meaning that it is a historical, not a trans-historical reality, and this is why historical hope runs right through the Old Testament, even though apocalyptic eschatologizes it and puts it back to the end of time. Despite the variations in Israel's hope, its essence consists in that "the resignation that confines God to the nebulous beyond of ideals and that goes with the immutability of the world is completely alien to it."[20] Israel holds to the fact that God can change bad and unjust reality into good and just reality as essential to its faith. Therefore, the Kingdom of God corresponds to a *hope in history*.

The second is that God's action impinges directly on the transformation of the whole of society, the whole of a people. Israel certainly understood the reality of individuals, of persons, for whom God has saving demands and plans: that their hearts of stone be changed into hearts of flesh (Ezek. 36:26ff). "Kingdom of God," however, formally designates the utopia of God for a whole people. Put in telling symbols, that conflict should turn into reconciliation, and so the wolf and the lamb may eat together (Isa. 11:6); that war should turn into peace, and so swords be made into ploughshares (Isa. 2:4); that injustice should turn into justice and life become possible, and so those who work the land may enjoy the fruits of the land and those who build houses may live in them (Isa. 65:21ff); so God may be the one who speaks first and writes his law on our hearts (Jer. 31:33). In short, that in contrast to the present reality, "new heavens and a new earth" may appear (Isa. 65:17). Our response to the Kingdom of God, then, has to be not just hope, but *hope as a people*, of a whole people and for a whole people.

The third thing is that the Kingdom of God appears as good news in the midst of bad things, in the midst of the *anti-Kingdom*, that is. The Kingdom of God will not arrive, so to speak, from a *tabula rasa*, but from and against the anti-Kingdom that is formally and actively opposed to it. The Kingdom of God is, then, a dialectical and conflictual reality, excluding and opposing the anti-Kingdom. Our response to the Kingdom of God has to be, therefore, in no way an ingenuous hope, but hoping against hope—in the late Pauline expression of Romans 4:18—and an *active and fighting* hope against the anti-Kingdom.

To sum up, the Kingdom of God is a utopia that answers the age-old hope of a people in the midst of historical calamities; it is, then, what is good and wholly good. But it is also something liberating, since it arrives in the midst of and in opposition to the oppression of the anti-Kingdom. It needs and generates a hope that is also liberating, from the understandable despair built up in history from the evidence that what triumphs in history is the anti-Kingdom.[21]

(b) Expectation of the Kingdom at the Time of Jesus: John the Baptist

Expectations of the Kingdom appeared in different shapes at the time of Jesus. The Pharisees and Sadducees scrutinized the signs of the times for evidence of the coming of the Kingdom. The Essenes and the Pharisees tried to hasten its coming through a life of purity, contemplation and observance of the law. There were also groups who tried to hasten its advent through armed violence aimed at bringing in a theocracy, though it is very unlikely that the armed anti-Roman Zealot movement was already in existence in the time of Jesus.[22] Some years after his death, the Zealots certainly appeared on the scene, formulating their goal in terms of the Kingdom of God. So Flavius Josephus tells of a messiah who sought to enter Jerusalem from the Mount of Olives with an armed band, seeking to install the Kingdom of God. Later, in 70 CE, when the Romans stormed the Temple, they met six thousand Jews awaiting the coming of the Kingdom of God.

Whatever shape they took, what is certain is that great expectations existed at the time of Jesus and that he was understood in relation to these, insofar as he confirmed them, modified them or replaced them. This can be examined through a little detour to analyze the figure of John the Baptist and his relation to Jesus; this will show what he taught about such expectations and also help to get to know Jesus, who was quite possibly a disciple of John.[23]

John the Baptist appeared in the desert, announcing God's imminent coming in terms of the "judgment of God," not the "kingdom of God,"[24] So the (redactional) formulation in Matthew: "the kingdom of heaven has come near" (3:2) would be designed to show the parallels between Jesus and John. But, although he did not use the terminology of the "kingdom," John did give a response to the expectations of his time, one unexpected for the force of its threat. God was coming and was coming eschatologically with imminent wrath. "Even now the axe is lying at the root of the trees" (Luke 3:9); hence the appeal to conversion: only this can save, not belonging to the people of Israel. John appears, then, as a prophet denouncing the sin of the people, announcing the coming of God and his radical judgment. Faced with this, there is one possiblity and only one: conversion, expressed in baptism for the forgiveness of sins and effected in "bearing fruit worthy of of repentance" (Matt. 3:8). In the midst of the wrath of God to come, John does proclaim something that is good news: the possibility of salvation in baptism, and something that is eschatological: the unification of the true Israel.[25]

This message and the person of the Baptist had a great influence at the time of Jesus, even on Jesus himself. The Gospels tell that he allowed himself to be baptized by John, and this event seems to be incontrovertibly historical. The communities could not have invented a scene in which Jesus appears being baptized with the rest of the people (Luke 3:21), without distinguishing himself from the rest (John 1:26, 31), and with a baptism that was specifically for the forgiveness of sins.

Furthermore, the fact that Jesus allowed himself to be baptized by John—a sign of inferiority in relation to John—cannot have failed to cause indignation in the early communities, when after Jesus' resurrection John's disciples continued to baptize (Acts 19:1-7) and competition between Jesus' and John's disciples continued to exist, a fact echoed in the Gospels and Acts: the fasting of John's disciples was contrasted to the non-fasting of Jesus' (Mark 2:18ff); Jesus' disciples also baptized (John 3:22ff)—though John states that Jesus himself did not (4:2-3)—and baptized more people than John's (4:1); disciples who had previously followed John became disciples of Jesus (1:35-42).

A final proof of the historicity of Jesus' baptism by John is that the baptismal scene was re-written so as to leave no doubt of Jesus' superiority over John, even though Jesus had accepted being baptized by John. In Mark, who seems to be using a pre-synoptic tradition, the baptism is described sparely (1:9). Matthew, out of doctrinal concern, prefigures the scene with a dialogue between Jesus and John, in which the latter at first refuses to baptize the former (3:14) and only accedes when Jesus persuades him that "it is proper for us in this way to fulfill all righeousness" (3:15). Luke passes over the name of the Baptist in silence and presents Jesus' baptism as something in the past, "when Jesus also had been baptized..." (3:21), so as to concentrate on the revelation of the Spirit to Jesus while he was praying (21b-22). John omits the baptismal scene (though he refers to it in 1:32-4) and concerns himself with the witness John gave concerning Jesus, of whom he says that he baptizes with the Holy Spirit (1:19-28). In short, John is made into a precursor of Jesus (Matt. 3:11ff; Acts 13:24ff).

That Jesus was baptized by John is, then, a historically certain fact. But this is not all. Jesus' relationship with John must have gone much deeper. He must have belonged to John's circle and had probably baptized on his own account. From the historical-religious aspect, Jesus was initiated in and depended on the Baptist's prophetic-eschatological movement. "Let us not in any way imagine that Jesus' relation to John the Baptist was a fleeting one."[26] Indications of this deep relationship are Jesus' praise of John as the greatest of the prophets and of those born of woman (Luke 7:26ff; Matt. 11:18ff) and the fact that he withdrew to a solitary place after hearing the news of John's assassination (Matt. 14:3-13). And let us not overlook one important fact: in Mark and Matthew, Jesus begins his own public ministry "after John had been arrested" (Mark 1:14; Matt. 4:12), which can, at least probably, be taken as meaning that John's arrest provided the existential motivation for Jesus to begin his own work, not just that the two were coincidental in time.[27]

The point of this analysis is that Jesus was to take up the mantle and some of the content of John's preaching in his proclamation of the coming of the Kingdom of God. Like the Baptist, Jesus appeared first and foremost as a prophet—though part of his language was taken from apocalyptic—announcing the close arrival of God, destroying the false hopes in Israel's prerogatives, proclaiming God's judgment not only on the gentiles, but also on Israel, rejecting those who trust in their own righteousness, welcoming notorious sinners, opening his preaching to all and not—as the Essenes and Pharisees did—to a separatist remnant. Like John, he offered the possibility of salvation. Neither Jesus nor John, though, offered a salvation connected with the salvific institutions of the Old Testament: the Temple, ritual, sacrifices; they offered something quite different: baptism in John's case, unconditional trust in God in Jesus' case, and true conversion in both.

(c) Jesus' Concept of the Kingdom of God

Jesus put forward his own concept of the Kingdom, as we shall see shortly. First, however, I should like to reflect briefly on the fact that Jesus came *following a tradition of hope for oppressed history*, that the first impression he made was above all *in continuity* with a hope-filled tradition.

The fact of the existence of this tradition is something not much alluded to in christology, even somewhat disdained, since the object seems to be first and foremost to find something specific to Jesus that will show his difference from other human beings so as to emphasize his unrepeatability. That is, we look for those things in Jesus that show him *in discontinuity* with the rest of the human race. Let me say that there is something very strange in this procedure.

To take a simple example: traditional christologies do not pay much attention to the parable of the good Samaritan, nor to the fact that Jesus lived as a good Samaritan, because, on the face of it, the message of this parable could be known independently of Jesus, and there is no need for it be something unique to Jesus. They would rather see Jesus working prodigious miracles impossible to anyone else, or showing a clear and explicit consciousness of his divinity, since this would prove his radical discontinuity from other human beings.

Christologies today do not base themselves on this sort of unrepeatable action peculiar to Jesus, but neither do they tend to give proper weight to what Jesus has in common with others. And if I regard this as a strange way of proceeding, this is why: Jesus' way of revealing the truth about God and human beings is through what is least esoteric and most common—love; and if we are looking for discontinuity, this is to be found not in the "beyond," but in this very love, a limitless love, valid to the point of the cross.

Whether there are discontinuities between Jesus and the rest of humankind as a matter of historical fact is something that needs examining, but we must also stress the deep significance of the continuity between Jesus and the positive traditions of humanity. To return to the Kingdom of God, we should first attach great importance to the fact that Jesus shared in expectation of the Kingdom, that he thought it possible, that he thought it something good and liberative. This view brings Jesus back to humankind, since humankind,[28] not just Israel, has forged these utopic hopes, and this is then an effective way of stating the true *humanity* of Jesus in historical and exegetical categories (as dogma was later to do in ontological categories), since it shows Jesus facing up to the question that has always preoccupied humankind: whether or not there is salvation for oppressed history. And Jesus appears tied into humanity in a specific manner: he is one of those who believe that it is possible to overcome the suffering of history. He belongs, then, to the current of those who hope in history, in the midst of oppression, who again and again formulate a utopia, who believe that justice is possible. And in this way we can say (in faith) that Jesus' humanity is *true* humanity.

In this particular sense, Jesus needs be seen not as the monopoly of Christians, but as belonging to the current of hope—expressed in religious or secular ways—of humanity, as belonging to the current of solidarity with the sufferings of history. And so Jesus himself provides the possibility of a universal, human ecumenism of all those who hope and work for a kingdom. This is why it is so understandable for non-Christians to ask Christians simply to "go back to Jesus."

Having said this, let us now look at Jesus' specific concept of the Kingdom of God, a specificity that can be enlarged later by examining the addressees of and Jesus' service to the Kingdom.

(i) The Kingdom of God is at hand. Just as the Baptist proclaimed the imminent coming of God, so Jesus says that the Kingdom of God is at hand. In the very early words of Mark 9:1, he says: "Truly I tell you, there are some standing here who will not taste death until they see that the kingdom of God has come with power." In

his parables, he states that the harvest is now ripe (Matt. 9:37 par.), that the fields are white, ready for harvest (John 4:35), that now there is new wine (Mark 2:22), that the hour of the bridegroom has come and there is no need to fast (Mark 2:18-20). He states that if he casts out demons, this means that the Kingdom of God has already come (Matt. 12:28). To the Pharisees' question about when the Kingdom would come, he replies that "in fact, the kingdom of God is among you" (Luke 17:21). In a word, the dawn of salvation has broken, the old times have passed away. "The eschatological hour of God, the victory of God, the consummation of the world is close. And indeed: very close."[29] And if at the end of his life Jesus did not see the closeness of this Kingdom quite so clearly, nor that it would come in the way he had envisaged, he nevertheless reiterated at the Last Supper his conviction that it will come: "I will never again drink of the fruit of the vine until that day when I drink it new in the kingdom of God" (Mark 14:25). This banquet will be the final banquet at which Abraham, Isaac and Jacob will be seated at table and to which will come pagans from the four points of the compass (Luke 13:28ff).

These words must have caused quite a stir. Jesus not only hopes for the Kingdom of God, he affirms that it is at hand, that its arrival is imminent, that the Kingdom should be not only an object of hope, but of certainty.[30] In systematic language, Jesus has the audacity to proclaim the outcome of the drama of salvation, the overcoming, at last, of the anti-Kingdom, the unequivocally saving coming of God. And the signs that accompanied his words upheld this hope.

(ii) The Kingdom is purely God's initiative, gift and grace. Jesus states that the Kingdom is a gift and purely a gift from God, that it cannot be forced by human action. The coming of the Kingdom is, then, shot through with gratuitousness; God comes out of gratuitous love, not in response to human actions.

This gratuitousness, however, is not opposed to human striving. The "growth parables" underline the fact that that the Kingdom of God and its final coming do not depend on human action, but neither is the growth a form of magic. I shall deal with the relation between gratuitousness and human action later, but for the moment let me just say that they are not opposed to one another, as is often supposed. Jesus himself, proclaiming the free gift of the Kingdom, does not draw a lesson of inactivity toward it, but rather carries out a whole series of actions related to the Kingdom. Whether he does so *because* the Kingdom is coming—and so he can show these signs—or *in order that* the Kingdom may come—and so its coming depends on his actions—cannot be elucidated by pure theory, since, existentially, the two aspects are united in Jesus; the main thing is the fact itself: Jesus actively served the Kingdom. And he obviously did not tolerate the anti-Kingdom, the situation of injustice, denouncing it with great force, even while thinking that it was not going to last long.[31]

And the same applies to those who heard him. The coming of the Kingdom demands a conversion, *metanoia*, which—to put it simply for the moment—is a task for the listener: the hope the poor must come to feel, the radical change of conduct required of the oppressors, the demands made on all to live a life worthy of the Kingdom.[32]

Gratuitousness and action are not opposed, then. The coming of the Kingdom of God is something that, on the one hand, can only be asked for, not forced; but on the other, the will of God has to be put into effect now on this earth. What is clear is the absolute loving initiative of God, which is neither forced nor can be forced— this being both unnecessary and impossible—by human actions. Clear too is that this gratuitous love of God's is what generates the need and the possibility of a loving human response. When a sinner is converted, it is God's goodness and mercy that moves the sinner to change. "The mercy of God we experience ... is the precondition, the basis and the foundation of the merciful behavior that ought to obtain among us."[33] In the words of 1 John, "Since God loved us so much, we also ought to love one another" (4:11). The gratuitous love of God both shows us what loving one another means and enables us to put it into practice.

God's gift is not opposed to human activity, or, more precisely, is opposed to only one thing: this activity being understood in a Promethean sense, being capable of causing or forcing God's action. What Jesus is rejecting, then, in affirming the Kingdom as gift, is that—as the Essenes, Pharisees and various armed movements claimed, in their various ways—we either can or should force the coming of the Kingdom. It comes purely from God's love. On this level, indeed, the only thing we can do is simply pray, as Jesus taught: "Your Kingdom come" (Matt. 6:10; Luke 11:2)

(iii) The Kingdom of God as eu-aggelion, *good news.* The coming of the Kingdom of God—in the understanding of the traditions preceding Jesus—means crisis for and judgment on the world and history. Jesus was no tranquilizer of consciences distancing himself from the Baptist. He shared his idea of judgment and, probably, expected the coming of the Son of Man at that time (see the apocalyptic discourse of Mark 13 par.). Nevertheless, this is not the most specific and original aspect of the proclamation of the Kingdom. Unlike the Baptist, what is imminent is not God's judgment—though this will come—but God's grace. And this is what Jesus expresses in a term not found in John the Baptist: *eu-aggelion,* the good news.

Jesus states that the coming of God's Kingdom is good and the ultimate good. Jesus, like the Baptist, requires conversion when he announces the coming of the Kingdom (Mark 1:14; Matt. 4:17), and later demands radical conversion. But, in itself, the coming of the Kingdom is, above all else, good news, as Matthew and Luke spell out: "The good news of the Kingdom of God." This is the vital core of Jesus' message: God is coming close; God is coming close because God is good, and it is good for us that God should come close. In Rahner's systematic language, God has broken for once and for all the symmetry of being possibly savior or possibly condemning judge. God is seen, in essence, as salvation, and God's approach is directly salvation.

Let us look briefly at the term *eu-aggelion* and how it relates to the Kingdom of

God. It appears frequently in the New Testament, and with a variety of meanings.[34] In the Synoptics, it is a central term and again has a variety of meanings. At the beginning of Mark's Gospel, when the evangelist himself is speaking, the term "good news" can refer either to Jesus himself or to what Jesus brings (1:1). But in other passages, where *eu-aggelion* is put into Jesus' mouth, it is used in a strict sense (8:35; 10:29; 13:10; 14:9) and it appears once as "the good news from God" (1:14). For Mark, then, the good news is what Jesus brings from God, though Jesus' person, life and destiny also form part of the good news.

In Matthew, *eu-aggelion* means "the good news of the Kingdom" (4:23; 9:35; 24:14). Luke avoids the use of *eu-aggelion* as a noun throughout his Gospel and it appears only twice in Acts: once on its own (15:7) and once qualified as "the good news of God's grace" (20:24). On the other hand he—and Q—make liberal use of the verb "evangelize" (ten times in the Gospel and fifteen in Acts), in the sense of "bring the good news to." In Luke and in Q, therefore, the word *eu-aggelion* is referred back to its meaning in Isaiah (61:1-3; 42:1-4; 51:16; 52:7; 59:21), "in whom the concepts of 'eschatological prophet' and 'bringing the good news to the poor' are tied one to another."[35]

The conclusion has to be that in the Gospels, Jesus is good news, but, with logical priority, the good news is what Jesus brings: the Kingdom of God. This is naturally so, since there is no way of separating the Kingdom of God Jesus proclaims and the good news Jesus himself brings. But sometimes they are one, even linguistically: the "good news of the Kingdom of God" means the Kingdom of God as good news.

This being so, the proclamation of the Kingdom of God is not only something true—this is how things are—but something that in essence has to be proclaimed with joy and must produce joy, as the Gospels also attest. And this, let me say in passing, imposes certain conditions on how it is proclaimed today and enables us to verify whether it has in fact been proclaimed. To proclaim something to be believed which, also, turns out to be good news, is not the same as directly to proclaim good news which is, also, true. And one way of verifying whether what has been proclaimed is good news is to check that it produces joy, since it would be a strict contradiction to proclaim it without producing joy. The joy of those who proclaim it and those who receive it is an essential condition of the proclamation at issue being good news, something frequently forgotten in the mission of the church, which is often more concerned with communicating a "truth" that has to be given and received in an orthodox manner, without bothering to present it with joy and to check whether or not it has produced joy.

In short, for the Kingdom of God to be *eu-aggelion* means that it must make its hearers rejoice. As Leonardo Boff has written, "Jesus articulates a radical aspect of human nature, its hope-principle and its utopic dimension. And he promises that it will now not be *utopia*, the object of anxious awaiting (cf Luke 3:14), but *topia*, an object of joy for all the people (cf Luke 2:9)."[36] Or, in the words of Raúl Aguirre, "Jesus gave religious expression to the actual situation of the immense majority of the Jewish people in the first century. The God of the Kingdom expresses the real hope of a people in great material difficulties, subjected to a cultural and political crisis of identity. This is why Jesus aroused undoubted popular support throughout the whole of his ministry."[37]

3. The Way of the Addressee: the Kingdom of God is for the Poor

I have already mentioned the subject of the "addressee" as one way of finding out what this Kingdom might consist of. The following logical consideration is relevant here: if the Kingdom of God is "good news," its recipients will help fundamentally in clarifying its content, since good news is something essentially relational, not all good news being so in equal measure for everyone.

In order to grasp what it means for the Kingdom of God to have specific addressees and so to be essentially partial, we need to remember that Jesus offered God's love to all, but not in the same way.[38] Certainly, Jesus did not come in the sectarian guise of his time, offering salvation only to those belonging to a particular group (Pharisees, Essenes, Zealots and the like), nor did he adopt a primarily antagonistic stance. He came rather as a positive evangelizer, concerned for the salvation of all and willing the Kingdom of God to be brought within the reach of all. As Schillebeeckx says, "Jesus' praxis and activity never had an anti, but a pro character."[39]

This, however, does not prevent Jesus from having a specific addressee in mind when proclaiming the Kingdom of God. All that can be deduced from it is that he did not exclude anyone from the possibility of entering into the Kingdom. But not excluding does not mean the same as addressing himself directly to certain people. And these are the poor.

(a) The Poor as Addressees of the Kingdom of God

In order to analyze who the addressees of the Kingdom of God are, let us start with this impressive quotation from Joachim Jeremias: "By ascertaining that Jesus proclaimed the dawn of the consummation of the world, we have not yet completely described his preaching of the *basileia*. On the contrary, we have not yet mentioned its essential feature... the offer of salvation Jesus makes to the poor.... The Kingdom belongs *uniquely to the poor*."[40] Jesus indeed understood his mission as directed to the poor: "... he has anointed me to bring good news to the poor" (Luke 4:18). This is shown too by his jubilant response to those sent by John: "the poor have good news brought to them" (Luke 7:22; Matt. 11:5). The first of his beatitudes, in Luke's version, proclaims: "Blessed are you who are poor, for yours is the kingdom of God" (6:20). These statements are basic for understanding what the Kingdom of God is for Jesus. They stand not in the line of discontinuity—as his audacity in stating that the Kingdom is at hand might—but in that of continuity, being rooted in the Old Testament. Yet, as Jeremias understands, they are the basic element for introducing us to the content of the Kingdom of God.

This relationship between the Kingdom of God and the poor is established in the Gospels as a fact, but more basically it appears as a relationship as of right, based on the very reality of God as this was shown in the Old Testament. This is what Jeremias means by that *"uniquely."* And this is impressively borne out by Puebla: by the mere fact of being poor, whatever the moral or personal situation in which they find themselves, God defends them and loves them, and they are the first ones to whom Jesus' mission is directed (cf. 1142).

This statement is still fundamental and is still, in my view, the touchstone for understanding the Kingdom of God, Jesus and the church's mission today. It is often diluted by taking as poor—and spiritualizing them—the poor mentioned in Matthew 5:3, or nullified by equating poverty with metaphysical limitation, so that all human beings can be included in the category of poor. It is also confusing to recall that poverty has various meanings in the Gospels (as Puebla itself does, 1148ff). The question here is not to deny that the "poor in spirit" or metaphysical "limitation" or different meanings of poverty exist—or that they can exist, and a good thing too—but to know which poor Jesus was thinking of when he said that the Kingdom of God belongs to them. This is the basic question now.

Descriptively—and following Jeremias once more[41]—the poor are divided into two classes in the Synoptics. On the one side are those who groan under some type of basic need in the tradition of Isaiah 61:1ff. So the poor are those who hunger and thirst, who go naked, strangers, the sick, those in prison, those who mourn, those weighed down by a real burden (Luke 6:20-21; Matt. 25:25ff). In this sense, the poor are those who live bent (*anawin*) under the weight of a burden—which Jesus often interpreted as oppression—those for whom life and survival is a hard task. In modern parlance, we could call these the *economic* poor, in the sense that the *oikos* (the hearth, the home, the symbol of what is basic and primary in life) is in grave danger, and that they are thereby denied the minimum of life.

On the other side, the poor are those despised by the ruling society, those considered sinners, the publicans, the prostitutes (Mark 2:16; Matt. 11:19; 21:23; Luke 15:1ff), the simple-minded, the littles ones, the least (Matt. 11:25; Mark 9:36ff; Matt. 10:42; 18:10-14; 25:40-45), those who carry out despised tasks (Matt. 12:31; Luke 18:11). In this sense, the poor are the marginalized, those "whose religious ignorance and moral behavior closed, in the conviction of the time, the gate leading to salvation for them."[42] These could be called the *sociological* poor, in the sense that being a *socium* (the symbol of basic interhuman relationships) is denied them, and with this, the minimum of dignity.

So the Gospels do not provide an absolutely clear-cut image of the poor Jesus was thinking of as addressees of the Kingdom, nor of course a strictly conceptual reflection designed to answer the questions we ask now about the meaning of poverty.[43] But neither can they be said to lack a basic vision of what the poor meant to Jesus. The poor are those who are at the bottom of the heap in history and those who are oppressed by society and cast out from it; they are not, therefore, all human beings, but those at the bottom, and being at the bottom in this sense means being oppressed by those on top. Both economic poverty and lack of moral dignity can express this being at the bottom. From a purely conceptual point of view, the two can be separated (Zacchaeus suffered the social shunning, but not the economic poverty), but both senses of being poor usually go together and converge in history, as happens today in the Third World. The poor are those close to the slow death poverty brings, those for whom surviving is a heavy burden and their chief task, and those who are also deprived of social dignity and sometimes also of religious dignity for not complying with church legislation. The poor are those who in Latin America are usually called the "popular majorities."

To these poor, Jesus showed undoubted partiality, so that what is now called the option for the poor can be said to start with him (though it goes back before him to the prophets, and indeed to God himself): partiality toward the economic poor, as shown in the beatitudes in Luke, and partiality toward the sociological poor, as shown in his standing up for publicans and sinners expressed with even more force, perhaps, than the former, precisely because their alienation on religious grounds was more provocative to him.[44]

Having said this, let me briefly characterize the poor as a social grouping at the time of Jesus, in order to shed light on the present discussion on what they mean, now that we are all asked to make a preferential option for the poor, and to show, above all, what the Kingdom of God meant for Jesus.

In the first place, one must stress that the Synoptics speak of *the poor in the plural*, not of poor individuals or the sum total of poor individuals, but of a reality—be it understood as a group or a class—that is collective and massive and sufficiently defined in historical terms. "The poor," in the plural, are spoken of in the beatitudes; "crowds" of the sick in the summaries; and the "multitudes" who listened to Jesus are often mentioned.

Looking at these groups or collectivity of poor in more detail,[45] the first thing to note is that they are *economically-sociologically* poor. The New Testament Greek word most frequently used to describe them is *ptochos* (from the verb *ptosso*, to crouch or bend down). It appears twenty-five times, and in twenty-two cases "refers to the economically afflicted and dispossessed."[46] In the other three cases, where it means spiritually poor (Matt. 3:5; cf. Gal. 4:9; Rev. 3:17), there is always some qualification added. And in the three places where Jesus relates the Kingdom of God to the *ptochoi* (Matt. 11:5 = Luke 7:22; Luke 4:18 and 6:20), the meaning is not spiritual. The conclusion is that for the New Testament and for Jesus "the term 'poor' is a sociological category, even in the three texts that mention good news to the poor."[47]

The second thing to note is that these are *dialectically* poor. In the Gospels, poor and rich are spoken of as different and contrasted groups. The New Testament does not in fact express this with the clarity and force of the Old. The contrast is rather between poor and envious. But even if it is not as explicit, this does not mean that the Old Testament context is not pervasive: "behind this understanding of rich and poor the class dialectic of the Old Testament is implicit."[48] The reversal of fate awaiting the poor and the rich in the Gospels—see the *Magnificat*—"has no meaning except that the understanding of poverty as a state of unjust oppression remains in force in the New Testament."[49]

It is, then to *these* poor that Jesus says the Kingdom of God belongs: those for whom the basic things of life are so hard to achieve, those who live despised and outcast, who live under oppression, who, in short, have nothing to look forward to; those who, furthermore, feel themselves cut off from God, since religious society forces them to introject this understanding—it is these whom Jesus tells to have hope, that God is not like their oppressors have made them think, that the end of their misfortunes is at hand, that the Kingdom of God is coming and is for them.

These poor are the majority, which is quantitatively important in itself, but important also for understanding the universality of the Kingdom of God, something to which liberation theology seems to have called attention. It is at least careless, if not hypocritical, to stress its universality—as a means of rejecting its partiality—since there is little universal about a universality that fails to take the majorities of this world into account. And the quality of these majorities also indicates that the Kingdom can come to be a universal reality: if life comes even to these—to whom it never has come—then one can indeed speak of the universality of the Kingdom of God.

If the poor, understood in this way, are those to whom the Kingdom is addressed, then it is from them that we can better understand what sort of Kingdom Jesus was thinking of. It is a strictly partial Kingdom and one whose minimum, but basic, content is the life and dignity of the poor.

(b) The Partiality of the Kingdom of God

As an eschatological reality, the Kingdom of God is universal, and open to all, though not to all in the same way. But the Kingdom is addressed directly only to the poor. And this being so, it is essentially "partial." This statement, so clear in the Bible, yet so difficult of acceptance—look at the interminable debates over the present "option for the poor," which had to be qualified into "preferential" so as to make the option less radical—has its roots in the Old Testament, which treats this partiality as something essential. While we so often use arguments from the Old Testament in order to understand Jesus, we now need to look briefly at the partiality that runs through it, in order to understand Jesus and the Kingdom he proclaimed.[50]

The founding event of the Old Testament, the exodus, shows God being partial to an oppressed people, revealing himself to them, not to all, liberating them, not everyone. And this partiality is a basic mediation of God's self-revelation. It is not that God reveals himself first as he is and then shows himself partial to the oppressed. It is rather *in and through* his partiality toward the oppressed that God reveals his own identity. And this pattern persists through the whole of the Old Testament. "Father of orphans and protector of widows...," God is defined as in Psalm 68:5. In the prophets God calls not the whole of Israel, but the oppressed within it "my" people.[51] Yahweh is defender of Israel, the *Go'el*, *"because* he defends the poor,"[52] and will go on being Israel's God to the extent that Israel defends them. H. Wolf finds the true *confessio Dei* in this exclamation: "In you the orphan finds compassion."[53]

The partiality of the Kingdom of God should not, therefore, surprise us. If Jesus apocalyptically stresses its eschatological character and imminent coming, he prophetically emphasizes the partiality of God as God of the poor. And this partiality of God, in terms of the Kingdom too, is present in the Old Testament. The "king awaited"—utopia—is not just any king, but the king who is partial to the oppressed. "The king's justice... does not consist primordially in pronouncing an impartial verdict, but in the protection given to the poor, to widows and orphans."[54] This was the way utopia was expressed in terms of kingship in Israel and the surrounding peoples: imparting justice "partially." The same is found in the language of the "awaited righteous judge": "Historically, when the idea of a righteous judge or what was later called a judge came into being, this was exclusively to help those who, being weak, were unable to defend themselves; the others had no need of him.... When the Bible speaks of Yahweh as 'judge' or the judgment exercised by Yahweh, it is thinking precisely of the meaning attached to the root *spt*: saving the oppressed from injustice."[55]

The internal logic of this partiality will be analyzed later in the context of the contrast between the God of life and the idols of death, which will show that partiality is not just arbitrary choice, but actively defending the poor because they are poor, and will also explain why Jesus was persecuted. Here I simply want to establish the fact and the difficulty—today as in the past—we have in accepting it. It is worth remembering that Jesus ends his reply to John's disciples, in which he sets out the signs of the Kingdom and the preaching of the good news to the poor, with the words "and blessed is anyone who takes no offense at me" (Matt. 11:6; Luke 7:23). How could good news offend? The reason lay in the fact that the relationship between God and humankind was being seen from the moral standpoint of the latter. For the Kingdom of God to come for the just had its own inner logic; that it should come without taking account of individual moral states was a scandal. The proclamation of good news to the poor simply because they were poor shook the very foundations of religion, and was the best way of showing God's gratuitousness in a world that idolized riches. "Therefore, the scandal derives from the good news and not primarily from Jesus' call to penance."[56] The offense taken by the non-poor is an indirect but effective proof of the fact that the Kingdom of God belongs to the poor simply because they are poor, and that God is revealed as essentially on the side of the poor simply because they are poor.

God's taking sides in this way seems to me to be a constant element of revelation. It is clearly shown by the choice God makes in support of some as opposed to and against others. The partiality that runs through the scriptures is therefore also a dialectical partiality. However obvious, we need to consider seriously how often scripture states what God and Jesus are against in order to show what they are for. This produces the frequent typification of two types of groups or persons: some accepted by God and others rejected by God.

In the Old Testament, Abel is opposed to Cain, Moses to the Pharaoh, the leaders of the Jewish people to the poor majorities. In the New Testament, the *Magnificat* contrasts the lowly with the powerful; Jesus contrasts the poor, those who hunger and thirst, with the rich, who laugh and have their fill; children with the wise; sinners with just; publicans and prostitutes with Pharisees and scribes and so on. We need to analyze exegetically what Jesus means in each of these cases, but not fail to see the wood for the trees in so doing. Jesus had a clear understanding of taking sides, and of not being accepted because of this, as the parables show. I shall examine these later, but for the moment let us just recall how Jesus formulated his partiality in effective terms: "The last shall be first."

(c) The Kingdom of God as a Kingdom of Basic Life

The poor are, to repeat, those for whom life is a heavy burden on the basic level of survival and living with a minimum of dignity. From Latin America, this is very clear: the poor are "those who die before their time," as Gustavo Gutiérrez constantly says. If the Kingdom of God is for the poor, then, it has to be in essence a Kingdom of life, and so Jesus sees it. According to Jeremias, the situation of the poor—even linguistically—was compared to death. "The situation of such persons, according to the thinking of the time, could no longer be called life. They are practically dead."[57] In this terminology, the proclamation of the Kingdom has to be translated: "now those who seemed dead are brought to life."[58]

In systematic language, Jesus saw poverty as contrary to God's original plan, as annulling it. In poverty, God's creation is vitiated and annihilated. The life that Jesus will bring goes beyond the basic fact of survival, but includes this fact as an essential component. This is what Archbishop Romero said: "We have to defend the little thing that is God's greatest gift: life."

There is no doubt that Jesus made great play of defending the life of the poor in the sense of the primary fact of being alive. For him, the law of Israel was the expression of the primal will of God. He seldom mentions the written Torah in the Gospels, but when he does he presents it as God's final will. And curiously—but logically—he concentrates on its second part, on those commandments that refer to the neighbor and protect life (Mark 10:19 par., see also the antinomies of Matt. 5:21-48). And when he gives examples of keeping the commandmments, he always shows a person in a basic situation of needing help to live: parents in need (Mark 10:17; Matt. 15:4: keeping the fourth commandment), the wounded man on the road (Luke 10:30: keeping the commandment to love one's neighbor). Jesus was a nonconformist in respect of the law, even to the point of "criticizing scripture itself."[59] But when what is at stake is defending basic life—the most specific requirement of the law—he defends it and requires it without hesitation.

Jesus' purpose to defend basic life comes out more clearly still in his criticism of the oral interpretation of the law made by the scribes: the *Halaka*. In criticizing these interpretations, Jesus is condemning the creation of human traditions that run counter to the primal will of God on the side of life: cutting off aid to parents in need (Mark 7:8-13; Matt. 15:3-9), forbidding eating corn plucked from someone else's field on the sabbath (Mark 2:23-8 par.).

Finally, Jesus gives central importance to the basic symbol of life: food and bread. He eats with publicans (Mark 2:15-17), a symbolic gesture that cannot be reduced to pure eating, but which includes it. He takes little account of ritual washing before meals (Mark 7:2-5; Matt. 15:2), the former being human institutions and the latter the divine will. He multiplies loaves to show—whatever the christological or liturgical intention behind the account might be—that the hungry must be fed, and the account explicitly tells that they ate and were filled (Mark 6:30-44 par.; 8:1-10; Matt. 15:32-9). At the last judgment those who have fed the hungry have found God (Matt. 25:35, 40).

Jesus also teaches us to ask for bread in the prayer that is most specifically his, a prayer on which Matthew and Luke coincide, though Luke presents only four of the petitions (Matt. 6:11; Luke 11:3). The meaning of *epiousion* is debated and may be either "what is necessary for everyday life" or "what is to come, what is tomorrow's." But even if one holds to the second sense on linguistic grounds, "it would be a crass error to suppose that this meant spiritualizing the asking for bread."[60] The bread of life and earthly bread are not opposed to each other. What people should ask is that the bread of life should come today, in the midst of their poor existence.

The passages cited above about life, meals and bread are not literarily related in the Gospels to those dealing with the Kingdom of God and the poor, but they are objectively related. They show Jesus' vision of God's creation—"and God saw that it was good"—as holding the prime place, and the primal evil of the anti-Kingdom consisting, precisely, in vitiating this creation, in producing poor. The Kingdom of God must, then, include as its least what is the greatest for the poor: life. For those who, today as well as yesterday, have life assured, this will hardly seem utopia, but for the poor it is.

In my view, of all the ways in which human beings can be divided up, the most basic is this: those who can take life and survival for granted, and those who cannot take precisely this for granted. For the former, the proclamation of life is not good news in itself, and they therefore tend to express the good news as fullness of life or, in religious language, as eschatological life. But it is good news—and very good—in itself for the latter, though their life too should not be limited to survival.

This distinction, on the basis of life, has great hermeneutical repercussions for understanding the reality of the poor in the time of Jesus. Here I must quote the following passage by G. M. Soares Prabhu, dealing with whether Jesus saw the poor in material or spiritual terms:

Western exegesis, which forms part of the vast ideological production of an opulent and intensely consumerist society based on principles diametrically opposed to those of Jesus, has inclined to the latter interpretation and has systematically tried to spiritualize the gospel understanding of the poor.... This tendency to spiritualize the poor and the beatitudes, which crosses all denominational boundaries and makes exegetes agree on this point when they would agree on hardly anything else, is a good indication of the degree to which exegetical currents are in fact determined by the spirit of the age.[61]

For the poor who cannot take life for granted, there is nothing esoteric or mysterious in the Kingdom of God providing this minimum. Nor is there for God, since this means the minimum of God's creation becoming reality. We no doubt need to speak of the eschatological fulfillment, but without forgetting the protology of creation; we need to speak of life in its fullness, but without forgetting life in its bare essentials. To appeal to the mystery and the maximum while devaluing the basic and minimum supposes a mistaken understanding of the God of Jesus. "The will of God is no mystery, at least insofar as it affects our neighbor and refers to love. The creator who comes into conflict with his creation is a false God."[62] The Kingdom of God cannot be opposed to God's creation, then, although the former reaches beyond the latter; it is in creation that a Kingdom of God that is good news for the poor has to begin.

(d) Making the Good News Real

As we know, the meaning of good news in Luke derives from Isaiah 61:1-2, which he follows in the passage where Jesus begins his public life (Luke 4:16-30). The importance Luke gives to the scene (and to what he relates immediately after) is undeniable: he places Jesus' visit to Nazareth at the outset of his public life, changing the place in which he appears later in Mark 6:1-6 and Matthew 13:53-8, and making it into a central passage. His account tells of Jesus' prophetic anointing (vv 18ff), the definition of his mission as evangelization (vv 18, 43), the content of his mission as the good news (v 18c) of the Kingdom of God (v 43), the urgency of proclaiming this (v 43) and the fact that it is now coming about (v 21). But the centre of the scene is held by verse 18b: "He has anointed me to bring good news to the poor."

Bearing in mind his dependence on Isaiah and the retouches Luke makes to the text, we can draw two important conclusions. The first is that the liberation of which Jesus speaks in Luke includes liberation from material want. Far from spiritualizing Isaiah, Luke reinforces his realism. So he replaces "to bind up the brokenhearted" (Isa. 61:1c) with "to let the oppressed go free" (Luke 4:18e, which in Isaiah is 58:6). He also leaves out the second line of Isaiah 61:2, "a day of vengeance of our God," to finish dramatically with the proclamation of the Lord's year of grace, "thereby presenting salvation as the jubilee year in which slaves are set free."[63] And this is the first important conclusion: the religious content of the new law includes "material liberation from any type of oppression, fruit of of injustice."[64]

The second conclusion is something I should like to stress more. Common sense tells us that proclaiming good news *to the poor* of this world cannot be a matter of words alone, since they have had more than enough of these. Good realities are what the poor need and hope for. And this is what "bringing good news" means in both Isaiah and Luke: "It will only be *good* news to the extent that it brings about the liberation of the oppressed."[65]

I am not trying to use the concept "bringing good news" as a premise for a speculative deduction of the need for Jesus then to carry out a certain practice, but both common sense and the meaning of the phrase in Luke do require this. And this is the subject of the next section.

4. The Way of the Practice of Jesus

I am using the word "practice" in its broad sense here, referring to Jesus' various activities, leaving till later the question of what his "praxis" in the stricter sense might have been. Through this practice, we are trying to establish what the Kingdom of God meant for him, but we first need to make an important previous— and polemical—observation.

In general, all theologies today accept that the Kingdom is a reality to which we have to respond in hope, so that if we were not beings who hope, we simply could not understand it. But, in strict logic, this hope could be mere expectation of the coming of the Kingdom without doing anything practical about it—an attitude that seems to sum up some christologies—or it can be hope accompanied by action to bring it about. It is therefore important to establish which kind of hope Jesus had and generated, whether purely expecting or acting, whether Jesus thought the Kingdom would come gratuitously, in which case all human beings could do was to pray for it to come, or whether he required his listeners to do something.

Let us pose a hypothetical question: If Jesus thought the Kingdom would come soon and gratuitously, why did he do anything? Why did he not simply accept the situation of his world if it was soon to be changed with the coming of the Kingdom? These purely logical questions can only be answered historically. Jesus proclaimed the Kingdom and did many things related to the Kingdom. This is shown programmatically in the Synoptics where their accounts of the beginning of his public mission describe him not only *proclaiming* the Kingdom, but carrying out related *activities*. "And he went throughout Galilee, proclaiming the message in their synagogues and casting out demons" (Mark 1:39); "and he cured many who were sick with various diseases and cast out many demons" (Mark 1:34; Matt. 8:14; Luke 4:40ff). And the summary in Acts 10:38 describes how Jesus "went about doing good, and healing all who were oppressed by the devil." The Gospels, then, speak clearly and at the outset of both "sayings" and "actions" of Jesus, as Vatican II says. In *kingdom* terminology, we can say that Jesus is both *proclaimer* and *initiator* of the Kingdom of God.

For hermeneutics this means that *kingdom* is not only a "meaning" concept— meaning hope—but also a "praxic" one, implying putting its meaning into practice:

that is, the need for a practice to initiate it, and thereby generating a better understanding of what the Kingdom is. (In passing: the act of "making" the Kingdom is the best indicator of the real existence of its counterpart: the anti-Kingdom. This might also explain why some theologies, which speak of the Kingdom and analyze it biblically, effectively silence the reality of the anti-Kingdom.) Here I want to analyze Jesus' practice as a means of establishing what the Kingdom is, specifically his "actions" in working miracles, casting out devils and welcoming sinners, as well as his "words" in parables and his "celebrations."

(a) Miracles: Calls for the Kingdom

From a historical point of view it is quite likely that Jesus soon detached himself from John the Baptist and the practice of baptism to follow his own course of activity through miracles, a contrast set out in his reply to John's disciples: Jesus heals the blind, the deaf, the lame and lepers (Matt. 11:5; Luke 7:22). It is equally brought out in the narrative: "That evening, at sundown, they brought to him all who were sick or possessed with demons... and he cured many who were sick with various diseases, and cast out many demons" (Mark 1:32, 34).

There can be no historical doubt that during the first main stage of his ministry Jesus worked miracles, which traditions have multiplied and magnified, and which diminished in number after the so-called "Galilean crisis." And as happens with other aspects central to the historical Jesus, the later New Testament writings hardly mention them. The conclusion to be drawn is that "Jesus carried out healings that astonished his contemporaries."[67] Nor can there be any doubt of the importance Jesus attributed to his miracles, to the point where he could sum up his activity in these words: "I cast out devils and carry out healings today and tomorrow."

(i) Miracles as liberative signs of the presence of the Kingdom.

(i) Miracles as liberative signs of the presence of the Kingdom. If miracles are to give some indication of what the Kingdom is, we first have to ask what they are, and to do so, need to avoid two misunderstandings. The first stems from the modern Western conception, which sees the essence of miracle as violating the laws of nature and therefore miracles as an expression of a supranatural power. But this is generally accepted not to be the biblical concept of miracle in the Old Testament. The Jews did not see nature as a closed system, and so miracles were not important for any supranatural element but for their share in the powerful saving action of God. This is why in the Gospel accounts they are never described by the Greek word *teras*, which denotes the extraordinary aspect of an incomprehensible event (in the New Testament it is used only in Hebrews 2:4), nor by *thauma*, which would be the Greek equivalent of our "miracle" (though they do say that the people were amazed and surprised). The terms used are rather *semeia* (signs, by which the happening is attributed to God), *dynameis* (acts of power) and *erga* (works, those carried out by Jesus). Jesus is not, then, shown as a professional thaumaturge like many who were around at the time.

The second misunderstanding consists in rushing in to consider the miracles directly in christological terms as expressing something that sets Jesus apart from other human beings, as if the miracles in themselves could give unequivocal access to the reality of Jesus, in this case to his supranatural powers, to his divinity as it used to be interpreted.

Jesus' miracles relate primarily to the Kingdom of God. They are first of all "signs" of the closeness of the Kingdom. As González Faus has pointed out, they are only signs; that is, they do not bring an overall solution to oppressed reality. They are, however, real signs of the approach of God, and so generate hope of salvation.[68] In this sense, miracles do not make the Kingdom real as structural transformation of reality, but they are like calls for it, pointing in the direction of what the Kingdom will be when it comes.

These signs occur in a historical context of oppression. The miracles are not, then, only *beneficent* signs, but *liberating* signs too. They take place in a history that plays out the struggle between God and the Evil One, since the Jewish mentality saw diseases, in the broad sense of the term, also as a sign of being under the power of the Evil One. The miracles are—and this is clearest in the casting out of devils— signs against oppression. This means that Jesus' miracles, like all his actions and praxis, should not only be understood from the Kingdom, but also—dialectically— from the anti-Kingdom. So we should stress not only their beneficent aspect *for* someone, but also their liberative aspect *against* someone or *from* something. This is important in understanding why Jesus' miracles generated hope and not just joy. They generated joy for the good they did, but they generated hope because they showed that oppressive forces can be routed. And this makes them, in the strict sense, signs of the Kingdom of God.

Jesus himself attached great importance to his miracles, since they were a sign of the approach of the Kingdom; to refuse them was to refuse the merciful closeness of God. So he bitterly reproached those who refused to see the coming of God in these signs: "if the deeds of power done in you had been done in Tyre and Sidon, they would have repented long ago in sackcloth and ashes" (Matt. 11:21). Closing oneself to his miracles as signs of the Kingdom was like closing oneself to God.

(ii) The miracles as plural salvations for the poor. In the Gospels, Jesus cures all sorts of people from diseases, but, as Schillebeeckx so rightly says, "in the miracle tradition we find a memory of Jesus of Nazareth, based on the impression he made above all on the simple country folk of Galilee, who were despised by all religious movements and groups."[69]

In the miracles, the poor saw salvation, and it is from the poor that we have to consider them. This needs to be emphasized not only because the addressee helps to understand the signs of the Kingdom, but also because, after the resurrection, the term *salvation* became absolutized and was presented as an indivisible and eschatological reality, expressed in the singular: *salvation* (from sins). But in the Gospels, salvation is not seen in this way. There are plural salvations in daily life, depending on specific oppressions. "So, saving means healing, exorcising, pardoning, through actions that affect body and life."[70]

The poor in need of salvation from their endless daily evils understood Jesus' miracles, while the apocalyptic groups who hoped for portentous prodigies as signs of the coming of the Kingdom did not. So in order to understand Jesus' miracles as liberative signs of the Kingdom—and to understand their ongoing significance—we have to put ourselves in the historical setting in which they happened: the world of the poor, since outside this they lose their necessary relationship with peremptory need for day-to-day salvation.

(iii) The christological dimension of the miracles: Jesus' pity. The primary christological significance of the miracles is that they show a basic dimension of Jesus: his pity.[71] The miracles not only demonstrate Jesus' powers as healer, whatever they may have been, but mainly his reaction to the sorrows of the poor and weak. The Synoptics keep repeating that Jesus felt compassion and pity for the sorrows of others, particularly the simple people who followed him. "He saw a great crowd, and he had compassion on them and cured their sick" (Matt. 14:14). He feels pity for a leper (Mark 1:14), for two blind people (Matt. 20:34), for those who had nothing to eat (Mark 6:34; Matt. 9:36), for the widow of Naim whose son had just died (Luke 7:13). And in at least four miracle stories, Jesus heals after someone cries out, "Have mercy on me" (Matt. 20:29-30 par.; 15:22; 17:15; Luke 17:13).

This pity is what at once explains and is expressed in Jesus' miracles, and what defines him in basic ways. Jesus appears as someone deeply moved by the suffering of others, reacting to this in a saving way and making this reaction something first and last for him, the criterion governing his whole practice. Jesus sees the suffering of others as something final that can only be reacted to adequately with finality. It is worth recalling that the verb used to describe Jesus' actions in the passages cited is *esplagjnizomai*, derived from the noun *esplagjnon*, which means stomach, bowels, heart, all symbols of what is deepest within a person. The reality of the suffering of others is what affected Jesus most deeply and made him react with finality from the inmost depths of his being.

In this suffering of others, the historical, material, bodily suffering at issue, Jesus saw something ultimate, not merely something penultimate compared to other evils—spiritual ones, sin—which were later to become the ultimate ones. Both are evils and Jesus was to liberate from both, but the *misereor super turbas*, the pity he felt for the poor, unprotected, humiliated crowds, was something foremost and ultimate for him, not to be superseded by anything.

Jesus' pity was not just a feeling, but a reaction—and so action—to the suffering of others, motivated by the mere fact that this suffering was in front of him. Pity is therefore not just another virtue in Jesus, but a basic attitude and practice. This is what the Gospels emphasize and what Jesus himself stresses in Luke by defining the complete man on the basis of pity: the Samaritan "moved with pity" (Luke 10:33), and by defining God himself on the same basis: the father of the prodigal son "moved with pity" (Luke 15:20). And this is what Jesus demands of all: "Be merciful, just as your Father is merciful" (Luke 6:36).

The Gospels show Jesus' pity as something first and last in various ways. He is upset when the healed lepers do not thank him, but his reason for healing them was not to inspire their gratitude, but pity. The father in the parable rejoices at his son's return, but his reason for embracing him is not a subtle tactic to get what he really wants—his son to ask his forgiveness and set his life in order—but pity. The good Samaritan is shown as someone carrying out the basic commandment, but in the parable he is described as acting not to carry out a commandment, but out of pity.

The attitude-practice of pity is not the only thing about Jesus, but it is the first and last. Other activities of his, including those that point to the transformation of society as such, can be understood as stemming from his immense compassion for the sufferings of the poor and afflicted, but it is his pity that provides his ultimate motivation. For Jesus, pity has to do with the ultimate, and therefore with God. It is something theologal, not simply ethical. This pity is what the Letter to the Hebrews was to raise to a christological principle by defining Christ (together with his total availability to God) as the man of mercy. And recalling this is still of supreme importance for the work of the church today. The church often carries out "works of mercy," but making pity for the suffering of the world the first and last criterion of its actions, which means not making itself the final criterion, and showing this in readiness to run grave risks in exercising pity, is very unusual. Personally, this is what most impressed me in Archbishop Romero. While deeply a man of the church, he put the suffering of the people before the institution and showed that he really put it first by not avoiding the risks this attitude brought not only to him, in his own death, but also to the institution: serious attacks on church bodies, the destruction of its means of communication (radio station, printing presses, offices), the assassination of its priests and so on.

The permanent value of Jesus' miracles derives from their being expressions of pity: they are powerful signs springing from sorrow at the sufferings of others and, specifically, of the poor people who surrounded him. And this is still valid and absolutely necessary today for understanding miracles both in secularized cultures that do not know what to make of them and in religious cultures where what is truly Christian about them needs disentangling. Jesus "has clearly indicated a valid direction for faith in salvation, that in which mitigation and final suppression of all human misery, of disease, hunger, ignorance, slavery and inhumanity of every sort make up the permanent and most important task for people in relation to their fellows."[72] But, let us remember, miracles are not just what are now called "works of mercy," beneficent aid; they are at the same time works that arouse hope in the possibility of liberation. And this means that present-day miracles have to be performed in the presence of and against some oppressive power. To illustrate this with a contemporary example, the works of mercy performed by Mother Teresa of Calcutta are praiseworthy because they bring help. But if they do not arouse hope that it is possible for the Kingdom of God to come—not just that individual wants will be alleviated—and if they produce no sort of conflict, then they cannot be compared to the miracles of Jesus.

(iv) The faith that heals externally and internally. Jesus himself, moved to pity as he was, did not work miracles for their own sake; he rather showed himself reluctant to appear as a professional wonder-worker. This is shown by the fact that accounts of miracles are often related to the faith of those who are healed. At times, faith seems to be the required condition for a miracle: "Do not fear, only believe" (Mark 5:36), Jesus tells the synagogue official, whose daughter had just died. And in Nazareth he could work no miracles because of their lack of faith (Mark 5:5ff). At times Jesus first establishes the existence of faith: "When Jesus saw their faith, he said to the paralytic... 'Stand up, take your mat and go to your home'"(Mark 2: 5, 11).

The most notable aspect, to my mind, however, is Jesus' repeated saying: "Your faith has made you whole" (Mark 5:34 par.; 10:52 par.; cf Matt. 9:28ff; Luke 17:19; Mark 5:36 par.; Matt. 8:13; 15:28), radicalized and elevated to a thesis in that other saying: "all things can be done for the one who believes" (Mark 9:23). What is meant here by "faith," which strictly speaking is neither a condition nor a result of the miracle, but what brings it about?

Certainly this "faith" has nothing to do with accepting doctrinal truths, nor even with confessing Jesus as the Christ. Faith here seems to have to do with God and in a very precise sense. It is accepting with deep conviction that God is good to the weak and that this goodness can and must triumph over evil. This faith is not historically evident, so its achievement is conversion, a radical change in one's very understanding of God, and so Jesus relates the proclamation of the coming of God's Kingdom to conversion, to accepting that it is both possible and good news for God to come close.

This faith has its own power. Through it, human beings are themselves transformed and empowered. This is why Jesus can make the scandalous assertion that "your faith has made you whole" without, linguistically at least, formulating it as "God, because of your faith, has saved you." Anyone who comes to make the basic act of faith in God's goodness has changed radically, is possessed of a power differing in kind from any other power, but still an effective power. "The power of faith is the power of good and truth, which is the power of God."[73] So Jesus can declare that for those who believe, "all things can be done" (Mark 9:23, even mountains moved (Mark 11:22ff). Those who believe in this way can be healed externally because they are healed internally.

This faith has to do with Jesus, but it is not so much faith in him as faith through him: Jesus makes faith possible. It is told that a power went out from him—the first indications in the Synoptics of the reality of the Spirit—a power that was contagious, that could change people. Here Schillebeeckx is quite right to say: "The mission of the earthly Jesus was to arouse *unconditional faith in God* among those who, temporarily or permanently, came into contact with him."[74] But this needs a qualification: this faith is in a God who, coming close, makes us believe in new possibilities actively denied to the poor in history. It is a faith that overcomes fatalism. It is faith in the God of the Kingdom opposed to the idols of the anti-Kingdom. This is why it is said that where there was no faith, Jesus could not work miracles (Matt. 12:23ff; 16:1ff; Mark 11:5; Luke 11:29ff).

Theologal faith is a gift from God, but from a God who imposes himself victoriously on non-faith, so that believers, now healed, are converted so as to become themselves principles of salvation for themselves. It is here that—as opposed to all miracle-working paternalism—the specificity of Jesus' miracles and the great delicacy of God are to be found: healing by making people heal themselves. Latin American experience provides analogies that can help us to understand this. Archbishop Romero helped the poor and the popular movements a great deal and did many concrete things on their behalf. But the most important thing he did was to give them faith in themselves: "You can, you are." And a peasant from Aguilares put this experience into these simple words: "Before we were not, now we are." This change is fundamental and this is what Jesus' miracles lead to.

(b) Casting out Devils: Victory over the Evil One

The casting out of devils can be considered in the same way as the miracles. Here I want just to deal briefly with what it—more clearly than the miracles—tells us about the dimension of struggle and triumph over the anti-Kingdom implicit in the coming of the Kingdom of God.

(i) The reality of the Evil One: the ultimate dimension of the anti-Kingdom. The ancient world, the Old Testament and Jesus' age all shared the conviction that the world was peopled by unknown forces that made themselves very present in people's lives and were harmful to them. Their world-view was impregnated and even dominated by demonology. Especially in Jesus' time, "an extraordinarily intense terror of demons ruled."[76] These forces acted above all through illness and especially through mental illness, to the point where demons possessed their victims really and totally. Disease and mental illness were not merely an evil whose elimination was beneficial, but a slavery from which people needed to be liberated.

Jesus made his appearance in this world enslaved by demons. Generally speaking, the New Testament shares this world-view, though it also radicalizes and transforms it. It radicalizes it by bringing all the different maleficent forces together as the Evil One, thereby giving this figure a universal dimension. While Judaism knew individual demons, Jesus stressed the unity of them all in Satan. The evil at work is therefore not the isolated actions of individual devils, but something that permeates everything. It is the negative power of creation, which destroys it and makes it capable of destroying, the power that was expressed in history and society as the anti-Kingdom. Jesus also states that evil has great power and knows that people feel helpless and impotent in the face of it. (To illustrate this from Latin America again: we not only have numberless calamities, but also this feeling of helplessness and powerlessness. The poor often feel helpless and powerless in the face of sickness—much in the manner of the Gospel narratives—but they feel so most in the face of historical calamities, which they not only suffer, but which are imposed on them in their total powerlessness and despair. From this point of view and to express their helplessness and powerlessness, I have proposed the following definition of the poor: "The poor are those who have all the powers of this world against them: oligarchies, governments, armed forces, party politics and, sometimes, churches and cultural institutions." The deepest impact of liberation theology, I believe, lies in helping the poor to overcome this feeling of helplessness and powerlessness, to believe that liberation from oppressive forces is possible.) Futhermore, the power of evil has not yet reached its zenith: it will be set up as a god (Mark 13:14). And this culminating point is eschatologized: at the end of time it will show its full power, which magnifies the formal parallelism between Kingdom and anti-Kingdom.

On the other hand, however, Jesus transforms the demonological world-view by stating that these powers, stronger than human beings, are not higher than God or stronger than God, but the reverse. Slavery to the Evil One is not the final human destiny; liberation is possible. Jesus himself "comes with the authority of God, not only to carry out mercy, but also, and foremost, to engage in the struggle against the Evil One."[77] Jesus' practice is the answer to the pressing questions of simple people on the possibility of overcoming the Evil One.

(ii) The casting out of devils and the characteristics of the anti-Kingdom. As a historical fact there can be no doubt that Jesus cast out devils. But just as he did not appear as a professional wonder-worker, though he worked miracles, so neither did he act as a profesional exorcist. Again, analysis of the terms used helps to understand this. The Gospels do not use the common terminology of the time to denote exorcisms: *exordikso* in Greek and *gadasar* in Hebrew, terms that appear in Jewish exorcisms and describe the function of magi and witch-doctors. Instead, Jesus' actions are described as *ekballo* (to send, expel) or *epitamao* (to warn) the devils.

What Jesus' actions in this respect show, then, is not the appearance of a great exorcist, but something far more radical. With Jesus there begins the destruction of the Evil One (see Mark 1:24), and thereby the approach of an end to tribulations. In his words, "If it is by the Spirit of God that I cast out demons, then the kingdom of God has come to you" (Matt. 12:28 par.), but it has come because it has the power to conquer the anti-Kingdom. The same can be said of the importance Jesus attached to his disciples' success in casting out devils (Luke 10:17, 19ff; Mark 3:14ff; 6:7 par.; Matt. 10:8).

Casting out devils, then, is an expression of the approach of the Kingdom, but of a Kingdom with specific characteristics, which appear more clearly in the miracle narratives. Above all, it shows that the Kingdom is coming in the presence of an anti-Kingdom that permeates everything, not that it is starting from a *tabula rasa*. The coming of the Kingdom is, therefore, not only beneficent but liberating. But it also expresses the fact that Kingdom and anti-Kingdom are formally exclusive, antagonistic realities. In the casting out of devils, this is seen on the level of the *mediators* of Kingdom and anti-Kingdom, Jesus and the devils; the characteristics of this relationship are thereby subjectivized. Through what happens to the mediators, we can learn something of what happens to the *mediation* (Kingdom and anti-Kingdom).

The fact that they are mutually exclusive is shown by the interpretation made of Jesus' own actions: either they come from God or they come from the devils. Jesus himself claims they come from God, since he casts out devils in God's name. His adversaries, however, claim that he operates in the name of the devils, that he himself is possessed (Matt. 12:24; John 7:20) and mad; Mark and John combine both accusations (Mark 3:21; John 19:20). A choice has to be made, then, between Jesus and the devils, which means having to choose between God and the Evil One, and also between what each generates: between the Kingdom and the anti-Kingdom.

The antagonistic dimension—how one acts against the other—is described with crude primitivism in the accounts of casting out devils. The devils resist and struggle, not wanting to be destroyed; that is, they act against Jesus. In these accounts, Jesus is shown as conquering them majestically in the first phase of his public life. But moving from the accounts of casting out devils to more existential passages, such as the temptations, the way Jesus had to struggle against the Evil One is clearly brought out, and, at the end of his life, the Evil One appears to have triumphed over him.

What the casting out of devils sheds light on is, then, the fact that the coming of the Kingdom is anything but peaceful and ingenuous. It happens against the anti-Kingdom and so its coming is a victory. It also clarifies, in an important though stylized fashion, the fact that Jesus' practice is struggle. This will emerge with still greater clarity in his confrontations with his historical adversaries, but here this struggle is raised to a transcendent principle: building the Kingdom implies, of necessity, actively struggling against the anti-Kingdom. And if the latter does not fight back, this means that the former has not truly been built (something always to be borne in mind in outlining and understanding the mission of the church).

(c) Welcoming Sinners: Liberation from Self and from Marginalization

In the Gospels, Jesus is frequently shown dealing with sinners or with those held to be sinners by the religious society of the time. There are also two passges where he is shown granting forgiveness of sins. What concerns us here is how all this relates to understanding the Kingdom of God.

(i) Welcoming sinners or forgiving sins? In many accounts, Jesus appears with sinners. He eats with publicans (Mark 2:15-17 par.), he talks to a woman of ill repute and even allows her to touch him in the Pharisee's house (Luke 7:36-50),

he lodges in the publican Zacchaeus' house (Luke 19:1-10), and talks to the woman of Samaria who has had five husbands (John 4:7-42). However historical each of these incidents may be, they demonstrate Jesus' approach as welcoming sinners, not acting as a harsh judge. This basic attitude of welcome is enlarged on in the parables. We have to go out in search of the sinner to save him (Luke 15:4-19; Matt. 18:12-14), and in the supreme parable of the prodigal son, Jesus shows how God feels toward sinners (Luke 15:11-32). Jesus also defends sinners against those who think themselves just and despise them (Luke 18:9-14), and defines his mission as having come to save not the healthy but the sick (Matt: 9:12; Luke 5:31). Finally, he makes the scandalous assertion that publicans and prostitutes will enter the Kingdom of God before the pious people listening to him in the Temple (Matt. 21:31).

In virtually all these passages there is no mention of Jesus forgiving sins; they are a direct demonstration of his tender and affectionate "welcome" to sinners. In two places, however, it is said that Jesus "grants" forgiveness: to the paralytic (Mark 2:10), and to the woman known as a sinner (Luke 7:48), but both these passages are not historical, but redactional, and so from a historical point of view, it is more accurate to speak of Jesus welcoming sinners than forgiving sins. (Mark 2:10 is trying to show that the Christ, confessed also as Son of God, has the power to forgive sins, an attribution not present in the traditions of the Son of Man. Luke 7:48 does no more than illustrate the content of the parable of the just man and the sinner going into the Temple to pray—Luke 18:9-14). This is important for understanding Jesus: just as he does not appear as wonder-worker or professional exorcist, neither does he appear directly as "absolving confessor" of sins. What he does to sinners is much more: he welcomes them. And in this way he proclaims the coming of the Kingdom of God. (In the terminology used here, forgiveness is good for the sinner, naturally, but existentially it does not express the totality and richness of welcome, which is a far better expression of God's initiative and gratuitousness; it includes absolution, but goes beyond it.)

Jesus' welcoming sinners should, then, be seen in the first place as a sign of the coming of the Kingdom and not, directly, as another way of showing Jesus' (divine) power. Like John the Baptist, Jesus recognized the sinfulness of human beings and required all to be converted, but unlike the Baptist, he stressed that the coming of the Kingdom is grace rather than judgment. So the coming of the Kingdom is good news for sinners too. And the fact that sinners cease feeling afraid at God's coming is a sign that the Kingdom is coming into being.

To understand this properly, we need to enquire a little further into who Jesus saw as sinners, although this classification cannot—in my view—be deduced from the words he uses, but from the sum total of his actions. On the one hand, there is the type of sinner whom, in present-day language, we could call "oppressor." Their basic sin consists in oppressing, placing intolerable burdens on others, acting unjustly and so on. On the other hand, there are those who sin "from weakness" or those "legally considered sinners" according to the dominant religious view.

Jesus takes a very different approach to each group. He offers salvation to all, and makes demands of all, but in a very different way. He directly demands a radical conversion of the first group, an active cessation from oppressing. For these, the coming of the Kingdom is above all a radical need to stop being oppressors, although Jesus also offers them the possibility of being saved. (How much success he had in this we are not told, though this is not an idle question for the present mission of the church. In fact the Gospels say very little on the subject. They briefly recount the conversion of Levi and exemplify what the conversion of oppressors implies in the story of Zacchaeus.) Jesus requires a different type of conversion from the second group: acceptance of the fact that God is not like the image they have introjected from their oppressors and the ruling religious culture, but true love; that God comes not to condemn but to save, and that sinners should therefore feel not fear but joy at God's coming.

This is what shows, in deeds, Jesus' welcome to sinners, and what he tells with impressive power in his parables. The God who is coming is a loving God, with more tenderness than a mother, one who seeks to welcome all those who think themselves unworthy to approach because of their sinfulness. This is a God who comes out to meet the sinner, embraces him and prepares a feast. The coming of the Kingdom is truly good news.

This does not mean that Jesus minimizes human sinfulness—though he does show what it basically consists of and distinguishes degrees—but that with the coming of the Kingdom, the tragic uncovering of sinfulness is simultaneously accompanied by welcome and forgiveness. It also means that the reason for Jesus' call to conversion, as distinct from John's, is not the imminence of judgment and fear of punishment, but the incredible goodness of God.

(ii) Welcome as liberation. Acceptance of one's own sinfulness does not now produce anguish or desperation, nor does it block off the future; it is therefore something liberating. If the miracles and the casting out of devils express liberation from physical evil and the power of evil, welcome expresses liberation of sinners from their own inner principle of enslavement. And it does so precisely because it is "grace" rather than "works." If forgiveness-absolution can be understood as what is conceded to sinners for what they do, at least in part, then forgiveness-welcome stresses God's grace and unconditional love. And this love is what achieves what neither pure moral demands, nor threats, nor social stigma can achieve. This is what liberates sinners internally from themselves.

Welcome is liberating also because it gives those despised and cast out by society back their dignity. Joachim Jeremias, commenting on the story of Zacchaeus, has these fine words: "The fact that Jesus wanted to lodge in his house, in the house of this despised man avoided by all, was inconceivable for him. Jesus gave him back his lost honour by staying in his house and breaking bread with him. Jesus granted him communion."[78] Jesus' gesture of friendship, the fundamentally human sign of "coming close," is what liberates, because in himself Jesus overcomes separation and opposition. This "coming close" or "allowing others to come close" is a distinctive feature of Jesus: he is shown approaching groups despised in his time: women, children, lepers. And in doing so he gave them back their dignity.

(iii) The reaction of the anti-Kingdom. As did his miracles and casting out of devils, so Jesus' welcoming sinners caused a scandal. His adversaries were indignant at his eating with publicans and sinners (Mark 2:16 par.). Redactionally, this scandal is shown at its most radical when his adversaries are scandalized at his "forgiving" sins: "It is blasphemy! Who can forgive sins but God alone?" (Mark 2:7). But the root of the scandal goes still deeper. Jesus, like the Baptist, offers welcome—forgiveness—independently of any cultic formula. God's forgiveness does not come mediated by any religious institution, there is no need to go up to the Temple and offer sacrifice. And, above all, his welcome to sinners is offered against the criteria sanctioned by religion. God offers himself in grace to those held to be sinners. This is another way of showing God taking sides: Jesus has not come to seek out the just (more accurately, those who considered themselves just), but sinners (more accurately, those held to be sinners). This new image of God is what causes the scandal because it overthrows what is most sacred: fulfillment of the law as what God reacts to with justice. Jesus breaks and finishes with this vision of God and in doing so puts an end to the law of purity in its cultic acceptance.

Jesus also unmasks what lies behind the unjustified scandal: who are true sinners and who are not. The accepted terminology of "just" and "sinners" did more than hide reality; it turned it on its head. This is what Jesus is saying in the parable of the two men who went up to the Temple to pray (Luke 18:9-14), told to "some people who trusted in themselves that they were righteous and regarded others with contempt" (v. 9). The apparently virtuous man did not go home at rights with God; the apparent sinner did. It is not actually said that the publican did not have his own sins, but degrees of sin are established and the basic sin pointed out: self-sufficiency before God—not accepting being welcomed by God—and despising everyone else. It can also be interpreted as saying that those who sin through weakness, let us call it, are by nature better disposed to being open to God's welcome. This same lesson appears, though in a different form, in the parable of the prodigal son, which is outwardly a story about two types of person. The older brother, though objectively the virtuous one, has not known God; the younger brother, the sinner, has let himself be welcomed by God and in doing so has come to know God.

The partiality and gratuitousness of God are what cause the scandal, because they upset official religious society, but they are also Jesus' way of saying that the Kingdom of God is coming as good news. Wherever sinners allow themselves to be welcomed by God, there the signs of the coming of the Kingdom are apparent.

(iv) God's delicacy: "Your faith has saved you." Finally, there is the fact that the expression analyzed in dealing with miracles reappears in Luke 7:50. In the story,

Jesus tells the sinful woman, "Your faith has saved you; go in peace." Again, Jesus' welcome-forgiveness does not end up as something extrinsic to the person concerned. God saves from within. The power with which the Kingdom approaches is a recreative power, not a magical one. This shows the supreme delicacy of God, who seeks to transform everything, body and heart, providing the strength for human beings to transform themselves. This then becomes a true transformation, intrinsic to each person, who will not fall back into dependency. Those welcomed and healed should be grateful for the gift—and Jesus complains when they are not— but they do not remain as it were enslaved to the giver. This is what is expressed by the supremely delicate "Your faith has saved you."

(d) The Parables of the Kingdom

Working miracles, casting out devils and welcoming sinners make up what Vatican II calls the "deeds" of Jesus. To these we need to add the "sayings," his practice of the word. The basic aspect of this is the very announcement of the coming of the Kingdom, to which Jesus added many other sayings: teachings, demands, prayers, apocalyptic discourses.... I propose here to concentrate on the parables, since they clarify important elements of the Kingdom of God.

(i) The parables as challenging and polemical accounts of the Kingdom. Jesus' parables have an undeniable historical core, even if in their present form they may be transformed by the early Christian communities.[79] So images originally used to explain the Kingdom of God have been applied later to Jesus himself (the bridegroom, the king, the merchant, the thief). Sometimes the imminent coming of the Kingdom is reinterpreted as a crisis caused by the postponement of the parousia (the parables of the thief in the night, the master returning late to his house, the lord who comes back from a long journey). Some parables have shifted the accent from the eschatological to the parenetic, the norms of daily life. Finally, there has been a reinterpretation of the audience to whom the parables were addressed; so parables originally addressed to the crowd are applied to the disciples, parables addressed to the leaders of Israel or Jesus' enemies are later redirected to the leaders of the Christian communities. These shifts, however, do not obscure the original meaning of the parables as parables of the Kingdom. Their purpose is to clarify what this Kingdom is, but in a very precise way stemming from the literary form of parable.[80]

Parables are stories based on events from daily life, but in order to understand them properly one needs to note, first, that they speak of the Kingdom without defining it. Jesus never says, "The Kingdom of God is a man who sowed seed or a shepherd who had a hundred sheep...," but "with the Kingdom of God it is like a man sowing good seed...."

Second, the content of these stories is such that interpreting the event related is an open question requiring, of its nature, its hearers to take a particular stance. They have to draw their own conclusions. Does it really mean that we should pay those who come late the same amount as those who have borne the heat of the whole day? Did the return of the prodigal son really merit a feast rather than the constancy of the elder son? "The parable does not force judgment: the listener is faced with two possibilities"[81] —to accept or not that the Kingdom is like this and not like that. It is then a story whose ultimate meaning is left in suspense until the listener decides; it does not allow for neutrality, but requires decision.

Thirdly, their specific content makes the parables challenging and polemical. This is implicit in their content: the Kingdom of God is not as the listeners expect, and it is also very often made explicit by their context: Jesus addresses the Jewish leaders, his adversaries. The same polemic that goes with his practice (and the controversies and condemnations we shall examine later) appears in the parables too. So Juan Luis Segundo calls the parables a means of de-ideologizing and conscientizing, not merely the preaching of a master of universal morality.[82]

(ii) The central message: the fact that the Kingdom of God is for the poor. The parables reproduce Jesus' basic message about the Kingdom in a different literary form. So they proclaim its imminence (the fig tree, Mark 13:28ff par.) and its novelty (the new cloth and the new wine, Mark 2:21ff par.). But their central message is the same as that proclaimed by Jesus' practice: the Kingdom of God is coming for the poor and outcast; it is partial, and therefore causes scandal.

The parables reproduce this central message; what changes is the audience, and therefore the presentation. It was the poor themselves who listened to the beatitudes, and Jesus ate with sinners; the parables, on the other hand, are addressed directly to Jesus' adversaries, those who criticize his partiality to the poor and sinners. So in the parable of the lost sheep and the lost drachma, Jesus is addressing the Pharisees and scribes who were complaining that, "This fellow welcomes sinners and eats with them" (Luke 15:2); the parable of the Pharisee and the publican going up to the Temple is addressed to "some who trusted in themselves that they were righteous" (Luke 18:9); the parable of the two brothers sent out to work by their father is addressed to the high priests and elders (Matt 21:23).

To this audience, Jesus repeats his central message: the Kingdom of God is for the poor, the weak and despised—though here he does it speaking of "God" rather than "the Kingdom of God". He tells his adversaries that God takes sides, is rich in mercy, tender and loving to the poor and little ones. The basic message is that this is what God is like and so the poor and sinners can await this God with joy and without fear. So the coming of the Kingdom is truly good news. This is shown by the parables of the lost sheep and the lost drachma (Luke 15:4-7; Matt. 18:12-14), the generous vineyard owner (Matt. 20:1-15), the Pharisee and the publican (Luke 18:9-14), the debtors (Luke 7:41-3) and, above all, the prodigal son (Luke 15:11-32), which Segundo calls the parable of the joy of God, the one that truly tells us who God is.[83]

What Jesus is doing with these parables is sallying forth to defend the poor and justify his own partial actions on their behalf. Jesus upholds the partiality of the Kingdom against those who do not accept it or reject it by simply saying "this is what God is like." In the stories he tells, Jesus is trying to convince his adversaries of the tragic situation of the "little ones": they are like a lost sheep, like a son in despair, like a destitute beggar... and hoping for compassion and mercy from them. But whether he succeeds in affecting them or not, he tells them how the heavenly Father reacts to smallness and weakness, how he rejoices when the little ones prosper and accept him as a good and loving Father. This is Jesus' ultimate justification of his practice and of the partiality of the Kingdom. "Such is God, so good. And because God is such, so I too am such, since I work through his command and in his place. Will they complain of the goodness of God? This is simply the justification of the gospel: *Such is God, so good.*"[84]

By means of this supremely positive message, Jesus unmasks the hypocrisy of his adversaries, and so his parables are strongly critical. He often introduces and contrasts two types of person (two brothers, a Pharisee and a publican, a rich man and a poor man...) and his adversaries tend to identify with one of them: the orthodox one, the "just" one.... Jesus then works a reversal that is also a strong criticism of his audience: the one whom you take to be "just" is not just, and therefore you are not just either. You, he tells them, are like the son who said he would go and work, but did not go (Matt. 21:28-31). Jesus ends the parable with these terrible words: "I tell you the tax collectors and prostitutes are going into the kingdom of God ahead of you."

Besides this central message, the parables clarify other elements of the Kingdom of God, particularly its "crisis" aspect. It cannot be that the Kingdom approaches and everything stays the same; time presses and something must be done. So Jesus warns his listeners not to be like those who do not respond to the children in the street (Matt. 11: 16-19; Luke 7:31-5), or like the barren fig tree (Luke 13:7), which will be cut down and cast into the fire, or like the man who sleeps and is robbed (Matt. 24:43ff; Luke 12:39ff), or like the foolish rich man who dreams of great harvests while the Lord is calling him to account that very night (Luke 12:16-21).

These parables of crisis, though with variants between Matthew and Luke, are addressed to the crowds, but some are expressly addressed to Jesus' adversaries, the rulers of the people. The warnings in these are extremely harsh. The *scribes* are told the parables of the nobleman going to be appointed king (Luke 19:12-27), the trusted servant (Matt. 24:45-51; Luke 12:42-6), the talents (Matt.25:14-30; Luke 19:12-27), the porter who should be awake waiting for his master's return (Mark 13:33-7; Luke 12:35-8). The conclusion is clear: faced with the imminent coming of the Kingdom they must put their talents to work; otherwise when the Lord comes he will put them from him and send them to share the fate of the hypocrites (Matt.24:51). The *Pharisees* are reproached for their actions and warned that they will incur God's wrath, since they are blind guides (Matt. 15:14), see the speck in another's eye and not the beam in their own (Matt. 7:3-5; Luke 6:41ff), are bandits and robbers instead of shepherds (John 10: 6-21). *Jerusalem*, which killed the prophets, is given the parable of the hen and chicks (Matt. 23:27; Luke 13:34). The whole of *Israel* is compared to a fig tree that does not produce fruit (Luke 13:6-9) and to salt that has lost its taste (Matt. 5:13; Luke 14:34ff; Mark 9:50).

All these parables show that the coming of the Kingdom is also a crisis. They are a jolt to consciences; you have to react in time and not just rely on Israel's status as chosen people. And in two classic parables, Jesus proclaims the basic requirement in the face of the coming Kingdom: you must be merciful to the needy (the good Samaritan, Luke 10:29-37) and do things for them (Matt. 25:36-46). This is the first and last requirement of the Kingdom and everything depends on it, including final salvation.

The parables also generate hope, the certainty that the Kingdom is coming. The parables of contrast (the mustard seed, Mark 4:30-32 par.; the yeast, Matt. 13:33; Luke 13:20ff; the sower, Mark 4:3-8 par.; the seed growing by itself, Mark 4:26-9) state that the Kingdom will grow from very small beginnings. But not just that. The Kingdom is already active, and we must put all our trust in that. This is based on the very reality of the good God, as featured in the parable of the unscrupulous judge (Luke 18:2-8) and that of the importunate friend (Luke 11:5-8). If these can be made to give what is asked of them, how much more will our Father in heaven give. "Take God seriously! He works miracles and his mercy to his own is the most certain thing there is," Jeremias comments.[85]

Finally, there are a few parables that express the joy produced by the Kingdom of God because it is good news. The parables of the hidden treasure and the pearl of great price (Matt. 13: 44-6) speak of the happiness produced by the Kingdom of God. God's happiness, shown in the parables of welcoming little ones, is matched by the happiness of those who find the Kingdom. And this is what these parables actually speak of, not directly—as they are usually interpreted—of ascetic willingness to give up everything. The latter derives from the former, not the other way round. "The good news of the coming of the Kingdom subdues, produces great happiness, directs life to the consummation of the divine community, brings about the most passionate bestowal."[86] And this leads to the final consideration in this chapter: the joy produced by the Kingdom.

(e) The Celebration of the Coming of the Kingdom

The coming of the Kingdom is good news, and is therefore incompatible with sadness. More, the Kingdom of God has to be celebrated with joy, since it would be a strange sort of good news if it did not. (And this joy is basic today for verifying the true faith of the true church. Obviously the Kingdom of God imposes hard conditions and building it involves suffering. But a church shot through with sadness, one that did not show and communicate joy, would not be a church of the *eu-aggelion*. A sad church is a sorry church, and this is the impression some of the mainstream churches give, even though they possess ample means, long tradition and great prestige within the universal church.) And this is what Jesus shows.

Besides proclaiming and embodying the Kingdom, Jesus celebrates it, especially in the form of meals. In the Gospels, meals are spoken of in the parables, in the miracles and in the multiplication of loaves. But Jesus also accorded them special importance in his own life: he ate with sinners and despised categories of people (Mark 2:15 par.; Luke 7:36-47), and, at the end of his life, said farewell to his friends at a supper (Mark 14:12-25 par.). After his resurrection, several of his appearances are also told in the form of meals (Luke 24:29-31; John 21:12ff; cf. Acts 10:41).

The importance accorded to meals as celebrative signs is present in all cultures, including that of the Old Testament, in which it becomes a sign of all the promises of the Kingdom of God:

> On this mountain the LORD of hosts will make for all peoples
>   a feast of rich food, a feast of well-aged wines,
>   of rich food filled with marrow, of well-aged wines strained clear.
> And he will destroy on this mountain
>   the shroud that is cast over all peoples,
>   the sheet that is spread over all nations,
>   he will swallow up death for ever.
> Then the Lord GOD will wipe away the tears from all faces,
>   and the disgrace of his people he will take away from all the earth,
>   for the LORD has spoken.   (Isaiah 25:6-8)

In this context, Jesus' meals are signs of the coming of the Kingdom and of the realization of his ideals: liberation, peace, universal communion. And all this not only has to be asked for and worked for, it also has to be celebrated. This—ultimate—communion of the whole human race is what needs celebrating because it produces joy; and therefore rather than "meal" in its purely nutritive sense, the terminology used is that of a feast, a wedding banquet. This is the happiness of the Kingdom: "Blessed is anyone who will eat bread in the kingdom of God!" (Luke 14:15).

As the Kingdom is also celebrated against the anti-Kingdom, however, Jesus attaches great importance to the presence at the table of those whom the anti-Kingdom habitually keeps from it. So he sits at table with publicans, with sinners and prostitutes. His parables stress that in the Kingdom those who are never invited will partake of the banquet: "the poor, the crippled, the blind and the lame" (Luke 14:21), people from the streets, "both good and bad" (Matt. 22:1-10). And this is also why—as I have said throughout this chapter—Jesus' meals are not only beneficent celebrative signs, but also liberative ones: those who for centuries have been prevented from eating together can now eat together. This is why Jesus eats with the poor and despised.

The tragedy is, once more, that the anti-Kingdom reacts. Instead of the sign being one of joy for everyone, including Jesus' enemies, they deeply distort the happiness of eating together and and accuse Jesus of being "a glutton and a drunkard, a friend of tax collectors and sinners" (Matt. 11:19). And they are most scandalized by the fact that he eats with publicans and sinners. Jesus counters their hypocrisy with the ironic comment that it is not the healthy who need a doctor but the sick (Mark 2:17) and backs this up with an Old Testament reference: that God desires justice, not sacrifice (Hos. 6:6, cited in Matt. 9:13, in the story of the meal with the publican Levi; cf. Matt 12:7). And he gives them a severe warning: the gentiles will sit at the table of the Kingdom of God and many of the Jews will be excluded from it (Matt. 8:11ff).

The trouble with his enemies is that they are absolutely blind to the Kingdom of God. It is the very fact that the poor sit at table that forms the great joy of God, and this is what we have to celebrate on this earth. So, if those who do not weep with those who mourn find conversion hard, it will be much harder for those who do not rejoice with those who do. If God's joy and the joy of little ones cannot move their hearts of stone, they will never have hearts of flesh and will have understood nothing of the Kingdom of God.

This joy is what Jesus communicates. He tells the parables of God's happiness with joy, he enjoys himself with the little ones, and it is with joy that he utters one of the very few prayers whose words have come down to us: "It was then that, filled with joy by the Holy Spirit, he said: 'I bless you, Father, Lord of heaven and earth, for hiding these things from the learned and the clever and revealing them to mere children'" (Luke 10:21; Matt. 11:25—JB).

Celebration of the Kingdom of God is the great sign that something of it has already arrived. Let me end this chapter by saying that this is still true in Latin America. This is a challenging and even scandalous fact for those outside, but of great importance to the poor themselves. The poor are experts in sufferings without end, but many of them do not give way to sadness. They have the capacity to celebrate what beneficent and liberative signs there are. And they celebrate it in community, like Jesus, around a table. The shared table is still the great sign of the Kingdom of God. This is what Fr Rutilio Grande SJ said in his famous homily in Apopa, in February 1977, a few weeks before he was assassinated:

> God, the Lord, in his plan, gave us a material world, like this material Mass, with the material bread and the material cup we are about to raise in Christ's toast. A common table with a big tablecloth reaching everyone, like this Eucharist. Everyone with a stool, and the table, tablecloth and place settings reaching everyone. Christ, at the age of thirty-three, celebrated a farewell supper with his closest friends and told them this was the great memorial of redemption. A table shared in brotherhood, with a place and a setting for everyone.... It is the love of shared fellowship that breaks and overthrows all types of barrier and prejudice and will overcome hate itself.[87]

Excursus 1

The Kingdom of God in Present-day Christologies

The subject of the previous chapter has been dealt with at some length because of its importance for christology in general. But it is also a fact that liberation theology has made it—for christological, historical and methodological reasons—its main concern; as Ignacio Ellacuría says: "Just what Jesus came to proclaim and bring about, the Kingdom of God, that is, is what should become the unifying object of all Christian theology, moral teaching and pastoral practice: what true followers of Jesus should pursue is the greatest realization of the Kingdom of God in history."[1] This being the case, we need to analyze how the Kingdom of God is understood today in various christologies and specifically in Latin American christology. Before doing so, let me make two prefatory comments.

The first is that, however strange this may now seem, the discovery of the Kingdom of God as Jesus' central concern is relatively recent, dating from within the last hundred years. In my view, this discovery is the most important for the church and for theology in many hundreds of years, with consequences that have made themselves felt in all basic theological fields (theo-logy itself, ecclesiology, morals, pastoral teaching), not only in christology.

To demonstrate the importance of this discovery, let us ask this purely hypothetical question: Would the church's mission, and even faith in Christ and God, be the same if Jesus, even having been raised by the Father and been proclaimed dogmatically as true God and true man, had not proclaimed the Kingdom of God? The answer is obviously No. And the recent history of the church confirms this. There can be no doubt that faith in Christ and the church's mission are different now—at least in principle—from what they were in previous centuries, and that this change, revolving round the church's new relation to the world, is seen as an improvement, as a faith and mission more in accordance with Christianity. The theological presuppositions of this change and improvement are based on Vatican II and Medellín, on the Kingdom of God moving the church to turn to the world.

Nevertheless—and this is my second prefatory comment—we must also be conscious of the difficulty of following this discovery through logically. While theoretically the Kingdom of God can be said to have been adequately integrated into christological and ecclesiological thinking, it is no easy matter to keep sight of it as the central element in theory, let alone in practice, since, if it is the most important element, it is also the most demanding and permanently judges faith and the church. Hence the importance of analyzing the actual significance of the Kingdom of God in theology.

1. The Rediscovery of the Kingdom of God as the Ultimate and Eschatological

In the nineteenth century, liberal German theology, for reasons discussed in the previous chapter, launched the famous call "back to Jesus." This led, on the one hand, to establishing the impossibility of writing a "life of Jesus"; on the other hand, however, analysis uncovered how basic the Kingdom of God was for Jesus. So in 1893 Johann Weiss published his *Die Predigt Jesu vom Reiche Gottes* ("the first attempt at a consistent eschatological interpretation of the gospel," according to OCD), and Alfred Loisy coined the famous lapidary phrase: "Jesus came to preach the Kingdom of God, but what he got was the church." In one way or another, the discovery was made that the decisive thing for Jesus was not himself or the church, but the Kingdom of God. And as a formal characterization of this Kingdom, it was described as the ultimate, the "eschatological."

(a) The Ultimate as Crisis of All that is not Ultimate

A first result of this discovery was to cause a crisis for the contemporary Christian understanding of historical reality and society, since the Kingdom of God, being the ultimate, threw all that was not ultimate into crisis. So what made the greatest impact in the discovery of the Kingdom of God in late nineteenth-century Germany was its dimension of crisis.

Adolf Harnack, for example, the last great exponent of liberal theology, in his famous work *Das Wesen des Christentums* (1900, Eng. trans. *The Essence of Christianity*, 1901) had put forward a figure of Jesus based on the paternal goodness of God, love for humankind and the infinite value of the human soul. This image of Jesus undoubtedly had exemplary value, but it also fulfilled a purpose of harmonizing and reconciling the values of nineteenth-century German society: divine justice and human order, throne and altar, religion and culture. Jesus is, then, presented as the one who fully embodies the aspirations of "man," that is of the bourgeois nineteenth-century citizen, imbued with idealism and an uncritical faith in progress. Society could continue on its chosen path unimpeded by Jesus.

This is the context in which the impact of theologians such as Weiss and Loisy (plus Albert Schweitzer with his brilliant *Von Reimarus zu Wrede* (1906, Eng. trans. *The Quest of the Historical Jesus*, 1910) has to be understood. Jesus was not a preacher of the universal morality that confirms the ideal essence of humankind.

The Kingdom of God he preached was not an extrapolation of middle-class aspirations, nor the harmonization of faith and history brought about one way or another since Constantine and the advent of Christendom. In more modern terms, it is not the foundation and justification for "civil religion" or "neo-conservatism" in the United States, or for the "national Catholicism" of Franco Spain, or for the "new Christian Europe" now looked for by the Vatican. None of this is the Kingdom of God and it is therefore hopeless to justify it in the name of the Kingdom. But this is not all: the Kingdom of God judges and actually critiques any historical and social structure. It therefore not only expresses the "eschatological reserve"—that society is *not yet* the Kingdom—but also and above all critiques society: it is *certainly* not the Kingdom. (The so-called "eschatological reserve" can be, and sometimes is, used casually by some first world theologies in order to safeguard the the truth of eschatology: nothing existing on this earth is yet the fullness of the Kingdom of God. But reading this from the Third World, it has a sarcastic ring, because here the not-yet is blindingly obvious and what obviously needs stressing is the certainly-not. This is why we insist that the Kingdom of God is not only a relativization, but also a very strong criticism of contemporary society.)

Rupture and critique are then the first outcome of the discovery of the Kingdom of God. Therefore, it first demands the de-absolutization of what passes for the ultimate, a basic change in our view of reality from faith. In the optimistic bourgeois environment of the last century, the discovery of the Kingdom of God came to say that things could not go on as they were and that they would not get better left to their own inertia and internal development.

(b) Defining the Kingdom as the "Ultimate": the What and When

What is ultimate relativizes and critiques all that is penultimate, as we have seen, but of its nature also introduces the temporal question: when the ultimate comes about. Analyzing replies to this question is important not only or mainly to satisfy curiosity—ever renewed in milleniarism movements—but because the apparently innocent question of *when in time* involves the more important question of *what in fact*. In other words, to know when the Kingdom of God will come, we need to know what it is.

Exegesis has traditionally furnished three replies to the question of when in time. Albert Schweitzer[2] thought the eschatology of the Synoptics referred to the future and only to the future. Jesus originally believed that the Kingdom would come during his lifetime (Matt. 10:23) and later thought that his death would hasten its coming (Matt. 26:29). The Christian community, disappointed by the non-arrival of the Kingdom, then located it in the future, at the end of time (Mark 13:32). So the Synoptics expressed an eschatology sequential in time: the ultimate would really come at the end. C. H. Dodd[3] interpreted the eschatological texts of the Gospels as texts speaking of events occurring in the present (contradicting his contemporary Rudolf Bultmann, who interpreted them in an ethical-existenialist sense). They show the Kingdom not as something still to come, but as something that has come about in the person and actions of Jesus. We need, then, to speak of a realized eschatology. Finally, Oscar Cullmann[4] tried to mediate between both positions. Jesus' preaching contains affirmations both about the present and the future concerning the Kingdom. Both are true, but there is a tension between them, and it is this tension that has to be analyzed. His reply is well known: the "already but not yet" of the coming of the Kingdom. With the coming of Jesus, the end of time has *already* begun, the Evil One and sin have *already* been overcome on principle. But what Christ is has *not yet* been revealed, and this will only be done at the end, on the day of judgment.

These authors try to establish exegetically when—in the temporal sense—the New Testament says the Kingdom will come. Their conclusions differ significantly, partly because they differ in the basic presupposition: *what* the Kingdom of God consists of. To give a systematic response today to the question of when the Kingdom will come, we need to clarify what we mean by it. Let us attempt this through two considerations.

(i) Jesus and Kingdom: mediator and mediation of God. We must first distinguish between the mediator and the mediation of God. The Kingdom of God, formally speaking, is nothing other than the accomplishment of God's will for this world, which we call *mediation.* This mediation—according to the whole history of the Old Testament and, in general, of humanity—is associated with a person (or group) who proclaims it and initiates it: this we call the *mediator.*

In this sense we can and must say, according to faith, that the definitive, ultimate and eschatological mediator of the Kingdom of God has *already* appeared: Jesus. We need not wait for another—even though before and after Jesus other mediators exist, related to him and authorized by him—which is no more than repeating, in kingdom terminology, the basic christological confession: Christ is *the* mediator. From this standpoint, we can also appreciate Origen's fine definition of Christ as the *autobasileia* of God, the Kingdom of God in person: important words that well describe the finality of the personal mediator of the Kingdom, but dangerous if they equate Christ with the reality of the Kingdom.

God's will for creation is not simply, however, that a definitive mediator should appear, but that human beings, God's creatures, should live in a particular manner, that history and human society should come to be truly after God's heart: in solidarity, peace, justice, reconciliation, openness to the Father.... This reality is the content of the Kingdom of God, what I have called its mediation.

Mediation and mediator are, then, essentially related, but they are not the same thing. There is always a Moses and a promised land, an Archbishop Romero and a dream of justice. Both things, together, express the whole of the will of God, while remaining two distinct things.

(ii) The signs and the reality of the Kingdom. We also need to distinguish between the "signs" and the "reality" of the Kingdom. As we saw when analyzing Jesus'

practice, his miracles, casting out of devils, welcoming sinners (and their modern equivalents) are signs of the presence of the Kingdom in history. They are, therefore, of supreme importance since they express something of the reality of the Kingdom, point to the direction this will take in its fullness and arouse the difficult hope that the Kingdom is really possible.

But these *signs* are not fully the *reality* of the Kingdom. The healings have not made the massive reality of sickness disappear, the casting out of devils has not cancelled the omnipresence of the Evil One, the multiplication of loaves still leaves hunger, welcoming sinners still leaves many outcasts, celebratory meals have not done away with sadness....

(iii) A new understanding of the "already but not yet." In what sense can one say, then, that the Kingdom of God has either come already or has not yet come, both in Jesus' time and now? We can say that it has come on the level of the mediator and that we do not need to await another eschatological mediator, although this does not exclude, but rather necessarily includes the appearance of new mediators mandated by Jesus. And it has come on the level of signs in the life of Jesus and in subsequent history.

It has not come, however, on the level of the reality of mediation: the world as a whole is not yet conformed to the heart of God, to put it mildly; to a very large extent it is positively contrary to the heart of God. In Paul's terminology there are still—most definitely—principalities and powers. And death—both in its meaning as human destiny and in its meaning as of being the product of historical sin—has still not been overcome, but rides where it will. Only at the end will God be all in all and only at the end will the Kingdom of God have come (1 Cor. 15:28).

This way of understanding the "already but not yet" is important if we are to avoid both despair and theological and ecclesial triumphalism. The first is forbidden by the fact that the mediator has already appeared and that hidden or obvious signs of the Kingdom happen—surprisingly and gladdeningly—in history. The second is forbidden by the cruel reality of history. It is good to proclaim the definitive appearance of the mediator; this should be done in liturgies and doctrines and experienced above all in personal faith and following of Jesus, but none of this should make precisely those who believe in a God "of the Kingdom" forget the tragic reality of history or hasten to intone triumphal canticles just because believers know and await a happy ending. And it would be worse—the most subtle of triumphalisms and the most dangerous root of alienation—to absolutize the real appearance of the mediator as if this alone were what God willed, while relativizing, ignoring or minimizing the magnitude of the anti-Kingdom.

If I might be allowed to use graphic and anthropomorphic language, we must not think that God is absolutely happy because his final plan has been fulfilled: that his Son should appear on the earth. We cannot think that either God or his Son are very happy when they look at the overall state of our world. Since the coming of the Son, God assures us that that he will not repeat what is said in Genesis: "And the LORD was sorry that he had made humankind on the earth, and it grieved him to his heart. So the LORD said, 'I will blot out from the earth the human beings I have created...'" (Gen. 6:6-7). But neither can it said that God is filled with peace and joy when he looks at his mediation, creation as it is, even though the mediator, the beloved Son, has already come.

2. The Kingdom of God in Modern Christologies

The discovery described above has had a great influence on modern theology since it has confronted it with the need to determine what the ultimate—what we can call the *eschaton*—is theologically, in order to organize and rank the whole of its content on this basis, without relegating its treatment of of the ultimate, in the sense of ultimate in time, to the "four last things": death, judgment, hell and heaven.

For hermeneutical reasons, this has also led theology to decide what is historically most important in reality—what we can call the *primacy*. And the relationship between *eschaton* and primacy has been sought within the hermeneutical circle. So human existence and its trust, hope, historical reality—which feature variously in christologies as the primacy in reality—will be placed in relationship to the *kerygma*, the resurrection of Christ or the Kingdom of God—which feature as the theological ultimate, the *eschaton*.

(a) Bultmann: the Eschatologization of the Mediator

Rudolf Bultmann has been a most determined defender of the eschatological nature of the Christian message, but has developed this from the paschal reality of Christ and not from the Kingdom of God. In other words, he has drastically shifted the stress from the mediation to the mediator, and his is therefore a theology that leaves the Kingdom of God out of account. Not that Bultmann is unaware that Jesus proclaimed the Kingdom of God, but neither the historical Jesus nor his message belong to his theology of the New Testament. "The preaching of Jesus does not belong to the presuppositions of the theology of the New Testament and does not form part of it."[5]

The basis of this stance is found partly in exegetical arguments: the Gospels do not lead us to Jesus, but to the faith of the first communities. Mainly, though, it is found in philosophical ones: what really holds the primacy is human existence in need of salvation, understood existentially-individualistically as authentic, open and freed existence, without basic reference to the exteriority of human beings and the transformation of history. Therefore, for Bultmann, neither the life of Jesus nor the Kingdom are central to Christianity.

In view of this, Bultmann's theology might appear to hold little interest for our current discussion. And yet, though he leaves out the Kingdom of God, he provides a most radical account of two dimensions that reappeared in christology with the discovery of the Kingdom: the eschatological and the critical. Bultmann shifts both dimensions to the mediator, but does so most radically:

The New Testament proclaims Jesus Christ as the eschatological event, as the action of God by which he put an end to the ancient world. In the proclamation, the eschatological event is always made present, and increasingly becomes an event in faith. For the believer the old world has come to its end, it is a "new creation in Christ"... he has become someone new and free.[6]

What there is, then, is the *eschatological* event, Jesus Christ. The ultimate is not in the mediation, but in the mediator. And, in turn, the mediator has become the ultimate not as the Jesus of history, but as Christ crucified and raised. This event becomes the ultimate for us by being proclaimed in the *kerygma*. This Christ preached is the one who places listeners under the unavoidable need to understand themselves and live according to an authentic life, life in faith, which allows salvation and the meaning of life to be bestowed by God, or to continue in their inauthentic life, closed in on themselves, destroying the possibilities of their human existence.

The eschatological ultimate is also *critical* of human beings. For the *kerygma* to be able to be salvation, the sinful being must be destroyed. "Those whom the action of God seeks to vivify are first destroyed by this same action."[7] The "new man" arrives in opposition to the "old man," just as the Kingdom arrives in opposition to the anti-Kingdom.

The eschatological ultimate is, finally, *good news*. There exists the possibilty of life in faith by which we accept that the cross of Christ is salvation for sinful humankind and bearer of the possibility of a new life, and that faith in the resurrection is, precisely, believing that the cross is a saving event.

In this vision of Bultmann's, Christianity is really eschatological, but the ultimate comes about purely in our inner subjectivity and has nothing to do with the exteriority of history, although Bultmann also proposes an ethic. The eschatological breaks into history when the *kerygma* is accepted, but any historical or social situation is equally far from or close to it. The ultimate is not measured by the achievement of the Kingdom of God, nor does its coming have anything to do with the final fulfillment of history. For the ultimate to come about depends solely on inner acceptance of the *kerygma*.

Bultmann's eschatology is, therefore, asocial and has nothing to do with building the Kingdom of God; it is also atemporal and has nothing to do with a future that can become fullness. (This also leads to Bultmann's demythologization project and, positively, to his existential reinterpretation of the language of the New Testament. Temporal language—in the end the angels will come from heaven, there will be all sorts of marvels, the dead will rise up and judgment be passed— should be reinterpreted as a way of affirming the finality and profundity of life here and now. Spatial language—humankind is set on earth between heaven and hell— should be reinterpreted as a way of emphasizing the existential alternative with which we are faced.) So his christology does away with the Kingdom of God. It concentrates on the mediator and the offer of salvation and liberation he brings: coming to be a "new man," triumphing over the "old man."

The limitations and grave dangers of this reduction, from our point of view, are obvious, but, as with any one-sided proposition brilliantly argued, Bultmann sheds some important light, in this case on the mediator. So I should like to end this examination by quoting a text on Jesus Christ in which Bultmann stresses the liberative aspect of Christ for humankind. He asks himself whether it is possible to know God through creation alone and concludes:

> Who is this man who can see creation truly as revelation? It would have to be the one for whom the world is no longer an enigma, who complains neither of pain nor need, who feels no anguish in the face of fate or death, who is not tormented by any inner excision. Where is the man who, without Christ, can say, "the world or life or death or the present or the future—all belong to you" (1 Cor. 3:22), who can say, "Who will separate us from the love of Christ? Will hardship, or distress, or persecution, or famine, or nakedness, or peril, or sword?... No, in all things we are more than conquerors" (Rom. 8:35, 37)? Only then will he see creation as the gracious revelation of God.

Such liberated persons are those who have faith in Jesus Christ. The ultimate is their faith, which allows them to live truly open to this world and freed from this world. This is, in turn, possible through the eschatological event of Christ. The mediator, for Bultmann, is truly mediator, since he liberates and saves.

(b) Pannenberg: the Eschatological as Anticipation of the Ultimate Future

Various theologians have reacted against the ahistorical existentialism of Bultmann (and the transcendentalism of Karl Barth), the most notable being Wolfhart Pannenberg. He declared as much in programmatic form: "History is the most embracing horizon of Christian theology."[9] With this he defends the historical method as the only valid one in theology—against all types of dogmatism and authoritarianism—and, above all, seeks to retrieve the essentially historical dimension of God's revelation. What is eschatological must, then, be sought in history.

(i) The ultimate: Jesus' resurrection as anticipation of the end of history.
Pannenberg sees the *eschaton* in the final future and the primacy of reality in the correlative trust-hope, an inspiration derived from Ernst Bloch, whom he thanks for rescuing the radical concept of eschatology and grasping the power of the future in human life and thought. The eschatological is the future, since only at the end will truth be decided, but also because, as what has not happened, it already shows its strength in the present.

On the basis of this conception of eschatology, Pannenberg interprets the figure of Jesus as an eschatological figure, but in a precise way and one different from

Bultmann. (His conception—justified in scripture—also allows him to reformulate all the major theological realities: understanding the reality of God as future power, understanding God's revelation as what happens at the end of history with anticipatory signs during history, resolving the problem of how to reconcile a creator God in the beginning with human freedom in the present....) For a start, the truth of Jesus' life and the claims he made have to be decided—as the Gospels demand they must be decided—in the future. As this, by definition, has not yet come, Jesus is eschatological, even if he in some way makes the end of history present now. And this is what happened in Jesus' resurrection, understood as anticipation (*prolepsis*) of the universal resurrection of the dead, in which the end of time, the absolute future, is made real. (Pannenberg insists on the fact that Jesus' resurrection is presented in the New Testament as the resurrection not simply of an individual, but of the "first-born." This means that in the New Testament Jesus' resurrection has, in anticipation, the character of the universal resurrection, of the end of time.)

(ii) The Kingdom of God enables us to live by the future. The eschatological is linked to what happened to the mediator in the resurrection. But if this is so, we need to ask what meaning Pannenberg gives to the Kingdom of God in his christology. This is not a purely optional question here, since Pannenberg himself is forced to face up to it by his consequent historical method: when he analyzes the life of the historical Jesus he cannot pass over the centrality of the Kingdom for Jesus.

This Kingdom must be said not to have come yet; it is, then, *future*, but necessarily adding that it is *imminent* future, and Pannenberg analyzes it on the basis of its imminent futurity in order to see in what sense it is also something ultimate. To do so, he insists on the effects on the listener of a proclamation of the Kingdom as imminent future: "Jesus has proclaimed the immediate proximity of the Kingdom of God. This message forced believers to abandon their everyday concerns, urged them to be converted to God, since the initiation of the Kingdom meant deciding the salvation or condemnation of each individual."[10] This proclamation of the Kingdom, at once imminent and future, is what enables us to understand it systematically as something ultimate, since it requires and enables us to live by the future, "to go beyond any fulfillment of existence and any presently real or possible security."[11] The proclamation of the Kingdom, then, uncovers the true human reality, "the openness of existence to God."[12] So if human beings accept this proclamation, it becomes for them good news and salvation: "Given that salvation consists in fulfilling the specific human determination, in the fullness of openness to God, this means it is already something present for those who long for the proximity of God preached by Jesus."[13]

Pannenberg's reasoning is at once simple and brilliant. The proclamation of the coming of the Kingdom as imminent enables and urges us to face up to the ultimate; but since, though imminent, it is still future, we can relate to the utimate only by realizing our essential anthropological dimension of openness, in this case through trust-hope. In this way, living only the Kingdom that is drawing near is to realize our human essence, and so salvation.

Pannenberg sees this systematic reasoning borne out in Jesus' own practice. "His healings provide immediate evidence of the fact that where the message of the proximity of God is accepted entire and in complete trust, salvation as such is already effected."[14] This is also why Jesus forgives sins in disregard to the law. In a word, "trusting in the coming of the reign of God is the only condition for participating in it."[15]

This understanding of the Kingdom as the ultimate is based, then, on the primacy given to human openness, trust and hope. Pannenberg then goes on to try to reclaim what is inescapably central in the Gospels: the relationship between the Kingdom and a way of life described generically as love. Those who accept Jesus' message come "to the authentic natural human relationship with God and can no longer live other than 'desiring the Kingdom of God above all,'"[16] which leads them to act as God acts, that is, to a life of service, forgiveness, mercy and love.[17]

In this, Pannenberg sees the present significance of the proclamation of the Kingdom of God. What matters in the here and now is no longer living by a hope insofar as this hope is imminent, but living by the future of God. In this way, what is not yet—and because it is not yet—already generates a reality in the present: trust, hope, unconditional surrender. In this way, too, Pannenberg puts forward a reinterpretation of Cullmann's solution. The "already but not yet" is not two continuous realities with differing values, in that the "already" is the beginning of a fullness that has "not yet" come about. The realities are rather discontinuous: the future, precisely, because it has not happened, allows a present of salvation to exist.

All this shows that Pannenberg places a positive value on the proclamation of the Kingdom of God announced by Jesus. In the end, however, the resurrection remains the basic factor, even when the ultimate is seen from the Kingdom of God. Asking himself whether the coming of the Kingdom has happened, Pannenberg states that it has, though in a partial and unexpected fashion, in the resurrection of Jesus himself. Put in other words, at present the proclamation of Jesus' resurrection functions as the equivalent of the proclamation of the Kingdom of God made by Jesus: "Jesus' resurrection justifies the hope for what is immediate that guided his life, and for the rest of humankind grounds the hope in the end that has already been accomplished in him."[18]

(iii) The (abstract) socio-historical dimension of the Kingdom of God. We have so far seen Pannenberg approaching the Kingdom of God from a metaphysical-anthropological standpoint, but in "The Kingdom of God and the Church,"[19] he also deals with its socio-historical dimension. This is worth discussing in itself, but also because it has become a model for an extensive body of theology.

Pannenberg notes that Jesus did not stop at proclaiming the Kingdom, but also demanded the practice of love, as the quintessence of justice, and that this shows a new dimension of the Kingdom, since "justice and love do not concern individuals alone, but also the structures of social dealings among human beings. In this sense, the Kingdom of God has a markedly political character." He also mentions the utopic dynamic toward justice, which sets the future of the Kingdom in motion, and recalls that the churches must shed light on history from the ideals of the Kingdom, must be prophetic critics of deviations from these, must avoid pulling back from involvement in society and, finally, must avoid triumphalism, since "the power of love is far from being the property or privilege of the churches." Elsewhere, he also recognizes that the Kingdom of God is "a kingdom of contradiction of the established powers."[20]

These statements are important. They show how discovery of the Kingdom of God has social implications and mark an advance on Bultmann's existentialist individualism. But they are hardly historical, and in this can be dangerous and even deceptive, without of course meaning to be so. Since this way of approaching the socio-historical dimension of the Kingdom has been and still is common in first-world christologies, let me make three basic criticisms.

The first is that Pannenberg, while appreciating the positive forces that stem from the proclamation of the Kingdom, insists on what is called the "eschatological reserve" (*der eschatologische Vorbehalt*), that is, the relativization the fullness of the Kingdom imposes on any historical configuration of reality and society. So he rightly stresses that nothing in history can be the Kingdom of God and reminds us of the dangers of making such an association, since real horrors have been committed in its name. And he stresses that "the authentic declaration that we are not God is still a decisive condition for true humanization."

Having established such a basic truth, however, we need to recall other equally basic truths. Although the Kingdom of God cannot be achieved on this earth, the ideal of the Kingdom serves to measure, on principle, *how much* of the Kingdom there is in particular social developments; it also serves to avoid all such developments appearing infinitely remote from the Kingdom by the standards of the Kingdom. The Kingdom of God certainly relativizes them, but it also *grades* them, and this is supremely important. The decisive point is how to measure, on principle, how much of the Kingdom of God exists as a social reality, and this is what many theologies fail to do.

By not analyzing the specific signs of the Kingdom, but subsuming them in "love"—actualized at best in forgiveness and mercy—the particular addressees of these signs are generally passed over, and thereby universalized. Universalizing the addressee means universalizing the content of the Kingdom: love. Then it becomes difficult to "measure" how much there is of *Kingdom*, not just how much goodness, to diagnose its true signs, to grade—not relativize indiscriminately—partial realizations of the Kingdom. In a word, the poor are not usually present in these christologies as an essential determinant of what the Kingdom is. So, although their statements are formally true and even important, they suffer from a lack of evangelical and historical perspective on the present. The contribution that faith and the churches should make, to set the correct signs of the Kingdom and to point history in the correct direction of the Kingdom, remains excessively vague and is very often hijacked by those who have no interest in seeing this Kingdom become a reality.

My second criticism is that the Kingdom of God is usually analyzed without its essential relationship to the anti-Kingdom. It is not that christologies do not mention sin, oppression and the persecution Jesus suffered, but that they fail to take serious account of the fact that the Kingdom is proclaimed in the presence of and in opposition to the anti-Kingdom. This ignores its dialectical and conflictual dimension and the agonistic nature of human existence stemming precisely from the fact that human beings have to choose between Kingdom and anti-Kingdom. So calls for the churches to propound the Kingdom—substantial in themselves— suffer from ingenuousness, since what really costs, on account of its risk and conflictivity, is the call to struggle against the anti-Kingdom. Let me add that in Pannenberg's own christology, this is coherently linked to his failure to give any socio-historical or theological valuation to Jesus' crucifixion and its causes, since the only thing that seems to concern him about the crucifixion is the fact of Jesus' death as a condition that makes the resurrection possible.

My third criticism is that, overall, Pannenberg's christology is addressed substantively to the individual, no longer in Bultmann's existentialist fashion, but still in the personalist expression of trust and hope: "The only contribution the church can make to society where its place cannot be taken by any other institution, is the personal integration of human life, which it carries out through our confrontation with the deepest mystery of life, with the eternal God and his purposes in the history of humanity."[21] I am not of course denying that this is a target, even a specific one, for the church and religions, but that a church that lives for the Kingdom of God can reduce its specific contribution to, or concentrate it precipitately on, the purely personal dimension.

In scripture, what corresponds to the Kingdom of God is a whole people, the people of God, within which the indivdual has to achieve self-realization. And this is still the case even though this realization, being personal, has its own autonomy and its own dynamic and is not mechanically dependent on being a member of a people, and even though individuals cannot delegate all their responsibility in faith, hope and love to the people. It is still true that in scripture it is essential for a person to achieve the trust and hope with which to respond to the Kingdom and to achieve the love with which to serve the Kingdom within a people. This being referred to a people—not just to another, a "thou"—is also essential for self-realization as a person, and, as much in Jesus' time as now, this reference is to a people "of the poor." In this case, personal transcendental hope must also be historicized as "the people's" hope and personal transcendental trust must also be historicized as trust in a God "of the poor."

In short, the vision of the Kingdom in this type of christology does not recognize the "partiality" of the Kingdom, does not stress—sometimes does not even mention—the anti-Kingdom and does not historicize the transcendental openness of the individual as "people's" hope and as trust in the God "of the poor."

(c) Moltmann: Following the Mediator to build the Mediation

As for Pannenberg, so too for Jürgen Moltmann, the *eschaton* is the future and the primacy is held by hope. In summary form, "the future as constitutive character" belongs to God;[22] the *eschaton* in history is the resurrection of Christ, because it points to the future; correlatively the human being is the being of hope. I do not intend to expand on this here, but to examine how Moltmann differs from Pannenberg's approach and his original contribution: the ultimate is the *mediator*, in that he must be followed, and the ultimate is also the *mediation*, in that this must be built in history; it is also both together, critiquing and struggling against what is negative in history.

(i) The ultimate as contradiction of the present: the resurrection of a crucified man.
A fundamental contribution made by Moltmann is his retrieval of the dialectical dimension of reality and, specifically, stressing its aspect of negativity. (In his first major work, *Theology of Hope*, Moltmann is inspired by Ernst Bloch, while his second and more definitive major work, *The Crucified God*, is more influenced by the critical philosophy of the Frankfurt School.) So, the present is not only or principally the "not yet" of fullness, a sort of *tabula rasa* with open possibilities not yet brought about, but is, concretely, poverty, oppression, injustice: in a word, sin. Therefore the present is not only distanced from the future but stands in contradiction to the future hoped for. And therefore, too, the future exercises a critical function with respect to the present and defines itself, in the present, as a power in and against the present.

Equally, the ideal person cannot be thought of as the whole person developed from the possibilities of the present-day person, but as the "new man" who, to become such, has to pass through the critique and negation of the present-day person. His hope is not just the positive realization of personal transcendental openness, but hope against the misery of the present. From this it also follows that hope is related to the future not only "expectantly," but also "praxically," operating against the misery in the present: it is, then, praxic hope. And this praxis is directed at the transformation not only of the individual person, but of society as such, since the future is anticipated in history not only in the crisis-transformation of the individual, but in that of society. The ultimate, then, can make itself present in history, but above all as contradiction and overcoming of present reality.

The theological roots of this approach, very different from Pannenberg's, lie in Moltmann's theo-logy and christology. The God of the future becomes definitive promise in the resurrection, but in the resurrection of a crucified person; this cross christianizes and concretizes the whole of theology. The fact that the resurrected one is the crucified one means that the hope with which we must respond to the resurrection is the hope of victims: "that the executioner may not triumph over his victim." The apocalyptic-transcendent aspect of hope is concretized through its prophetic element and so hope is also hope for the historical present and requires transforming praxis.

In this sense, one can say that the eschatological event, the *eschaton*, is the resurrection of Christ for Moltmann as well, but in a very different sense from that of Bultmann or Pannenberg, since it is the resurrection of a crucified man.

(ii) The ultimate of the mediator: following the one crucified. The eschatological can happen in history in personal form, since we can live in the presence of the ultimate in history, not only through personal transcendental openness to God, but in the hope and following of the risen crucified one.

Believers are those whose hope is based on the resurrection of a crucified one. This means that Christian hope embraces the scandal of there being a crucified one and a crucified history. It also means that the resurrection—being that of a crucified man—is an expression of justice to victims, not only of an afterlife in the beyond, and this is what Moltmann sees as the final purpose of apocalyptic.

Injustice, overcome in the resurrection, is not just a factor in the cosmic drama, but a real injustice, and as such drags believers back into the present history of poverty and suffering. And it does so in a particular way: "Suffering presupposes love. If we do not love, we do not suffer."[23] In this way the resurrection's promise of plenitude places us "in the time of love," in a "life of solidarity with the oppressed."[24]

What happened to the mediator in his resurrection draws believers back to their present history, and by trying to live this adequately, eschatologically, they meet the historical fact of the mediator. "Not any life is an occasion for hope, but the life of Jesus is, since he laid the cross and death on himself in love."[25]

What Moltmann is stating, then, is that it is already possible to live in history eschatologically, realizing at once the present hope in the resurrection of one crucified and the love shown in Jesus' life. In resurrection terminology, we can live now as raised under the conditions of history. In historical terms, we can live now with the love of the crucified Jesus. And this is nothing other than the following of Jesus:

> The way and destiny of Jesus Christ are for faith the roots of anticipation, or rather, of the gift anticipated, of the coming Kingdom of human beings in the midst of the kingdoms of this world. The crucified one incarnates the new humanity which corresponds to God in the midst of the conditionings of inhumanity which contradict God.... But it is precisely in this way that human beings are enabled to make these conditionings change, to make the world a better country and abolish external and internal slavery.[26]

(iii) The ultimate of mediation: the Kingdom of God for the poor. A better world and one without slavery: this is the Kingdom of God. Moltmann has developed this

systematically in his book on the church[27] (from which quotations in this section are taken) which marks a notable advance on other contemporary first-world theologies by bringing out the partial and community nature of this Kingdom, its addressees the poor and, above all, the presence of the anti-Kingdom. In his analysis, Moltmann decides what the Kingdom of God should be today on the basis of what it was for Jesus.

(a) First, Jesus "announces the good news of the Kingdom to the poor and summons captives to the coming freedom of God. The content of his message is the God who is coming and the liberation of the people." (b) Second, the poor are described realistically: "the poverty alluded to here goes from economic, social and physical poverty to psychic, moral and religious poverty.... The poor are all those who, bodily or spiritually, live on the margins of death and to whom life has given nothing." (c) Third, the poor are described historically and dialectically, in relation to the anti-Kingdom: "all those who suffer violence and injustice without being able to defend themselves from these are poor"; they are, then, the impoverished, the oppressed. "The concept opposed to *poor* is that of *oppressor, violent*, those who oppress the poor and reduce them to penury in order to enrich themselves at their expense." (d) Fourth, Jesus offers these poor not only a word, but signs of liberation. The Kingdom of God is therefore something that has to be built. (e) Fifth, it is from this partial standpoint that Jesus' message gains its true universality. The good news is for all, but "it can be heard as good news only by accepting one's own poverty and in communion with the poor... (in) solidarity with the humble and burdened." (f) Sixth, this Kingdom of God is made present in history in community, collective form: "The concrete form taken by the Kingdom of God is the community of the blind who see, the captives who are freed, the poor who are blessed and the sick who are healed. With these the exodus of the whole people begins. They make up the community of the wretched, praising and giving thanks to God here and now."

This Kingdom of God preached in this way by Jesus has value for the present, has become a force determining the present, acting "through the word and faith, promise and hope, prayer and obedience, power and the Spirit." The important thing to note here is that the Kingdom acts, and not only formally, as Pannenberg has it, through being still in the future and requiring and enabling a hope, but because, though future, it has basic concrete content: the putting of Jesus' ideal into actual practice.

Expressed graphically, Moltmann tackles the problem by asking what the present reality of the true church should be. That it should be for the Kingdom is not a problem: this consists in where this true church is made real, "in the community manifested through word and sacrament or in the latent brotherhood of the universal judge hidden in the poor?" His reply is that the church should be present "*there where* Christ is waiting for it, in the little ones, the sick, the imprisoned." So Moltmann historicizes and reformulates the marks of the true church on the basis of its service to the Kingdom and its characteristics. Oneness is achieved as "a communion of believers with the poor"; holiness, above all in "the signs of its suffering, of its persecution on account of its resistance to the world and its poverty"; catholicity, in taking sides, "through choosing the little ones, while the powerful incur God's judgment"; apostolicity, in that mission which "leads inevitably to conflict, opposition and suffering."

Moltmann, then, takes the Kingdom of God seriously, as the mediation of the ultimate, a reality that has to be both hoped for and built against the anti-Kingdom, in taking sides with the poor and according to the norm laid down by the mediator. In Latin America he has been criticized for his lack of historical specificity, and I shall show later how Latin American christology historicizes the Kingdom of God. But seen from within the history of christology, we must note his major and specific retrieval of the Kingdom of God, in which he has been influenced not only by exegesis, but also, in fact, by the theology of liberation.[28]

(d) Kasper: the (Abstract-Universal) Kingdom of Love

I propose to finish this brief survey with some comments on the christology of Walter Kasper.[29] To determine what this Kingdom is, Kasper briefly addresses the question of its addressees acording to the Gospels (pp. 84ff) and on some aspects of Jesus' attitude. Among these he distinguishes, "in the first instance, the forgiveness of sins" with its resultant "rejoicing at having encountered the boundless and unmerited mercy of God" (p. 86). He also deals with the miracles, which show that the "well being" established by the Kingdom of God "is not just a spiritual state, but affects human beings as a whole, including their bodies" (p. 95). With regard to the addressees, Kasper emphasizes, on the one hand, that there is a certain partiality in the Kingdom, since "Jesus proclaims it with the stress on God's love and compassion for sinners" (p. 66), though he hastens to qualify this partiality, which has nothing to do with "what is thought of today as social concern or revolution," since "God is a God of people, people of all sorts" (p. 67). The conclusion he draws in these chapters—analyzing Jesus' activity and message—is the universalization of the Kingdom of God: the salvation of the Kingdom of God consists in the love of God, communicated by God, coming to rule in and through people. Love shows itself as the meaning of being: "[Love] is the wholeness of man and the world" (p. 87). And this Kingdom comes about in every individual:

> Everyone can know that love is the ultimate, that it is stronger then death, stronger than hatred and injustice. The news of the coming of the Kingdom of God is therefore a promise about everything that is done in the world out of love. It says that, against all appearances, what is done out of love will endure for ever; that it is the only thing which lasts forever (p. 87).

These words, fine and true in themselves, are disconcerting. Love, meaning, hope and promise are all central realities in the Gospels and in the whole of the New Testament, and they are also realities that bear directly on the Kingdom of God as Jesus preached it. What is disconcerting and disappointing is that they should be presented—and with such a degree of abstraction—as a result of an inquiry into what the Kingdom of God is in the Gospels. What is here said of the Kingdom could equally be said of Jesus' commandment to love or Paul's hymn to love and hope (1 Cor. 13; Rom. 8:31-9) or love in 1 John. It is not that what he says is not true in itself, clearly, but that he does not see how it helps to clarify the specific and concrete content of the Kingdom of God preached by Jesus, and that he gives the impression rather of hiding an important aspect of this. The conclusion is that the Kingdom of God—the symbol of basic wholeness for Jesus and the concept he uses most— becomes practically interchangeable with other theological realities and so loses its specificity.

The reason for this universalizing abstraction of the Kingdom of God is that Kasper does not undertake a serious analysis of whom the Kingdom is for, the poor and their poverty; he rather de-historicizes them, without analyzing the actual conditions under which they lived in Jesus' time—or our own for that matter. This makes him anxious to tell us that "the revolution Jesus brings is the revolution of unrestricted love in a world of egotism and power" (p. 68), and, naturally, that "class-war slogans find no direct support in Jesus" (p. 69).

This biblical analysis of the Kingdom of God is rather superficial in comparison with the authors examined earlier and even shows a certain fear of letting New Testament texts speak for themselves, whatever the results. Above all, it is hermeneutically limited and biased. Apparently, Kasper's limit of understanding the meaning of poverty is set by the metaphysical limitation of all human beings and the more specific limitation of being separated from God by sin. His limit of understanding the meaning of salvation is set by love "in itself"—while it is surely very difficult to know what it consists of—historicized at most as forgiveness.

But there are other poverties that cannot be interchanged with metaphysical limitation and there is another love of God directed not only at the sinner, but at the poor. That the Kingdom of God includes what Kasper says is therefore correct. But he is not correct in reducing it to this, let alone in making it the central element of the Kingdom of God: the good news of God to the poor of this world. To say nothing of the little importance Kasper attaches to the anti-Kingdom, which will be analyzed in the excursus devoted to God and idols.

3. The Kingdom of God in Latin American Christologies

The foregoing survey should have shown how the "ultimate," the *eschaton*, features in different ways in first-world christologies, depending on what is considered the "primacy" in reality. It should also help to understand, by way of contrast, what is specific to Latin American christology. (I have reviewed only a few; there are others more akin to Latin American christologies. The christological thinking of José Ignacio González Faus, for example, has developed along lines in accordance with Latin American thinking, as can be seen from a comparison of the first edition of his *La humanidad nueva* and the latest, and with his *Acceso a Jesús* [1987] as well as his numerous articles in the *Revista Latinoamericana de Teología*.)

Latin American christology follows the main lines of modern theolgy: naming a theological "ultimate," the *eschaton*, as the organizing and ranking principle of everything else, and naming a "primacy" in reality. In Latin American theology, the primacy is held by "liberation," understood fundamentally as "the liberation of the poor," without reducing the whole of reality to this, but seeing the whole of reality from this point of view. And this primacy has a corresponding *eschaton*, the ultimate and eschatological, the "Kingdom of God." This is not deduced from such and such an explicit affirmation, though these exist, but from the specific task of this theology, from what it is most concerned with and analyzes in greatest detail, from what it relates most often to what its primacy is: the liberation of the poor.

At its outset, Gustavo Gutiérrez's *A Theology of Liberation* gave a clear new emphasis to the eschatological focus of theology (chapter 11), but placing this at the service of its greatest problem: liberation and salvation in history (chapter 9). He concluded that the Kingdom of God is the most appropriate reality for expressing the utopia of liberation, though in this book he did so not from a biblical standpoint, but from that of the teaching of the church, particularly the documents of Vatican II (chapter 12). Since then, christological and ecclesiological studies have all given great importance to the Kingdom of God and have made it the central and final reality *in actu*, or at least something more central and more final than other theological concepts. As we saw at the start of this excursus, this was explicitly stated by Ignacio Ellacuría.

(a) Reasons for making the Kingdom of God the Ultimate

Considering the Kingdom of God as the ultimate in liberation theology is not arbitrary, but due to several convergent reasons. Let us look at these.

(i) Before theology there is the *pre-theological*, and for liberation theology this is the specific reality of the Third World. Now, in this world, the utopia hoped for is not any utopia, but the hope that life, as the primal fact of surviving, the dignity of outcasts and basic solidarity—justice, in a word—may be possible. Therefore, without being naive or anachronistic, there is no doubt that the Third World, much more than the others, presents a historical reality somehow analogous to that in which the very notion of a "Kingdom of God" arose. The *locus theologicus* of this theology, understood here not only as a categorical *ubi*, but also as a substantial *quid*, is therefore akin to the Old and New Testament theological setting of the theology of the Kingdom of God. We are therefore at the pre-theological, but hermeneutically decisive, level on which the *Horizontsverschmelzung* (mingling of horizons) takes place; this enables us to understand the biblical notion of the Kingdom of God today, but more importantly, forces us to take it seriously into account.

(ii) Furthermore, still in general terms, liberation theology possesses certain *formal characteristics* that correspond to the "Kingdom of God" more easily than to other theological concepts. It is, in effect, a *historical theology*, with a basic concern to historicize all the transcendental realities of faith. It is a *prophetic* theology, centrally concerned with denouncing and unmasking historical sin. It is a *praxic* theology, in that it sees itself as the ideological arm of a praxis directed at transforming reality. It is a *people's* theology, which sees in the people—in their double sense of "collectivity" and "oppressed majorities"—the primary targets of its activity, and, in a sense, also the authors of theological activity and certainly the agents of faith. For all this, the Kingdom of God provides advantages not offered by other theological concepts.

Despite accusations of "reductionism" from its detractors, liberation theology sees itself as definitely an all-embracing theology and thinks it can better express this inclusiveness from the Kingdom of God and from liberation. The Kingdom of God offers theology a totality that enables it to be just *theology*, and a specific historical embodiment of this totality that enables theology to be theology *of liberation*. The totality can be formulated generically as "transcendence in history," and the "Kingdom of God" facilitates this, since the "Kingdom" is history and the "of God" is transcendence. "What this conception of faith from the Kingdom of God does is place God in indissoluble conjunction with history," overcoming "the (earthly) Kingdom and (celestial) God duality."[30] Liberation theology, then, claims to have found in the Kingdom of God a totality from which it can deal with all theological subjects and also rank them in accordance with their closeness to the ultimate mystery, now formulated as Kingdom of God.[31]

(iii) Looking at the history of theology, liberation theolgy also holds that by making the Kingdom of God central it is easier to avoid serious practical dangers for theology. To mention just two of these: it overcomes the grave danger of equating the Kingdom with the church, and does so in a precise way. The church, on the one hand, cannot escape from the world, since the Kingdom is world; on the other, neither can it conform to the values of the world, become worldly, since the Kingdom is of God. Taking the Kingdom of God seriously is what enables and forces the church to be of the world but not worldly. And the most important thing is that the Kingdom provides a criterion of verification concrete enough to see if and to what extent this danger is present (something that cannot be seen so clearly if other theological realities are taken as the ultimate).

The second example is that, through what it denies, the Kingdom of God points out the historical malice of the world for what it is, as sinful structure, as anti-Kingdom, and again clearly points to degrees of sin: "It is not that structures can sin, as some claim liberation theologians say, but structures demonstrate and actualize the power of sin and, in this sense, make people sin and make it supremely difficult for them to lead the lives that belong to them as children of God."[32]

(iv) Finally, this theology makes the Kingdom of God central for strictly christological reasons. This means, as we have seen, that it retrieves the historical Jesus and so retrieves and makes central the Kingdom that Jesus preached, while applying it to the historical present, as we shall see.

Before tackling this subject, however, we need to meet a reasonable objection, since analyzing the figure of Jesus necessarily leads to another all-embracing reality that could feature as the ultimate: his resurrection. However, liberation theology deliberately chooses the Kingdom of God and not the resurrection as "ultimate." Let us see why.

Jesus' resurrection, understood as first-fruits of the universal resurrection, undoubtedly presents major claims for featuring as the ultimate: absolute making whole and salvation, and so absolute liberation. Correlatively, it unleashes a radical hope going beyond and against death, all of which is important and is generally taken up in christologies. But furthermore, Jesus' resurrection can be interpreted—on the basis of exegesis, not just abritrarily or manipulatively—in such a way that it sums up and sheds light on specific elements important to liberation theology.

So it can be said that Jesus' resurrection is not just the revelation of God's power over nothingness, but the triumph of justice over injustice; that its direct promise is not the universal hope of an afterlife, but a partial hope—which can later be universalized—for the victims of this world, the crucified of history; that it can unleash a radical hope now in history, since if God has shown the power of freeing from death, God will have more power to free from oppression; that it is not only a symbol of individual hope, but also of collective hope, since Jesus' resurrection is presented in its very essence as the resurrection of a "first-born," which must necessarily be followed by the resurrection of many others; that it expresses the importance of the corporeal-material dimension, since, unlike other symbols of afterlife, such as those of Greek and Oriental philosophy, it is the whole human being that is raised; that it can somehow be already experienced in history, historicized therefore, by making its specific power felt in a particular way of acting out the following of Jesus in joy and freedom, realities that both reflect the making whole signified by the resurrection within the limitations of history. The resurrection can express central tenets of faith, such as the final eschatology and the absolute gratuitousness of God, even better than the Kingdom of God.

All this is true and appreciated by liberation theology. Despite this, however, if Jesus' resurrection is to function as the ultimate for a theology of this sort, an immense interpretative effort is clearly needed, which is not necessary if the ultimate is the Kingdom of God. The resurrection of itself possesses great power for expressing the ultimate meaning of history, final utopia and radical hope, but it does not possess so much power for showing how we have to live now in history and guide it toward utopia.

Furthermore, as happens with any symbol of the ultimate one chooses—including that of the Kingdom of God—the resurrection also has its limitations and dangers, not maybe as pure concept, but in practice. There is no need to be shocked by these words, since anything we human beings touch, however good and holy—prayer, the struggle for justice, the very idea of God—is subject to our limitation and concupiscence. So history shows that a precipitate and one-sided penchant for the resurrection can and usually does encourage an individualism without a people, a hope without praxis, an enthusiasm without a following of Jesus: in short, a transcendence without history, a God without a Kingdom. History is witness to this from New Testament times to our own days: look at the community in Corinth and modern Catholic, Protestant and sectarian charismatics. Liberation theology is particularly sensitive to this danger.

All this has to be understood correctly. Of course I am not saying that Jesus' resurrection is not a central reality for faith and for theology, and liberation theology in fact gives it the greatest importance and uses it as an expression of the ultimate. José Miranda criticizes Marx precisely on the basis of the resurrection, accusing him of not daring to conceive a transformation of reality that goes so far as to include "the resurrection of the dead."[33] All I am trying to say is that Jesus' resurrection is not considered as apt a reality as the Kingdom of God for featuring as the ultimate and organizing and ranking the whole of faith and theology. The resurrection will be very much taken into account, but from within something more all-embracing, the Kingdom of God.

(b) Systematic Characterization of the Kingdom of God

Liberation theology starts from the Kingdom of God preached by Jesus, but applies it historically to the present for the obvious reason that the Kingdom did not come in Jesus' time and the present requires that we set it in history. We are conscious of the risks inherent in doing do, but believe it better to run these risks:

> The gospel invites us to creative fantasy and to formulate ideologies born not from an a priori magnitude, but from analysis and from the challenges of a situation seen from the standpoint of a liberative project. In this situation, Christians in their faith should not be afraid of taking a concrete decision with the risks of failure this implies, a decision that can be the historically mediated coming of the Kingdom.[34]

Let us look now at how liberation theology assembles and historicizes the formal elements of the Kingdom as they appear in the Synoptics, a process that distinguishes it from many other present-day theologies of the Kingdom.

(i) The Kingdom of God in the presence of and against the anti-Kingdom. Liberation theology sees it as a basic task to establish, methodologically and systematically and in the first place, the *reality of the anti-Kingdom*, since the present situation of Latin America is not just a not-yet, but a certainly-not, so that the utopia of what the Kingdom might be has to focus first on eradicating the anti-Kingdom. This theology begins, then, with asserting the extremely grave sin of injustice, repression and oppression that denies and opposes utopia. This was a feature of both Medellín and Puebla, as we saw in the previous chapter.

The salvation brought by the Kingdom—though this is not all the Kingdom brings—will, then, be *being saved in history* from the evils of history. What the benefits of the Kingdom might be is determined above all by the actual situation of oppressed human beings and not by an *a priori* decision about what salvation might mean. "Salvation is always salvation *of* someone, and in that someone, *from* something."[35] The salvation brought by the Kingdom comes, therefore, in history. So with Jesus, the content of salvation was dictated by the reality of his listeners, and his actions (miracles, casting out of devils, welcoming sinners) were beneficial because they brought good where there had been specific ills.

These benefits brought by the Kingdom are a direct contradiction of the anti-Kingdom and this makes the Kingdom *liberating*. It not only has to produce benefits, but to liberate from ills. The anti-Kingdom is not just the absence or the not-yet of the Kingdom, but its formal contradiction. Building the Kingdom means destroying the anti-Kingdom; saving human beings means liberating them from their slaveries. This is the liberative aspect of Jesus' actions against oppressors in history (the rich, the scribes, the Pharisees, the rulers) and against the transcendent oppressor, the Evil One.

The coming of the Kingdom stands in *combative relation* to the anti-Kingdom. They are not merely mutually exclusive, but fight against one another, and this is massively evidenced in Latin America: the Kingdom is not being built from a *tabula rasa*, but in opposition to the anti-Kingdom, and the present persecution of those who are mediating the coming of the Kingdom is effective proof of this. This persecution, in its turn, becomes the criterion of whether the Kingdom is actually being built. Those who carry out purely beneficial activities are not persecuted, which means that they have not struggled against the anti-Kingdom, and this, in turn, means that their activities are not, strictly speaking, signs of the Kingdom, since they are not activities like those of Jesus.

Liberation theology, then, finds it absolutely necessary to take the anti-Kingdom into account. In this way it distinguishes itself from other theologies of the Kingdom, does justice both to the gospel and to the situation in Latin America and unmasks ingenuous, superficially attractive and alienating visions of the Kingdom. And, though this may not seem much, it provides a guide to what the Kingdom should be through denial and overcoming of the anti-Kingdom.

(ii) The Kingdom belongs to the poor. Liberation theology takes absolutely seriously the question of who the Kingdom is for and reaffirms that it belongs to the poor. This is what it sees in the Synoptics and what it maintains, looking at it historically, for the present. Juan Luis Segundo, after a lengthy analysis of the texts, insists: "The Kingdom of God is not proclaimed to all. It is not preached to all.... The Kingdom is destined for certain groups, it is theirs, it belongs to them. It will be a cause of joy to them alone. And, in accordance with Jesus, the dividing line between joy and sadness that the Kingdom must draw passes between rich and poor."[36] The same is implicit in the text from Puebla already quoted (1142): God loves the poor and defends them simply because they are poor, regardless of their personal and moral situation.

This partiality with regard to who the Kingdom is for is still essential in liberation theology. Partiality is maintained because it cannot be any other way in the cruel world we live in, and let me say quite bluntly that liberation theology's guts are wrenched by the inhumanly poor and cruelly oppressed masses, and in this resides its final argument for partiality, an unprovable but decisive argument, and one that finds its proof in Jesus.

Together with this partiality, another theme being developed at present is what might be called the "analogy of the poor" as addressees "and" as builders of the Kingdom, an analogy that is not pursued—as in other theologies—in order to annul partiality, but to determine in history today—when the Kingdom has not come for the poor—who these are and what they mean for understanding the Kingdom of God. Ignacio Ellacuría made a rigorous analysis of this analogy, and the citations in the following paragraphs are taken from his work.[37]

The poor are, first of all, those who are materially poor, that is, economically and sociologically poor, the great majority of people living in the Third World. Here liberation theology makes its own the concept of poor in the Synoptics (and distances itself from Marxism, which did not include the poor in this sense as agents of history)[38]: "This real material nature of poverty cannot be replaced by any spirituality; it is the necessary condition for evangelical poverty, though not its only condition."

In the second place, the poor are those who are impoverished, oppressed. They are then dialectically poor, "being dialectically dispossessed of the fruit of their labor and of labor itself, as of social and political power, by those who have enriched themselves and seized this power by this dispossession."

In the third place, the poor are those who have carried out "a conscious appreciation of the very fact of material poverty, an individual and collective appreciation." This is a first expression of the spirit in which poverty has to be lived, noting that "spirituality is not here a substitute for the material fact, but a crowning of it," and that "being materially rich and spiritually poor is an inassimilable and insuperable contradiction from a Christian point of view."

In the fourth place, the poor are those who turn this conscious appreciation into organizing the people and praxis. This does not imply belonging to a particular party or organization, but does involve "the brute fact that the poor have to organize themselves as the poor to banish this collective and originating sin of the riches-poverty dialectic." Here lies the political significance of the poor, more evident in the Old Testament than in the New, though not totally absent from the latter.[39]

In the fifth place, the poor are those who live their material situation, their conscious appreciation and their praxis with spirit, with gratuitousness, with hope, with mercy, with fortitude under persecution, with love and the greatest love of giving their lives for liberation. In a brilliant systematic synthesis of the beatitudes according to Matthew and Luke, Ellacuría concludes:

> For this reason, even though it may appear a deviation from the literal text, the true translation of poor in spirit is "poor with spirit," that is, those who take up their real poverty in all its immense human and Christian potentiality from the

standpoint of the Kingdom. The material fact of poverty is not enough, just as substituting material poverty by a spiritual intentionality is not enough. We have to incarnate and historicize the spirit of poverty and we have to spiritualize and conscientize the real flesh of poverty.

In this analogy of the poor we must not forget the *analogatum princeps*, the materially poor. The Kingdom of God is directed to them simply because of what they are and they are its direct addressees. What the analogy sheds light on is that— as the Kingdom of God has not yet reached the poor—they are also the principal agents of its building in history. In them lies the indispensable material condition for putting history on the right road to the Kingdom of God, and from this material condition of poverty—in a connatural way not found in other material conditions— arises the spirit to build the Kingdom.

We can participate in various ways in the fullness of the concept of "poor" and this is why we speak of analogy. The theological-systematic ideal is one that embraces all the elements enumerated, but the important thing is that we must share in some of them if speaking of the poor in a Christian sense is to have any meaning. Once again, everything begins with material poverty. The Kingdom is for the poor because they are materially poor; the Kingdom is for the non-poor to the extent that they lower themselves to the poor, defend them and allow themselves to be imbued with the spirit of the poor.

This is also the formal solution to the controversial question of how the non-poor share in the Kingdom. The solution cannot lie in ignoring the material nature of poverty and supposing that there can be a poverty in spirit in and for itself with no relation to material poverty. The spirit of the "poor in spirit" should not be judged by how the non-poor relate to their riches, whether they are attached to them or not, but by how they relate to the real poor. The solution has to be found in the line of lowering themselves to material poverty in the form of real *kenosis*, of real service to and support of the materially poor, of sharing in and taking on the fate of the poor. Here too we find the analogy of how the non-poor become recipients of the Kingdom, but the central and vital element in this is to establish a real relationship with the materially poor and with real poverty.

Finally, the poor have at the present time another decisive significance for understanding the Kingdom of God: their "evangelizing potential" (Puebla, 1147). They become good news for the church (and for the whole of humankind), both because their very condition of poor moves it "to conversion" and by incarnating "in their lives the evangelical values of solidarity, service, simplicity and openness to accepting the gift of God" (*Ibid.*).

This meaning of "poor" is of prime importance and is less evident in the New Testament owing to the expectation of the imminent coming of the Kingdom. Now, twenty centuries later, we say of the poor not only that they are those for whom the Kingdom is meant, as the Synoptics say, that they are not just the builders of the Kingdom, but that they bring good news, that they are an *eu-aggelion*. But they are not this irrespective of their primary material poverty. The Puebla text speaks of the "poor and oppressed," that is, those who are materially poor, and of the base Christian communities, that is, communities whose members are materially poor. Their potential for bringing about conversion stems from their ability to challenge, that is, from their very materially oppressed existence. Their evangelizing potential stems from the fact that they live out their material poverty in a particular spirit. It is, then, in their material poverty that the appropriate conditions exist for giving rise to the specific kingdom values that the poor offer to all as good news.

(iii) The historical dimension of the Kingdom. Liberation theology takes the essentially *historical* dimension of the Kingdom of God most seriously. This means that it does not leave its appearance to the end of history (though its fullness will appear only at the end) but insists on its actual realization in the present of history. The Kingdom of God cannot ever be fully realized in history, since it is utopia; this does not remove it from history, however, but obliges us to make it present through historical mediations and to bring it about at all levels of historical reality; utopia becomes a source of ideologies functioning to configure history.[40]

With this insistence, theology reformulates and corrects the interpretation of the eschatological reserve as purely relativizing, and insists that already in history "we must take account" of the fact that it is truly God who reigns. And because the Kingdom is liberating, account must be taken of this reign at all levels where slavery occurs: physical and mental, personal and social.[41]

Liberation theology finds the basic argument for this historicization in Jesus himself, as has been analyzed above. It thereby disproves statements such as those in Rudolf Schnackenburg's classic work: "the salvation proclaimed and promised with the Kingdom of God is a purely religious dimension," and the conclusion he draws: "because of its religious nature, Jesus' message concerning the Kingdom of God has a universal destination."[42]

In order to distance himself from this type of interpretation and to stress the historicity of the Kingdom, Juan Luis Segundo describes it as a "political" reality,[43] since this is what it was objectively for Jesus, too, though he proclaimed it for religious reasons. Its content is still political, not in opposition to the religious dimension, but by differentiation from the purely transcendent or individual dimension.[44] The religious and political dimensions have really no reason to be mutually exclusive, whether they are seen as different aspects of human existence or, still more so, if they are taken on different levels: that of subjective motivation and that of objective motivation. As history repeatedly shows, religion can be a powerful motivation in politics and the truly religious dimension of the Kingdom of God does no more than reinforce its political dimension, since concepts such as that of the Kingdom "are the more decisive politically the more they are pushed, to put it plainly, by religious motivations."[45] This is so true that one must beware of political fanaticism especially when it is motivated by a religious message.

Whether one calls it political or simply historical, what liberation theology stresses is that the Kingdom of God happens in history as this is transformed, since what God seeks to transform is the sum total of history, and it would be a contradiction for God to reign without any transformation being made visible in history.

(iv) The popular dimension of the Kingdom. The Kingdom of God is essentially "popular" in character, both in the qualitative sense (the people as the *poor* majorities) and the quantitative sense (the *majorities* being the poor). Liberation theology characterizes it as such because of its historical concern for the liberation of the poor majorities, but also because of its biblical roots.

However forgotten it may be—certainly in practice, though upheld in words— we must remember that, since the Old Testament, God and people have been correlatives, and that, *a fortiori*, Kingdom of God and people of God are correlatives. "There will be a Kingdom of God when there is a people of God and to the extent that there is one; there will be a people of God when there is a Kingdom of God and to the extent that there is one."[46]

The reasons for forgetting this fact lie in the hasty equating of the people of God with the church, as though God's primary relationship were with the latter and not with the former. They also lie in the individualization of the person, as though individual persons acceded directly to God and God to them. For the church to see itself as people of God is correct, and at the present time it is absolutely vital to stress this against the devaluation of the definition being attempted in certain quarters. But this must not make us forget that God's primary election is of the poor of this world, of the majorities God defends and seeks to save, of which the church should be a privileged sign. And that persons as such relate to God is also correct, and we even need to underline the individual dimension of persons in their relationship with God to show what cannot be taken away from such a relationship. But, biblically, persons are such within a people, open to giving to and receiving from the others who make up this people.

Having cleared up these possible misunderstandings, we need to return to the basic proposition: the correlation between Kingdom and people. "The Kingdom of God is for the people and only when the people of God has been formed will we have reached the fullness of the Kingdom."[47] The first phrase should be obvious from our analysis of the actions of Jesus. Although salvation (the miracles, the welcoming of sinners) is often described as coming to particular persons, we are here dealing with "signs" of the Kingdom pointing to a greater whole. Let us not overlook the fact that the plural is often used: Jesus cures "the multitudes," "the poor" are blessed.... And the ideal of the Kingdom as such, symbolized in Jesus' meals, is a reality for a collectivity, for a people. There is no point in repeating, as is often done, that the Kingdom of God is a kingdom of justice and solidarity if it is not directed at a collectivity. Without people there would be no Kingdom of God, although hypothetically there could be individual salvations and the eventual sum total of them all, a model that has of course been very prominent in the history of the church.

But the ideal of the Kingdom of God is not described as this, but as salvation for a people and as being built up as a people with specific internal relationships within that people.

The second phrase—"only when the people of God has been formed will we have reached the fullness of the Kingdom"—is, properly understood, virtually tautological. To the extent that the true people of God comes into being, so the Kingdom of God is made present. This means that both the definitive Kingdom of God and the definitive people of God are interchangeable formulations of utopia. When humankind becomes a single people and a true people in which relationships of justice and solidarity reign, then the Kingdom of God will have come.

(c) The Systematic Concept of the Kingdom of God

To end this survey, we need to inquire into what is meant systematically by the Kingdom of God. An answer is not easy to put into words, but let me suggest the following definition: the Kingdom of God is the just life of the poor always open to a "more."

(i) The content of the Kingdom of God: the just life of the poor. Our systematic concept should make clear, on account of the primacy given to them in the Old Testament and the Synoptics, and because of their massive presence in the world today, that the poor are those to whom the Kingdom is primarily addressed. That its content should be their "just life" needs some explanation. I say "life" because this is what the historical and utopic dimensions of the Kingdom concentrate on, and I add "just" to show the formally liberative nature of the Kingdom.

I insist on the "life" of the poor as the central nucleus of the Kingdom because, in the Third World, poverty means closeness to death and "life" suggests that with the coming of the Kingdom the poor will no longer be close to death. This produces a reassessment of God's creation, of protology, and in a very precise sense: in the Third World, life does not function as something "given," something that once assured can lead to what is truly human and so the place in which one can talk of the Kingdom of God as wholeness. In the Third World, life is not the "given," but what from time immemorial and still today has to be "put." The Kingdom of God is the eschatological dimension, paradoxically, since it is the protological dimension, God's ideal "least," expressed in God's creation. That life should be "just" expresses first and foremost the aim that life should come to be real in opposition to the anti-Kingdom. It expresses the ways of justice needed to build life. It expresses the relationships of solidarity and dignity in the Kingdom. And it expresses the basic condition for the existence of the Kingdom.

The "just life" relates the systematic concept of the Kingdom with the gospel concept of it. It is the good news for millions of human beings, it is what promotes establishing signs of the Kingdom and what leads to denunciation of the anti-Kingdom. And let me add that making life possible is today what still causes conflict, persecution and death. All of which lends meaning to the formulation that the Kingdom of God is the just life of the poor.

(ii) The historical transcendence of the Kingdom of God. "Life" is a reality that is by its very nature always open to a "more"; it is something dynamic that points to a development of itself to fulfill itself on various levels, with new possibilities and new demands. "Life" can therefore point to what is fulfilling and utopic in the Kingdom of God, to what is shot through with historical and theologal transcendence. Let me illustrate its historical transcendence in the first place by what I have referred to elsewhere as the "phenomenology of bread," the symbol of life.[48]

The Kingdom of God begins with bread, the prime symbol of life and the overcoming of death. But this bread is always more than bread. Its very reality implies the question of how to get it, which introduces the praxic dimension of human life into bread. And once it has been obtained, the question of how to share it arises spontaneously, so we then have, at the same time, the ethical dimension of bread (the need to share it), its community dimension (bread as shared) and its primary celebratory dimension (eating together at table).

Bread obtained and shared by some immediately becomes a question of bread for others, other groups and other communities, finally bread for a whole people. And this gives rise to the social and political dimension of bread and the question of the liberation of a whole people, which in turn brings a whole host of questions about how to obtain bread for all, through what activities, working ideologies, theologies, ways of being church and so on.

None of this happens mechanically, but at each stage of the reality of bread the need for spirit appears: mercy to stir our hearts at the sight of those without bread, courage to struggle for bread, fortitude to stand firm in the face of conflicts and persecutions, truth to analyze the reasons why there is no bread and to find the best ways of overcoming these. Bread, then, mobilizes all the powers of the human spirit and confronts it above all with the question of whether or not it is capable of loving, of whether or not it is capable of the greatest love. And so, bread brings self-giving, generosity, heroism and even the greatest love of laying down one's own life.

Bread also has its sacramental dimension. So in El Salvador we celebrate the feast of maize, and those who gather to celebrate it not only eat, but sing and recite poems, and this feast begets and expresses community, and produces joy.

The good news of bread moves us to thank God who made it or it can make us ask why God allows there not to be bread and it not to be shared. It moves us to follow the Jesus who multiplied loaves to satisfy hunger or it can make us ask why history forces death on such as he. It can make us ask if there is something more than bread, if there is a bread of the word, necessary and good news, even when there is no material bread, if it is true that at the end of history there will be bread for all and whether it is worth working for it in history, even though at times darkness seems to cover everything, whether the hope that there will be bread is wiser than resignation to the lack of it....

This phenomenology of the "more" involved in bread, however effective this description of it, claims only to show how "life" always develops into "more." This is why liberation theology emphasizes, on the one hand, the historical-material aspect of the Kingdom of God, the bread that is life and denial of death, and why it has to speak, on the other, of an "integral" liberation. In doing so, it is not merely trying to balance "material" liberation by adding "spiritual" liberation in order to avoid accusations of "reductionism," but is being faithful to the primary material dimension that is life, in which there is always the seed of more life.

By beginning with material bread and not setting limits to the dynamic inherent in bread itself, liberation theology can and must state that the Kingdom of God is the radical overcoming of death and that it is the expression of life and life in abundance:

> By being so vivid and massive in Latin America, the historical experience of death—and not just of sorrow—death from hunger and from poverty and death from repression and various forms of violence, shows the huge need for and irreplaceable value of material life in the first place, as primary and basic gift, in which everything else must be rooted, everything else being ultimately development of this primary gift. This life should spread out and fulfill itself by internal growth and in relation to the life of others, always in search of more life and better life.[49]

Historical transcendence, which I have here analyzed on the basis of bread, is, I think, present in all theologies, each of which develops, explicitly or implicitly, phenomenologies analogous to mine, starting from relationship to a "thou" or from concern for one's own salvation or from transcendental experience... in order to unfold the fullness of life. How this "unfolding of life" comes about existentially in and for each person is a highly personal affair. Liberation theology begins methodologically with the primary fact of life, but, in homage and fidelity to life, finds itself in the dynamic of the more. The Kingdom of God has its own historical transcendence. And this is so because bread is always more than bread.

(iii) The theologal transcendence of the Kingdom of God. This historical transcendence is—or can be—the mediation for the theologal transcendcence of the Kingdom. Liberation theology states that the Kingdom is really of "God," but insists that, since God is a God "of the Kingdom," God appears in a particular way.

As far as the "content" of God is concerned, if the Kingdom is like this, theology can call God God of life, but, more specifically, God of the life of the poor, God of the life of victims, and this brings back today the basic truths that Jesus expressed about God in his personal relationship with God and in the way he spoke about God in his parables. The flagrant inhumanity to which the poor are subjected manifests the humanity of God in the form of loving self-abasement, tenderness, happiness when the poor cease being so. What we saw when analyzing the parables is still true in stating that God wishes a Kingdom for the poor. Such is God, *so good.*

As far as the "mystery" of God is concerned, the just life of the poor effectively brings us into a God different from the usual God of thought, since the reason for the Kingdom belonging to the poor is simply that God is like that. God being like that is not what natural, let alone sinful, reason thinks or can think, and the partiality of the Kingdom becomes the historical mediation of what is novel and unthinkable in God. It is a powerful way of affirming the mystery of God. *Such is God*, so good.

I want to insist on the theologal transcendence of the Kingdom, because liberation theology is accused of lapsing into reductionism and required to stress the transcendent dimension of the Kingdom of God. I consider this unjust, because this theology does accept the transcendence of God quite naturally. But it is ironic above all because, by making the life of the poor central in the Kingdom, theology magnifies the mystery of God.

A God of the life of the poor is not, in effect, the thought God, and still less so is the God who is so often subject to the power of the anti-Kingdom, so that the greater God appears as the lesser God, a scandal I shall analyze in dealing with the cross of Jesus. As Ignacio Ellacuría succintly wrote: "God the Father had, or produced, many poor sons, among them his only-begotten Son, his well-beloved, when he became incarnate in history. This is a prime and massive fact, which no one seeking to speak of God can ignore."[50] What I want to emphasize now is that while christologies have drawn *theologal* consequences from the scandal of Jesus' cross—from St Paul to the christologies of the crucified God—not many of them have drawn the same consequences from the fact of the Kingdom being for the poor. So it is right to be on one's guard not to reduce the Kingdom to the historical dimension and to integrate God into it. But it is wrong not to introduce into the mystery of God the fact that this is a God of a Kingdom of the poor. Then God becomes a lesser God, and this maintains the mystery of God, more so than many declarations of orthodoxy.

This lesser God, however, is ultimately a greater God, the utopia that, from the future, continues to give hope and constantly inspires the building of the Kingdom of just life for the poor. As utopic principle, this God goes on instigating good things for the poor, in history and against history: hope, the struggle for justice, peace, community.... And this God goes on enabling us to combine in history such apparently irreconcilable things as the struggle for justice and work for peace, efficacy and gratuitousness, action and contemplation, activity and spirit.... As long as all this remains a reality, God is being seen to be present in the Kingdom, and the Kingdom is being seen to be "of God." In this way, in the historical dimension, building the Kingdom is walking toward God, till all the principalities—the anti-Kingdom—are overthrown and God is all in all: the definitive Kingdom of God.

Chapter 5

Jesus and God (1)
Jesus and a God-Father

Jesus proclaimed and served the Kingdom of God and for this was sentenced to death. In all this—like any human being—he was faced with the need to find and give meaning to his life and history. For him, this meaning was undoubtedly religious, and he expressed it by saying that what underpins reality is not an absurdity but something positive, and that this something positive is not an impersonal force, but something good and personal, a God whom he called Father.

The Gospels leave no room to doubt the radical experience Jesus had of God; they present it as something absolutely central to his life. Before beginning to analyze it, however, we need to stand back and evaluate the fact itself. Jesus comes across as a true human being in this theologal dimension too. He, too, had to interact with God, seek and dialogue with God, question and rest in God, open himself up to God and let God be God. Again, in all this Jesus is seen as just like anyone else, except in sin.

The task of this chapter is to examine what Jesus thought about God, what experience he had of God. The difficulties are obvious: first, because of the very nature of the subject, since God is the hardest reality to put into words, even harder than the utopia of the Kingdom; second, because it is extremely difficult, if not impossible, to penetrate Jesus' inner psychology, particularly on this point. Nevertheless, Jesus' relationship to his God made a deep impression on the people and on his disciples, and the Gospels have retained important signs of this.

As in the previous chapter, I propose to begin with a brief analysis of what ideas of God Jesus could have had, followed by an examination of the outer expressions of what his basic inner attitudes were—prayer, trust, openness and faith—which can serve as a guide to the answer to the question: who was God for Jesus?

For methodological reasons, I am leaving the illustrations Jesus gave of the true God in confrontation with his adversaries to the next chapter. Let me say too that this analysis cannot be separated from that of the Kingdom of God in the previous chapter, since the God of the Kingdom is inevitably part of it, nor from the subsequent chapters on the cross of Jesus. The explicit treatment of the God of Jesus in this chapter is therefore somewhat artificial, but I find it methodologically convenient in order to advance our understanding of what the "Kingdom" of God is, and what the "God" of the Kingdom was for Jesus.

1. Jesus' Ideas about God

It is not easy to establish what concrete elements of the tradition of Israel Jesus incorporated "conceptually" into his own vision of God, and he certainly does not provide any "doctrine" about God. Kessler gives the following reason for this:

> We must be very careful when speaking of the ideas about God that Jesus had. For Jesus produces no formulatable and teachable "ideas about God." He rather acts in such a way that the specific and actual decisions he takes are different from those of others around him. And he comments on his way of acting through parables or images, so that from his way of acting, together with his preaching— which tells the story of an event—and from their mutual interaction, we can intuit: God is like this or this, or rather, God behaves in such and such a way.[1]

According to Gustavo Gutiérrez, how Jesus contemplates God has to be deduced above all from how Jesus "puts God into practice."[2]

Having said this, however, it is possible to sketch out what ideas Jesus could have had of God, derived from the Old Testament. These can be divided into the content of the reality of God and the way in which God is God.

(a) Looking into the *content of the reality* of God, the Gospels show various traditions at work in Jesus' words and deeds; he embodied these in his life, bringing them together only existentially, as they remain distinct.

Jesus used the *prophetic* tradition about God, in which God is shown as taking sides and defending the poor, the weak and the oppressed, acting against the injustice that made them so and promising a utopia in which life and justice are possible. This tradition is also responsible for the vision of a God who relates demandingly with creatures, requiring personal, inner conversion, giving prophets their calling, which then requires everything of them, even their life. This tradition is basically that of the God of the Kingdom and there is no need to elaborate on it further.

Jesus is also seen to be influenced by the *apocalyptic* tradition, which lays stress on the absolute future of God, emphasizing that God and God alone will transform reality and will do so at the end of time, since the present time is not capable of receiving God. This tradition also relates to that of the God of the Kingdom, in its expectation of the imminent coming of the end and its concept of the overall and absolute transformation of reality.

Jesus also uses the *wisdom* traditions, in which the emphasis is on a creator and provident God, who looks after his creatures and sees to their everyday needs, who allows the good and the bad to grow up together in history, leaving the imparting of justice to the end. This tradition relates directly to the idea of a creator-provider

God and is formally distinct from the eschatological vision of the God of the Kingdom.

Finally, toward the end of his life, Jesus links in with what we might call the *existential* traditions (present in all theodicies) concerning God. These are the traditions of the Lamentations of Jeremiah, of the Teacher of Ecclesiastes, of Job, telling of the times when all that can be heard is God's silence. This tradition appears only sporadically in the Old Testament. It is essentially different from and even contrary to that of the God of the Kingdom.

All these traditions are present in Jesus in one way or another, according to the Gospels, and from a strictly conceptual viewpoint they are difficult to reconcile. If one reads the passages as they stand, the God of prophecy does not emerge in the same way as the God of apocalyptic, and the God of the Kingdom is certainly not the God of the wisdom or silence traditions.

In search of a solution to unify this diversity, some commentators seek one concept that can prevail over the others, while others respect the differences. To give a classic example of the diversity: the God who comes eschatologically and the provident wisdom God presuppose different views of God. Specifically, the God who proclaims his imminent coming and the end of the world can hardly be reconciled with the God who makes the sun rise on the good and the bad, who cares for the daily life of creatures, since he looks after the flowers of the field and the birds of the air.

Some see the solution to this problem in the God of eschatology revealing the true God of creation, thereby making the wisdom and eschatological traditions highly compatible.[3] Others see them as incompatible and unified only by the fact that "God is God."[4] Without going into the strictly exegetical question here, I think it better to keep the diversity and novelty of visions of God—particularly that of God's silence—a diversity that Jesus progressively integrated in his life existentially, not only or mainly conceptually.

(b) Turning to the formality of the reality of God, God's transcendence, this is brought out clearly, though in different ways, in the Gospels. Jesus states that God is transcendent through being creator (Mark 10:6; 13:19) and above all because of God's absolute sovereignty: God has power over life and death and can destroy both body and soul in hell (Matt. 10:28); God's name must be respected and should not be sworn by (Matt. 5:33-7; 23:16-22); before God, we are servants (Luke 17:7-10), or slaves (Matt. 6:24; Luke 16:13). Jesus, then, brings out God's transcendence, and also the impossibility of grasping God (Matt.11:25ff; Luke 19:21ff), and he emphasizes this by the way he speaks about God: "Jesus developed a particular way of expressing himself, giving an unusually wide space to the circumlocution of the name of God by means of the passive voice (*passivum divinum*)."[5]

This view of transcendence has a lot in common with other religious and even philosophical traditions. What makes Jesus' view special is that it captures the transcendence of God, the unthought and unthinkable, essentially as grace. God acts through grace and as grace, as was sketched out in the previous chapter. By content—God is what is good—and by the unexpected and unmerited way in which God makes this goodness present for us in history, God is gift and grace.

In this way, Jesus breaks with a traditional and widespread view of transcendence that concentrates and reduces it to the infinite distance between God and creatures, and to the infinite difference in power between God and creatures. Jesus accepts this distance and difference, but states that God's transcendence becomes present specifically in breaking down this notion of transcendence. The infinitely distant makes itself radically close. Jesus also changes the notion of what transcendent power is, that it consists in achieving what is beyond natural human capabilities and doing so without reference to us: "So we have the impossible: not as a supernatural event belonging to the world of beyond with absurd consequences in this world, but that poor, impious and evil human beings can, unexpectedly, once more call themselves human."[6]

(c) This quick survey shows that the idea of God Jesus had is made up of several elements that cannot easily be synthesized on a purely conceptual level. For Jesus, God clearly had a content that, in the most general terms, is being "the good," and had a form that is "transcendence." What this actually means, how the two things interrelate, what aspect should be emphasized above others, in other words, who God was for Jesus, cannot be resolved, in my view, merely from a conceptual analysis of the words Jesus used. Here, as with the Kingdom of God, we have to look at Jesus in action for the reality of what he is and does to embody and grade the concepts in which he expressed himself.   If there is one thing that seems to give unity to the various notions of God Jesus had, it is his walking always with a God-mystery and embodying always a God-of-the-Kingdom. In the words of Micah: "to do justice, and to love kindness, and to walk humbly with your God" (6:8).

This is what I am going to examine in the rest of this chapter, but at the outset it needs to be said plainly that Jesus faced up to an ultimate reality that he called "Father" and this father is always the ultimate for Jesus, that is, "God." Father, because of the absolute trust Jesus reposed in the ultimate as father; God, because of his complete openness to this Father, whom he allows to be God. God is father, and he lets his heart rest in him, but the Father is still God and will not let him rest. The personal ultimate for Jesus is, then, God-Father, and his relationship with him is one of trust-availability. For Jesus, God was, and to an increasing degree, a supremely dialectical reality: absolute intimacy and absolute otherness.

2. Jesus' Prayer

Let us begin with Jesus' prayer, even though this was not the only, or even the most important, element for showing his relationship with God. Jesus' prayer shows that he addressed himself to God, and above all, to what sort of God he addressed himself.

(a) As the pious Jew that Jesus was, it is to be supposed *a priori* that he prayed, and the Gospels provide unequivocal evidence of this. The Synoptics show Jesus as a prayerful Jew: he blesses the table (Matt. 15:36; 26:26 par.); he observes the sabbath and prays with the community (Luke 4:16). From a minute analysis of the texts, Joachim Jeremias concludes: "In all probability there was not a single day in Jesus' life when he would not have recited the table prayer, before and after eating."[7]

Yet it is Jesus' personal prayer that tells us more about his God that this formal type of prayer, and the Synoptics speak of this too. According to them, Jesus' whole life unfolded in an atmosphere of prayer. In Luke, his public life begins with a prayer (3:21) and in all the Gospels his life ends with a prayer, interpreted variously as one of anguish, of hope or of peace, but definitively as addressed directly to God (Matt. 27:46; Mark 15:34; Luke 23:46; John 19:30). His public life from beginning to end is strewn with innumerable allusions to prayer. Jesus is shown praying at moments of vital decisions: before choosing the twelve (Luke 6:12ff), before teaching the Our Father (Luke 11:1), before curing the epileptic child (Mark 9:29). Jesus prays for particular people: for Peter (Luke 22:32), for his executioners (Luke 23:34). He alludes to prayer on important occasions, as when he says that some types of devils cannot be cast out without prayer (Mark 9:29) or when he relates prayer to strength of faith (Mark 11:23f). The Synoptics also relate that Jesus used to retire to pray on a mountain, in a garden, in a wilderness (Mark 1:35; 6:46; 14:32; Luke 6:12...), and Luke introduces this custom into one of his summaries: "But now more than ever the word about Jesus spread abroad; many crowds would gather to hear him and to be cured of their diseases. But he would withdraw to deserted places and pray" (5:15f).

The fact that Jesus prayed is, then, certain. Although the pasages cited are theologically tinted, especially in Luke, and influenced by the situation of the communities, there can be no doubt that Jesus made a deep impression by the way he prayed. And this fact needs reflection for understanding Jesus' God.

(b) The first aspect to bring out is that the Gospels do not show Jesus praying ingenuously, as though ignorant of the pitfalls attendant on prayer; on the contrary, he condemns many types of prayer.

He condemns mechanical prayer: "When you are praying, do not heap up empty phrases as the Gentiles do; for they think they will be heard because of their many words. Do not be like them, for your Father knows what you need before you ask him" (Matt. 6:7-8). He condemns vainglorious and hypocritical prayer: "And whenever you pray, do not be like the hypocrites; for they love to stand and pray in the synagogues and at the street corners, so that they may be seen by others" (Matt. 6:5). He condemns cynical prayer: "The Pharisee, standing by himself, was praying thus, 'God, I thank you that I am not like other people: thieves, rogues, adulterers, or even like this tax collector'" (Luke 18:11). He condemns alienating prayer: "Not everyone who says to me, 'Lord, Lord,' will enter the kingdom of heaven, but only the one who does the will of my Father in heaven" (Matt. 7:21). And he condemns oppressive prayer: "Beware of the scribes... they devour your widows' houses and for the sake of appearance say long prayers" (Mark 12:38, 40).

All these passages show Jesus—or, more accurately, the first communities reflecting on prayer on the basis of their memories of Jesus—as conscious of the numberless ways in which prayer can be spoiled: spiritual narcissism, vanity and hypocrisy, verbosity, alienating and oppressive manipulation.... Jesus was certainly not ingenuous with regard to prayer. He knew that all we human beings do is subject to sinfulness, including prayer. So he denounces the spoiling of prayer, whereby praying is not basically putting oneself before God and allowing God to come before one. Nevertheless, despite all these pitfalls, Jesus urges others to pray and prays himself. It is important to stress why: in prayer we express, in concentrated form, the experience of ultimate meaning and this—whatever form it may take—is irreplaceable and unchangeable in human experience.

Turning for a moment to the Kingdom of God, let us recall that Jesus devoted his life to its service—which implies both action and reflection—and also put it into words, "proclaimed" it, which is something other than embodying, reflecting on and teaching it. The importance of the proclamation and what makes it something irreplaceable and unchangeable lies in the fact that in this proclamation the ultimate meaning of the Kingdom—its being good news and its gratuitousness—is concentrated in one dense word.

The same is true of Jesus' relationship to God. Responding and corresponding to God is a matter of listening to God's word and putting it into effect, which is what Jesus' whole life consisted of. But expressing the ultimate and all-embracing nature of this God, what there is of otherness and absolute nearness in this God, is what prayer is for. None of this detracts from the reflection needed and the action demanded: rather the contrary. As we shall see, Jesus' prayer is historically situated and related to his actions, but in itself, prayer is a distinct reality, a recapitulation of the whole of meaning and the meaning of wholeness, a placing oneself truly before God.

The actual way Jesus placed himself before God in prayer is what sheds light on the reality of his God. So I propose to analyze here two of Jesus' prayers, the content of which is given in the Synoptics, leaving his prayer on the cross to another chapter.

(c.i) "At that time, Jesus said, 'I thank you, Father, Lord of heaven and earth, because you have hidden these things from the wise and the intelligent and have revealed them to infants'" (Matt. 11:25; Luke 10:21).

This is a prayer of praise and thanksgiving, the formulation of which can better be understood against the apocalyptic background of the communication of revelation (Dan. 2:20-23), the content of which is the Kingdom of God (Dan. 2:44).[8]

The prayer is historically situated, though we cannot be sure of the actual words or when Jesus said them. It is clear that some time had passed in which Jesus had been evangelizing in deeds and proclaiming the Kingdom, and that a basic conflict had already arisen with the leaders of the people, who disagreed with him and maliciously opposed him. This prayer, then, presupposes Jesus' actions.[9]

In this context, Jesus gives thanks to the Father because it is precisely the "infants" who have understood him. This fact is brought home to Jesus and he puts it into words before God. What appeared impossible has become possible. And this prayer by Jesus shows who God is for him: a God with a will—"Yes, Father, for such was your gracious will" (Matt. 11:26)—a God who takes the side of the little ones and is a good and loving God to them. Jesus' reaction to this God is to rejoice that God should be like this and to thank God for it. In a scene charged with meaning, then, this prayer sums up Jesus' experience of his God and expresses it in joy. Or, looking at it the other way around, this joy shows what God is for Jesus: that which produces joy because it is good, someone in whom one can truly trust and whom one can call "Father."

(c.ii) "And going a little farther, he threw himself on the ground and prayed that, if it were possible, the hour might pass from him. He said, 'Abba, Father, for you all things are possible; remove this cup from me; yet, not what I want, but what you want'" (Mark 14:35-6; Matt. 26:39; Luke 22:41-2).

This account of the prayer in the garden, as presented by Matthew, is a compilation, but the nucleus of the scene and the prayer is historically certain, since "the christological scandal aroused by the pericope makes it very hard for us to think of it as freely invented."[10] The original nucleus consists of Jesus expressing his realization that he was going to be handed over to death, that his soul is sorrowful and that he asks the Father to free him from that hour.[11]

The prayer is, then, historically situated: it stems from the risks Jesus ran by his actions and unfolds into Jesus' decision to take on his own death. It is a situation of crisis, of ultimate crisis, and in it Jesus turns to prayer and in this expresses the whole of the meaning of his life. He asks that God "might make the kingdom come without suffering preceding it,"[12] but in the end delivers his "I" to God. This "I" which the Gospels have shown as source of supreme authority before the law, the "I" that has sent the disciples out, the "I" that has cured sicknesses and cast out devils, this same "I" is what is now being handed over to the will of the Father.[13]

The *Abba*-Father still resounds in this prayer, as in the earlier one of jubilation, but what this prayer reveals directly is not Jesus' trust, but his absolute self-surrender. What this prayer reveals of God is not the scandal of being good news to "infants" but the scandal of total obscurity. God remains as the unfathomable mystery for Jesus, and Jesus lets God be God.

(d) To sum up this account of Jesus' prayer, we can say that the very fact of Jesus praying shows that he had a final point of reference with a personal meaning, before which he placed himself, both receiving and expressing this. This prayer is something distinct from his actions and from his possible analytical reflection on how to build the Kingdom; it is a reality in which he expressed the meaning of his life before God, in relation to the building of the Kingdom, a meaning affirmed or questioned by actual history. This is why Jesus' prayer is seen as a quest for the will of God, as joy at the coming of the Kingdom, as acceptance of his destiny; in short, it is seen as trust in a good God who is Father, and as self-surrender to a Father who is still God, mystery.

3. Trust in a God who is Father

The Gospels clearly show Jesus placing his trust in God, though ultimately they cannot describe the source of this trust. It is, however, real, and supposes—logically and in fact—that for Jesus God was really good to him, as is sealed by the term in which he addresses God: *Abba*.

Saying that God is "something good" for Jesus can seem fairly minimal, but it is of great importance. It means that the ultimate definition of God is not power, as with the pagans, nor thought, as in Aristotle, nor judgment, as in John the Baptist, but goodness. Jesus is convinced that God is good to him and to all beings. In the words of Karl Rahner already cited, God has forever broken the symmetry of being possibly salvation and possibly condemnation. God is in essence goodness and salvation for us.

I propose to examine this using Jesus' words about God, and also his actions, which cannot be explained without this experience of a good God.

(a) The Goodness of God

There is nothing in Jesus' life that shows God and human beings in competition or God being jealous of human happiness. God is jealous, and very jealous, of other gods, as we shall see in the next chapter, but not of human beings—very much the opposite in fact.

(i) According to Jesus, human beings are the most important thing for God; their cause is God's cause.[14] They are of more value than other creatures (Matt. 6:26) and nothing created can be used against them, not even what is conventionally accepted as serving God. Hence the sharp statements about offering gifts and forgetting people (Matt. 5:23ff; Mark 12:33), people being more important than the sabbath (Mark 2:23-7 par.). God is shown as having no rights over against humankind; God's rights are rather those that promote human beings. God is good and is essentially on our side. Later—on the cross—God is shown as being even at our mercy, but not even this risk can remove God's original reality: being good for us.

This is the starting point for understanding what is central in Jesus' teaching and his own life. In the summary of Acts 10:38 it is said that Jesus "went about doing good." Jesus, of whom exalted things will be said and to whom sublime titles will be attached, is shown here as the proto-sacrament of the good God, as the one who went about embodying the goodness of God in this world. This enables us to understand the words Jesus addressed to all: "Be perfect, therefore, as your heavenly Father is perfect" (Matt. 5:48); "Be merciful, just as your father is merciful" (Luke 6:36). Jesus has nothing better to offer than his God. The final logic working in Jesus, in my view, is not so much presenting God as one who requires obedience to a commandment—"be good"—as presenting God as good news: "what is good for you is to reproduce the goodness of God."

(ii) For Jesus, not only is God good to human beings, but God's goodness has to be described as love. We know that the New Testament word used for "love" is *agape*, not *eros*; that is, a love that rejoices in the well-being of others and only on account of the well-being of others, while *eros* also implies self-gratification to some extent. John says, absolutely and directly, that God is *agape* (1 John 4:8), and this is what Jesus embodies in the Gospels. The unique distinction of this love is tenderness.[15] Just as Isaiah describes God as more tender than a mother, so Jesus compares God to the father who comes out to greet the returning prodigal son, embraces him and celebrates his return (Luke 15:11-31). In his paroxysm of joy that God should be so, Jesus declares that God "is kind to the ungrateful and to the wicked" (Luke 6:35).

Here, again, lies the logic of the "commandment" to love in the Synoptics (Mark 12:28-31; Matt. 22:34-40; Luke 10:25-8) and of the "new commandment" in John (13:34-5). This is undoubtedly a commandment, just as it is in the Decalogue of Leviticus. In the first letter of John it can also be read as a commandment: "love one another" (4:11). However, if not necessarily from an exegetical standpoint, I think these commandments can be systematically interpreted in a deeper sense: "God is like this, be you likewise." Love is not a commandment imposed arbitrarily, as though it could equally well not have been imposed. God imposes what God is, and "imposes" it because this is what is good for us. The "I am the LORD" with which Leviticus ends, the basis of the commandment, "you shall not take vengeance or bear a grudge against any of your people, but you shall love your neighbor as yourself" (Lev. 19:18), can be interpreted in the same way.

This is also how we should understand the commandment to love one's enemies (Matt. 5:43; Luke 6:27-35), not as the greatest—arbitrary—test God puts us to, but because "such is God," as Matthew and Luke end their passages: the heavenly Father is "perfect" (Matt. 5:48), he is "kind to the ungrateful and the wicked" (Luke 6:35).

Finally, this is how we should understand the deepest and most vulnerable arguments Jesus puts forward to demand conversion—though he recalls the threat of eternal fire—and his arguments against his adversaries, as we saw when analyzing the parables: such is God, so good.

This view of God as goodness, as love, as tenderness, is essential in Jesus and forms the central nucleus of his experience of God. In this the whole New Testament was to be very faithful to him, each writing in its way. "God so loved the world," say John and Paul. Perhaps the letter to Titus puts it at its simplest, echoing Jesus' own tone: "the goodness and loving kindness of God our Savior appeared…" (3:4).

(b) The Good God is neither Authoritarian nor Oppressive

Jesus' experience of the goodness of God makes him relegate other mediations of divinity to a lower plane, or drastically alter them. God is absolute and transcendent, lord and judge, but not authoritarian or despotic. So Jesus can preach and present himself as both servant and free.

(i) Jesus presents himself as one having authority, but not as authoritarian. He criticizes the existing civil and religious powers, and teaches, by word and deed, that authority is service in freedom.[16]

Power, which so often in civil, religious and church life passes itself off as divine mediation, is not so for Jesus. He rather shows that its historical embodiments become the exact opposite. So Jesus not only asserts that he has come not to be served but to serve (Mark 10:45); he refuses to allow himself to be served, but makes himself a servant (Luke 22:27; John 13:1-15). He tells his disciples that "Whoever wants to be first must be last of all and servant of all" (Mark 9:35).

Reviewing the rulers of his time—in a sentence that sums up thousands of years of history—he also tells the disciples: "You know that among the Gentiles those whom they recognize as their rulers lord it over them, and their great ones are tyrants over them," ending succinctly: "But it is not so among you" (Mark 10:42-3). Jesus' observation is based on accumulated experience, but his logical argument against the way things are is absolutely simple: God is just not like that.

Power tends to be associated with an authority that imposes, and Jesus distances himself from this too. He speaks with conviction, with authority, but does not impose. "Jesus does not impose, threaten or intimidate, and rarely commands or reprehends."[17] He is often shown arguing, appealing to the reason of his audience or even of his adversaries, not laying down the law. From a detailed analysis of the texts, González Faus comes to an important conclusion: the verb *epitiman*, to intimate, something so characteristic of authority, is used of Jesus' words when he is addressing devils, forces of nature, sickness, things hostile to human beings; when it is used of his words addressed to persons, it is to forbid them to reveal the "messianic secret," that is, to prevent his messianism from being falsified. From this use of language, he deduces that Jesus does not speak to people to impose on them, nor is he shown as authoritarian: "Jesus exercises his authority avoiding prohibition and dissipating fear."[18]

Above all, Jesus goes beyond imposition and authoritarianism by putting his words into practice, by giving an example, as John's Gospel succinctly recalls: "I have set you an example" (13:15). This means that "it is not permissible to say that Jesus is shown in his requirements like a master giving orders; we should rather say that he is the friend who helps us to do God's will."[19]

Jesus' actions present us here with a particular picture of God. We cannot deny power to God without falling into some kind of logical contradiction, but Jesus denies the oppressive and authoritarian aspects of power. God is not like that. However difficult it may seem for us to conceive, the correlative of power in God is not our servile submission, but our freedom. "Now God is seen as that power which allows human beings their freedom and responsibility for themselves."[20] We could say that just as we must allow God to be God, Jesus tells us that God allows us to be ourselves. Not that God makes no demands on us: God sometimes makes very heavy ones; we have to carry them out in a fittingly human manner, in freedom and out of conviction, rather than from coercion and imposition.

If we inquire where Jesus gets this view of God from, there are no explicit arguments to put forward, but Jesus' concentration on the goodness of God sheds some light. For Jesus, goodness is not just one aspect of the reality of God, but a reality that expresses the essence of God and therefore has the force of God. Jesus believes that goodness (and truth) are forces that change and transform things, and that they exercise a specific intimation on others when they are seen as visible and palpable in history. Jesus does not exclude the reality of power in God, but sees it primarily as the force of goodness (and truth).

(ii) Jesus presents himself devoid of authoritarianism, but with sovereign freedom.[21] The Gospels clearly show Jesus as a free person. Besides his obvious freedom with regard to the law and the sabbath, he chooses his followers with all naturalness from among pious Israelites and equally from the ranks of publicans and armed groups. He eats with his friends and also with Pharisees, with publicans and prostitutes. He lets himself be accompanied by men and women. He visits the rich and curses them in no uncertain terms. He pays no heed, then, to public opinion, even to that based on religious values. And this freedom is seen in sovereign form, along with great bravery, in his denunciations and unmaskings, as we shall see in the next chapter. He insultingly denounces oppressors, those who scandalize the little ones, who lead the people astray, and he pays no heed to the consequences to himself that stem from this conduct.

What characterizes this freedom Jesus shows, and where does he get it from? Jesus' freedom should not be seen primarily in the light of modern "liberal" ideas of freedom as freedom to exercise one's own rights, nor should it be seen in existential terms, as an aesthetic fulfillment of humanity. The examples given above do not show Jesus directly asserting the exercise of freedom "for its own sake" as a great good, though he would not of course exclude it; what he is saying is something far more profound: that there are no limits to or constraints on doing good. (He would not of course be against modern freedoms, which in fact are largely based on the vision of humankind that stems from Jesus and Paul.) This is freedom for the sake of the good of others, and here there must be no limits or obstacles: not social opinion, not success or failure, not even the law and the sabbath. Jesus' freedom is then, paradoxically, freedom to "enslave oneself" to doing good. As Paul, the great defender of freedom, would put it: "I have made myself a slave to all, so that I might win more of them" (1 Cor. 9:19).

The apogee of Jesus' freedom is seen, then, in John's expression, in the free laying down of his own life: "No one takes it from me, but I lay it down of my own accord" (John 10:18). To let the paradox stand, it is then an enslaved freedom, because it is a freedom in the service of goodness, not in Jesus' own service.

This enables us to understand better where the root of Jesus' freedom lies: in the goodness of God. It is not as a radical protest, but as an echo of the heavenly Father's mercy, that Jesus cures the man with a withered hand on the sabbath, and justifies doing so with the unanswerable argument: "Is it lawful to do good or to do harm on the sabbath...?" (Mark 3:4). The goodness of God is what frees for goodness, and through this sets us free from ourselves. Free persons are those who have been set free, and this is the image Jesus puts forward. "Loved in order to love," as one might paraphrase the First Letter of John (4:11). "Free to love," as Gutiérrez puts it.[22] "Set free in order to set free," might be a definition of the free Jesus. His experience of the goodness of God is what sets Jesus free and makes him free. And

Jesus uses his freedom for goodness. Here, it seems to me, lies the root and meaning of his freedom. This shows the deeper sense of what God's goodness means as a force that creates freedom.

(c) Jesus' Trust: "Abba, Father"

The foregoing shows Jesus' conviction that God is good and that it is good for there to be God. Within himself, Jesus relates to this good God with trust, and this has become enshrined in the term he uses to address God: *Abba*, Father.

In the Old Testament and in Judaism prior to Jesus there was a strong resistance to addressing God as Father. Yet when the Gospels transmit a prayer of Jesus, or put one into his mouth (on twenty-six occasions, with the exception of Mark 15:34 par.), Jesus addresses God as Father,[23] which can be said as a mark of respect as much as one of familiarity. Nevertheless, the relative ambiguity of the term "father" is clarified by noting that Jesus used the Palestinian Aramaic term *Abba*, the historicity of which is not open to doubt.

To understand the significance of Jesus using the term *Abba* to address God we need to bear in mind that such an invocation is not found in Jewish prayers, for the reason that *Abba* was the term used by children to address their father. So it implies a great familiarity and trust, and this is why the Jews did not use it. "The fact that Jesus should dare to go so far as to speak to God like a child speaking to its father, with simplicity, intimacy and security, was something new, something unique and unheard-of."[24]

This singular fact has given rise to christological deductions stressing the difference this shows between Jesus and other human beings as far as being "Son" is concerned, and this is borne out by the occasions on which he distinguishes between "my" father and "your" father, as we shall see in another chapter. Here, though, I want to focus on the totally original way in which Jesus relates to God: with the simplicity and trust a child would show to its father.

This trust toward God shows that Jesus regarded God not only as what is good, but as someone in whom one could trust and rest, someone who gives meaning to human existence. One might say that Jesus is not only grateful for God's goodness, but rejoices in the fact that God is like this, a bountiful father not frightening out of majesty, but impinging through loving closeness. So, too, Jesus comes close to people, especially to those in most need of goodness, the poor and sinners. So, too, Jesus opens out to all, time and again, while being realistic about the limitations of the human condition and our tendency to egoism.[25] And what upholds him in this arduous task is his original experience that "human life is wrapped in the incomprehensible goodness of God."[26]

This goodness of God produces joy in Jesus and he rejoices that God is so. He rejoices when the little ones know God, when sinners feel no fear of God, when the poor trust in this God. And this joy spreads to others. Jesus "included sinners and publicans in the kingdom, authorizing them to repeat this one word: *Abba*, beloved Father."[27] And when he teaches people to speak to God he begins neither with obligation nor techniques of prayer, but with good news. When you pray, say "Our Father" (Matt. 6:9; Luke 11:2). "Our" is the reality of the Kingdom, "Father" is the reality of God.

This is what God is for Jesus, a bountiful father in whom one can trust and rest. This experience of God's goodness permeates Jesus' activity of doing good and bestows final meaning on his person, because he sees that reality itself is charged with God's goodness. His trust, then, is not just a psychological trait, nor an ideological product. It stems from the primary experience that at the back of reality there is something good, that God is Father.

4. Openness to a Father who is God

Jesus' relationship to the Father was one of complete closeness, but not one of possession. In this, too, Jesus lived his creatureliness in depth: having to be referred to God without being able to seize the pole of that reference. In other words, Jesus' experience of the close Father did not annul, but magnified his experience of the mystery of God.

In general terms, this is borne out in the Gospels and other New Testament writings when Jesus' "obedience" to God is mentioned. One must add straightaway that Jesus obeyed God alone and that the only text that mentions his obedience to other human beings—his parents—uses different terminology: "he was subject to them" (Luke 2:51).

This obedience on Jesus' part should not be understood in terms of the concrete, categorical obediences demanded of and carried out by human beings; that is, it cannot be reduced to fulfilling divine precepts, still less understood as Jesus' chosen way to achieve his own moral perfection, as it has usually been interpreted, in order to provide a motivation for obedience in the religious life, for example. Jesus' obedience was rather a fundamental and foundational attitude of his life: an active openness to God, which certainly included doing God's will, but which at a deeper level was a radical reference to God as to someone who was radically "other" for Jesus, to whose word he had to be actively open in order to grasp his own identity.

Jesus' openness to God was a going out of himself toward God, and its realization was therefore something fulfilling for Jesus as a creature. But it was also an emptying out of himself and a going out time and again against himself. In this, Jesus also partook of the human condition, and this was very much present in his theologal relation to the Father. In other words, Jesus had to let God be God, with the problems this involved. This is expressed in more theological terms in the writings of Paul and John and the Letter to the Hebrews, in more historical form in the Synoptics.

(a) Jesus' "Conversion"

The expression "conversion" of Jesus will strike a strange note if by conversion one understands, essentially, the process of abandoning evil to do good, of turning back to the God one has previously abandoned—the process insistently called for by the prophets of Israel. Conversion undoubtedly usually comprises both stages, but not necessarily. The logic of the second week of the *Spiritual Exercises* of St Ignatius, for example, is based not simply on the choice between good and evil, but on choosing the specific good that God wills. Following the metaphorical language of "turning back" to God, conversion consists in abandoning one's "own" place, however good this may be, and meeting God "there" where God wishes to be met.

In this strict sense there is no doubt that we can and should speak of Jesus' conversion, since his God moved in relation to him and moved him. What the Gospels show is that Jesus let himself be moved by God. We can demonstrate this simply by asking whether Jesus' theologal vision at the beginning of his public life, as it is shown in the Synoptics, is the same as it was at the end of his life, or whether it altered significantly.

We have already seen that at the outset of his public life Jesus proclaimed the Kingdom of God and its imminence, gave abundant signs of this, called disciples to accompany him on his mission, castigated the sin of oppressors, demanded a faith-trust of the poor and of sinners, prayed in exultation and thanksgiving. In this first major phase of his life, Jesus, in his own specific way, presented the image of a Jew inheriting the best religious traditions of his people, setting out to embody these traditions in the hope that they would bear fruit. Even though he undoubtedly revealed his own specific experience of God, he still showed a relative continuity with the experience that had preceded him.

By the end of his life, however, his theologal vision was very different. He no longer speaks of the closeness of the Kingdom—though he still hopes for it at the Last Supper, but without clarifying how it will come nor what its signs will be— or performs miracles: indeed, he forbids them. The call to follow him issued to the disciples is not to enthusiastic mission but to carry their cross. Sin is no longer something to be simply denounced and castigated, but something one has to bear. His prayer is not of exultation, but of complete self-abandonment to the will of God. And at the end, on the cross, Jesus does not speak of the Kingdom of God, but launches a tortured cry to God.

There is, then, no doubt that the theologal vision presented by Jesus at the end of his life was very different. It still contains the formal elements there at the beginning: God, mission, sin, following, prayer, but their historical embodiment is quite other. His vision is now dominated by the mystery of God and what there is of mystery in God. The subject matter may be the same, but Jesus has been through a process of embodying it, not only conceptually, but historically. He set out to change history according to the will of God, but history changed him in relation to God. In this context, Jesus' conversion represents the openness that enabled him to respond to God in history, wherever God might lead him, the openness that enabled him to allow God to be God.

(b) The Temptations

Jesus' conversion or gradual conversions were not achieved peacefully, as though his closeness to the Father guaranteed him continual clarity of vision with regard to the Father's will or as though the changes required of him affected only the outer aspects of his person—sufferings included—while leaving his innermost being untouched and immersed in the peace of God. The Synoptics (and the Letter to the Hebrews) explicitly and clearly state that Jesus was tempted, meaning that his conversion to God was achieved through trial. In this too Jesus shows his full humanity.

All the Synoptics state that Jesus was tempted after his baptism and before beginning his public activity (Matt. 4:1-11; Mark 1:12-13; Luke 4:1-13). The setting of the temptations at this stage of Jesus' life is out of place and, even stylistically, can be seen to be an interpolation. It is then, a theological reflection on Jesus, though based on his life.

The fact that the temptations are placed at the beginning of Jesus' public life is, however, very significant. They are effectively set between his baptism—which might be interpreted as Jesus realizing what his mission is to be—and his starting on this mission. This means that what the temptation will bear on is not simply Jesus' acting out of the human condition, with its inherent limitations and sinfulness, but what is most specific to and typical of Jesus: his relation to the Kingdom of God and his relationship with God. The temptation will therefore bear on Jesus' messianism and sonship. In this sense, the temptations are concerned not with some particular ethic, but with what is deepest in Jesus, his ultimate attitude to God.

Before examining their actual content, let me stress that the temptations refer to Jesus himself and are not just moralizing and edifying examples for others, even though the scene is obviously intended as an encouragement to Christians in their trials. But the primary concern is christological: Jesus was really tempted. There are no Docetist touches in the account, as though Jesus were pretending to be tempted without really being so, merely to set us an example. The temptation was something real for Jesus, as shown by the fact that in Mark's version it is the Spirit that drives Jesus out into the wilderness, an idea that could not have come from the community, since the Spirit is precisely the helper in overcoming temptation. Furthermore, Luke 22:28, "You are those who have stood by me in my trials," belongs to the earliest tradition and precludes a merely moralizing interpretation. So there can be no doubt that the temptation assailed Jesus in his real being, that his self-understanding "felt threatened by extreme crises of self-identification."[28]

"The temptation is to regionalize (the Kingdom of God) and particularize it down to one political model, one ideology of the common good or one religion:"[29] more specifically, it is to do with the type of power Jesus is to use in his mission. This becomes temptation—because it is attractive—in Luke above all, when Satan shows Jesus his concept of power over the kingdoms of this world. The temptation itself, however, is not concerned with a regional issue, the particular means and tactics to be employed in service of the Kingdom, but on the overall messiahship of Jesus: whether to carry this out with the power that controls history from outside or with immersion in history, with the power to dispose of human beings or with self-surrender to them. In short, the temptation bears on two ways of exercising messiahship—a decisive choice, since the two ways are mutually exclusive. Jesus is confronted with a disjunctive, "and this disjunctive was, as a problem, very real in his life."[30] Concretely, the three temptations "imply that the purely political dimension was not far from Jesus' mind."[31]

In his temptation, Jesus was confronted directly with the question of his messiahship: with what power to serve the Kingdom of God? But through his messiahship he was also confronted with the question of the power of God, and so with God. In the account, Jesus argues with Satan, who is assigned the role of tempter. This stresses that it is a real temptation and helps to show how much conflict and struggle temptation means for human weakness. But read at a deeper level, the scene shows that it is not a matter of convincing Satan of who Jesus is, but of Jesus having to convince himself of who he is, what his messiahship is to be. So Charles Schütz interprets the scene as a dialogue between Jesus and God.[32] The numerous quotations from the Old Testament with which Matthew and Luke illustrate the scene show that the real background to the temptation is the reality and will of God, which Jesus has either to accept or to reject. Like Jeremiah or Job before him, Jesus has to place himself before God in a situation of darkness, difficulty and solitude.

All the Gospel accounts relate that Jesus overcame the temptation: that he let God be God. This victory, however, is related in different ways. In Mark, Jesus seems more like the victor than the tempted from the beginning. So his account needs no denouement; it is only later that the objective reason for Jesus' victory is given: he is stronger than Satan (3:27). In Matthew and Luke it is implied that the devil retired vanquished, but Luke adds "until an opportune moment" (4:13).

This last observation indicates that temptation was not something that happened only at a particular time and place in Jesus' life—at the beginning of his ministry and in the wilderness—but that it was rather the climate in which his life unfolded, accentuated near the end in the garden. His temptation took place in real history, not just in the wilderness. Jesus did not overcome temptation by fleeing from history, but by immersing himself in it and its conflictivity, even though this was to bring him to his greatest crisis and temptation: "This is your hour, and the power of darkness" (Luke 22:53). The fact that Jesus did not flinch from temptation or from the real place in which it took place shows that he let God be God and that he let himself be carried by God wherever this might lead.

(c) The "Galilean Crisis"

The Gospels show the temptation at its most acute in Jesus' passion, but before this they all, though in different ways and for different theological reasons, describe Jesus as going through a crisis that divided his public life into two main parts.[33] This has been called the "Galilean crisis," since Jesus left the heart of Galilee and went first to Caesarea Philippi and then to the Syro-Phoenician border. This geographical rupture in his activity was used by Jesus to express another, deeper rupture affecting him personally: the leaders of the people had rejected him, his disciples had failed to understand him and even the crowds had abandoned him. In short, his early mission had failed and he had to ask himself whether and how to continue.

The historicity of this crisis is debated today, or at least played down,[34] but before analyzing it, let us look at how the Gospels describe it. In the Synoptics, the one who brings it out most strongly is Mark. In his chapter 8, the Pharisees are still asking him for a sign. This means that they have not understood him, and he leaves them (v. 13). Nor have his disciples understood him (v. 21), not even Peter, who, far from understanding, has completely misread his person and mission, and receives the terrible reproach: "Get behind me, Satan! For you are setting your mind not on divine things but on human things" (v. 33). Jesus refuses the title of Messiah, which Peter has called him, referring to himself instead as Son of Man (v. 31, see 9:30; 10:32), and reinterpreting following him as taking up one's cross (v. 34).

Of the other Synoptics, Luke basically follows Mark's account, though not as emphatically (Luke 9:18-26). Matthew relates this break in his chapter 13 and explains it according to his concerns for the community. Jesus stops speaking to the crowds and concentrates his activity on the disciples, because "to you it has been given to know the secrets of the kingdom of heaven, but to them it has not been given" (v. 11). In Matthew's parallels to Mark, he does not bring out the basic misunderstanding on the part of the disciples; on the contrary, Jesus praises Peter for his faith and calls him the rock on which the church is built (Matt. 17-19).

John recounts the change of scene with a wealth of details. After the discourse on the bread of life (6:22-59), the Jews abandon Jesus: "Many of his disciples turned back and no longer went about with him" (v. 66), and only the twelve remained. Two attempts to stone Jesus are recounted (8:59 and 10:31), with the detail that Jesus was excommunicated by his people. Shortly afterward, he retires to the other side of the Jordan (10:40) and goes to visit his friends Lazarus, Martha and Mary, at some risk to his life (11:8, 16).

The likelihood of the crowds abandoning Jesus has been analyzed and questioned by R. Aguirre.[35] From a detailed exegetical analysis, he concludes that "chapter 6 of John does not imply a change of attitude on the part of the people or a lessening of his popular appeal."[36] Rather, his acceptance by the people is what makes him dangerous to the leaders of the people. Aguirre's justification for this conclusion, drawn from the four Gospels, is this:

> In fact his entry into Jerusalem takes place amid popular rejoicing (Mark 11:8-10). During the discussions in the temple during his final week, the authorities seek to arrest him , but the people support him and prove his best protection (Mark 12:12; 14:2). In a passage of exceptional importance historically, related of the final phase of Jesus' ministry, it is stated that it is just his popular appeal that makes him dangerous, since he can become a pretext for the Romans to intervene (John 11: 47-54). His arrest will take place under cover of night and through the betrayal by one of his followers (Mark 14:43-50 par.)[37]

If this is so, the historical content of the Galilean crisis cannot be Jesus' abandonment of the crowds, as C.H. Dodd suggests: "It was not so much opposition threats as the misguided enthusiasm of his supposed followers that prompted a temporary withdrawal from the scene."[38] As we shall see in a later chapter, the first thesis is much clearer than the second, and, as Aguirre says: "Jesus never fled from the people, but only from the authorities."[39]

In Mark, the crisis is presented in a different guise and the evangelist really insists on it. As Jesus' mission continues, fewer people understand him, including and above all the disciples, as is also reflected, from an independent source, in John 6:60-71. Jesus might well have thought that the people were no longer a sufficient support, though he is not said to abandon them, but the main point at issue is that he could no longer trust in his disciples. It is not the crowd, then, that constitute the main problem—whether they have understood him or not—but the lack of understanding on the part of the disciples.[40] Jesus has to change tactics, and on the way up to Jerusalem he gives his disciples radically different instructions (Mark 10:31-45).

For our purposes here, whatever the actual historicity of the crisis—though Mark's account is thoroughly plausible—and whatever its setting in time and place, the main issue is that the Gospels show Jesus changing his approach, at least externally, and in doing so they are seeking to say something important. Geographically, Jesus withdraws northwards—which could be reinterpreted as a temptation to shun publicity and reduce his following to a small group with the characteristics of a sect: limited numbers, with strong internal cohesion—but later goes toward Jerusalem, which could be interpreted as having overcome the crisis and the temptation.

It is probably not possible to determine what reasons came together to form Jesus' purpose. But it seems clear that a new factor had entered his mind and that he had to resolve the problem. The clearest elements, historically, seem to be his knowledge that he was being persecuted by the leaders of the people and the lack of understanding on the part of some of his closest followers. In any case, toward the end of his life, the Gospels show him no longer speaking of the Kingdom of God, nor working miracles—forbidding them, indeed—nor casting out devils, nor welcoming sinners; his discourses concentrate more on attacking the chiefs of the people and defending himself.

Jesus has changed and this change has not been simply a peaceful evolution. Whether one calls it a "crisis" or not, whether it can be dated and located as "Galilean" or not, is secondary for our purposes here. The important thing is that Jesus is shown being faithful to God to the end, and this fidelity is expressed as going up to Jeruslaem, where he is going to meet God, again in a new form, in his passion and cross.

(d) Jesus' Ignorance

Conversion, temptation and crisis are all realities through which Jesus is shown allowing God to be God. His readiness for all this shows Jesus as the one who truly surrenders himself to God. Finally, we have to consider one of the presuppositions that accompany this self-surrender: Jesus' ignorance, the correlative to his active readiness to listen to the word of the Father, since without the former, the latter makes no sense.

In theology, the subject of Jesus' ignorance has been debated for dogmatic reasons and different interpretations of the Gospel accounts have been found to disguise it, the most extreme being that through the hypostatic union of human and divine nature in Christ, his human nature would partake of the omniscience of his divine nature.[41] An unbiassed reading of the Synoptics, however, forces one to examine the subject, and in my view it has a real positive value, in that it helps us to understand that Jesus' experience of God was truly theologal, and again shows him in complete solidarity with everything human.

The fact that Jesus went through the human process of learning what he did not previously know seems to be taken for granted in the Synoptics, and Luke in fact has no hesitation in saying so outright: Jesus "increased in wisdom" (2:52). It should not surprise us to find this type of ignorance, including what might be called the "normal" mistakes that human beings make, in Jesus' life. Only an anthropology such as the Greek, which sees ultimate perfection in knowledge and therefore in the absence of all ignorance and error, could be scandalized by it. But, as Karl Rahner says in speaking of Jesus' "error" from a different anthropological perspective, "for the historical subject, and so for Jesus too, this 'erring' is better than knowing everything beforehand."[42]

Nevertheless, the most striking feature—as also appeared from our examination of the temptations—is that Jesus' ignorance and mistakes as reported in the Gospels are not confined to everyday matters, which are not mentioned, but appear on the theologal level. Put summarily, it is not that Jesus did not know about God, but that his human understanding could not embrace everything in God.

If we start with Mark 9:1—"Truly I tell you, there are some standing here who will not taste death until they see that the kingdom of God has come with power" (par. Matt. 16:28; Luke 9:27; see also Mark 13:10 and Matt.10:23 on Jesus' belief in the imminent coming of the Kingdom)—we can see that Jesus' ignorance is not of detail but affects something as central to him and as important in itself as when the Kingdom is to come. The nucleus of these words appears to be historical and shows Jesus not merely not knowing, but making a mistake; nor can one answer this by saying that the Kingdom had in fact come in Jesus, since even if what the Kingdom is was (later) interpreted in this sense, Jesus himself did not see it in this way. This must have been striking enough for these "error" passages to have been replaced later by the communities with simple "not knowing" ones: "But about that day or hour no one knows, neither the angels in heaven, nor the Son, but only the father" (Mark 13:32).

The Gospels, then, have no hesistation in saying of Jesus, who is presented as holding a position of absolute trust in and closeness to the Father, that he did not know the day of God's coming, an igorance or error that involves not merely quantitative aspects, measurable in months or years, but also a qualitative reality by definition. On this point, Jesus simply does not know. It is a mystery that belongs to God and to God alone.

The positive aspect here is that not knowing the day of the coming of the Kingdom is the noetic precondition for unconditional openness to God. Jesus, mistaken about or ignorant of that day, finally does not force the secret out of God. In systematic language, Jesus respects the transcendence of God absolutely, and so his not-knowing has nothing of imperfection about it, but expresses his own creatureliness and "having simply shared in our lot… (since) a genuinely human understanding has to have an unknown future before it."[43] By accepting this not-knowing, Jesus is open to God as a creature.

The fact that Jesus could not combine trust in the coming of the Kingdom with knowledge of the day of its coming is no indication of imperfection, but makes him participate in the human condition that makes it possible to be a hearer of the word. The limitation of his categorical knowledge is the historical condition for making his surrender to God real:

> Jesus' surrender to his mission and to the one who sent him, the Father, does not necessarily go with omniscience or infallible prescience. Rather, the limitation of Jesus' understanding, even from the point of view of his own relationship to God, belongs to the perfection of the surrender of his person to the future of the Father.[44]

This brief survey of the conversion, temptation, crisis and ignorance of Jesus has focused on his active surrender to God, concentrating on the hard and obscure elements in this, since I believe that this is the best way of clarifying what it means to allow God to be God. This is not a question in the realm of ideas only, but one of a truly historical approach, enabled and questioned by history and realized within history. History provides knowledge and also verifies not-knowing, but in his "not-knowing" of the day of God, Jesus "knew" God, since he allowed God to be God. The fact is that "the mystery goes on being mystery eternally."[45]

5. Jesus' Faith

Absolute trust and complete openness to God, taken as a whole, can be understood as what the scriptures mean by faith. For Jesus, God is someone to whom, in the final analysis, human beings have to relate in faith, and, for its part, faith can be reposed only in God. So one can, and in my view must, say that "Jesus was an extraordinary believer and had faith. Faith was Jesus' mode of being."[46]

The reality of this faith of Jesus', in its actual content, has been presented throughout this chapter, and Jesus' practice of this faith forms the content of this volume, so there is really no need to analyze his faith in itself. Nevertheless, the New Testament itself speaks of Jesus' faith, and furthermore, since the concept is novel and even shocking, analyzing it as faith is pedagogically useful in order to bring out the truly human nature of Jesus and, conversely, to show what true faith should be for human beings. Before going on to examine what the New Testament says about Jesus' faith, a preliminary reflection is in order.

(a) The Treatment of the Subject in Theology

The expression "Jesus' faith" can still sound shocking and polemic, aside from any analysis of the New Testament texts, since there is a presupposition that Jesus *could not* have faith. This a priori derives above all from the scholastic notion of faith. So St Thomas states that "the object of faith is the unseen divine essence... but Christ saw God fully in the first moment of his conception... therefore there could not be faith in him."[47]

This supposes a particular concept of what faith is, a scholastic and non-biblical concept, and a type of argumentation starting from the hypostatic union.[48] But above all it has one important consequence: it cannot be reconciled with the figure of Jesus presented by the Synoptics, and makes Jesus no longer like us in all things. He might be called one of us, but in the depths of human nature, he is not like us. Jesus' humanity could be brought out at different levels, personal-existential, social, too, and even political, but if his faith is not accepted, Jesus would remain infinitely distant from us and—paradoxically for theology—one would be saying that faith is not essential in defining what is human. Acceptance of the true humanity of Jesus, then, is put to the test in admitting or not admitting that Jesus had faith. Without admitting it, talk of Jesus the man cannot go beyond being pious, unreal talk.

Theology has for some years now faced up to this disturbing anomaly of a Jesus shown without this basic depth of humanity. To give just two examples: first, writing from a theological standpoint, Hans Urs von Balthasar, in his article *Fides Christi*, analyzes Jesus' life as a life in faith with regard to God similar in kind to our own:

> The fidelty of the whole Son of Man to the Father, a fidelity granted once and for all, yet realized anew at each moment in time. His absolute preference of the Father, his nature, his love, his will and his commandments to all his own desires and inclinations. His imperturbable perseverance in this will, come what may. And, above all, allowing the Father to be the one who disposes, not wishing to know anything beforehand, not anticipating the hour.[49]

Second, writing from a purely exegetical standpoint, W. Thüsing has analyzed "Jesus as the 'believer'" and stated that Jesus' faith is the key to understanding not only his earthly life, but also christology and all theological subjects.[50]

(b) Jesus' Faith in the New Testament

Theology, then, has come to terms with Jesus' faith, but it is also mentioned in some passages of the New Testament. The expression is infrequent and after the resurrection there is, understandably, a concentration on the relationship of the believer with the person of Jesus, so *faith in Christ* is stressed more than the *faith of Jesus*. Furthermore, once Jesus is seen in his fullness, the aspects of him that emphasize his "pilgrim" nature, including his faith, tend to be shifted into the background. Nevertheless, the Synoptics and even highly theological writings such as the Letter to the Hebrews do mention Jesus' faith.

(i) Jesus' faith in the Gospel of Mark. In Mark 9:23, Jesus says to the father of the epileptic boy: "If you are able!—All things can be done for the one who believes." Here "the one who believes" is none other than Jesus himself, who, in effect, bases the miracle on his faith, as is confirmed by verse 29: "This kind [of demon] can come out only through prayer"—prayer that exegetes equate with faith. What is being claimed, then, is directly that Jesus possessed the power that comes from faith, and indirectly he himself is declared to be one who has faith.

There is another indirect confirmation of Jesus' faith in 11:22ff, where Jesus again brings together faith and the possibility of doing the impossible, moving mountains. And as what precedes this passage is the disciples' surprise that the fig tree Jesus cursed (11:14) has withered away to its roots (11:20), the implication is clear: Jesus has achieved the impossible because he has faith.

In these passages Jesus is declared to be one who has faith. There is no clarification of the content of his faith, his relationship with a God-Father—though it is equated with prayer—except for one of the characteristics of faith: its power in history. The important fact, though, is that Jesus—or at least as Mark interprets him—refers to his own faith and is declared to be a man of faith.

(ii) Jesus' faith in the Letter to the Romans. Romans 3:21 says: "But now, apart from law, the righteousness of God has been disclosed, and is attested by the law and the prophets, the righteousness of God *dia pisteos Iesou Xristou*," which can be translated either "through faith in Jesus Christ" or "through the faith of Jesus Christ." Thüsing inclines to the second tradition, which would mean: "What is in God is revealed through Jesus and Jesus brings this revelation about precisely in the one who 'believes,' that is, who is radically and trustingly obedient."[51] As I would put it, the reality of God, our justification, has been revealed in the fact that Jesus responds and corresponds to God.

J.O. Tuñí also translates as "the faith *of* Jesus" in the context of his analysis of how Paul puts on the humanity of Christ. What Paul tries to incorporate into himself is "the inner life of Jesus": his compassion, his mercy, his love, his self-surrender and what is innermost: his faith.

(iii) Jesus' faith in the Letter to the Hebrews. While there might be debate on whether Romans 3:21 deals with the faith *of* Jesus, this is very clear in Hebrews: "looking to Jesus the pioneer (*archegos*) and perfecter (*teleiotes*) of our faith" (12:2). The statement is clear and radical, meaning that Jesus is the one who first

and fully lived in faith. It is important to stress that this text is speaking of the actual faith of Jesus, and not of Jesus as author, object or meritorious cause of our faith—interpretations motivated by the *a priori* assumption that Jesus could not have faith.[53] The *archegos* is the initiator of faith and the *teleiotes* the one who brings it to perfection.

In the context of the Letter, this affirmation is clearly designed to inspire a weary and discouraged community (10:32ff; 12:3ff); the faithful are offered the example and encouragement of Jesus, the believer by definition, after being offered a host of witnesses to faith (ch. 11). In other words, just as Paul presents Jesus as the firstborn among many, reaching all fullness in the resurrection (Rom. 8:29; 1 Cor. 15:20; Col. 1:18; see Rev. 1:5), so Hebrews presents Jesus as the firstborn in faith, the first to have lived wholly and fully in the state of pilgrim man.[5]

This faith describes the totality of Jesus' life and does so in expressly historical terms like those of the Synoptics. Jesus' life, and so his faith, is a process, coming and having to come to perfection (2:10; 5:9); it is historical, passing through suffering (2:10, 18; 12:2), through cries and tears (5:7), through learning obedience (5:8). Jesus' faith is simply the history of his faith.

Its basic component might be described with the two essential features that characterize the true priest: fidelity to God and mercy toward brothers and sisters (2:17). This fidelity and mercy can be taken as equivalent to Jesus' openness and trust—his faith—which we have examined as shown in the Synoptics. Fidelity in Hebrews is allowing God to be God. Mercy in Hebrews is exercising the goodness of God, the grounds for Jesus' trust. The Letter to the Hebrews can serve, then, as a theological synthesis of Jesus' faith in the Synoptics, which in turn can be seen as the historical expression of Hebrews.[55]

6. Who is God for Jesus?

The substance of this chapter (and the previous one) can be summed up by saying that God is the one to whom Jesus responds and corresponds in faith. And it is from the manifestation of Jesus' faith that who God is for him is ultimately deduced.

God is the totally good, Father, the love that lies at the origin of all, guarantor of the meaning of life and the one in whom he can rest. And Jesus qualifies this love. It is partial love, love that can be described in human language as infinite tenderness. It is a love freely offered that does not terrify through terrible majesty, but is offered and imposed through its invincible closeness to what is little and lost in this world. So Jesus, in the tradition of tender language about God—"bridegroom," "mother"—reformulates this in terms of *Abba* and rejoices that there is God.

Jesus rests in this Father, but the Father in turn does not allow him to rest. God appears to him as father, but the Father appears to him as God. God goes on being mystery, being God, not man, and therefore different from and greater than all human ideas and expectations. God becomes temptation for Jesus when he has to discern true saving power. God becomes enigma for him by absolutely holding back the day of the coming of the Kingdom, which Jesus had thought close at hand. God becomes mystery for him when God's will goes beyond the logic of the Kingdom and demands an undreamt-of suffering at the end of which lies the cross. God becomes scandal to Jesus when he listens to God's silence on the cross.

On two points, however, Jesus has clarified the mystery of God. First, the greater God appears to him as the lesser God, present in what is poor and little—the silent God on the cross comes later. Second, the mystery of God has ceased to be an enigmatic mystery and has become a luminous mystery in one respect: love. Where human beings exercise true love, there is God.

There is, then, a positive theo-logy in Jesus, since he affirms that God is Father and dares to proclaim that the final reality of history is the saving approach of God to the poor, the triumph of the victim over the executioners. But there is also a negative theo-logy in maintaining that the Father is God.

7. Conclusion: "Messiah," "Son," "Brother"

These last two chapters, which I consider basic for an understanding of Jesus, have examined his constitutive relationship to the Kingdom of God and to God-Father. Jesus' mission has been shown to be doing history in God's way, and his own historical path to be making himself a human being in the presence of God-Father.

In one sense nothing has been said yet of Jesus that would completely differentiate him from other human beings, nor has he been presented methodologically, despite his audacity in proclaiming the closeness of the Kingdom and in addressing God as *Abba*. And yet there is no doubt that Jesus presented in this way draws us to him; there is something human and whole in him that evokes the best that is in us. So, even if we have not been "doing christology" in the conventional sense, our examination is extremely important.

Leonardo Boff has put it with his usual devotion and force: Jesus was not original in the sense of bringing something completely new—completely differentiated from us, in my terms—but because "he says things with absolute simplicity and sovereignty. All he says and does is diaphanous, crystal-clear, obvious. People recognize this at once. All who come into contact with Jesus meet themselves and what is best in them: all are brought back to their esentials."[56] This is perhaps the most important thing these two chapters have to say to all of us: a Jesus-based ecumenism is possible, but they also provide something specific for believers and for christology. This can be summed up in three points.

(a) After the resurrection, the Jesus movement was to change into faith in Jesus Christ and christology was to make its appearance: who this Jesus Christ in whom we believe is. This came to be expressed in dignified titles to show *that* there was faith in Jesus Christ (*fides qua*) and *what* was confessed in this faith (*fides quae*). The first is the leap of faith, which nothing can force; the second, however, needs historical support not to be arbitrary.

Now, on the basis of all we have examined, Jesus, in proclaiming and initiating the Kingdom of God, followed the line of the anointed one, the "messiah" who responds to the hope for salvation of a poor and oppressed people. And by his relationship to God-Father he followed the line of "son," of the human person who responds and corresponds to God. This does not force us to confess him as *the* messiah and *the* son, but makes it credible so to confess him. And above all, it gives specific content to his messiahship and his sonship, so that both things can no longer be voided of meaning or distorted in the abstract concepts of "messiah" and "son."

(b) We must also add—as is not usually done much in christologies—that the "messiah" seeks followers and the "son" wants all to call God Father. This means that Jesus can be seen as related on the same level to all other human beings. He comes as a human being, but in a specific way, in the manner of a "firstborn" and, above all, of a "brother."

This restates the Letter to the Hebrews, which systematizes the Synoptics, by calling Jesus "one who in every respect has been tested as we are, yet without sin" (4:15). But it adds two important elements: Jesus' solidarity with all others in their weakness and trials (2:18)—put forward as evidence of his true humanity—and Jesus' brotherliness: in moving words, he "is not ashamed to call them brothers and sisters" (2:11)—also a sign of true humanity.

In this way the possibility of formulating and, above all, of correctly understanding christological dogma is being built up. Starting from Jesus' actual relationship to God and the Kingdom of God, and from his actual relationship with his "brothers and sisters," it becomes possible to confess what his true divinity and true humanity actually consist of.

(c) Finally, we need to point out—though it may seem obvious—that this picture of Jesus not only makes it possible to assent to his *truth*, but presents him as *good news*. The Kingdom he proclaims and his proclamation of a God who is Father are evidently good news, but it is also good news that the mediator—"messiah" and "son"—should be as he is. The mediator of what is good is shown as good himself. This needs to be stated not only for a priori dogmatic reasons, but also because this is how Jesus appears and how he is. A mediator deep down, close to and defender of human beings, especially close to and defender of what is belittled in humanity, the poor and oppressed; a mediator who makes the essence of humanity, mercy and faithfulness, present on earth, is good news.

Christology, in this case, both can and must assent to the truth of Jesus Christ, but also has to express his being good news. And in itself, as christology, it both can and must be shot through with the gospel characteristic of good news and exude joy. Otherwise, it will not correspond to the mediator.

Chapter 6

Jesus and God (2)
Jesus' Prophetic Praxis as
Upholding the True God

We have already examined various of Jesus' deeds and sayings, which I have called his "practice," meaning the broad sweep of his activities in the service of the Kingdom. The Gospels, however, also contain other activities, particularly verbal ones, in the form of debates with and unmaskings and denunciations of his adversaries, which I propose to call his "prophetic praxis." This praxis is also at the service of the Kingdom, but it mainly brings out the reality of the historical anti-Kingdom, and is related to Jesus' theologal experience in upholding the true God and denouncing idols. This chapter, therefore, refers back to the previous two and prepares the way for the next, on Jesus' destiny.

1. Prophecy and Anti-Kingdom

Before analyzing Jesus' prophetic praxis in detail, we should engage in some reflection on its specific content.

(a) Prophetic Praxis

Jesus' activities examined so far were "signs" of the presence of the Kingdom, but in themselves did not make the Kingdom present nor were they aimed at bringing about the total transformation of society, though they laid down the lines the Kingdom should follow and aroused the hope that the Kingdom was possible in the midst of an oppressed reality. Nevertheless, Jesus hoped that the Kingdom as such was going to become a present reality. We can, then, inquire as to whether Jesus carried out any activity whose correlative was the Kingdom of God as such.

This type of activity can be found in his controversies, unmaskings and denunciations. In these, Jesus is addressing collectivities, whether one calls them groups or classes. Jesus denounces the scribes, the Pharisees, the rich, the priests, the rulers, in the plural and not just as individuals. The factor common to all of them is that they represent and exercise some kind of power that structures society as a whole. Unlike the demands for individual conversion, which Jesus undoubtedly made and which might be seen as most typical of him, here he summons whole groups to change as groups and so the whole of society to change. The controversies, in effect, bear on realities (the law, the Temple) in whose name society is structured. The denunciations call this structure oppressive, an expression of the anti-Kingdom. The unmaskings show that the anti-Kingdom seeks to justify itself in God's name.

I call this group of activities "praxis," then, because its correlative is society as such and its purpose the transformation of society as such. This does not mean to say that we should look to Jesus for theories of society and its transformation, still less in the modern sense of the term "praxis" as a transforming social activity guided by an ideology and carried out by the organized people as privileged subject, but it does mean to say that Jesus, objectively, faced up to the subject of society as a whole—including its structural dimension—and sought to change it. So I call this type of activity his "praxis," as distinct from the "signs" examined earlier, though we have seen that in the parables Jesus carries out a process of de-ideologizing.

Jesus carries out this praxis through the word, without making use of any other type of tool of social transformation. In modern terms, Jesus would be doing something like carrying on an ideological, de-ideologizing and denunciatory struggle. Directly, he is denouncing and unmasking the anti-Kingdom, but *sub specie contrarii* he is proclaiming what a society in accordance with the Kingdom of God should be.

I am calling this praxis *prophetic* and not simply messianic for the sake of clarity. Both terms here have a systematic, rather than a strictly biblical, sense. By messianic practice I mean positive contribution to the coming of the Kingdom; by prophetic praxis I mean direct denunciation of the anti-Kingdom. My analysis will not, then, be guided by the use of the word "prophet," applied to Jesus in the Gospels (as it was not guided earlier by the use of the terms "messiah" and "son"), but by the objective fact of his praxis. Nonetheless, through his prophetic practice I seek to situate Jesus within the current of the classic prophecy of Israel—quotations from which appear in the Gospels—and its concern with denouncing and unmasking real injustice and oppression.

(b) The Theologal-Idolatric Structure of Reality

In order to understand Jesus' prophetic praxis, with its purpose and consequences, we need some overall framework for interpreting reality. This framework has to be historical, and so we need to know something of the social reality at the time of Jesus. "Jesus' practice, being that of a historical agent, cannot reveal its meaning without being set against the sum total of objective conditions of his time, in the economic, social, political and cultural spheres, from which it has often been isolated. Like all human practice, that of Jesus does not represent an absolute beginning nor can it be understood simply on the basis of itself. Christ had to intervene in an existing force-field, of interactions and conflicts that were not his to control or avoid, and in relation to which he therefore had to define himself. Jesus' practice thus forms part of a broader social whole."[1]

Here, however, I want to concentrate on examining the theologal-idolatric structure of reality, an aspect that is no less historical and influential. History contains the true God (of life), God's mediation (the Kingdom) and its mediator (Jesus) as well as the idols (of death), their mediation (the anti-Kingdom) and mediators (oppressors). The two types of reality are not only distinct, but conflictually disjunctive, so mutually exclusive, not complementary, and work against each other.

This structure of reality is what explains Jesus' prophetic praxis and the theologal dimension of this praxis. It is needed because the positive proclamation of the Kingdom has to be made in the presence of the anti-Kingdom. Its purpose is to overcome and destroy the anti-Kingdom by upholding the true God. This is carried out in the midst of conflict, and therefore implies struggle. And if the mediator appears to be vanquished in this struggle, then the very structure of reality is what becomes the question of the meaning of history. Why did the anti-Kingdom reject the Kingdom and its mediator, Jesus? In other words, this raises the question of why sin has power, power meaning that the tragedy of history certainly includes putting the mediator to death, but going beyond this. The anti-Kingdom determines the whole structure of society and puts many human beings to death.

2. Jesus' Controversies: God is Controversial

In many Gospel passages, Jesus is shown debating with his adversaries and having to defend himself, personally, against their insinuations and accusations. But there are also passages where the debate turns directly on Jesus' vision of social and religious affairs. It is these I wish to consider under the heading "controversies."

(a) Direct Controversies in the Synoptics

At the beginning of his Gospel, Mark brings together five controversies (2:1 - 3:6),[2] which appear also in Luke (5:17 - 6:11) and, divided into two sections, in Matthew (9:1-17; 12:1-21). I propose to examine them as they appear in Mark.[3]

The five controversies are: one, the healing and forgiving of the paralytic (2:1-12); two, eating with sinners (2:15-17); three, the question of fasting (2:18-22); four, plucking grain on the sabbath (2:23-8); five, curing the man with a withered hand (3:1-6). In their final redaction, all these accounts have the same structure of controversy, but they can usefully be divided into two groups the better to appreciate the exact nature of the controversy and its significance, whether this is purely casuistic or truly theologal.

Two, three and four have various features in common. They recount things being done that by their nature and in the society of Jesus' time were in themselves controversial: eating with sinners, not fasting while others did, taking something not one's own. This is the nucleus that arouses the controversy: Jesus and his disciples are shown breaking with accepted and required social norms—keeping separate from publicans, fasting and respect for private property. So these doings are in themselves controversial and Jesus and his disciples are naturally challenged over them.

The core of one and five is a miracle, an activity that need not in itself have unleashed a controversy. In their final version, however, the facts are made controversial by the circumstances added to them. In the first episode, Jesus is shown claiming the power not only to heal, but also to forgive sins. In the fifth, Jesus carries out the cure on the sabbath. So in these episodes the controversy arises not because of a social fault, but because it is linked to a religious dimension. The fourth controversy also changes its significance when the primary fact of plucking ears of grain in someone else's field is supplemented by the observation that this was done on the sabbath.

What is the really controversial element in these episodes? The debate apparently turns on social and religious rules, but I would say that what is really at issue is a vision of the reality of God. Set in the form of an argument, what is being debated is in the name of what God are certain practices upheld, whether social or religious. In systematic terms, what Jesus is maintaining, and defending with his actions, is that his God is a God of life and that this is the basis on which the goodness or badness of religious and social rules and practices must be judged. Let us take the controversy of the grain plucked on the sabbath as an illustration.

In its final version, the account of the disciples plucking heads of grain on the sabbath and the underlying theological intention are to show Jesus as lord of the sabbath and the supremacy of human beings over any purely religious ordinance. But at the bottom of this controversy lies something more fundamental than the correct use of religion. According to M. E. Boismard, in the earliest version the controversy is not about the sabbath, since when Jesus defends himself by arguing what David did in taking and eating the bread of the Presence (vv. 25-6), there is no mention of the question of the sabbath. So what the Pharisees were questioning would be not that the grain was taken on the sabbath as that it was taken from someone else's field. It is therefore a purely human and not a directly religious problem, and a very basic human problem: the disciples were hungry and plucked the grain to satisfy their hunger. What Jesus is stating in their support is that "in cases of need (here, the disciples' hunger) all laws have to yield to a necessity of life."[4]

Beyond this basically human question, however, Jesus is putting forward his vision of God against his opponents' view of God. For people to go hungry cannot be justified in the name of God when this hunger can be satisfied. Any law or custom that prevents their hunger from being satisfied is against the will of God. In this way, the two dimensions of the controversy, the human and the religious, are drawn together.

What is controversial, then, is God. Jesus' opponents are against plucking the grain from someone else's field and as their final justification invoke the will of God, the sabbath. Of course God wants us to have life and not go hungry, they are saying, but what we cannot do—they conclude triumphantly—is violate God's command. This radical posing of the question is what gives Jesus ground for an equally radical response: the God in whom he believes is not one who claims rights over us when these rights are what enable us to live.

In the accounts of the five controversies, and in parallel texts, the Synoptics show Jesus arguing in various ways to justify his radical and obvious message of the God of life to his opponents. So he appeals to their mercy and ultimate good sense, even when their reaction is obstinate and hypocritical: "Is it lawful to do good or to do harm on the sabbath, to save life or to kill?" (Mark 3:4; Luke 14:2f). How can it be wrong, Jesus seems to be asking, to heal a sick woman on the sabbath: "Ought not this... daughter of Abraham whom Satan bound for eighteen long years, be set free from this bondage on the sabbath day?" (Luke 13:16). Sometimes he uses arguments *ad hominem* and accuses his opponents of hypocrisy: "If one of you has a child or an ox that has fallen into a well, will you not immediately pull it out on a sabbath day?" (Luke 14:5; 13:15; Matt. 12:11). Sometimes he argues "biblically," citing the Old Testament, as in the case of David and the bread of the Presence (see 1 Sam. 21:2-7; Mark 2:25-6).

His basic argument, however, is one of principle: God does not wish religious observance to get in the way of human observance, but quite the opposite. So in Matthew's version of the five controversies, the lapidary phrase from Hosea 6:6, "I desire mercy, not sacrifice" (9:13, eating with publicans; 12:7, plucking grain) is quoted twice. Doing the will of God is treating people with justice, not observing religious rules, as also in Matthew 5:23-4: "So when you are offering your gift at the altar, if you remember that your brother or sister has something against you, leave your gift there before the altar and go; first be reconciled to your brother or sister, and then come and offer your gift."

This argument has been immortalized in Jesus' succinct saying: "The sabbath was made for humankind and not humankind for the sabbath" (Mark 2:27). In the Synoptics, its justification is christological: "the Son of Man is lord even of the sabbath" (Mark 2:28 par.), but on a deeper level it is theologal: any supposed manifestation of the will of God that runs counter to actual human life is an automatic negation of the deepest reality of God.

To understand more fully how radical Jesus' statement about the sabbath was, let us recall how its observance was regarded at the time: "According to Jewish understanding, God himself celebrates the sabbath in the heavenly world with all the angels; the chosen people, Israel, must take part in this celebration; the commandment of the sabbath is an order for the people of Israel to honor God in the highest degree."[5] According to this, observance of the sabbath is not just an arbitrary commandment of God, but what makes a correct relationship with God possible, something to which God's people must correspond by celebrating it with thanksgiving and as a real privilege. (Accepting that it is only by analogy, this understanding of the sabbath, as God's own celebration in which God's creatures are allowed to take part, can also form part of effective understanding of the

Christian liturgy and eucharist. It is as though God had presented us with a liturgy in which we could take part, and as though this taking part provided the greatest actualization of being Christian. That God's gift should be celebrated is obvious, necessary, humanizing and divinizing. But to think that we have been given, in the liturgy, the best, if not the only form, of celebrating God, seems to me dangerous and far from Jesus' example.) Humankind being for the sabbath, then, means the people being for God. In this context, Jesus' words must have struck terror, since "this horizon (of the sabbath) is surprisingly dislocated in Jesus' statement."[6]

This is what underlies the controversies: the reality of God in relation to us and our reality in relation to God. Jesus' purpose is simply to state what the truth of this relationship involves. In modern terms, Jesus seeks to carry out a process of "illustrating" the image of God. However logical their own image of God might have seemed to the Pharisees, Jesus says: God is not like that. And what must be insisted on—since the problem is still a real one—is that the Pharisees' image of God was at least a reasonable one, and so the novelty of Jesus' vision must not be played down, as though he were tilting at the Pharisees just because they were monsters of casuistry and hypocrisy, as they have been depicted. The problem is deeper and is posed for all of us in our religious condition or equivalent secular condition: how we relate to what is "ultimate" for us: God, country, church, party, and certainly riches and power. The conclusion is that, for Jesus, "right service of God not merely *can* be, but *must necessarily* be service of humankind."[7] This "illustration" of God is the other face of the coin of the positive message of the God-of-the-Kingdom and the God-Father. What the controversy does is shed light by opposing, by rejecting what is denied. And in this way—by affirming and denying—we come to know what we are positively stating.

Jesus, it should be said, sheds light on the truth of God in a provocative fashion. In the fifth controversy, he unnecessarily, and therefore provocatively, heals on the sabbath day, when he could have waited till the following day—let us say—to solve a non-emergency human problem. And the question he addresses to his opponents is a maximum objective provocation: "Is it lawful to do good or to do harm on the sabbath?" It is not surprising that the scene ends with the Pharisees conspiring with the Herodians as to how to get rid of him.

(b) The Controversy over the Greatest Commandment

The passages on which is the greatest commandment do not have the same formal controversial structure as those just analyzed, though in Matthew they come in a sequence in which the Pharisees approach Jesus during his last week in Jerusalem in order to tempt him (22:34), and in Mark they come after Jesus has been arguing with the Sadducees (12:28).

There is nothing wholly new in Jesus' answer to the question of which is the greatest commandment, since his reply comes from Hellenistic Judaism. His reply, however, was not unnecessary, since there was considerable debate on the subject,[9] and Jesus insisted on the importance of grading the commandments at a time when "there was no lack of declarations which explicitly forbade making distinctions as to which was most important,"[10] since the whole of the law came from God. And Jesus insisted, above all, on the basic issue: putting love of God and love of one's neighbor on the same level.

The final version of the Synoptics, each in its own way, reflects the surprise Jesus' reply must have caused, a surprise he himself provoked.[11] In Mark, a scribe comes to him with the controversial question: "Which commandment is the first of all?," to which Jesus replies by quoting Deuteronomy 6:4f: "You shall love the LORD your God with all your heart." The surprise comes when, without being asked, Jesus adds what in Mark is called the second commandment: "You shall love your neighbor as yourself," quoting Leviticus 19:18. In Matthew, Jesus replies in the same way, but the final version adds, "and the second is like the first." Luke places the correct formulation of the first commandment in the mouth of a lawyer, but then Jesus goes on to tell the parable of the Good Samaritan so as to leave no doubt as to who loves his neighbour, and to discomfort those who were supposedly professionals of the first commandment, the priests and levites (10:31ff), but who fail to observe the commandment of loving one's neighbor, while the Samaritan observes this but does not appear to obey the first.

Putting love of God and of one's neighbor on the same level is already scandalous, but his reply becomes more scandalous in what appears to be Mark's original version, which does not even mention love of God. According to the reconstruction made by M.E. Boismard, the original text would read: "and one of the scribes said to him, 'Well, Master,' and asked him, 'Which is the greatest commandment of all?' Jesus replied: 'It is: you shall love your neighbor as yourself; there is no greater commandment (than this).' And no one dared to question him further."[12]

This reconstruction of the original text can at least be said to be coherent with other passages in the Synoptics. Textual analysis shows that, surprisingly, the expression "love of God" appears only in the texts cited and in Luke 11:42: "But woe to you Pharisees! For you tithe mint and rue and herbs of all kinds, and neglect justice and the love of God." The paucity of such texts gives one pause for thought, the more so taking into account that this text in Luke is a later version of the parallel in Matthew, where love of God is not mentioned (Matt. 23:23).

It is also worthy of note that in the scene where the rich young man comes up to Jesus to ask him what he must do to merit eternal life (Mark 10:17-22 par.), Jesus replies by quoting those commandments that refer to obligations to one's neighbor and omitting the first three commandments. It is also surprising that in Matthew 5:21-48, and chapters 6 and 7—which are a catechesis on the radical way to behave as a Christian—there are abundant prescriptions on how to behave toward one's neighbor and minimal indications of duties of a religious nature. Paul too reinforces this: "For the whole law is summed up in a single commandment, 'Your shall love your neighbor as yourself' (Gal. 5:14); "for the one who loves another has fulfilled the law" (Rom 13:8). And John's theology makes this out to be a new commandment (1 John 2:8; 4:11; John 13:34; 15:12, 17).

These findings are still surprising, which is why Braun states that the juxtaposition of love of God and of neighbor is only "an *apparent juxtaposition*," since Mark would be talking about love of one's neighbor.[13] But how do we reconcile all this with Jesus' experience, examined earlier, of living from God and for God, trusting in God as the greatest good and rejoicing in this? Obviously the answer cannot lie in ignoring God, so it must be in changing our notion of God, so that in loving our neighbor we are honouring and loving God, really responding to God.

What Jesus seems to presuppose in what he says and does is what 1 John later clarifies, in a truly surprising piece of reasoning. God is love, he says. We know this because God loved us first, and revealed this love by sending his Son into the world. And from this, instead of concluding that we must love God, John draws the surprising conclusion: "Beloved, since God loved us so much, we also ought to love one another" (4:11). And he repeats the same concept in other words speaking of being *in* God and abiding *in* God; this can only happen *in* loving one another (4:16). Again, God is simply like this.

In systematic terms, we might say that Jesus really requires us to respond with total and utter seriousness to God, to "love God with all one's heart," as Deuteronomy says. But at the same time he says that this responding to God means corresponding to the reality of God, doing to others as God does to them and to us. God created us creators, in Bergson's words. The love of God makes us loving to others, in the logic of the New Testament. This is the ultimate we have to be and do, because this is how God is and what God does. God is ex-centric, willing what is good, life and solidarity for all. What God wants is this and nothing more than this. When we realize this, God is in us and we are in God.

This is the substance of the basic "illustration" of God that Jesus draws from his controversies. Whether these are formulated as social or religious controversies, what lies at the root of them is correct relationship with God (and in this, God is controversial), which consists in correct relationship with our brothers and sisters. Jesus does not draw this picture for purely theoretical reasons, but for its practical consequences: according to the particular God they accept, so human beings behave, and so they structure society into the form of Kingdom or anti-Kingdom.

3. Jesus' Unmaskings: Manipulating God

Jesus shows that people not only have differing visions of God, and even contrary ones—hence the need for his "illustration" of the true God—but that they even use their vision to defend their own interests—and hence his need to "unmask" false visions of God. More specifically, he shows that people oppress each other and justify doing so in the name of God, that the human tragedy consists not only in a purely noetic error concerning God (culpable or not), but in that we are capable of producing false and oppressive images of God and passing them off as the true God.

That we human beings should be capable of doing evil is already tragic enough, but is it possible for us to commit aberrations *in the name of God*? Scripture is fully conscious of this and of its consequences, to the extent of repeating that "The name of God (and Christ) is blasphemed among the Gentiles because of you" (Rom. 2:24; 2 Pet. 2:2; James 2:7; Ezek. 36:20-22).

(a) Ignorance and Lies

The reason this is possible lies in the human condition, which always tends to "cover up"—as the Watergate and Irangate scandals showed—the evil we commit and, furthermore, tends to justify it. Scandal and cover-up are, then, correlatives. And for religious persons, the greatest opportunity of doing both things lies in invoking the name of God. It is understandable that sin should tend to hide, and this is part of its intrinsic malice. That it further tends to pass itself off as the opposite of what it is, is tragic but true. "Indeed, an hour is coming when those who kill you will think that by doing so they are offering worship to God" (John 16:2).

Human beings are, therefore, not only limited beings—beings whose ignorance needs to be overcome—but sinful beings—beings whose lies must be unmasked. For Jesus, then, "illustrating" is not only affirming the truth about God, but unmasking the lies that suppress the truth of things and the truth about God, primordial sinfulness denounced in Romans 1:18 and John, where the Devil is called not only an assassin, but a liar. And, most importantly for our present purpose, keeping the truth of God locked up is done for one's own benefit and to justify keeping other people locked up. The name of God is used as religious justification for oppressing others, and this is what must be unmasked.

(b) Unmasking the Mechanisms of Oppressive Religion

The classic case of unmasking the oppressive image of God occurs in Mark 7:1-23 (Matt. 15:1-20). The occasion is provided by a simple event: the Pharisees and some scribes who had come from Jerusalem ask Jesus why his disciples are eating with unwashed hands, that is, committing an impurity and breaking with the tradition of the elders, to which the Pharisees were deeply attached. This is simply an example of ritual purity, which, according to the Synoptics, Jesus and his disciples disregarded without a qualm: omitting ablutions before eating (Luke 11:38), breaking the sabbath (Mark 2:23ff; 3:1ff; Luke 13:10ff; Matt. 12:9ff, etc.) and the law of fasting Mark 2:18ff par.), being touched by a woman with a hemorrhage (Luke 8:43ff), touching a bier (Luke 7:14), touching a leper (Mark 1:41).

When the Pharisees attack him, Jesus gives two types of answers. The first refers to the value of human religious traditions (Mark 7:6-13) and the second to true purity (vv. 14-23). In his reply, Jesus shows what truly human traditions are, but above all unmasks their production and use as mechanisms for ignoring the true will of God and therefore being able to oppress others with a clear religious conscience.

(i) In the first part, Jesus exposes people who produce their own traditions that contradict God's commandment. This contradiction is clearly exposed by the example Jesus himself gives: in the name of a human religious tradition, parents in need can be left without support from their children (v. 12), while it is clearly God's will that children should look after their parents (Exod. 20:12; 21:17; Deut. 5:16; Lev. 20:9). By means of these created religious traditions, people therefore do exactly the opposite of what God wills, "thus making void the word of God" (v. 13) and denying others their rights.

Jesus is not against the production of human traditions, or denying that the word of God—in this case, "honour your father and mother"—needs to be interpreted, nor does he give the impression of being an anarchist who would like to abolish all institutions and traditions on principle. Jesus is not rejecting explaining the word of God, but this particular explanation. He cannot tolerate the will of God being interpreted in the exact opposite sense to the obvious one given it by God. And let us note once more that the example he gives bears on a tradition—coming from God—to do with defending the lives of people in need. Jesus seeks to come out in support of God's honor, we might say, and to come out in support of human life. He cannot allow God to be used to defend the opposite to what is clearly God's will.

The remark with which Mark ends the story shows the worst of it. The cruel twisting of the fourth commandment Jesus unmasks is just an example of much more general conduct: "And you do many things like this" (v. 13). What is vitiated is the general run of religious traditions, not just some human explanantion of them. In modern language, it is using religion itself against humankind. What Jesus insists on is that this is to go against the essence of religion based on his God, who, essentially, upholds the weak. It is not difficult, then, to understand Jesus' anger at the way religious people manipulate his God. (And maybe here is the place to think about the manipulation of theology, its ideologizing role, in tolerating—not to say encouraging—the oppression of others in the name of God.)[14]

(ii) In the second part of his reply, Jesus gives an explicit answer to the question of what is pure and impure as posed by the Pharisees. The basis of his answer is that what goes into a person from outside cannot defile (vv. 15, 18), meaning that a person's good or evil cannot be measured by holding to external traditions or proscriptions (eating without washing one's hands, touching a corpse or a leper). So he "put an end also to the Old Testament legislation with its distinction between pure and impure animals and foods"[15]—"(Thus he declared all foods clean)" (v. 19). This questioning of exteriority as a criterion for fulfilling the will of God is a harsh accusation of his opponents and a basic declaration of principle, since, taken to its logical extreme, it means "casting doubt on the presuppositions of the whole liturgical ritual of antiquity, with all its practice of sacrifice and expiation."[16]

Up to this point, Jesus has been illustrating what external traditions really consist of, and proclaiming, in principle, freedom in their regard. But he does not stop here—he is not just a "liberal"—but adds (without being asked) what true human evil consists of. Evil comes from within a person, as is shown unequivocally by its outer manifestation. This is: "fornication, theft, murder, adultery, avarice, wickedness, deceit, licentiousness, envy, slander, pride, folly" (v. 22). In this catalogue of "real" evils, Jesus unmasks the use of legal proscriptions to distract attention from and cover up these evils. And, to the point here, Jesus exposes the fact that these real evils are those that God condemns unequivocally—the true religious tradition—because their effect is, directly or indirectly, to inflict harm on one's neighbour.

(iii) The logical presupposition of all this is that Jesus sees the will of God as something absolutely clear, written in all our hearts and not to be overlaid by any human-made religious tradition. If it is, it is with the aim of obscuring the true will of God. "In the account of it given by Jesus, God's will is simple: there is nothing incomprehensible about it."[17]

Religious traditions produced by human beings neither can nor should obscure the brightness of the will of God. We are not to detract from God's glowing mystery, let alone cancel it out, by rules and ritual or outer solemnities. Jesus goes to the depths of the human heart and tells us that there we know what God's will is. And we know this because we are, above all, "religious" beings, creatures of God. What the Pharisees seek is to annul original human creatureliness in the name of subsequent piety. (It is not otiose here to recall that God created creation—the repetition can stand—and not religious observance. It is true that the created creature is transcendentally religious, open to God. But creatureliness and its transcendental piety have absolute priority over any particular form of religion. This seems often to be forgotten, as though God's final will for humankind were the observance of particular religions.) The Pharisees also see themselves as humanizing people, but when piety is used to go against creatureliness, religion becomes an oppressive mechanism. "The creator who comes into conflict with creatures is a false God and false gods make even the pious inhuman."[18] This is the objective tragedy and/or subjective hypocrisy of the Pharisees. And this is what Jesus unmasks.

4. Denunciation of Oppressors and Their Idols

Jesus' denunciations are directed mainly at oppressive groups, collective sinners, who produce structural sin, rather than at individuals. Jesus makes not only the Evil One—a trans-historical reality—but also historical agents responsible for the anti-Kingdom. I propose to concentrate on his denunciations of the rich, scribes and Pharisees, priests and rulers, as those who hold economic, cultural, religious and political power, noting that sometimes, as always happens, these powers cannot be confined to one group or another, but overlap the categories.

(a) Denunciations of the Rich

The order of the groups I have chosen to analyze Jesus' denunciations is to some extent arbitrary. By beginning with the rich, I am attributing to Jesus a vision that would see the economic sphere as determining everything else, and so representing the most basic oppression. In general and as narrated, Jesus confronts the scribes and Pharisees, and the high priests at the end of his life, most often and most directly; his confrontation is directly set in a religious context rather than an explicitly political or economic one. But this in no way detracts from the harshness of his denunciation of the rich, nor from the clear-sightedness of his basic intuition of the great evil there is in wealth. The rich do not usually appear as direct opponents of Jesus, but they are certainly very much present in his denunciations: "Woe to you who are rich" (Luke 6:24). This is an absolute denunciation of the rich and their riches that nothing can soften. In the curses, Luke "inveighs against the rich quite simply, against those who really have their fill now, against those who laugh now, against those who are praised and esteemed by the world. This is not a matter of spiritual dispositions, but of actual situations; it is not even a matter of attitudes, but of near-physical attributes."[19]

(i) Jesus tells these rich people, first, that their riches are bad for them. Riches here do not mean an abundance of possessions, which are sometimes blessed in the Old Testament, but—by implication—the offensive abundance some possess in contrast to the inhuman poverty of others. If the term "abundance" describes a source of blessing in the Old Testament, the term "riches" implies a motive for cursing in the New, and Jesus again and again explains what sounds like a paradox, then as now: riches are a curse.

Riches imply, above all, the dehumanization of the rich, because they set their hearts on treasures (Luke 12:34; Matt. 6:21), which cannot provide true life (Luke 12:15). This is a first condemnation of riches, out of wisdom, so to speak, but still decisive, since Jesus seeks the good of all. Only those who put their hearts in God and seek the Kingdom of God are truly humanized. Jesus wants us all to be really human and truly happy, but he has a "theory" of what it means to be human and happy, according to which this is to be found in the content of the beatitudes, not in riches.

Riches are what make it most difficult, if not impossible, to open ourselves to God. This is shown in the scene of the young man who wanted to follow Jesus (Mark 10:17-22 par.): "He was shocked and went away grieving, for he had many possessions" (v. 22); this contrasts with the preceding scene of Jesus and the little children—symbol of "little ones" in general—which ends with "for it is to such as these that the kingdom of God belongs" (v. 14).

Riches ultimately mean damnation. The rich have had their consolation; they will be hungry, will mourn and weep (Luke 6:24-5). Riches will be of no use to them on the day of judgment (Luke 12:20). Hence the sharp statement: "It is easier for a camel to go through the eye of a needle than for someone who is rich to enter the Kingdom of God" (Mark 10:25).

This denunciation of wealth is clear, even though throughout history people have sought all manner of subterfuge to obfuscate it. Many ways have been sought to reduce the size of the camel or enlarge the eye of the needle, but to no avail. That Jesus meant what he said seriously is shown by the disciples' reaction: "Then who can be saved?" (v. 26), to which Jesus replies: "For mortals it is impossible, but not for God" (v. 27), which in turn should not be seen as a respite for the rich, since this real miracle does not mean that God could make riches and salvation compatible, but that "God makes possible the renunciation of riches that seems impossible to us."[20]

This is the real fate of the rich according to Jesus, and it is absolutely coherent with what he says about the poor, which finds a parallel in the Letter of James, redolent of Old Testament prophecy. I give it here as the best commentary on Jesus' own words:

> Come now, you rich people, weep and wail for the miseries that are coming to you. Your riches have rotted and your clothes are moth-eaten. Your gold and sliver have rusted, and their rust will be evidence against you, and it will eat your flesh like fire. You have laid up treasure for the last days.... You have lived on the earth in luxury and pleasure; you have fattened your hearts in a day of slaughter (James 5:1-3, 5).

There can be no clearer evidence of the evil of riches for what they make the rich do. Nevertheless, this evil is derived; it is not the primary evil of riches. Jesus makes this clear by linking riches in a double pattern of opposition: riches work against the poor and riches work against God. In other words, riches are a relational problem and their ultimate evil lies in this relation.

(ii) I have already said that in the New Testament (with the possible exception of James) the causal opposition between rich and poor, as impoverishers and impoverished, is not as clear as it is in the Old Testament, especially in the prophets, but this does not mean that it is absent from the New.

The first thing to remember is that Jesus not only juxtaposes but opposes rich and poor. The parable of the rich man and the poor Lazarus (Luke 16:19-31) most vigorously expresses the difference in situation between the two, and shows in the most pathetic terms that the fate of the poor man depends on the rich man: "[He] longed to satisfy his hunger with what fell from the rich man's table" (v. 21).

This opposition is set out formally in the beatitudes and woes of Luke 6:20-26. Poor and rich are introduced, but as opposed to one another, and Jesus addresses opposed words to each. "The formal contraposition between the blessings and the curses places two social groups in divided contradiction: on one side, the rich, the satisfied, those who laugh; on the other, the poor, the hungry, those who weep, the despised."[21] The comparison is one of formal contraposition, admitting no complementarity, and recalls the contraposition, inversion rather, of the Old Testament recalled in the *Magnificat*: "He has filled the hungry with good things, and sent the rich away empty" (Luke 1:53).[22]

The least that can be said of Jesus' vision as shown in these passages is that the co-existence of rich and poor is insulting and therefore intolerable, and the obvious implication is that the rich must help the poor, even if this means they cease being rich in the process. But in one passage at least, Luke reflects on riches no longer as simply dehumanizing and insulting, but as "dishonest," using the adjective here not to distinguish one out of many possible sorts of riches—as though there could be honest as well as dishonest riches—but as descriptive of riches as such. The moderate Jerusalem Bible (which here calls money "tainted") comments: "It is called 'tainted' not because those who possess it have come by it through dishonest means, but also, more generally, because there is always some injustice at the root of all fortunes." Several Fathers of the Church read the verse in this way: Clement of Alexandria used it to argue that all wealth is unjust and therefore it is right to hand over even the worthiest money. St Jerome is even sharper on the point: "For all riches proceed from injustice, and unless one has lost, the other cannot find. So this proverb seems to me most true: either a rich man is unjust or he has inherited from an unjust man."[24]

Riches are, then, for Jesus a grave social evil, and the intrinsic reason for this consists in that they are unjust. This is brought out clearly in Luke's Gospel. From his detailed study of this Gospel, C. Escudero Freire concludes that the rich are "oppressors of the poor" and that situations of poverty are "caused by the oppressor."[25] In simple terms, remember that in the only recorded conversion of a rich man in the Synoptics, that of Zacchaeus (Luke 19:1-10), Jesus rejoices at it, but not because of the welcome Zacchaeus accords him, and not before he promises to give back what he has stolen. Zacchaeus ceases to be a sinner because he has stopped being a rich oppressor.

There is no doubt that Jesus castigated wealth and Luke's Gospel is the best record of this. It might seem strange that it should be just this Gospel—which provides the most tender account of Jesus, showing God's mercy to sinners—that speaks out most virulently against the rich and their wealth. But there is no paradox in this; coherence rather: this Gospel also shows Jesus most passionately defending the poor. This is an indication that the ultimate evil of riches is relational: the oppression of the poor. James can again serve as a commentary on this section:

> Listen, my beloved brothers and sisters. Has not God chosen the poor in the world to be rich in faith and to be heirs of the kingdom that he has promised to those who love him? But you have dishonored the poor. Is it not the rich who oppress you? Is it not they who drag you into court? Is it not they who blaspheme the excellent name that was invoked over you?... Listen! The wages of the laborers who mowed your fields, which you kept back by fraud, cry out, and the cries of the harvesters have reached the ears of the Lord of hosts (James 2:5-7; 5:4).

(iii) Jesus not only analyzes the evil of riches in relation to the poor it produces, but also presents it in absolutely antagonistic relation to God: "You cannot serve God and wealth" (Matt. 6:24; Luke 16:13). In this way, he brings out the final theologal evil of riches and explains why riches reach such a degree of evil. Here it is not just a matter of riches removing one from God, but of them acting directly against God. The God-riches opposition could have been deduced simply from the poor-rich opposition, but Jesus mentions it specifically and brings out its meaning.

The term *mammón*, used here for riches, can mean various things in its Old

Testament usage: fortune, profit (licit or illicit), money handed over to a judge as a pledge, a bribe paid to a judge.... Nevertheless, the term and its equivalents "appear mainly in texts concerned with social denunciation."[26] The most important feature to note here, though, is that Jesus classes it as a "master," that is, makes it act as a god, and presents God and *mammón* as mutually exclusive: "No one can serve two masters; for a slave will either hate the one and love the other, or be devoted to the one and despise the other" (Matt. 6:24). Riches act, then, as an idol (whose nature and characteristics will be examined in the following excursus).

The fact that riches must be referred to as an "idol," not merely as a "danger" or "temptation," that they might even be called the idol by definition, is decisive. In Amos, "if there is one god who dominates the upper class of Samaria and to whom this offers worship, it is money."[27] In Jesus' words, one can debate whether he is using *mammón* as just one example of an idol, or putting it forward as the idol by definition; whether or not there are other idols, however, "the fact that Jesus, in seeking to specify a possible rival to God, refers to *mammón*, shows that this subject was of capital importance for him and that he considers riches the greatest danger when it comes to serving God."[28]

We can say, then, as a conclusion to this section on Jesus and the rich, that riches are not only a partial evil allowing some complementarity with good. They are a radical evil because they are an idol: they act against God, dehumanize those who render them homage and need victims in order to survive. Jesus did not use these words, but this is what he was saying. And this intuition runs through the New Testament in various forms: "... the pride in riches comes not from the Father but from the world" (1 John 2:16); "the love of money is a root of all kinds of evil" (1 Tim. 6:10).

(b) Denunciations of the Scribes and Pharisees

Jesus' attitude toward the law is complex, and so has been interpreted in different ways. He has been called a nonconformist and even revolutionary with respect to the law, or conservative and even traditional in going back to its origins. What strikes me as clear is that Jesus defends the law insofar as it is God's law, acting in support of human beings. It also seems clear that he upholds it as a "free man," playing with the paradox "law-freedom."[29] Here I want to examine his attitude to the law not directly, from Jesus' "liberalism," but from his denunciations of use of the law to oppress people, and specifically, his denunciation of two social groups closely involved with the law and deriving great social influence from this: the scribes and the Pharisees.

The scribes were the doctors of the law, and so possessed, one might say, intellectual and ideological influence. The Pharisees were fervent observers of the law, and so possessed religious influence. In a deeply religious society, both represented a great power, that of ideology and symbolic exemplariness; Jesus' great preoccupation was with how they used this: to bring people to God or to oppress them.

We have already seen that in his activity outside Jerusalem and also in it during his last week—though then his opponents were the ultimate political leaders of the people, the high priests—Jesus is often shown debating with scribes and Pharisees and unmasking them (even if the degree of harshness in his attacks on the Pharisees has later been exaggerated). What matters is to find out why.

Classic examples of these denunciations are Luke 11:37-53 and Matthew 23:1-36. In their final arrangement, the denunciations are preceded by anathemas that are also found in Mark 12:38-40 (against the scribes). Essentially, Jesus is denouncing the vanity and hypocrisy of the scribes and Pharisees: "They do all their deeds to be seen by others; for they make their phylacteries broad and their fringes long. They love to have the seats of honour at banquets and the best seats in the synagogues, and to be greeted with respect in the market places" (Matt. 23:5-7; see Luke 11:43; Mark 12:38f). And with all this they claim to remind people of the the will of God and to be those who best comply with it.

Given this, Jesus denounces their hypocrisy, puts the people on their guard against them (Mark 12:38) and tells them not to imitate them (Matt. 23:3). It is their hypocrisy that Jesus seeks to denounce directly in these passages, and it is this that provokes his severest judgment: "They will receive the greater condemnation" (Mark 12:40; Luke 20:47). Although the denunciation is aimed directly at hypocrisy, its content points to something more fundamental: the scribes and Pharisees oppress the people. Vanity is bad, Jesus seems to be saying, and hypocrisy is worse, but what is absolutely intolerable is oppression, which makes the vanity and hypocrisy something not only insulting, but cruel.

In Mark 12:40 the scribes are condemned because they "devour... widows' houses" while saying long prayers for the sake of appearances. That is, they oppress the poor with the added malice of doing so under the cloak of religion. This is their basic sin, to which their hypocritical vainglory is added. "Beware of the scribes," Jesus says, obviously echoing—for the reason he adduces—the harsh denunciation of priests in Hosea 4:8: "They feed on the sin of my people; they are greedy for their iniquity."

In Luke 11 and Matthew 23 oppression also features as the ultimate evil of the scribes and Pharisees. Both lists have much in common and I follow the analysis made of them by Boismard,[30] who sees Luke's text as the earlier one, differentiating between denunciations of scribes and Pharisees. The first three are directed at the Pharisees, whose hypocrisy is thrown back in their faces:

Luke 11:39-41: they clean the outside of the cup and are full of greed and wickedness internally;
Luke 11:42: they tithe herbs and forget justice;
Luke 11:44: they are like unmarked graves that cannot be seen (Matt. 23:27 explains this: they are white outside but full of corruption inside).

These curses clearly point up the inner/outer contradiction: the outer is good while the inner is bad. And this inner badness is expressed both internally and externally: they are full of greed and wickedness within and forget justice outwardly, and this—justice—is exactly what they "ought to have practiced" (Luke 11:42). The solution to this incongruity lies not in reconciling inward and outward attitudes so as to avoid hypocrisy at least, but in doing good: "So give for those things that are within; and see, everything will be clean for you" (11:41).

The anathemas against the scribes do not so much stress their hypocrisy as directly attack their oppressive and objective wickedness:

> Luke 11:46: they load people with heavy burdens without lifting a finger to help them;
> Luke 11:47-51: they build tombs for the prophets, but their ancestors killed them and they approve of their ancestors' deeds;
> Luke 11:52: they have taken away the key of knowledge and deny others access to it.

These are above all denunciations of objective wickedness, irrespective of inward disposition: they actually do place intolerable burdens on the people, applaud those who killed the prophets, deny knowledge to the people....

In the final arrangement of Matthew's text, an expression directed to the scribes and Pharisees is repeated: they are blind (Matt. 23:17, 19, 26) and blind guides (23:16, 24). They also do all they can to make converts and when they win these make them worse than themselves (23:15). This is Jesus' ultimate denunciation.

So the scribes and Pharisees, the teachers and fervent practitioners of the law, neither teach nor observe it in truth. They do not help the people, but hinder them. Worse, they oppress them and are able to oppress them because of the ideological and symbolic-exemplary power they possess through their close identification with the law.

(c) The Denunciations of the Priests

During his lifetime, Jesus did not come into frequent contact with the priests, and these do not feature as his main opponents, except at the end of his life, when he comes up against the Sanhedrin and the high priest. But there is one passage that shows Jesus in conflict with religion as such: the expulsion of the traders from the Temple in Jerusalem.[31]

In the three Synoptics this scene is placed during his last days in Jerusalem (Mark 11:15-19; Matt. 21:12-17; Luke 19:45-8), while John places it at the beginning of his public life (2:14-16). That the event, in its essentials, took place, is certain,[32] though the details and theological purpose of the narrative are highly debatable. The cleansing of the Temple could be a prophetic gesture, an exemplary correction of abuses, an unmasking of Israel's false sense of security, a call to conversion, even a "Zealot-inspired" action.

The basic question is whether Jesus' action shows him opposed to the Temple as such or against the abuses committed in it and in its name. It is not easy to answer this on the basis of the texts, nor should we look to Jesus for an answer to our modern systematic questions. Abuses were certainly being committed in the Temple, and to a greater than normal extent. Joachim Jeremias comments: "The priests have made the Temple a robbers' den, from the shelter of which wrongdoers constantly emerge to do their misdeeds. The priests are abusing their vocation, which is to perform the rites to the glory of God. Instead of doing this, they devote themselves to business and making profits."[33] But it does not follow from this that Jesus was against the Temple as such.

Nevertheless, in the three Synoptics, Jesus uses two Old Testament quotations about the Temple, Isaiah 56:7 and Jeremiah 7:11, which at least suggest that the reality of the Temple of Jerusalem was very far from what the true temple should be. Isaiah 56:7 speaks of a new temple, an eschatological temple for all the peoples, and condemns the exclusivity and hypocritical superiority of the Jews. Jeremiah 7:11 is the conclusion to a long oracular passage on genuine worship and of invective against the Temple, which is worth quoting in full:

Hear the word of the LORD, all you people of Judah, you that enter these gates to worship the LORD. Thus says the LORD of hosts, the God of Israel: Amend your ways and your doings, and let me dwell with you in this place. Do not trust in these deceptive words: "This is the temple of the LORD, the temple of the LORD, the temple of the LORD." For if you truly amend your ways and your doings, if you truly act justly one with another, if you do not oppress the alien, the orphan and the widow, or shed innocent blood in this place, and if you do not go after other gods to your own hurt, then I will dwell with you in this place, in the land that I gave of old to your ancestors forever and ever. Here you are, trusting in deceptive words to no avail. Will you steal, murder, commit adultery, swear falsely, make offerings to Baal, and go after other gods that you have not known, and then come and stand before me in this house, which is called by my name, and say: "We are safe!"—only to go on doing all these abominations? Has this house, which is called by my name, become a den of robbers in your sight? You know, I too am watching, says the LORD (Jer. 7:2-11).

It is unlikely that Jesus would have spoken these words, but the Synoptics interpreted his actions in the light of them, and rightly so, since they cohere with all Jesus' practice: Jesus distances himself from and criticizes alienating and oppressive worship. Furthermore—and these do seem to be his actual words, since the Gospels echo them frequently—Jesus spoke of "destroying the temple," which was to lead him finally to the cross. At the beginning of the apocalyptic discourse, Jesus says of the Temple that "not one stone will be left here upon another" (Mark 13:2; Matt. 24:2; Luke 21:6). In the testimony given against him (Mark 14:58 par.), in the taunts from the foot of the cross (Mark 15:29 par.) and in the martyrdom of St Sebastian (Acts 6:14), we are reminded that Jesus wished to destroy the Temple. These words are likely to be historically accurate, since the first Christians had not broken with the Temple, though they had with sacrifices, and "day by day... spent much time together in the temple" (Acts 2:46).

What did Jesus mean by this? In theological language, he is proclaiming that the setting in which we meet God has radically changed. In Matthew this was to be defined as the community, "where two or three are gathered in my name" (18:20), and justified christologically: "I am there among them." Then, more radically, he claims that the place we meet God is in the poor (25:31-49). John expresses this change still more directly, and in terms of the "temple": "The hour is coming when you will worship the Father neither on this mountain nor in Jerusalem... the hour is coming, and is now here, when the true worshipers will worship the Father in spirit and truth" (John 4: 21, 23).

So Jesus is highly critical of the Temple and its implications: rites, sacrifices, the priesthood. He is critical for theologal reasons, but it is also likely—on the basis of all we have seen so far—that he is critical for historical reasons also. The Temple of Jersualem was, in effect, the centre of the economic, political and social life of the country. All major political decisions were taken there (by the high priests), the treasury was kept there, and the priestly caste benefitted from association with it. It was a source of work for the inhabitants of Jerusalem, while it was a source of burdens and taxes for the country peasants. And it sanctioned the superiority of the Jews over other peoples.

Besides being the place of worship by definition, then, the Temple expressed a whole way of life and structured society in a particular way. And Jesus was against this. "Destroying the Temple" is a symbolic expression denouncing the reality of the false god and the oppressive structure of society, upheld by religious power and justified in the name of religion.

5. Conclusion: Jesus the "Prophet"

Jesus' denunciations also included those of political power. However, he is not shown directly confronting the ruling political authorities in the course of his public life, nor did he make criticism of Roman rule a central feature of his prophecy during his ministry in Galilee. He was certainly conscious that the expectations he generated among the people placed him in danger from Herod, whom, according to Luke, he roundly insults: "Go and tell that fox..." (13:32). This is not to say that his mission did not have a clearly political dimension,[34] or that he was not conscious of the political impact he made on the people, but in the context of his denunciations, he addressed the groups discussed above more than political rulers as such.

The following chapter will analyze the political dimensions of Jesus' conflict as expressed in rejecting the "Temple" and the "*pax romana*" as socio-political structures, which was to lead to his death. Here let me just cite his lapidary phrase in response to the ambitions of the sons of Zebedee: "You know that among the Gentiles those whom they recognize as their rulers lord it over them, and their great ones are tyrants over them" (Mark 10:42; Matt. 20:25; Luke moves this passage to the Last Supper, 22:25). So Jesus throws the governors' oppression of the people back in their face too.

To conclude this whole chapter, I should like to stress that Jesus not only proclaims the Kingdom and proclaims a Father God; he also denounces the anti-Kingdom and unmasks its idols. In doing so he strikes at the roots of a society oppressed by all sorts of power: economic, political, ideological and religious. The anti-Kingdom exists and Jesus, objectively, gives an account of what its roots are. And he is not content with denouncing the Evil One, a trans-historical reality, but denounces those resposible for the anti-Kingdom, who make up a truly historical reality.

In this praxis, Jesus can be seen to be in the line of the classic prophets of Israel, of Amos, Hosea, Isaiah, Jeremiah, Micah..., and in that of the modern prophets, Archbishop Oscar Romero, Bishop Emiliano Proaño, Martin Luther King, Jr ... in their confrontation with the anti-Kingdom and its idols. Jesus' basic stance is defending the oppressed, denouncing the oppressors and unmasking the oppression that passes itself off as good and justifies itself through religion. This praxis is what makes Jesus like the prophets in his fate too: the anti-Kingdom reacts and puts him to death.

Excursus 2

The Question of God:
God of Life and Idols of Death

Jesus' prophetic praxis shows that the "question" of God arose in his time too and that he "illustrated" the reality of the true God. This question was to reach its culminating point in what happened to Jesus on the cross (and in the resurrection), but it needs examining at this stage, since the posing of the question of God and the way Jesus illustrated it are still highly topical. And I have to say that for Latin American theology, despite what might be thought in other latitudes, this question is decisive.[1]

1. The Question of God as Atheism or Idolatry

"Illustrating" God is a process that has operated since ancient times. Greek philosophy was already suspicious of the image of God: "The gods of the Etruscans are fair and the gods of the Ethiopians are black"; and a major part of this philosophy—"natural" philosophy—consisted in demythifying the gods of various religions. Western thought has also demythified this image and has also unmasked a particular image of God as alienating. The historical conclusion of this process has been the route to atheism, which also puts itself forward as liberating.[2] Whether it is so in fact is something that is now being questioned in the West. So Rostand has said: "Construct a God or reconstruct man," and Horkheimer put it clearly toward the end of his life: "Theology will be liquidated. But with it will disappear what we call 'meaning'."[3]

Atheism, then, has failed to eradicate many of the evils it sought to, but the reason for bringing it in here is that in Western theology the question of God has been posed, understandably, as that of the existence or non-existence of God. This means that this theology has taken atheism very seriously and has sought to find an answer to it. For our purposes, however, the important point is that it has been atheism that has forced the question of God to be posed in theology and has, in effect, become its dialectical pole of reference.[4]

Jesus sheds no particular light on this way of posing the question of God, since

180

neither for him nor for his audience was the existence of God in any doubt, and of course for Jesus it was God that made people human. In general, the same is true today for the great masses of the people of Latin America: "God is for them something as concrete and as identified with their life as the experience of love, the experience of struggle.... God is their skin, their very experience of life."[5]

But if instead of posing the question of God from atheism we pose it from idolatry, then Jesus does shed very important light on the question of God. This is what I want to discuss in this Excursus, but first let me say a few words about the novelty of posing the question of God from idolatry.

(a) Atheism and Idolatry in Theology

Shortly after Medellín, Juan Luis Segundo voiced the suspicion that theology was covering up the problem of idolatry; as I would put it, that the Western world was victim and made others victims of a colossal theological deception in making idolatry a thing of the past. So his 1970 book on God started from the following proposition: "Our reflection begins much more interested in the antithesis—apparently out of fashion—*faith-idolatry* than in the—apparently topical—*faith atheism*."[6] The reason he gives for this is that we confront ourselves more radically and are forced to decide about ourselves at a deeper level if we face up to the vision of what is ultimate for us, whether this is a real God or not. By means of this image, we ask if our existence is to be one of service or domination, and this question can arise whether our self-understanding is explicitly believing or atheist. "I believe that the image people have of God divides them more deeply than deciding whether anything real corresponds to this image or not."[7] What is decisive in this proposition is whether the image is idolatrous or not, since idolatry is by its nature a praxic concept, which, whether we know it or not, leads us to produce victims.

Despite this, the subject of idolatry has been absent from the theology of the First World. In the field of Old Testament exegesis, J. L. Sicre in 1979 published a doctoral thesis with the relevant title "The Forgotten Gods." In the Introduction he states that "idolatry seems to have become a museum piece, with no great interest or actuality for most scripture scholars."[8] The reason for this oversight seems to lie in the ingenuous—more likely unconsciously prejudiced—presupposition that idolatry is expressed basically on the religious and cultic level and is therefore not a problem for enlightened, not to say secularized, Western societies. So, as Sicre observes: "Idolatry is almost always studied from the dual perspective: the cult of Yahweh and the cult of pagan gods. A strictly cultic focus, and based on questions many centuries old."[9] The Old Testament, then, has not been used to show the meaning of idolatry for our age. The most serious aspect of this is the presupposition that it could not be a problem for the enlightened Western world.

The same is true in systematic theology: it is not idolatry, but atheism that serves as the usual dialectical pole for considering the question of God. An important example of this is Walter Kasper's book on God.[10] He is very conscious of the question of God for today, but from the outset approaches it from the challenge of atheism. He establishes the general difficulty of faith in the existence of God, deepened today because the problem is mainly an atheism that lives in people's hearts. Since atheism is the challenge, this is what needs analyzing. So theology needs to be "theological theology"; if it is, it then becomes the only possible response to modern atheism and will safeguard the reality of God and of humanity. The book ends with the declaration that faith in the Trinity is the answer to modern atheism. Kasper concentrates the question of God on atheism, believing that this is the most universal problem for the average people of the twentieth century, and seeing it as the most radical dialectical pole for *theo*-logy. A word about both these arguments.

With regard to the first, Kasper and other first-world theologians know very well that empirically things are not so, that the "average twentieth-century" person is still in a minority—though maybe a growing one, in the Third World as well. But even supposing that they accept this, they go on propounding the question of God, as though of right, on the basis of atheism. (In the section of his book devoted to "The Question of God Today," Kasper cites only classic philosophers and theologians, plus a few moderns, virtually all German. Liberation theology gets a passing mention, lumped together with European political theology, with no recognition of its methods or content, and ending with the judgment that it is probably "victim, in its turn, of more deadly reductions.") The logical outcome of this approach is that any other way of posing the theologal debate will be meaningful only as demonstrating an earlier phase of the debate and under the hypothesis that it will come to be debated on the basis of atheism in all places. This is certainly an important warning to third-world theology, but both the presupposition and the hypothesis are accepted uncritically in this book.

This must make us think carefully for two reasons. The first is pastoral. If the theoretical direct confrontation with atheism can be seen not to have produced good fruits in upholding, let alone extending, the faith, then one might have to think—pastorally—of other approaches. The second, and more important, is the absence of any suspicion that by posing the question of God in this way they are playing into the hands of oppression—ignored as a fundamental problem, hypothetically, by both believers and unbelievers—and that theology is not even conscious of this. Consciousness of this is precisely what we seek by approaching the question of God from idolatry.

With regard to the second point, it is not that Kasper does not mention idolatry, which he does at various points, but that he does not analyze it deeply, since he reduces it to the absolutization of what is not God, nor does he make it anything central to the question. This is still atheism, and so the basic problems to examine and answer are still "the question of the meaning of existence," "secularization," "praxis that prescinds from its transcendent basis," the difficulty of language about God.... The aim of theology is still to show the idea of God as basis and goal of all reality, to make human freedom possible and to save the transcendence of the human person..., all important questions no doubt, but all showing that atheism remains the basic point of reference. Idolatry is seen as no more than the other face of the coin of atheism: whenever God is truly denied, what is not God is absolutized and becomes an idol.

This transcendental statement is true, but leads nowhere, since it does not say what verifies what: atheism idolatry or the other way round. This, however, is very important, since in historical terms it is not clear that those who declare themselves atheists immediately become idolators, or that those who do not declare themselves idolators—something no one would do in a secularized world—are automatically believers.

Furthermore, this is to approach idolatry from "natural" reason, which is not specifically Christian. The greatest problem and danger in doing this is the lack of historical focus on what is being absolutized. To give a banal example, to absolutize a stamp collection is not the same as absolutizing one's own political party or one's own possessions. They can all act as an idol, but the results will be very different. If one argues that this is stating the obvious, then at least one is recognizing the need to understand idolatry analogously and the need to determine its *analogatum princeps*. And to do so, it is not enough to overcome atheism and affirm the existence of God and God's formal transcendent dimension. We have rather to determine a central content in God, and hence the importance for Christian theology of analyzing who the God of Jesus is and what is opposed to this God, and to use this analysis seriously, something that Kasper does not do consistently. What he does is to deduce the universalization of the reality of God from his universalization of the figure and activity of Jesus. The fact that the Kingdom of God is for the poor, for example, does not feature in his vision of God, or, as a result, in his assessment of idols.

(b) Idolatry in the Theology of Latin America

In Latin America, examination of the figure of Jesus has led us to place great emphasis on the actual reality of the Kingdom of God and the God of the Kingdom, and to analyze what is opposed to them as something absoutely central. The Kingdom is opposed by the anti-Kingdom and the "God of life" is opposed by the "divinities of death." In this way—besides the fact that our history demands it— the subject of idolatry is perforce introduced, and a criterion of importance is introduced from the outset. If God is the God of the just life, the *analogatum princeps* of idols is determined by their capacity to generate death through impoverishment. The idols and their victims in history become correlatives.

(i) In 1979, the Puebla document was bold enough to mention idols and to list those most active in working against the true God at the present time (405, 491, 493, 497 and 500). The theological analysis Puebla makes of idols is not wholly satisfactory, since it limits itself to the (transcendental) statement that any element in human life can become an idol: "wealth, power, the State, sex, pleasure, or anything created by God—including their own being or human reason" (491), an analysis that would be shared by first-world theology. Nevertheless, Puebla has the great merit of giving specific examples of idols and of grading them (just as Paul, however he may have thought of them, graded the charisms in 1 Cor. 12-14). Puebla puts wealth first in its list of idols, then power, then the State... and in practice those it devotes most attention to are wealth (493-7) and political power (498-506). In these paragraphs, and above all in its first chapter, it analyzes the terrible fruits of these idols and describes the faces of their victims (27-50, on poverty and political oppression). Taken as a whole, then, the Puebla document presents a sufficiently clear picture of the idols. These really exist, some (it would appear) are more important than others, and, for certain, they produce victims.

(ii) Archbishop Romero, helped in this by Ignacio Ellacuría, analyzed idolatry with greater theological precision and historical illustration.[11] For Romero too, what makes idolatry possible lies in our capacity to absolutize what we have made, but he does not begin with this; he begins with a dynamic basic assertion, at once transcendental and historical: "idolatry offends God and destroys human beings,"[12] the second statement being a verification of the first.

Archbishop Romero did not stop at reiterating the transcendental possibility of idolatry, but analyzed it historically and so differentiated between the subjective capacity for absolutizing what is not God and the concrete objective reality that is absolutized. Specifically, in the actual state of El Salvador, he distinguished between the idols of wealth/private property and national security on the one hand, and the idol of the popular front on the other.

By being absolutized, all these elements become idols, but what absolutizes them is different by nature. "This absolutizing of the front differs from the other two I have mentioned in that they are basically evil, as I have said. On the other hand, the absolutizing of the front starts from something basically good."[13] The results are different as well. The first two inevitably lead to the death of the poor. The third, while working for a needed justice and liberation, usually tends to make its adherents fanatical and can lead them to make others innocent victims. So the way to overcome both types of idolatry is also different: by eliminating them, in the case of the first two; by humanizing it—through pastoral work and presence as far as the church is concerned—in the case of the third.

Keeping sight of *what* is being absolutized and not only the capacity to absolutize enables Romero to grade these idols, a theoretical and practical matter of the greatest importance. His criterion for grading them is determined by what is most opposed to the God of life, and so to the life of the poor, by what generates death on the greatest scale and in the cruellest and most unjust ways. This criterion in turn supposes a particular view of God, which Romero expressed succinctly: "The glory of God is a poor person who lives"; "We have to defend the least that is God's greatest gift: life."

This means that the *analogatum princeps* of idolatry is the absolutization of inbuilt wealth/private property, which becomes, in Medellín's famous phrase, "institutionalized violence" (Peace, 16). This idol is the worst and gravest of all because of what it produces, but also because it begets other idols: the doctrine of national security in the interests of the idol of wealth. And, indirectly, it also begets the response, good and just in itself, of the popular front, which nevertheless can itself become an idol.

Finally and decisively, Archbishop Romero analyzed idolatry on the basis of the victims it produced, a decisive criterion for knowing whether and to what degree idols exist. Idols dehumanize those who pay them homage—that is, those who adore them end up as victims of the idols they venerate—but their deepest evil can be seen in the other victims they produce: a world of the poor and oppressed, subject to the slow death of poverty and the violent death of repression. These victims have to be produced, since the idols need them to subsist—which is why idols and victims are correlatives—and so Romero compared present-day idols to the mythical god Moloch:

> The omnipotence of these national security regimes, their total disregard of the individual and human rights, the total lack of ethics in the means they use to gain their ends, turn national security into an idol, similar to the god Moloch, in whose name numerous victims were sacrificed every day.[14]

(iii) Latin American theology recognizes the various forms idolatry can take and knows our transcendental capacity for absolutizing any created thing[15]—hence, too, its insistence on spirituality[16]—but it takes the basic idol very seriously on account of its human and theological repercussions. Idolatry is not only a radical ethical distortion, but a theological distortion too. That is why we speak of idols in a real, not figurative, sense as divinities of death. So our current definition of the true God as God of life gains new theologal strength and accuracy.

From this standpoint, Latin American theology examines the question of God from the origins of present-day Latin America. "Millions of human beings were sacrificed on the altar of gold and silver. Gold and silver became the new gods."[17] Leonardo Boff, analyzing what happened five hundred years ago, asks: "Why so much violence?... Only to enable the Christians to achieve 'their basic goal, which is gold',"[18] and this is the basic thesis of Gustavo Gutiérrez's book *Dios o el oro en las Indias* (God or gold in the Indies). Then it was called gold, today it has more sophisticated names, but its results are the same, "the same history is repeated with new protagonists," as Ellacuría said.[19] The basic fact is that old and new idols produce victims. In the simple, recent words of two Panamanian bishops: "Gold, a god that begot victims. The dollar, an idol that delivers death."[20]

Latin American theology has taken such statements seriously; they are not important for ethics alone—and they are far more than pious rhetoric. It has examined and analyzed idolatry theologically from the basic criterion of the death-life of the masses of the people. As a brief summary, this is what it says: (a) In the first place—and this it shouts from the rooftops—idols are not a thing of the past, nor realities that occur only in the religious sphere, but currently and really exist: they are actual realities that shape society and determine the life and death of the masses; (b) these realities are classed as idols in the strict sense, since they take on the trappings of divinity: ultimateness (they are "transcendent" and there is no appeal beyond them, as witness the strictly theologal saying "business is business"), self-justification (they do not need to justify themselves to us), untouchability (they cannot be called into question and those who do so are destroyed); (c) the idol by definition, originator of all the others, is the economic configuration of society, which is unjust, structural, lasting, with many other organs at its service: military, political, cultural, juridical, intellectual and often religious, which partake analogously of the being of the idol; (d) these idols demand rites (the cruel practices of the ruling capitalism in our countries) and an orthodoxy (the ideology that goes with these), and promise their followers salvation (making them like the rich and powerful of the First World), but dehumanize them, de-Latin-Americanize them and de-fraternalize them; (e) finally, and decisively, these idols, through their adherents, produce millions of innocent victims, whom they despatch to the slow death of hunger and the violent death of repression.

In Latin America, then, we remember—with force and in detail—the "forgotten" gods, and this memory—as the intitial quotation from Juan Luis Segundo showed—is decisive for theology and for christology. In relation to idolatry, as a minimum, the faith we have in God should be actively anti-idolatrous, and the primary task of our enlightenment will therefore be not to demythify, but to de-idolize God. Put positively, God will be a God of life on the side of the victims, and knowing this God will promote life.

Posing the question of God from the standpoint of idolatry in this manner forces theology and christology to be essentially dialectical and in a very precise way. By this I mean that in order to affirm the truth of God positive affirmation is insufficient if we do not at the same time adduce the negative affirmation. In simple terms, nothing of real import has been said, despite appearances, by stating that one does (or does not) believe in God, without adding what god one does not believe in or which god one is fighting against; the same goes for stating that one believes in Christ, without adding which mediators one does not believe in and is fighting against. So we need to say two things to express a complete truth: a Yes and a No. In other words, the Christian temptation to think we are of God because we are not of this world has long been denounced; here we go a step farther: the temptation to think we are of God when we can be of an idol.

Let us now look at how Jesus and the biblical tradition make possible and in fact demand this way of approaching the question of God.

2. Jesus and the Question of God: Demythifying Divinity

The Gospels often show, and do so on very important points, Jesus proceeding dialectically to explain what he meant and to leave his listeners in no doubt of what he did mean. We have already seen the numerous antitheses between two types of persons in the parables, so that what is really being said of one is clarified by the opposite being said of the other. We have also seen that in his controversies and unmaskings Jesus clarifies what the Kingdom is and what God is by rejecting what his adversaries say they are. But sometimes, even in the same formulation, Jesus puts forward mutually exclusive and paradoxical alternatives: "those who want to save their life will lose it, and those who lose their life for my sake will find it" (Matt. 16:25); "he who is not with me is against me." In this way—dialectically—Jesus illustrates the positive message he wishes to convey. And this is also what he states of God: "No one can serve two masters" (Matt. 6:24).

Jesus poses the question of God dialectically from the existence of various gods among whom we must choose and—in the explanation of the inexorable nature of having to choose—makes clear what this choice means: to serve one master means hating the other. In plain terms, Jesus asks people not only if they believe in God, but what god they do not believe in "and" what god they "hate." Jesus calls these gods that must be hated, not just ignored, "masters" and, by setting them against God, calls them gods.

So Jesus describes idolatry in all clarity and, indeed, gives it the characteristics already systematically examined here. For Jesus, the idol is not a "religious" idol but an actual reality: *mammón*, wealth. This is an idol that offers salvation to those who worship it (this is the presupposition of the rich whom Jesus disabuses and castigates), but a false salvation in Jesus' eyes. And it is an idol that produces victims through the worship offered to it: the poor. I have already said that Jesus is not as explicit as the prophets on the causal (structural) relationship between rich and poor; directly, he opposes the poverty of some to the envy of others. But it is plain that he sees this envy producing fruits harmful to the poor, producing victims. And Jesus stresses, finally, that we must hate the idol, even though we know—as we shall see in the next chapter—the results that can stem from this. Jesus, then, knows "the struggle of the gods," "the mutual hatred of the gods" and the need to choose.

In John's theology, the question of God surfaces in another way and system-atically more radically. The leaders of the Jews claim to know God and Jesus treats their claims with irony. They say: "He is our God," but Jesus judges: "you do not know him" (John 8:54ff). Jesus does not interpret this not-knowing as noetic error (nor as atheism) but as idolatry, as clinging to other gods, to the "devil," whom he calls a "murderer" (8:44). As for worship of the true God, this consists in loving one's brothers and sisters, to which he opposes another worship that consists in dealing death: "All who hate a brother or sister are murderers, and you know that murderers do not have eternal life abiding in them" (1 John 3:15).

Paul's theology also approaches the question of God from idolatry in Romans 1:18-32. The original fault is not simply not to know God, but to suppress the truth through wickedness (v. 18), which leads to a specific negation of God: exchanging the truth of God for lies and so adoring creatures rather than God (v. 25). The results of this idolization of creatures are their own dehumanization (vv. 26ff) and outward conduct that, in our terms, makes victims of others: wickedness, evil, covetousness, malice, envy, murder, strife… (vv. 29ff).

The simple, but vital conclusion is that the New Testament and Jesus shed light on the question of God by making people take account of the existence of other contrary gods (*mammón*, the devil), and therefore faith in God must, at very least, be an anti-idolatrous faith. And Jesus sheds light on idols by declaring that their worship is dealing death to others. The idolator, in our terms, is the murderer in John's, and wicked, evil, covetous... in Paul's.

This dialectical and anti-idolatrous vision of God is rooted in the essence of the faith of Israel. It is set out programatically in the formulation of the first commandment: "I am the LORD your God, who brought you out of the land of Egypt, out of the house of slavery; you shall have no other gods before me" (Deut. 5:6-7).

In the first place, this formula should be seen as dialectical: they must accept the Lord "and" not have other gods. Scripture provides many reasons for this. The Lord is the one who has saved them, while other gods do not save, since they are lifeless, as the passage about Elijah on Mount Carmel admirably describes, and Jeremiah later expressed: "(they) went after worthless things and became worthless themselves" (Jer. 2:5). But the lifelessness of the other gods—on which theology lays so much stress when speaking of idols—is not the only or the most important aspect of the "other" gods of the first commandment. "The prophets drew from this [first] commandment a completely new conclusion when they applied it to the divinization of earthly instruments of power."[21] Then, though lifeless with regard to saving, these gods forged and adored by men cease to be lifeless and become very active. According to the prophets, then it is useless to put one's trust in idols, actualized in foreign powers and wealth, but furthermore—and this is the decisive point— these idols produce victims: orphans, widows, refugees, the poor, the weak, the miserable..., victims whom God calls "my" people in Isaiah and Micah. These victims are the evidence of the evil of the idols, not just their inability to save their adherents. And this is the objective reason for not adoring other gods: because their reality is essentially the contrary to the reality of the Lord. If the Lord produces life, the others produce death.

Furthermore, in "the vision of Micah 6-7, the principal victim is God himself, since the injustices of society, its lack of justice and loyalty, are an attack on God's plan and the covenant he made with the people."[22] It is not just that God and other gods exist, but that they are "rivals," as can also be deduced from the first commandment; they are mutually exclusive and are in combat. Syncretism is impossible thanks to the very nature of the true God: there can be no rapprochement between the God of life and the idols of death. Faith in God must be essentially not only monotheist or monolatrous, but anti-idolatrous. In systematic terms, the formulation of the first commandment is not arbitrary, but tautological, since giving life and giving death cannot coexist. If the Lord is held to be God, one cannot, in any sense, hold other gods to be God, since they are essentially incompatible.

Let me end by recalling that Jesus shared this prophetic view of idols and that he illustrated this view with the idol of wealth, as J. L. Sicre shows at the end of his book. Jesus "roundly condemns wealth as the great rival to God [Matt. 6:4), which chokes the message of the gospel [Matt. 13:22]. The choice between Yahweh and Baal, set out by Elijah on Mount Carmel and applied by the other prophets to that between Yahweh and the empires, is applied by Jesus to Yahweh and Mammon, god of wealth. This is the idolatrous temptation of his time. Jesus does not limit himself to saying, like Ezekiel, that silver and gold cannot save on the day of wrath [7:19]; he expressly affirms that they condemn us, that they are our greatest temptation."[23]

3. Jesus and the Question of God: Orthopraxis

The subject is familiar, but it needs examining in this strictly theologal context. Jesus states that we must act against idols in order to be able to serve God, but what concerns him is that God should be served in truth. What does this service consist of? Clearly, the usual orthodox verbal response is not enough: "Not everyone who says to me, 'Lord, Lord,' will enter the kingdom of heaven"...; the response has to be one of praxis: "[doing] the will of my Father" (Matt. 7:21). This is not to oppose orthodoxy and orthopraxis, nor can they be opposed, since they are realities that respond each to different aspects of the reality of human beings. What has to be clarified is what is at the service of what, and in doing this, Jesus also sheds light on the reality of God. To clarify this, let us briefly look at its roots in the Old Testament.

The second commandment forbids making images of God (Exod. 20:4ff; Deut. 5:8ff), which, seen from the present, would seem to be more in the line of classical enlightenment: we need to purify the image and idea of God of all anthropomorphism. It is true that the second commandment forbids equating the transcendent God with anything material or simply created. But its purpose goes deeper than this. José Miranda says that the reason for it is that images cannot speak, and so cannot challenge. It is just this capacity to challenge us that constitutes the specific element of the reality of God. "The God of the Bible cannot be grasped as neuter; he ceases to be God the moment his intimation ceases."[24] For this reason, God has no appearance, but only word, a voice. So God said to Moses: "You heard the sound of words but saw no form; there was only a voice" (Deut. 4:12).

This shows the specifically biblical "illustration" of God: accepting God means allowing oneself to be challenged by God; if we "in any way neutralize our being-challenged, it is no longer God we adore."[25] And we need this illustration, because "we have many means of silencing this challenge."[26]

If God is word, voice, then we must necessarily listen and answer, and in this we achieve our right relationship with God. In listening, on the one hand, we have to let God appear as God, whatever such manifestation may be (such as the always scandalous manifestation of God's partiality toward the victims of this world) and whichever the path along which God leads us may be; on the other hand, we have to put the word we have heard into action.

This is to affirm the irreplaceable and essential nature of orthopraxis, since without it we simply do not enter into a right relationship with the God of the Bible.

But we have to be clear about what our response entails. This is nothing other than doing what God himself does. Answering God's voice is corresponding to the reality of God. Doing the will of God is becoming like the reality of God. Hence the familiar words of Jeremiah and Hosea: "Did not your father... do justice and righteousness? Then it was well with him. He judged the cause of the poor and the needy... Is not this to know me?" (Jer. 22:15ff; Hos. 6:4-6). Here, I feel, is the final justification of the superiority of orthopraxis over orthodoxy. This derives not only from the commonsense knowledge that ultimately we express our humanity more in doing than in saying, but from the fact that the specific doing of justice remakes the reality of God in history. And here too lies the relationship between an anti-idolatrous faith and an orthopraxic faith. What we have to do is exactly the opposite of what the idols do: if they beget victims, we must defend these, "do justice," in Jeremiah's words.

Orthopraxis is, then, response to God, corresponding to God's reality. And this is, ultimately, what God wants. The basic foundation of orthopraxis is extremely simple: it is good that God should be a God for the victims of this world, and it is good that we should be the same. There seems to be no way of going beyond this reasoning.

To go back to Jesus: we should not look to him for these systematic reflections, but I see this logic at work in both his own activity and his teaching about God. Jesus sheds light on God in proclaiming that love of God and love of neighbor are inseparable, not as something arbitrary, but because this is how God is and this is how we correspond to God. Jesus also proclaims—and here lies the deepest aspect of his teaching process—that by loving our neighbor we prove our love for God. Let us look at two classic texts.

The parable of the good Samaritan is concerned with how to respond rightly to God. The parable, as with so many of them, presents us with two types of persons, of varying affinity to Israelite orthodoxy: one type represented by the priest and the Levite, the other by the Samaritan. We can read various oppositions into the contrast: priests and lay people, believers and Marxists, devotees of the interior and exterior life... but the most meaningful opposition is the most obvious one: two respectable Jews, both intimately associated with their religion, and a Samaritan, from a group despised at that time for being of impure race, mixed with the pagans. In simple terms, the orthodox-religious and the heterodox-mistaken-religious. For Jesus' listeners, "if all had gone according to normal expectations, the one the victim of the assault could least have expected help from would be the Samaritan."[27] And this is just where the illustrative effect of the parable comes in. What matters is not religious orthodoxy, Jesus would say, since you can see how those two behaved (despite efforts to make the actions of the priest and the Levite appear reasonable).[28] What finally counts before God is to do God's will, which—as this parable once again shows—consists in going forth in support of victims. So we all, Jews or Samaritans, respond to God by corresponding to the reality of God.

The parable of the last judgment illustrates the same point with even greater clarity.[29] All stand before God and expect to be judged by their relationship with God. The judgment, however, is made on a different basis: mercy showed or not showed to the poor. What is being taught is shown in the absolute supremacy given to the practice of mercy, and in the way this is pressed home, leaving no escape route: "While those who are being judged logically expect to be judged according to what thay have done to God, it emerges that their works of mercy to those in need become the decisive factor, because God has identified with the poor, the hungry, the sick, the imprisoned."[30]

This parable is not only decisively enlightening in regard to salvation; it is also definitively illustrative of God. Faced with the surprise shown by many: "When did we see you hungry, thirsty...?," Jesus states the ultimate irrelevance of "seeing" and the supreme importance of responding to the challenge that comes from reality itself. It does not count for the motivation for an action to be explicitly religious, doing something for God's sake: what counts is the action itself. And to close off any possible loophole, since "they" are arguing with God, Jesus replies: the fact is that God is precisely there; the fact is that the challenge posed by reality is the challenge posed by God.

This theologal supremacy of orthopraxis comes out in several places in the New Testament: "If I have all faith, so as to remove mountains, but do not have love, I am nothing" (1 Cor. 13:2). "Religion that is pure and undefiled before God, the Father, is this: to care for orphans and widows in their distress," says James 1:27 succinctly. And John's theology says the same with daylight clarity and expressly teaching intent: "Those who say, 'I love God,' and hate their brothers or sisters, are liars; for those who do not love a brother or sister whom they have seen, cannot love God whom they have not seen" (1 John 4:20); "Whoever says, 'I have come to know him,' but does not obey his commandments, is a liar, and in such a person the truth does not exist" (1 John 2:4); and in positive terms: "whoever says, 'I abide in him,' ought to walk just as he walked" (2:6). We need enlightenment about God, therefore, because we are not only limited and ignorant, but also sinful, "liars," and our lies on the theologal level are expressed as supposedly "knowing" God without truly "walking" just as God does. And this "walking," once more, is expressed in love for our brothers ands sisters, in following the road Jesus took.

Who is God, then, for Jesus? In positive terms, we have already seen this: a mystery who is Father and a Father who is still God. This is the reality of God, and this cannot be interchanged with anything else. But in order to be able to state something so positive, Jesus shows how human beings tend to distort and manipulate it. We have seen this descriptively in his controversies, unmaskings and denunciations. The conclusion, in technical language, is the following: *This* God-Father is antagonistic to and in conflict with the other gods, and therefore faith has to be anti-idolatrous. *This* God has no appearance, but has a voice, and therefore faith has to be praxic, responding to the will of God. *This* God has a word that remains constant: that human beings should make his reality come about in history; this consists in defending the weak, and therefore faith has to be a work of mercy, of justice, of love. And *this* God does—disconcertingly—have an image, a preferred place in history: the faces of the poor and the oppressed, and therefore faith has to be incarnate and partial.

As I said at the outset, Jesus does not have much to say on the question of God if this is approached purely from atheism, from whether or not God exists. But he has a lot to say, and is still saying it today, if we ask who God is and what to do with God. Jesus does not show *that* there is a God, but he does show *what* God there is.

PART III

THE CROSS OF JESUS

Chapter 7

The Death of Jesus (1)
Why Jesus was Killed

There is no doubt that Jesus died a violent death. This is stated by the primitive *kerygma*, both in its more historical version—"those who killed both the Lord Jesus and the prophets" (1 Thess. 2:15), and in its theologically amplified version: "handed over to you according to the definite plan and foreknowledge of God, you crucified and killed by the hands of those outside the law" (Acts 2:23). The four Gospels confirm it with total clarity. They give the maximum importance, and the maximum space, to the passion and death of Jesus, to an extent that makes them nothing more than the story of the passion with a long introduction (M. Kähler).

Jesus' violent death presents two related but distinct problems: "Why was Jesus killed?" (a historical question about the causes of his death), and "Why did Jesus die?" (a theological question about the meaning of his death).[1] Both are given an answer in the New Testament. The first is explained in terms of Jesus' history, and the second is not, strictly speaking, answered, but referred to the mystery of God.

In this chapter I shall analyze the historical reasons for Jesus' death, leaving its theological meaning for the next chapter. I then add a chapter on "the crucified God," something already done in European theology with Jürgen Moltmann's well-known book, and end with a meditation-discussion on "the crucified people," something not usually done in christologies, even though later ones, in dealing with Christ's resurrection, speak of him as the head of a historical body.

It should be unnecessary to mention the importance of these chapters for Latin America, where the cross is ever-present. Among us the question is not, as it keeps being described in Europe, how to do theology *after* Auschwitz, but doing it *in* Auschwitz, that is, in the midst of a terrifying cross, and that is why I said at the beginning that the title of this book is not obvious, and that it might well have been called *Jesus Christ Crucified*. Nonetheless I think that these chapters are important too for all the other worlds, which are to a large extent responsible for and at any rate witnesses to this historical cross—not onlookers, it is to be hoped.

I want to say also that the cross of Jesus points us to the crosses that exist today, but that these in turn point to that of Jesus and are—historically—the great hermeneutic to enable us to understand why Jesus was killed and—theologically— express in themselves the question that cannot be silenced, the mystery of why Jesus died. The crucified peoples of the Third World are today the great theological setting, the *locus*, in which to understand the cross of Jesus. I say this because, especially in these chapters, a series of important questions appear which do not receive an unequivocal answer from exegesis: the meaning Jesus gave to his own death, the historicity of Jesus' trials, Jesus' last words on the cross, and so on. I have nothing to contribute to the exegetical elucidation of these questions. The point I do want to make is that the cross that dominates the Third World greatly illuminates the coherence with which the passion and death of Jesus—as a whole— are described.

1. Persecution: The Climate in which Jesus Lived

There can be discussion about whether Jesus was a revolutionary, directly in the religious sphere and indirectly in the social, political and economic spheres, or simply someone who interpreted radically the best elements of Israel's heritage. What needs no discussion is the fact that Jesus' preaching and activity represented a radical threat to the religious power of his time, and indirectly to any oppressive power, and that that power reacted. Jesus was essentially a "a man in conflict,"[2] and because of this was persecuted. This man in conflict got in the way, and, in the simple words of Archbishop Romero, "Those who get in the way get killed." Jesus, surrounded by conflict, got in the way, in the last resort because he got in the way of the other gods and got in their way in the name of God.

We have already seen that Jesus put forward an *exclusive* alternative. But since this alternative is also in the form of a *duel*—one against one—it makes perfect sense that Jesus was attacked, rejected and eliminated. Put in the terms suggested earlier, the divinities (Jesus' God and the idols) are fighting. So are the mediations (the Kingdom of God and the anti-Kingdom). That is why the mediators (Jesus and his adversaries) are also in conflict: "Whoever is not with me is against me" (Matt. 12:30; Mark 9:40).

This is what the Gospels show with complete clarity, although it is impossible to say exactly when the hostility from the leaders began. Whatever the case, just as we said earlier that temptation was, as it were, the inner climate of Jesus' life, it needs to be said here that persecution constituted its outward climate. "The Gospels seem more likely to be historically correct when they state that ... popularity and enmity had been part and parcel of Jesus' life from the start."[3]

The controversies we examined earlier show how the problem is framed objectively. "If his critics were not prepared to admit that [his healing powers] betokened 'the finger of God,' there was (in their view) only one alternative... The inference followed: 'He drives out devils by the prince of devils'; in other words, he was a sorcerer."[4] And we all know what people do with sorcerers, especially religious people.

In a moment I shall analyze the atmosphere of persecution that surrounded Jesus, and if I do so in more detail than usual, it is to stress that his death really had historical causes and Jesus must have been very well aware of this. (It is also to justify giving Jesus the title "persecuted," which is so important in Latin America because of the scale and cruelty of persecution.)

(a) Persecution according to the Synoptics

Whatever the historical chronology of Jesus' persecution, at the very beginning of his public life we hear of two scenes of threats and persecution. Luke describes the first serious attack against him in the scene of the beginning of his mission in support of the poor. The discussion turns on Jesus' signs in his own region, Nazareth, where he is unwilling to repeat the signs he had done in Capernaum. What is involved here might be a reminder that "No prophet is accepted in the prophet's hometown" (Luke 4:24; Mark 6:4; Matt. 13:57; John 4:44), but the conclusion of the account is that his fellow townspeople, full of anger, threw him out of the town and wanted to throw him over a cliff (Luke 4:28ff).

Distinct from this incident, which is more local and like a village squabble, Mark also mentions the persecution of Jesus very early in his Gospel and for weightier reasons. After describing the fifth controversy, when Jesus carried out cures on the sabbath, he shows the reaction: "The Pharisees went out, and immediately conspired with the Herodians against him, how to destroy him" (Mark 3:6 par.). Furthermore, according to the composition of the scene, they already "watched him, to see whether he would cure him on the sabbath, so that they might accuse him" (Mark 3:2 par.).

In the stage before Jerusalem, the evangelists describe how many of the questions the scribes and Pharisees ask Jesus are designed to put him to the test, to observe him and find a saying they could use to accuse him. Thus they put him to the test in connection with divorce (Mark 10:2; Matt. 19:3), with a sign from heaven (Matt. 16:1; Mark 8:11; Luke 11:16), with healing on the sabbath (Luke 14:1). Luke ends the section on denunciation of the scribes and Pharisees with these words: "When he went outside, the scribes and the Pharisees began to be very hostile toward him and to cross-examine him about many things, lying in wait for him, to catch him in something he might say" (Luke 11:53ff).

Luke has stressed the gradual nature of these threats more exactly than the other Synoptics. In 6:11 the scribes deliberate because Jesus has healed on the sabbath. The same occurs on a larger scale in 11:53—the journey up to Jerusalem had already begun—and in 13:31 the Pharisees themselves warn him that Herod wants to kill him, although their intention may simply have been to get Jesus to leave that place. No sooner has he reached the Temple in Jerusalem than the scribes and chief priests are looking for him to kill him. (19:47; 20:19).

The culmination of this gradual persecution is clear in all the Synoptics. Once Jesus is in Jerusalem, before Judas' betrayal, it is clear than plots against him are multiplying, and that the leaders—now a more diverse group, including especially the chief priests—want to get rid of him. All the Synoptics describe five scenes in which Jesus' life is at risk. In the story about the payment of tribute to Caesar (Mark 12:13-17 par.) the Pharisees and the Herodians are sent "to entrap him in what he said." In the story about the resurrection from the dead (Mark 12:18-23 par.), the Sadducees try to discredit him. The passage on the cleansing of the Temple (Mark 11:15-19 par.) concludes with the deliberation of the chief priests and the scribes to put him to death. The passage about the parable of the murderous vinegrowers (Mark 12:1-12 par.) ends with their desire to arrest him because they realize the parable is directed against them. Finally, Mark and Matthew introduce at this point the passage about the greatest commandment (Mark 12:28-34; Matt. 22:34-5) and present the scene also as an insidious temptation for Jesus. All these passages end with a summary before Judas' betrayal: "The chief priests and the scribes were looking for a way to arrest Jesus by stealth and kill him" (Mark 14:1; Matt. 26:3; Luke 22:1).

(b) Persecution in John's Gospel

John's Gospel is the one which shows with the greatest wealth of detail that persecution followed Jesus throughout his life. In the passages I shall quote in this section, "the Jews" frequently appear as those responsible. In fact, however, Jesus' main enemies are not the Jews in general, but the Pharisees—associated on five occasions with the "chief priests." In the passion it is the chief priests who are the main enemy, though they have also been mentioned earlier, and from John 18:3 onwards it is only the chief priests, without the Pharisees, who appear as Jesus' deadly enemies. From a historical point of view, the Pharisees' responsibility is exaggerated, and reflects the church situation after the year AD 70, when the church distanced itself from the synagogue; on the other hand, the responsibility attributed to the priestly aristocracy is historical.[5]

As I have said, in John there is a detailed analysis of the climate of persecution throughout Jesus' life. As early as the beginnings of his first stay in Jerusalem, Jesus is suspicious of the Jews (2:24). On his second stay, "The Jews started persecuting Jesus, because he was doing such things on the sabbath ... [and] were seeking all the more to kill him, because he was not only breaking the sabbath, but also called God his own Father, thereby making himself equal to God" (5:16,18).

When he went up to Jerusalem for the feast of Tabernacles, he "went about in Galilee; he did not wish to go about in Judea, because the Jews were looking for an opportunity to kill him" (7:1), and asked themselves, "Where is he?" (7:11). And in the Temple Jesus asked them, "Why are you looking for an opportunity to kill me?" (7:19). "Then they tried to arrest him; but no one laid hands on him, because his hour had not yet come" (7.30). "The Pharisees heard the crowd muttering such things about him, and the chief priests and Pharisees sent temple police to arrest him" (7:32). In new discussions about Jesus "some of them wanted to arrest him" (7:44), and in a discussion with the Pharisees Jesus bears witness to himself while teaching in the Temple, "but no one arrested him, because his hour had not yet come" (8:20). At the end of the speech "they picked up stones to throw at him, but Jesus hid himself and went out of the temple" (8:59).

The parents of the blind man cured by Jesus are afraid to make a statement "because they were afraid of the Jews, for the Jews had already agreed that anyone who confessed Jesus to be the Messiah would be put out of the synagogue" (9:22). At the feast of the Dedication, after Jesus had spoken, "the Jews took up stones again to stone him" (10:31); "they tried to arrest him again, but he escaped from their hands" (10:39).

On the way to Bethany to visit Lazarus' family, "the disciples said to him, 'Rabbi, the Jews were just now trying to stone you, and are you going there again?'" (11:8). After the raising of Lazarus many disciples believed in him; the Pharisees met with Caiaphas' council and "from that day on they planned to put him to death. Jesus therefore no longer walked about openly among the Jews" (11:53-4). At his last Passover festival, "the chief priests and the Pharisees had given orders that, anyone who knew where Jesus was should let them know, so that they might arrest him" (11:57).

(c) Jesus the Persecuted

I have gone through the Gospels in some detail because the persecution of Jesus shows a number of important things.

(i) First and foremost, even if not every detail is historical, the Gospels show a constant and increasing persecution, such that Jesus' end was not accidental, but the culmination of a necessary historical process. Jesus' death should not be interpreted as a "tragic ending," such as might be produced by an *idolum ex machina*, analogous to the "happy ending" produced by a *deus ex machina*. "Time," as a structural dimension of reality, is against Jesus. It is important to stress this in our time in order to grasp the element of culmination present in the murders of today's martyrs, and not to reduce them to a very cruel historical accident, but to understand them as something that could be seen coming, because history in itself is cruel.

(ii) The Gospels name various types of people as responsible for the persecution: Pharisees, chief priests, scribes, Sadducees and Herodians, though from a historical point of view we need to determine where the fundamental responsibility lies. The important point is that all of them are groups that, directly or indirectly, hold some type of power: economic, political, religious, ideological, as religious models, military and police..., and that all these groups come together, in fact, in persecution. Once more, it is a sign that the whole context is reacting against Jesus. The analogy with what happens today could not be clearer, and it is important to emphasize it in order that we do not think that Jesus suffered a peculiar fate rather than one common in such cases.

(iii) The people, the masses, whom Jesus chose as his audience, do not appear among those responsible for the persecution. There can be discussion about whether or not they understood Jesus' message properly, but they do not persecute him; on the contrary, they are an objective protection for Jesus, because "fear of the people" is an obstacle to his arrest.[6] Recognizing this helps us also to understand who Jesus' activity was aimed at, and puts us on our guard—from a historical point of view—against the hasty theological generalization that what brought about Jesus' death was everyone's sins in equal measure. Again, analogy is extremely important here. In the Gospels there is no suggestion that the people betrayed Jesus or sought his death and therefore, that Jesus died for the sins of all equally. It is very important to keep this in mind in the historical *analysis* of why Jesus was killed and why crucified peoples exist today, whatever the conclusion of any subsequent analysis of the relationship between sin and the death of Jesus.

(iv) The causes cited for the persecution are various, some historical, others theological interpretations (especially in John). Nevertheless, at root they are no more than Jesus' condemnations of oppressive power, specifically, of religious power, in the name of which others were justified. The persecution arises because Jesus attacks the oppressors (historical dimension), who in addition justify oppression in the name of God (transcendent dimension). By attacking them, he defends their victims.

(v) Real, constant and increasing persecution shows objectively that "the conflict is not something isolated, accidental,"[7] and, subjectively, that it is a process that "Jesus accepts with increasing lucidity..., not only suffers it but also provokes it."[8] This makes it clear that Jesus must have been aware of the possibility of a tragic outcome. This point is important to make us aware of Jesus' freedom and, ultimately, of his love. If the cross, in the sublime theologies of Hebrews, Paul and John, is to be the manifestation of love, a historical proof of this—so abundant in our day—is that Jesus deliberately stays in the conflict while aware of its consequences. This brings us to the next section.

2. Jesus' Consciousness in the Midst of Persecution

(a) Awareness of a Probable Death

Jesus knew that Herod, the Sanhedrin and the Romans had power to execute people and that the persecution against him could lead to this. Nevertheless he stood up to the persecution, which confirms his faithfulness to God and the depth of his compassion for human beings.

From a historical point of view, fear of a possible tragic end presented itself to Jesus after what happened to John the Baptist. There is no doubt that Jesus knew of John's violent end at the hands of Herod: "his beheading is one of the most secure historical facts,"[9] and this certainly gave him food for thought. It is certain that the "Herodians," as enemies of Jesus, rarely appear in the Gospels, but it was common knowledge that Jesus had been initiated into John's group and had been baptized by him, and Herod too eventually heard of Jesus, a fact that Mark associates with the story put about by some people that Jesus was John the Baptist risen from the dead (Mark 6:14).

Matthew and Mark testify to the deep impression made on Jesus by the violent death of the Baptist, which may have been interpreted by Jesus as also an omen for him. Certainly, after hearing the news of John's death, Jesus withdrew to a lonely place (Matt. 14:13; Mark 6:30). According to Matthew, in the transfiguration scene Jesus refers to the Baptist as Elijah who has already returned (Matt. 17:13), and says that "they did to him whatever they pleased," and will do the same with the Son of Man (Matt. 17:12).

Jesus is aware, moreover, that what happened to John was no accident, but the fate of prophets, as various texts show. He recalls the failure of Elijah and Elisha in their country (Luke 4:25-7), denounces those who persecute and kill prophets (Luke 11:50; Matt. 23:34), and curses Jerusalem for killing the prophets (Luke 13:34; Matt. 23:37). In John the good shepherd is the one who gives his life for the sheep (John 10:11, 15).

Jesus, then, suffered persecution, knew why he was suffering it and where it might lead him. This persecution, consciously accepted, is the measure of his faithfulness to God. It reveals him as a human being who not only announces hope to the poor and curses their oppressors, but persists in this, despite persecution, because this is God's will. The final violent death does not come as an arbitrary fate, but as a possibility always kept in mind.

This fact is what later allowed his death to be interpreted as freely accepted and, therefore, as an expression of love. But it also shows that Jesus knew and accepted the battle of the gods, and the negative power of history, which puts prophets to death. The journey to Jerusalem, despite and through persecution, is the geographical translation of Jesus' faithfulness in the midst of the battle of the gods.

(b) The Meaning Jesus Attached to His Own Death

Jesus was aware that persecution could bring him to death, but we also have to ask what he himself thought about this death, because Jesus does not look like a fanatical madman, but like a normal man who would have had to think about this. More specifically, what positive element, if any, did Jesus see in the fact that he might die in this way? In other words, what contribution, if any, did a violent death make to Jesus' cause, the Kingdom of God, and how could this violent death be reconciled with the confidence he had placed in God the "Father"?

Let it be said from the start that the historical Jesus did not interpret his death in terms of salvation, in terms of the soteriological models later developed by the New Testament, such as expiatory sacrifice or vicarious satisfaction. "Neither the veiled (Matt. 12:39 par.; Luke 12:50; 13:32-3; Mark 10:38-9) nor the open predictions (Mark 8:31 par.; 9:30-2 par.; 10:32-4 par.) of the passion contain any allusion to the death as salvation or propitiation."[10] In other words, there are no grounds for thinking that Jesus attributed an absolute transcendent meaning to his own death, as the New Testament did later.[11] This does not mean, however, that Jesus did not look for a meaning for his own death, that he did not see it in continuity with and supporting his cause. All prophets, religious or not, have done this, because it is not possible to accept dying completely, and no prophet wants to accept that his cause will die completely:[12]

> Jesus does not resign himself to an "It is written," but perceives the will of God, his Father, which asks him to persevere to the end in the role he has entrusted to him. While he seems not to have either "willed" or "desired" death, he faced it clearly as the path of radical fidelity.[13]

In the Gospel texts it is impossible to find an unequivocal statement of the meaning Jesus attached to his own death, since the majority of these texts are strongly marked by the post-paschal situation in which a clear transcendent saving dimension was already being ascribed to Jesus' death. Nevertheless there are signs of what Jesus thought, and we shall examine them in the account of the Last Supper,[14] interpreted not in isolation, but in relation to the whole of Jesus' life.

The four versions of the Last Supper are based on two traditions, the Pauline-Lucan, deriving from Antioch (1 Cor. 11:23-7; Luke 22:14-20), and the Markan-Matthean, deriving from Jerusalem (Mark 14:22-5; Matt. 26:26-9). They combine two elements, the farewell supper and the institution of the eucharist, the first more historical and less liturgical, and the second more liturgical and less historical. As a whole the accounts of the Last Supper are liturgical accounts, but with a historical background.[15] From a historical point of view, we may conclude that Jesus, on the evening before he was captured, organized a solemn supper, which he accompanied with a blessing and gestures and words of farewell. The literary form of these words and gestures—the "testamentary form"—itself "expresses the desire of the person bidding farewell to guarantee the continuity of his or her life and, as far as possible, the continuance of his or her person among their friends."[16]

This account reveals, first, the attitude with which Jesus himself faced his imminent death and, second, the possible meaning his death could have for others. As regards the first, in a text the historicity of which is already established, Jesus says, "Truly I tell you, I will never again drink of the fruit of the vine until that day when I drink it new in the Kingdom of God" (Mark 14:25 par.). In these words Jesus expresses the certainty of his death, on the one hand, and on the other his own hope. This is eschatological hope for the coming of the Kingdom of God, the definitive coming, reinforced in the expressions "that day" and "new."[17]

So far the account is clearly historical. Jesus wishes to share the end of his life and reaffirm his cause. "Jesus foresees his end, but does not despair of the meaning of his death, but positively establishes his firm hope in the triumph of the Kingdom and of his personal cause."[18] Jesus does not say specifically *what* the meaning of his death consists in, but insists that his death is not meaningless for him, since it does not nullify his hope—which he formulates, moreover, in terms of the Kingdom of God—which is consistent with the trust he places in the Father.

The positive meaning of his death for his cause is what is expressed in the texts about the institution of the eucharist. In very general terms, his death will be something "good" for others, for all. If we take together all the salvation themes in the four texts in their present redactions, they tell us that the bread— Jesus' body— is "given for you" and that the wine—his blood—is "shed for many," "for the forgiveness of sins," as a "new covenant."

I have already said that this interpretation is post-paschal, but that its overall positive sense of salvation does contain an important historical core that points to what Jesus thought about his own death. The crucial point is that Jesus says that his life is "for," "on behalf of" (*hyper*) others, and that this produces positive fruits in others. It is an understanding of Jesus' life as service, and in the end sacrificial service.

What may be the most historical element, the actions and words of offering bread to his disciples, must be interpreted as offering salvation, salvation that at this solemn moment is Jesus' own sacrifice. The gesture of offering them the cup — though the words here are heavily theologized—is an invitation to his disciples to participate in his death. These gestures are nothing other than signs, at a moment of special solemnity, of what Jesus' whole life had been and of the legacy he is leaving to his friends. Jesus says to them, "I have set you an example, that you also should do as I have done to you" (John 13:15).

This connection of a life and death devoted to service appears in other passages in the Gospels, and clearly in Mark 10:45: "For the Son of Man came not to be served but to serve, and to give his life as a ransom for many," a text that Luke— independent here of Mark—places in the Last Supper, after the institution of the eucharist. These texts about service, with Luke 12:37b and John 13:1-20, are all "part of the Last Supper tradition."[19] According to this whole tradition, at the supper Jesus interprets his own death as service, the continuation and culmination of his life. His death is not, therefore, absurd and useless, either for him or for others. Jesus directly offers to all people the meaning of a life of service, and this is what he proposes to his disciples.

Can we be any more precise about the meaning Jesus gave to his own death? It is certainly not at all plausible that he should have looked for one in the theoretical models developed later by the New Testament, vicarious expiation, expiatory sacrifice, and so on, as we shall see in the next chapter. We can ask whether Jesus thought that his death would hasten the coming of the Kingdom of God—an idea totally remote at the beginning of his mission—as Schürmann's well-known thesis asserts,[20] that is, that his death was an explicit service to the coming of the Kingdom. This possibility is open, but it cannot be pressed.

What is clear is something else. Jesus goes to his death with clarity and confidence, faithful to God to the end and treating his death as an expression of service to his friends. Paraphrasing Micah 6:8, we can say that Jesus saw with clarity right to the end what God demands of every human being: "you must go on doing justice and loving tenderly." He also saw with clarity that we must continue "humbly" walking with God in history. He saw that this is good and required of him, and that it is good, and so required, of others. In this sense, we can say that

Jesus went to his death with confidence and saw it as a final act of service, more in the manner of an effective example that would motivate others than as a mechanism of salvation for others. To be faithful to the end is what it means to be human.

Whether and how Jesus changed this attitude in the events from the garden to his death on the cross, whether and how his own self-understanding was challenged by these events, are issues I shall examine later as far as possible. However, with regard to what we have seen so far, I want to say that Jesus remains a faithful and compassionate prophet. He is faithful to God, because he is aware of his novel destiny and accepts it. He is merciful toward human beings because—in the Synoptics this is described in this context by the term "Son of Man"— he proclaims that his life is service to the end and that—when all that he has left to give is his life—he interprets this giving of it as a service to others. What the threats and the increasing persecution did not change in Jesus, although they gave it a very new shape—was his constitutive relatedness: in relation to God he remains the person who is faithful; in relation to human beings, the person who serves. What is added by his acceptance of death is that he is faithful and merciful "to the end."

3. Jesus' Trial

Jesus was sentenced to death and died on a cross, a punishment for slaves and subversives. Before this, however, there was a trial, at which the reason for such a death was given: why Jesus was killed. The important point for us is to stress that there was a reason, which may have been valid or invalid from a strictly legal point of view, and that this reason was based on what Jesus did and said.

The account in the Gospels of the political trial, and even more of the religious trial, is extremely controversial[21] from a historical point of view, and I can add nothing to clarify it. My analysis here will be in terms of the model I put forward above. The divinities and their mediations are at war, and so therefore are their mediators. Jesus' trial is the trial of a mediator, but it is held to defend a mediation, and this is done in the name of a god. In other words, Jesus' trial is also the trial of his God. From now on we can appreciate the tragedy about to occur. Jesus will be sentenced to death in the name of a god, and Jesus and his God seem to lose the case.

(a) The Religious Trial

It is clear historically that Jesus came into conflict with the religious leaders, and it is also clear theologically that he was condemned in the name of a divinity. John describes, in very theologized form, a bitter religious conflict between Jesus and the Jewish leaders in the Temple, at the feast of the Dedication (John 10:22-39). In the Synoptics this appears during the last week in Jerusalem. What the Synoptic traditions chose to turn into history, in the religious trial is "the growing hostility of the Jewish leaders (especially the leaders of the priests), which in John reaches its climax at the feast of the Dedication."[22] Ordering events in this way makes the alternative "to death" appear between the chief priests and Jesus. It stresses that they wanted "to put him to death" (Mark 14:55; Matt. 26:59) and the conclusion is that "he deserves death" (Mark 14:64; Matt. 26:66). What is important is to know why.

The historicity of the religious trial or trials is much discussed, as I said. The interrogation before Annas could have been a private interrogation (John 18:12-23), and the interrogation before the Sanhedrin would have taken place the following morning with the intention of preparing the charges to be laid before Pilate, who had the power of execution (Mark 14:53-64 par.).

According to John, in the first interrogation, in Annas' house, Jesus was questioned about his disciples and his teaching. This could be interpreted as a questioning of Jesus' orthodoxy and, more dangerously, an inquiry into his movement, which could have gone on gaining force and in this way have become a danger to the established religion. However, Jesus' reply provided no grounds for a charge, although one of the guards reacted to Jesus' freedom, which he took for insolence, and slapped him (John 18: 19-23). According to the Synoptics, there was another interrogation next morning before the Sanhedrin. The reason for the sentence appears when Jesus blasphemes by declaring himself to be the Christ (Matt. 26:64; Mark 14:62; Luke 22:67; cf John 10:24). Accordingly, he is deemed guilty of a capital offence.

This reason for the sentence, understood as blasphemy in the strict sense, seems to be editorial. The real reason lies elsewhere. Schillebeeckx,[23] for example, thinks that the people who made up the Sanhedrin were against Jesus for various reasons, but were also respecters of the Law, and would not have condemned him without a legal basis. This could be contained in the text of Deuteronomy 17:12: "As for anyone who presumes to disobey the priest appointed to minister there to the LORD your God, or the judge, that person shall die." On this view, the legal basis for the condemnation could have been that Jesus remained arrogantly silent before the court that was questioning him. On the other hand, it does not seem absolutely clear that the Deuteronomy text could have been interpreted against Jesus. This is the source of the ambiguity reflected in Mark: on the one hand he states that the Sanhedrin pronounced sentence of death (Mark 14:64), and on the other that the next morning they reached the decision to hand Jesus over to Pilate (Mark 15:1). Schillebeeckx's conclusion about the Sanhedrin's conduct is that "everybody was against Jesus, but when it came to legal validity, there was no general agreement. Only at this point does the guilt of the Sanhedrin begin. There was no lack of unanimity about handing Jesus over to the Romans!"[24]

The crucial issue is why they were all against Jesus. According to Boismard, the reason appears in the charge brought against him that he wanted to destroy the Temple (Matt. 26:61; Mark 14:58; cf John 2:19). Whether or not such an accusation at the moment of the trial is historical, this does seem to be the underlying objective reason. If we remember what we saw previously about the Temple and what it meant in Jesus' time—the structuring core of Jewish society—

it is completely comprehensible that the chief priests, above all, who were at the same time religious and political leaders, and themselves rich,[25] would have wanted to get rid of him.

As a historical conclusion, Boismard's view seems very plausible. "We may reasonably believe that the authors of this death were primarily the members of the priestly caste, irritated at seeing Jesus set himself up as a religious reformer of the cultural practices current in his time."[26] A reasonable systematic conclusion seems to be that Jesus was convicted for wanting to destroy the Temple, because he not only criticized certain aspects of it, but also offered a distinct and opposite alternative, which implied that the Temple would no longer be the core of a political, social and economic theocracy in Israel's life.[27]

If all this is the case, the reason for Jesus' condemnation is absolutely consistent with his rejection right through his life. The anti-Kingdom (a society structured round the Temple in this case) actively rejected the Kingdom and its mediators actively rejected the mediator. What the religious trial makes clear—even at an editorial level—is that the gods too are at war. "Jesus became involved in conflict because of the way he spoke about God and made him present in the world."[28] The chief priest appeals to God: "I put you under oath before the living God" (Matt. 26:63). And "in the name of the living God"—tragically and ironically—he sends him to his death. Jesus is condemned in the name of a god.

(b) The Political Trial

In the Gospels, especially in Luke, there is a tendency to attribute ultimate responsibility for Jesus' death to the Jewish leaders, not to Pilate.[29] Nevertheless, Jesus died crucified as a political offender and died the type of death that only the political power, the Romans, could inflict. The reason for the conviction, on the other hand, is formulated in political terms: he claimed to be the king of the Jews. This seems to be confirmed by Pilate's offer to exchange Jesus for Barabbas, a political subversive.

Strictly speaking, the narratives do not contain a trial of Jesus, but the basic historical fact might be called "the episode of the people calling for the release of Barabbas."[30] However, within this context we find Jesus' so-called political trial, in which two types of charges are used to secure his conviction. One is based on supposed politically subversive actions of Jesus and the other, which in the end secured the conviction, on the religious-political opposition to Rome that Jesus objectively represented.

In the first area, what is historically most probable is the account in Luke 23:2 and John 19:12-15:[31] "We found this man perverting our nation, forbidding us to pay taxes to the emperor, and saying that he himself is the Messiah, a king." I want to say something about each of these three elements.

The historical context of the charge of subversion may be the insurrection referred to in Mark 15:7, and the Jewish leaders may have wanted to implicate Jesus in this,[32] although the Gospel narratives give no support for such a suggestion. The most likely situation is that the Jews wanted to portray the really subversive elements of Jesus' preaching as "politically dangerous" before Pilate,[33] and in order to make this convincing they associated him—as is still done today—[34]with politically subversive groups or actions. It is fairly obvious that prophets like Jesus automatically become dangerous in political terms, and it is a frequent occurrence that in order to eliminate their influence they are falsely implicated in specific events.

The passage about paying taxes to the emperor (Mark 12:13-7; Matt. 22:15-22; Luke 20:20-6) is presented as having been a political trap for Jesus. Luke makes this explicit by calling the Pharisees (Mark and Matthew) and Herodians (Mark) who came to put the question to Jesus "spies," and reinforces the point by adding at the end: "in order to trap him by what he said, so as to hand him over to the jurisdiction and authority of the governor" (Luke 20:20). As is well known, Jesus replied in the famous words, "Render to Caesar the things that are Caesar's and to God the things that are God's." With this reply Jesus distanced himself at once from the Roman dominators and the anti-Roman subversives:

> In concrete fact, the nationalist theocratic interpretation of the state is not the alternative Jesus proposes when faced with the problem of Roman domination. On the one hand, the nationalist emphasis interests him relatively little; on the other hand his real interest lies in what is happening to people whoever their oppressors and rulers may be.[35]

Finally, in John, Jesus' answer to the charge that he is proclaiming himself a king is that he is a king and has a kingdom. It is well known that John's main interest in dealing with the issue is christological,[36] which is consistent with the whole of his Gospel, in which the Synoptics' Kingdom of God gives way to the kingship of Jesus. The kingship is real, though impotent and weak, and the opposite of what we expect, as is shown by the composition of the scene *sub specie contrarii*: Jesus the convicted prisoner proclaims himself king before Pilate (18:33-38a), mockery from the soldiers in the scene of enthronement and coronation (19:1-3), epiphany before the people with the purple cloak and crown of thorns (19:4-7), and the "Crucify him" as the acclamation (19:15). We learn that the kingship is real, however, from the fact that throughout the whole interrogation scene John presents a clear inversion: Jesus appears more as judge than accused, and Pilate more as accused than judge, and this is so because Jesus is the truth.

If Jesus is really a king, the question arises what his kingdom consists of. "My kingdom is not from this world. If my kingdom were from this world, my followers would be fighting to keep me from being handed over to the Jews," says Jesus (18:36). In this way Jesus rules out the possibility that his kingdom is—merely— a kingdom of this world and political, or, more precisely, that his kingdom is like those of this world and his mission like that of a politician.

This statement is so often quoted to defend faith against any involvement in politics that it needs to be carefully studied, on the basis of the Gospel text. The idea that Jesus' kingdom is not of this world is completely consistent with what Jesus says in the Synoptics. In their terminology, the world is the anti-Kingdom; in John's the world is, by definition, what is in opposition to God, what cannot open itself to the light and truth. Therefore Jesus says not only that his kingdom is not of this world, but also that it is a crisis and judgment for the world (the equivalent of the unmasking and condemnation in the Synoptics).

John, however, not only explains what Jesus' kingdom is not, but also gives positive information: "You say that I am a king. For this I was born, and for this I came into the world, to testify to the truth" (18:37). "Coming into the world" is something real, something which happens in the world, and is done for a purpose, to bear witness to the truth. Jesus' coming forces people to take a position on the truth. Though in a different way from the Synoptics, John in essence stresses that there is a Kingdom and an anti-Kingdom, the world of truth and the world of lies, both real and historical,[37] which cannot be contrasted as "spiritual" and "material." Ellacuría comments, analytically, that the truth referred to is the truth that clarifies and judges, and that in terms of this truth we have to shape the world and overcome evil.[38] The fact that in this case the true kingdom is defined as a kingdom of truth in no way means that the concept is not historical or even political, and present-day history shows how historical truth is, how much historical reality it produces, and how historical and political are the reactions against those who utter the truth.

After these observations, let us return to the course of the trial. It is very important to remember that the charges against Jesus had no success before Pilate (John 18:33), who does not even seem to have been surprised at the claim that Jesus wanted to be a king (John 18:33). The conclusion, rather, is that he tried to free him. All the Gospels, moreover, introduce the Barabbas scene (Matt. 27:15-23; Mark 15:6-14; Luke 23:17-23; John 18:39-40)—which is historically improbable—as Pilate's last excuse for freeing Jesus. The people, however, choose Barabbas, and call for Jesus' crucifixion, although both Matthew 27:20 and Mark 15:11 specify that it was the chief priests who persuaded the crowd to call for Barabbas, and in John the shout "Crucify him" is uttered only by the chief priests and the guards (19:6). Next a final charge is brought before Pilate: "We have a law, and according to that law he ought to die, because he has claimed to be the Son of God" (John 19:7). Pilate does not react, though he became even more afraid, but still wanted to release Jesus (John 19:12).

In the Gospel account, then, many very different accusations are made against Jesus, and none of them convinces Pilate, which could be due to a desire not to make the Romans responsible for Jesus' death. Nevertheless Pilate finally sentences Jesus to death; it is therefore very important to discover why. In the narrative the Jews do not yet accuse Jesus of any specific act, but say grandly, "If you release this man, you are no friend of the emperor. Everyone who claims to be a king sets himself against the emperor" (John 19:12). This alternative, and not the specific accusations, is what makes Pilate give way and, though wanting to save him, sentence Jesus to death (John 19:16).

Because Pilate has to choose within this necessary disjunctive, Jesus dies. From a historical and legal standpoint, Jesus' conviction, as described, is not only unjust, but also has very little logic, but in terms of the theologal structure of history it is a necessity. In systematic language, at the trial there is a confrontation between two "mediators," Jesus and Pilate, representing two "mediations," the Kingdom of God and the Roman Empire (the *pax romana*). While at the level of the mediators the progress of the trial is a sequence of individual irrationalities, its deep logic is clear: the "total encounter" between Jesus and Pilate.[39] The confrontation between the mediators reveals the confrontation of the mediations and, above all, that of the divinities that lie behind them: the God of Jesus or Caesar. It is curious that the Gospels put into the mouth of the Jews the words that make Pilate realize the exclusive alternative: it is impossible at one and the same time "to be a friend" of Jesus and of the emperor: every king "sets himself against" the emperor (John 19:12).

This "not being able to be a friend" of two gods is the equivalent of the inevitability of "hating" one of them spoken of by Jesus. The inevitability of "setting oneself against" one of them reflects the theologal structure of reality, and from this point of view the specific charges—which may in fact have been strictly based on legality—made by the mediators are secondary. Caiaphas summed it up without circumlocution: "It is better for you to have one man die for the people than to have the whole nation destroyed" (John 11:50).

The need to put Jesus to death is, therefore, of a higher order: we have to choose between Jesus' God and Pilate's god, between God and the emperor. The ultimate reason why Pilate can send Jesus to his death while recognizing his personal innocence is the invocation of a god (such as made by the high priest earlier), and so "It can be said... that Jesus was crucified by the Romans not merely for tactical and immediate political reasons of peace and good order in Jerusalem, but basically in the name of the state gods of Rome who maintained the *pax romana*."[40] And if one asks how a religious man like Jesus could be so dangerous to an empire, and have so much political influence, the answer is that religion touches and moves the foundations of society in a radical way. Prototypically, this appears in the fact that the chief priests prefer that Barabbas should be released and not Jesus, and Pilate acts accordingly, even though Barabbas is a well-known rebel. That is why we can say that the trial before Pilate was genuinely "political." As Ignacio Ellacuría remarks of it, "In short, Jesus represented a greater threat to the existing society and to its socio-political religious organization (than Barabbas)."[41]

4. Jesus' Death as a Consequence of His Mission

Why Jesus was killed is very clear in the Gospels. He was killed —like so many people before and after him—because of his kind of life, because of what he said and what he did. In this sense there is nothing mysterious in Jesus' death, because it is a frequent occurrence. There is indeed an immense tragedy in this, though not primarily because it happened to Jesus—who was later recognized as the Son of

God—but because it occurs to many human beings, also sons and daughters of God. The fact that it was the Son of God who was killed adds an incomparable depth to the tragedy, but it is not its first expression.

Jesus was killed because he got in the way, of course. But we need to be clear that this "getting in the way" is a general getting in the way, not specific, not particular charges against one or other group. It is the getting in the way that comes from the simple fact of a particular incarnation, but not—as we too easily say—in the world, but in a world that is anti-Kingdom, which acts against the Kingdom. Jesus became incarnate in this world, and not in another, he acted against this world of necessity—in the name of the Kingdom—and this world reacted against Jesus also of necessity. As Ellacuría says, "Jesus and his enemies represent two contrasting global visions, which seek to direct human life in different directions; they are two practical visions, which take the contradiction into the sphere of everyday life."[42] What happens is that the global (the Kingdom of God) is expressed in the everyday, the details of Jesus' life, but these in turn are the expression of the global vision, of the Kingdom of God. Because of this, seen in terms of the global vision, the specific judgments passed on Jesus are very deeply logical, and even the redactional changes are very well chosen.

In the religious trial, the chief priests invoke God to convict Jesus, and Jesus answers them with a practical blasphemy: "Acting as a destroyer of real forms of oppression is my way of invoking God."[43] In saying this he is saying that there are two ways of invoking God, and especially that there are two gods to be invoked, who are definitely opposed. In saying this Jesus is continuing his movement to show what God is like, which he is soon to do with his own life: there are gods who kill. The conclusion is terrifying: "the cross itself is incomprehensible without the collaboration of God-fearing judges."[44]

In the political trial, Jesus is accused of being an enemy of the emperor, an issue Jesus says nothing about in the Gospels. What is certain, however, is that Jesus did not see in the *pax romana*—he would have known something of the empire—a world after God's own heart, and his life, with more or less awareness on this point, objectively went counter to it. As a result, the sentencing of Jesus to death was not a regrettable error, as Bultmann claims,[45] but a necessity.

Jesus' death was not a mistake. It was the consequence of his life and this in turn was the consequence of his particular incarnation—in an anti-Kingdom which brings death—to defend its victims. If nothing more had happened after his death, if faith in Jesus had not arisen after the resurrection, his end would have been recorded in history like that of so many others. Doubtless the question would have remained why a just and innocent person should have died and, ultimately, the question raised by any death. And the answer, to anyone bold enough to ask such questions, would be simply, "History is like that." A religious person could add, "We must face it: sin has power, more power than God."

However, that was not the case with Jesus. His disciples insisted that he was alive, and living abundantly. One would think that after such a statement there would no longer be any need to continue wondering about Jesus' death. But exactly the opposite happened: precisely because after the resurrection he was recognized as the Son of God, the quest for the meaning of his death became more urgent, sharpening the question, "Why did Jesus die?"

Excursus 3

Jesus and Violence

Latin America is an extremely violent continent, primarily because of the omnipresent and cruel structural injustice, and also the repression by armies and death squadrons. It has also had—although the new world order now makes them historically less likely—armed revolutionary movement in which, for the first time, Christians have participated, and have done so because of their faith. Bishops and theologians have thrown light on both types of phenomena, but we also need to analyze, if only briefly, whether and how Jesus throws light on the problem of violence and its solution.

(a) The Latin American church has made a valuable contribution in tackling this question in a different way from usual and trying to give it a comprehensive solution,[1] and so has liberation theology, which, despite what is usually said about it, has as "one of its fundamental aims to achieve liberation from violence."[2]

The fundamental novelty consists in two points already sketched out in Medellín: (1) the production of a scale of types of violence and their historical and moral evil, beginning with structural injustice, which Medellín called "institution- alized violence" ("Peace," 16), and (2) the application of the principle of a legitimate response of insurrectionary violence "in the case of evident and prolonged 'tyranny that seriously works against the fundamental rights of man and which damages the common good of the country'" ("Peace," 19),[3] not only to persons, but to "clearly unjust structures" (*ibid*.) Nevertheless Medellín also warns very seriously of the grave evils of insurrectionary violence and prefers—for gospel reasons and because of the geo-political situation of the continent—the paths of peaceful revolution (*ibid*.).

In El Salvador, Archbishop Romero dealt with the subject in his third and fourth pastoral letters.[4] He began by ranking violence according to its historical and moral evil and its capacity for generating other types of violence. In these terms, the primary and worst of all types of violence is structural injustice, which generates, on the one hand, repressive violence by the state and ultra-right-wing groups to maintain it and, on the other hand, the violence of popular insurrections as a response. His moral judgment was absolutely condemnatory of the first two types, while on the third he followed the traditional doctrine of the just war. As a rider to all this, he stressed the primary necessity to fight first of all against structural injustice, the need at the same time to explore other avenues to a solution—in the case of El Salvador even in his time, dialogue—and in all circumstances the principle of never turning violence into a cult, even if it may be justified.[5]

Starting from theological premises, Ignacio Ellacuría addressed the issue on various occasions in all its complexity, analyzing violence in terms of the historical forms it has taken and seeking a solution, on the one hand, from philosophical and theological principles and, on the other, from what realism allows.[6] In short, he picks up, amplifies and deepens the following points from Medellín and Archbishop Romero: (1) Structures are not only unjust—something the church had been formally teaching for some time—but also formally violent; (2) The evil of this unjust violence is not to be measured in terms of an abstract common good—which was the usual practice—but in terms of the harmful consequences it produces for the mass of the population and on what they need for subsistence; (3) It is this type of unjust violence that of its nature generates the violence of repression (from armies and paramilitary groups) and this repression provides the *analogatum princeps* for terrorism—very often state terrorism—since terrorism must be judged objectively by the terror it seeks to cause and not in terms of the actions of what are conventionally called terrorist groups; (4) Revolutionary violence is the objective, and very often historically inevitable, response to the two previous forms of violence to affirm the denial of life denied, survival in the face of the empire of death and liberation from what prevents the achievement of a minimum level of human life. In principle, it represents the struggle of the oppressed and repressed for their liberation; (5) The revolutionary struggle must be guided by the principle of proportionality: cultural gains must be won by a cultural struggle, political gains by a political struggle.... Material life can only be taken when material life is at stake; (6) The theoretical legitimacy of this struggle must not lead to confusion about its evils, those of war in itself and—whatever the moral idealism—those of its negative sub-products: the dynamic of violent actions, the exaltation of making political power into an end when it should be a means. Ellacuría's conclusion, taking into account especially what is happening in El Salvador, is the following:

Armed struggle is always an evil, greater than people think, which can only, as a concession, be used when it is certain that it will avoid greater evils. But: this evil cannot be measured by a supposed abstract common good which makes peace, understood as the absence of war, the highest good, but by the necessary good of the poor majority. And this good of the poor majorities is, first and foremost, the satisfaction of their basic needs and effective respect for their basic rights. It is precisely the negation of this necessary good that permits and legitimates revolutionary violence, but by the same token becomes the basic criterion of its use.   To the extent that the struggle favours, extends and consolidates this good, this struggle is justified and, to a point, obligatory; to the extent that it is an obstacle to it, not in the short term but in the medium term, this struggle is unjustified in practice, whatever theoretical justification it might have.[7]

(b)   In this real context we must return to Jesus to see what light he may have to throw on the matter. It needs to be clear from the outset that in this case, as in others, it is not enough to look for a saying of Jesus to settle the issue, nor is it easy to find anything like a "teaching" of Jesus about insurrectionary armed violence, not even in the sense in which there can be said to be a teaching of Jesus about religion, wealth or power. Moreover, his expectation of the imminent coming of the Kingdom would also make it anachronistic. Nevertheless, we do need to analyze what light Jesus sheds on this complex problem.

I have already analyzed Jesus' judgment on originating violence (oppression by the powerful) and his struggle against it, and I shall not dwell on that here. What I want to look at now is his position on the anti-Roman armed groups of his day, whether or not they were formally constituted as such in his lifetime.[8]

Above all, there is an important point that must be stressed: the Gospels portray any number of attacks by Jesus on the scribes, the Pharisees, the priests and the rich, but there is no sign of such attacks or criticisms against armed groups or actions. It is also a fact that Jesus had Zealot sympathizers among his followers,[9] certainly Simon called "the Zealot" (Luke 6:15); probably Judas Iscariot, whose name may be a transliteration of *sicarius,* "knife-man"; "Boanerges," "son of thunder," a name which may have Zealot echoes, and perhaps Peter. The cleansing of the Temple, Jesus' fierce attack on Herod—"Tell that fox"—his irony at the expense of those who govern without mercy, could all be understood in terms of Zealot attitudes. In Luke 22:36 he tells his disciples to sell their cloaks and buy swords and in fact there were swords in the garden on the night of his arrest, according to Luke 22:49. Jesus' expression "carry your cross" may also derive from the Zealot movement, which demanded unconditional commitment to the end, to death on the cross.

On the other hand, it needs to be borne in mind that Jesus also called and admitted among his followers a publican, a collaborator with the Romans, and that he ate with such people as a sign of the approach of the Kingdom. On the problem of paying taxes, his position did not have the clarity of politically correct anti-Romans. And though in Luke he orders swords to be bought, in Matthew he condemns their use (Matt. 26:52). In the Sermon on the Mount, he breaks with the friend-enemy model popular with the zealots, does not call for vengeance, but for forgiveness ("Love your enemies and pray for those who persecute you," Matt. 5:44). Luke gives the supreme example of this when Jesus forgives his executioners (Luke 23:34). And where his own fate was concerned, Jesus—hard and verbally aggressive to the point of insult when defending the poor and oppressed—offered himself without resistance to his persecutors: "Have you come out with swords and clubs as if I were a bandit? When I was with you day after day in the temple, you did not lay hands on me" (Luke 22:52-3).

Jesus, then, did not himself belong to any type of armed group or advocate Zealot attitudes, although, from the point of view of the leaders of the state, appearing in the company of people who had belonged to such groups was not a recommendation. Nevertheless, his activity had obvious socio-political implications of a different stamp from the attitudes of the powerful and closer to those of the Zealots, which explains how he could be presented with some plausibility as close to those who sought the end of Roman domination by force of arms.

What the whole history of Jesus shows is not the apolitical character of the Kingdom he proclaims nor pure pacifism—understood as an absence of struggle—as the way to build it, but a different understanding of how to do it. The Kingdom he glimpses does not mean getting back into power, and so Jesus did not share the heady religious nationalisms or the theories of political theocracy upheld by the Zealots. This Kingdom, in contrast, was to be expressed and established by the best of human values: by the power of truth, justice and love. It was to be established—and this is the greatest difference from all other groups—by grace. At all events, this "obsession"—let's call it that—of Jesus' with the kingdom meant that he could appear close to others obsessed with liberation from the Romans. Cullmann may be wrong in his analysis of Zealotism, but he may be basically right in claiming that "The whole of Jesus' public life was in relation to Zealotism; this constituted, so to say, the background to his activity."[10]

(c) These facts, sufficiently clear in the Gospels, do not, however, even when taken as a whole, allow us to produce anything like a doctrine of Jesus on violence as a way of transforming society today,[11] and the expectation of the imminent coming of the Kingdom would make it anachronistic. Nevertheless I believe that Jesus' activity taken as a whole provides guiding principles for today,[12] and I will summarize them in four propositions:

First, Jesus' practice and teaching demand absolutely the unmasking of and a resolute struggle against the form of violence that is the worst and most generative of others because it is the most inhuman and the historical principle at the origin of all dehumanization: structural injustice in the form of institutionalized violence. It follows that we have to unmask the frequent attitude of being scandalized at revolutionary violence and the victims it produces without having been scandalized first and more deeply at its causes. The conventional violence of revolutionary or liberation movements is not in general a primary phenomenon— though aggression is part of human biology and psychology—[13] but derivative, and those who produce the primary violence and those who benefit from it should be very careful about being scandalized at response violence.

This is a present-day application of Jesus' condemnation of hypocrisy we examined earlier: the scribes and Pharisees are unjust themselves and generate oppression. Today we need to condemn the terrorists in white gloves, who hide the steel under the glove, and those who, once response violence has been triggered, "appropriate the surplus value generated by violence...a surplus value of fear."[14]

The struggle to unmask structural injustice—institutionalized violence—is, therefore, Jesus' first lesson on violence, and one that also lends credibility to the proclamation of the utopia of peace and condemnations of response violence.

Second, all violence, even violence that may be legitimate, is potentially dehumanizing: "Violence triggers an inner logic which in the end destroys those who exercise it."[15] Violence, even legitimate violence, generates a series of evils and harmful byproducts such as are produced in any struggle, especially armed struggle.[16] In Jesus' name we have to condemn all these evils on moral grounds, of course, but also in the name of accumulated historical wisdom, which Jesus made ample use of in the Gospels: "All who take the sword will perish by the sword" (Matt. 26:52).

What is certain is that Jesus' principles support Archbishop Romero's constant thesis: it is wrong to put all one's trust in violence to solve problems that have many aspects, it is wrong to let the military level dominate the struggle; violence should never be turned into a cult, which is not just a subjective problem, but one which arises out of the inherent dynamic of a struggle.

Third, Jesus offers as an alternative to violence the utopia of peace as a goal to achieve and as a means to achieving it. Let us remember that Jesus, who was in no way naive about the human condition, also frequently suggested utopias: be good as your heavenly father is good, be prepared to lose your life to win it, never take oaths, give all that you have in alms...; and Jesus puts forward the scandalous utopia of the beatitudes: happy are you the poor, the persecuted, the pure in heart....

At this fundamental level, peace and work for peace as a utopia is Jesus' first demand. The symbols of "peace," called for and exemplified by Jesus, vulnerability before one's persecutors, turning the other cheek, loving one's persecutors, forgiving one's executioners, are utopian and their value derives, not from being the keeping of a commandment (which might anyway be understood as an arbitrary demand), but from their being connected with the utopia of peace. The fact that Jesus insist on it stems from his conviction that utopia, though never wholly achievable, produces benefits and is humanizing. At all events, without utopian gestures, which means gestures of "grace," of peace, there is no breaking the spiral of violence—a gesture of "law."

These positive values are those that, in the long run, sustain the Kingdom of God and without them any social structure degenerates; even though it may begin as a positive sign of the Kingdom, it becomes something different and even contrary. Utopian principles cannot be realized in history, but they do initiate good things. This must have been Jesus' fundamental conviction, starting with the great utopia of the proclamation of the coming of the Kingdom and the love of his Father, God.

Finally, all violence always needs redemption. The first form of violence— the original and the origin—can only be redeemed when it is eradicated, which, historically, presupposes a counter-violence. The second form of violence—originated, the response—can be redeemed by actively doing violence to the dynamic of violence itself. We must add to this that, in Christian terms, all "redemption" has a specific structure with an element that is necessary, though by no means sufficient: bearing the evil from which we have to be redeemed. This means fighting against the roots of violence, but also bearing it. As historical violence comes from injustice, we have to bear injustice, which means taking the side of the victims of injustice and its violence, the poor majority, and bearing their fate: violence cannot be redeemed unless it is borne in some way.[17]

We cannot know for certain what Jesus would say today about violence. It is true that the church—which itself has been involved in wars and, in the past, often in cruel and unjust wars—has developed teaching to bring a little clarity into an area that is inherently obscure. Today I think that what "Jesus would say"—if it is legitimate to use the expression—has one very clear element and an element that cannot be deduced from what he said and did. It is clear that he would denounce the violence of injustice, which triggers all other forms of violence, and it is clear that he would say to armed groups what Archbishop Romero said. But I do not think that we can deduce from his life and his words what he would say about the legitimacy of an armed insurrectionary struggle.

Bishop Pedro Casaldáliga, when asked about this in El Salvador, usually replied with fear and trembling, that he would rather give his life than take someone else's, but that he has no right to forbid anyone to take up arms to defend the victims of horrible abominations and to try to change the centuries-old structures that make these possible. Nor were Archbishop Romero and Ignacio Ellacuría extreme pacifists or simplistic about the problem. Both made peace their basic thesis, but also admitted the antithesis of the possible legitimacy of an insurrection—at all events, they understood its inevitability—and always insisted on the synthesis: effective work and struggle for justice, and so for peace. And by their lives and violent deaths they tried to redeem the violence in El Salvador.

The violence of our world is so deep and so inhuman that it requires a response, and there is no doubt that this has to be historical, because the forms violence takes are historical. But violence is also so complex that there does not seem to be a single response that is adequate and embraces the innumerable problems it poses, even in terms of the gospel of Jesus. Nevertheless, although the gospel does not give us total clarity, it allows and obliges us to say something specific, which would be the specifically Christian contribution to solving the problem of violence. This contribution cannot be reduced to affirming or denying the possible legitimacy of an armed struggle against injustice. In my opinion, it cannot be said that an armed revolution is automatically anti-Christian, but this in itself does not tell us what is the most specifically Christian contribution to a revolution.

To say this with a specific example, since it makes no sense to talk about this outside a real context, I want to recall what Ignacio Ellacuría said in the situation of El Salvador, with centuries of massive injustice and repression. His words are both complicated and clear, but they convey the essential point. And they have the taste of a testament:

> [Christian faith] regards violence as intrinsically related with evil and only explicable in a world of sin in which in the last resort death prevails over life, egoism over altruism, thirst for revenge over love, grasping over giving. From a realistic point of view, it is inevitable, even for a Christian, to accept certain forms of violence, according to the principles and reservations described earlier, whenever it is non-terrorist liberating violence, related especially to liberation from the death which strikes the poor majority of the Third World.
>
> But it would seem that from a more Christian point of view, that of the perfection of discipleship of the historical Jesus, Christians who are doubly Christian in their lives and actions, the first and most audacious in combating all forms of injustice, should not use violence. It is not that violence is always and in all cases to be rejected by a Christian, but Christians as such do not normally give their specific witness through violence. Nor is it a matter of wanting to leave the "dirty work" to others, while the Christian remains one of the "pure" who don't dirty their hands. It is a matter of giving the fullest and most comprehensive witness that life is above death and love is above hate. This attitude would be acceptable and effective if Christians were willing to risk even martyrdom in defence of the poorest and in the fight against oppressors with the witness of their word and their life. There are different gifts in the church, and different callings from the Spirit. While the personal vocation of each individual must be respected, provided it is genuine, it does not seem audacious or cowardly to claim that the Christian vocation calls for the use of peaceful means, which does not mean less effort, to solve the problem of injustice and violence in the world, rather than violent means, however much these may sometimes be justified.[18]

Chapter 8

The Death of Jesus (2)
Why Jesus Died

In the last chapter I analyzed the historical and theological logic that led Jesus to his death: the battle of the divinities and their mediators. In this chapter I want to analyze the meaning of that death, why Jesus died. The question is obligatory for particular reasons, since it was not just any human being who died on the cross, but the Son of God.

The New Testament has a precise answer to this question *after* the resurrection. In general, it tries to explain two points, distinct though related. The first turns on the *explanation* of the fact in itself: how is it possible that Jesus should have died on the cross, that is, how can we reasonably come to terms with a fact that is inherently scandalous? The answer—which in the end is no answer—is that it is part of the mystery of God. The second question turns on the *meaning* of the fact: whether in this fact, inherently evil for Jesus and apparently negative for everyone, there is something good and positive; and the answer is that through the cross of Jesus God has bestowed salvation. The cross, in short, was something immensely positive. This is what I shall analyze shortly, but first I want to make three prior observations.

The first is that the first Christians, in their attempt to find some possible explanation and some possible meaning for the cross, were no different from any human being faced with the crosses of history, although this cross caused them particular perplexity. The second is that this approach, though perfectly comprehensible, can also be dangerous if thereby the scandal inherent in the cross of Jesus and the crosses of history is blunted or deprived of its force. The third observation is that both the explanation Christians offered for the cross and the meaning they assigned to it are, in the last resort, products of faith. No empirical argument compelled them, but their faith moved them to say, haltingly and obscurely, that, despite everything, something immensely positive took place on the cross. The New Testament's explanatory and soteriological models do not "prove" anything

219

in the strict sense. They are expressions of faith, more specifically of a hope-filled faith in God, in the ultimate goodness of God and history.[1]

1. The "Explanation" of the Cross in the Mystery of God

To the question "Why did Jesus die?," the first Christians gave various answers, which I shall discuss here in logical, not necessarily chronological, sequence.

A first step was to treat the cross as a prophet's fate (1 Thess. 2:14ff; Rom. 11:3), an explanation taken up later by the Gospels (Matt. 23:27; Mark 12:2ff), the Q source specifying that it was an example of Israel's rejection of the prophets (Luke 11:49ff; Matt. 23:34ff), and all the Synoptics adding that the prophet rejected will return to judge his executioners (Luke 12:8ff; Matt.10:32ff; Mark 8:38). This explanation is understandable, because it is based on Israel's own tradition and explains the early persecution suffered by the Christian communities themselves. So 1 Thessalonians 2:14ff. combines the persecution of the communities, the fate of the prophets and that of Jesus.

Explaining the death of Jesus as that of a prophet undoubtedly explains why Jesus was killed. Israel's history and that of the human race bear witness to this, and can be fitted into the battle of the gods. However, it does nothing to explain the meaning of this death. On this level, it is mere statement rather than explanation—that is the way history is: it kills prophets—but it does not explain the meaning of history's being like this. The problem is exacerbated in the case of Jesus' death because in the New Testament Jesus is not simply a prophet, but "more" than a prophet, and this "more" is essential to the new faith. The question therefore becomes, not "Why did a prophet die?," but "Why did the Messiah, the Son of God, die?"

A new step was taken in the explanation of the cross with the assertion that it had been foretold in the scriptures. This was an important theological argument for Christians who had come from the Jewish faith, and necessary for their apologetic when they presented themselves before Jews to preach a "crucified" Messiah. Why should it be a surprise that the Messiah should die by crucifixion if this was already prophesied in the scriptures? This comes through the beautiful account of the disciples on the road to Emmaus: "Oh, how foolish you are, and how slow of heart to believe all that the prophets have declared! Was it not necessary that the Messiah should suffer these things and then enter into his glory?" (Luke 24:25-6). This type of argument must have appeared at an early stage, because it is already present in the extremely ancient text 1 Corinthians 15:3-4: "Christ died for our sins in accordance with the scriptures." In Mark, Jesus himself—in what are called prophecies *ex eventu*, after the event—also interprets his death as foretold (Mark 8:31; 9:31; 10:33 par.).

But again, although there is an appeal to scripture, we are given no real explanation of the fact that Jesus, the Messiah and Son of God, should meet his end in this way. So the process takes a further step, the most theologal: Jesus died "according to the definite plan and foreknowledge of God" (Acts 2:23; 4:28). What is more, we are told that the cross "was necessary" (Luke 24:26), an expression that becomes a technical term to explain the reason for the cross.

We need to examine carefully this process of pushing back the explanation for the cross to God himself. The first thing it shows is that, in itself, the cross has no meaning directly discoverable by human beings. We may understand the historical reasons for the cross—Jesus' cross and those of so many others—but as to the "why?" of the cross, judgment is suspended. If there is an explanation, it must be hidden in God.

The appeal to God, in the last resort, to find a meaning for the cross at least in God, shows on the one hand the despair of human beings of finding this meaning for themselves, which is a sign of honesty in the face of what in itself is only tragedy and scandal. And it shows, on the other hand, the obstinacy of these same human beings in maintaining that there must be some meaning, in other words, that history is not absurd, that hope continues to be a possibility. They locate this meaning in God.

Both these things, our human despair of finding a meaning for the cross and the hope that it has one, even if only in God, are vitally important. At root, it is simply one way of answering the question of theodicy, Jesus' own question on the cross, and the question of so many human beings throughout history: how can we reconcile evil and injustice with God? I think the way the New Testament deals with this is very honest, because just when it seems to be giving the most convincing explanation of the reason behind the cross, it abandons all attempt at explanation—because the only answer is in God. And, on the other hand, in maintaining that the cross may have a meaning—even if only in God—it expresses the hope that absurdity is not the last word about history. However, this hope is not drawn from "knowledge" of the mystery, but from "faith" in this particular God with this particular plan.

The positive side of referring the meaning of the cross to God is clear, but it also has an element of danger. It is natural that Christians should look for an answer to this question "Why?," because an answer always brings some kind of peace for the intellect and calm for the emotions, even in the realm of atrocity. Going from uncertainty to knowledge is always felt as a relief. The danger is that in having our own answer to the "Why?"— God's plan—we dull the edge of the scandal of the cross, as I said before, because in the end it could not be explained. And it would be even more dangerous—as shown by all arguments based on Anselm—to claim to know that and how, in God, Jesus' cross becomes something logical and even necessary. If this were the case, Jesus' cross would not reveal anything about God, it would not give any help at all in understanding God. God, understood in advance, is what would make it possible to explain the cross, but then the cross would tell us nothing about God.

2. From the Cross as Scandal to the Cross as Salvation

Even if the "Why?" of the cross were explained by the appeal to the mystery of God, there would still remain another obvious question: why was this God's plan and not something different? This question is not a mere theoretical exercise or pure creaturely arrogance. Furthermore, for Christians coming from the Jewish tradition it was inescapable, for a particular reason. The God whose plan was Jesus' cross is not just any God, nor is his mystery just any mystery. For the Jews and for Jesus, God is a good God, who frees the oppressed, who wants his Kingdom to come; he is a God whom Jesus calls Father. This essential goodness of God does not rule out his being mysterious, nor that he should have an unfathomable plan, but that a good God's plan should be for his Son to die on a cross seems a cruelty incompatible with his goodness. The goodness of God and the bare fact of his Son's cross seem incompatible. So the intellectual question—why did Jesus die?—leads naturally to the salvation question: what did Jesus die for?—what good, if any, is there in Jesus' cross, if this was a good God's plan?

The formal answer, from very early on, is that Jesus' cross is something supremely good because of its effects on human beings. In the language of the whole New Testament, through Jesus' cross, God saved us from sin. In the formulation of the primitive *kerygma*, Jesus was crucified "that he might give repentance to Israel and forgiveness of sins" (Acts 5:31). Jesus crucified is the salvation of Israel (John 11:50), and so he is the salvation of the "nation" (John 11:51ff.), of "all" (2 Cor. 5:14ff; 1 Tim. 2:6), of the "world" (John 6:51). In this way we have come from the first question, "Why the cross?", to the second, "What was the cross for?" This salvational "what for?" was to occupy the New Testament and subsequent theology. Before analyzing it, however, I want to say two things about this method.

The first is that the good that God brings through the cross is salvation, but salvation came to be understood in the specific sense of salvation from sin. "Salvation from sin" was to be the positive all-embracing term, in the singular, for what the crucified Jesus brings, as distinct from the plural salvations brought by the Kingdom of God proclaimed by Jesus. The positive aspect of this concentration is that it functions as something all-embracing, and certainly it refers to a crucial and determining dimension of human existence. The danger is that within this all-embracing salvation the plurality of salvations brought about by Jesus of Nazareth is not made explicit: salvation from any sort of oppression, inner and outer, spiritual and physical, personal and social.

The second point is that there are two levels in this argument that need to be distinguished. That God wishes to save and wishes to do this through Jesus was not in doubt for the first Christians. But what specifically in the cross makes it a mediation of salvation, and in particular, of forgiveness of sins, required explanation. Here, then, we are moving on two levels: on the level of faith, the deeper level, where we affirm that there is salvation in the cross, and on the level of analysis, the more theological level, where we have to show how there can be salvation in the cross.

There is nothing to object to in this approach, but two dangers need to be mentioned. The first is to think that these models really "explain" the salvation the cross as such brings, when they are only a way of saying, reasonably, that the cross manifested God's saving love. The second is, again, dulling the edge of the scandal of the cross in itself: there is now nothing scandalous in God's letting his Son die because only in that way could he have achieved the greater good of salvation. This presupposes that before the cross we already know who God is and, here, specifically, how a God who wanted to save human beings from their sins would have to act.

Let us look at the main theoretical models the New Testament uses to present the relationship between the cross and salvation. On this point, as I have said previously, I have nothing to add to what others have said, though subsequently I shall try to discuss these models in terms of today.

(a) Sacrifice

In various places in the New Testament the figure and action of Jesus are described in cultic sacrificial language: sacrificed paschal lamb (1 Cor. 5:7), the lamb who "ransoms" (Rev. 5:9), the "blood" of Christ, which points to the sacrifice of the cross (Rom. 3:25; 5:9; Eph. 1:7; 2:13), the blood shed, for "you" or for "many" in the words of the Last Supper (Mark 14:24; Matt. 26:28; Luke 22:20). It is well known that the Letter to the Hebrews, using cultic sacrificial language, declares that all sacrifice and all priesthood both before and after Christ has been abolished, but, even with the radical transformation the Letter brings, it uses sacrifice as a theoretical model to explain the saving importance of Jesus' cross. Let us look, then, at what the model means in itself.

Both in the Old Testament and in religion in general, sacrifice is one of the human institutions created to solve the central problem of human beings: how, as limited creatures, to bridge the infinite distance separating them from God, a distance which, moreover, has become qualitatively, intrinsically unbridgeable, because of the sin of creatures. Sacrifice is what bridges this distance, according to the following logic. Seen in terms of human action, in sacrifice human beings present to God what is most vital and dear to them and in this way recognize God's sovereignty. In order to offer sacrifice to God they separate the offering from the world of creatures, introduce it into the sacred world, make it sacred ("sacrifice" = *sacrum facere*, "to make sacred"), and not only set it apart from the profane world, but even destroy it. In this way human beings believe they can gain access to God, and this is symbolized in their eating part of the victim offered—which is now God's possession—and sprinkling the altar of God and the people with the blood of the victim. And, seen from God's side, if God accepts the sacrifice—and this is the crucial element—then the unbridgeable distance has been bridged, and human beings enter into communion with God: there is salvation.

This theoretical sacrificial model is the one the New Testament uses to explain how Jesus' cross can bring benefits and salvation. The Letter to the Hebrews radically criticizes the way Old Testament sacrifices were carried out, but maintains the terminology of sacrifice, and even a revised theoretical understanding, to explain the saving effect of the cross. The essence of the critique of Old Testament sacrifice is that these sacrifices cannot overcome the separation between human beings and God, because God did not accept them and so they do not achieve the effect expected of sacrifice. Jesus' sacrifice, on the other hand, produces communion, because he has been accepted by God, has "entered into heaven itself" (9:24) and so can save (7:25). He appears "on our behalf" (9:24), has secured "eternal redemption" (9:12), "bringing many children to glory" (2:10), bestows sanctification (10:10), enables us to "enter the sanctuary," "approach" God (10:19ff). And in terms of salvation from sin, the Letter says that Christ "has made purification for sins" (1:3; 10:11-14), purified "our consciences from dead works to worship the living God" (9:14), and "from an evil conscience" (10:22). The basic point is that Christ's sacrifice, unlike other sacrifices, has been accepted, and therefore can bring salvation. The same logic is presupposed in the other New Testament passages that stress the newness and superiority of Christ's sacrifice: it is a "fragrant" sacrifice (Eph. 5:2), "without defect or blemish" (1 Pet. 1:19).

We shall see later *why* Jesus' sacrifice—Jesus himself historically sacrificed— has been accepted by God, according to the New Testament, and so can save.[2] What I was concerned to point out here was that the New Testament uses sacrifice as a theoretical model to explain that the cross was not an absurdity, but salvation.

(b) The New Covenant

Another explanatory model of the cross's saving effect is that of the covenant. The idea that the covenant between God and human beings is salvation is essential to the Old Testament faith, and one of its most specific ways of describing salvation. Since the covenant was sealed by the shedding of blood, Jesus' cross could be interpreted as the blood of the new covenant. According to the logic of the comparison, Hebrews recalls that "not even the first covenant was inaugurated without blood" (9:18), and in the logic of superiority it says that in Jesus a covenant superior to that of Sinai was made (8:6), a new covenant, foretold in Jeremiah 31:31-4, a text quoted in Hebrews 8:6-13 and 10:16ff.

This understanding of Jesus' cross as salvation is also offered in the accounts of the Last Supper, which are already theological interpretations. First, Jesus' words over the cup are interpreted in a sacrificial sense as an action for the benefit of human beings, blood "poured out for you," say the Synoptics, and Matthew adds "for the forgiveness of sins." However, in addition the three Synoptics and 1 Corinthians 11:25 explain that this blood produces a new and definitive covenant between God and human beings.

This theoretical model of sacrifice includes the salvation produced by sacrifice, forgiveness of sins, but in itself the model includes a wider-ranging salvation, as can be seen from the text of Jeremiah 31:31-4 on the new covenant. What this new covenant is we learn from the Letter to the Hebrews in the passage that follows the quotation of this text from Jeremiah. The new covenant is a new way of life for those graced by it. In short it is "full assurance of faith", a "confession of hope without wavering" and "love and good deeds" (Heb. 10:22-4; cf. also chapters 3, 4 and 11 on faith, 12 and 13 on hope, and 12:14 - 13:21 on charity).

(c) The Figure of the Suffering Servant

Another model used to explain the salvation brought by the cross is that of the mysterious figure of the Servant of Yahweh, described in Isaiah 42:1-9; 49:1-6; 50:4-11; 52:13 - 53:12.

The New Testament makes frequent use of these passages to explain important phenomena of the election and earthly mission of Jesus and his way of carrying it out. Parts of Isaiah 42:1-9 are explicitly quoted in Matthew 12:18-21; 11:10, and implicitly in John 1:32-4 (election), Matthew 3:17 and John 8:12 (to be a light for the Gentiles), and Luke 4:18; 7:23 (to open the eyes of the blind).

The last song—the novel, scandalous one, which presents the Servant as suffering—was at first probably used only to provide a few phrases to describe the way Jesus died: "like a sheep he was led to the slaughter" (Isa. 53:7, quoted in Acts 8:32), "and he was counted among the lawless" (Isa. 53:13, spoken by Jesus in Luke 22:37, to show the fulfillment of scripture).

These last references were very useful to record and describe "biblically" how Jesus died, but not to explain the meaning of his death, because in none of these quotations do we yet find the most novel and scandalous element of Servant theology. The Servant is the product of our actions: "he was wounded for our transgressions, crushed for our iniquities" (v.5), "stricken for the transgression of my people" (v. 8b) "bore the sin of many" (v. 12), "shall bear their iniquities" (v. 11), and through this brings salvation , "upon him was the punishment that made us whole" (v. 5), "by his bruises we are healed" (v. 5), "... shall make many righteous" (v. 11), "made intercession for the transgressors" (v. 12). And the Servant himself is glorified: "when you make his life an offering for sin, he shall see his offspring" (v. 10).

These passages are unique in the Old Testament, and were not easily applied to Jesus, because they assert that a human being sheds blood, innocently, in the place of and for the benefit of those who deserved to do so, interceding for them, for their justification and healing. In Israel, before, during and after Jesus' time, such an idea was unthinkable, because human sacrifices were forbidden.[3]

It is therefore not easy to discover how the New Testament came to apply this Servant Song to Jesus. Possibly it was done by non-Palestinian Jews in Syrian Antioch, because there was a tradition there that was similar in a way, though not exactly the same, to that of the Suffering Servant. This tradition can be found in the fourth book of Maccabees, which tells the story of the struggles of the pious Jews against King Antiochus IV Epiphanes, who forced the Jews to reject their religious traditions. As is well known, many Jews died in this persecution, but something new and specific happened that forced the Jews to rethink their faith: innocent children died. Their innocence, which made them the same as the Servant, provoked the inevitable question of the meaning of their deaths: what meaning can death inflicted on an innocent have for a believer in Yahweh?

The book's answer is twofold. On the one hand, it says that these dead people will receive justice from God: they will rise again. However, on the other hand, it looks for some positive meaning in the very fact of innocent death: the innocent did not die for their personal sins, but as substitutes and in expiation for the people.

This tradition may have helped to link Jesus with the Suffering Servant. It appears in various layers of the New Testament. The ancient hymn in Romans 3:25 (composed in Antioch) says of Jesus that "God put [him] forward as a sacrifice of atonement by his blood ... [and] passed over the sins previously committed." Paul also says, "He made him to be sin who knew no sin, so that in him we might become the righteousness of God" (2 Cor. 5:21), that is, God made the curse inherent in sin fall on Jesus. Galatians 3:13 connects the curse with "hanging on a tree." In John the theology of the Servant is connected with that of the expiatory lamb of Leviticus: "Here is the lamb of God, who takes away the sin of the world" (John 1:29). In 1 John, Christ is called "the atoning sacrifice for our sins" (2:2; 4:10). In Hebrews, Christ makes "a sacrifice of atonement for the sins of the people" (2:17), and in 1 Peter we are told that "he himself bore our sins in his body on the cross, so that, free from sins, we might live to righteousness" (2:24).

The fundamental idea is repeated throughout the New Testament. Jesus is innocent, the sufferings he bears are those that others ought to bear and by bearing them he becomes salvation for others. Once again, this is not an explanation, but a profession of faith: something positive took place on Jesus' cross.[4]

(d) Salvation through the Cross in Paul

I have mentioned some of Paul's arguments in the previous sections, but he also has other ways of stressing the saving effect of the cross.

(i) Above all, Jesus' cross is central, alongside and "in spite of," his insistence on the resurrection. Its centrality derives from its being the way Paul directs the Christians to Jesus of Nazareth and corrects and criticizes the fundamental distortion of Christianity, defined in general terms in his criticism of the Corinthians: "No-one speaking by the Spirit of God ever says 'Let Jesus be cursed!'" (1 Cor. 12:3). Christian life cannot consist of the enthusiasm of the Corinthians, who thought they were already living the risen life—and so did not wait for the resurrection—and in order radically to correct their talkative enthusiasm he points them to Christ crucified. His approach can be seen in two eloquent phrases at the beginning of the letter: "Jews demand signs and Greeks desire wisdom, but we proclaim Christ crucified, a stumbling block to Jews and foolishness to Gentiles, but to those who are the called, both Jews and Greeks, Christ the power of God and the wisdom of God" (1 Cor. 1:22ff), which he confirms with a personal declaration: "I decided to know nothing among you except Jesus Christ, and him crucified" (1 Cor. 2:2) and illustrates from their experience: "I came to you in weakness and in fear and much trembling" (1 Cor. 2:3).

This preaching of the crucifixion is essential because the truth of the faith depends on it. But it is also saving, because the very fact of its being scandalous makes the cross an authentic "revelation" of God. The cross becomes an unmasking of all sinful human excuses for not accepting the revelation of the truth about God. You can accept God or not, Paul says, but if you accept him on the cross, scandalous and unsuspected as it is, then you have really accepted God and have accepted that he himself has showed himself to us, and not that we reached him by our own efforts.

(ii) In the second Letter to the Corinthians Paul stresses the saving power of the cross without offering "proofs" of it, but with incomparable power. Rather than explaining, he glosses, so to say, what salvation through the cross consists of. His synthesis is that the negative aspects of human existence have become positive. Christ "died for all, so that those who live might live no longer for themselves" (5:15). "Though he was rich, yet for your sake he became poor, so that by his poverty you might become rich" (8:9). "He was crucified in weakness, but lives by the power of God. For we are weak in him, but in dealing with you we will live with him by the power of God" (13:4). "In Christ God was reconciling the world to himself, not counting their trespasses against them, and entrusting the message of reconciliation to us" (5:19).

These are not attempts to explain how the cross brings salvation, but a grateful proclamation of the fact: the deepest weakness has been transformed into strength, poverty into wealth, egoism into altruism, division into reconciliation, negative into positive.

(iii) Finally, Paul tries to explain that the cross saves because it has freed us from the law, which has become a curse. For Paul the law comes from God and is good; sometimes he calls it a training for Christ. But the existential human situation—and Paul's own experience as a Pharisee, a fervent Jew—convinces him that the law has become a curse: the law prescribes what one should do, but does not give one the strength to do it. The law shows human beings their radical inability, their condemnation to failure: "scripture has imprisoned all things under the power of sin" (Gal. 3:22); "All who rely on works of the law are under a curse" (3:10).

What "the law" illustrates here is the existential situation of human anguish and failure, and what Paul wants to emphasize is that Christ has freed us from this situation. Since the situation of condemnation comes from the law, Christ's liberation is analyzed in terms of its relation with the law. What enabled Christ to free us is the fact that he himself was "born under the law, in order to redeem those who were under the law" (Gal. 4:4-5). This liberation became real on the cross. "Christ redeemed us from the curse of the law, by becoming a curse for us" (Gal. 3:13).

3. The Manifestation of What is Pleasing to God

The New Testament asserts, as we have been seeing, that Jesus' cross brings salvation, and to explain this its theologians make use of various theoretical models, some better-known (sacrifice, covenant), others more surprising (the Servant's vicarious expiation), others again totally new (liberation from the law). I have insisted, however, that, strictly speaking, these models do not explain anything, and so I have to state, at least, the essential point they were trying to make in asserting that the cross brings salvation, and what this can say to us today.

First of all, it is important to emphasize that the New Testament does not insist that the pain of the cross, in itself, produces salvation. After a detailed analysis of the texts, González Faus concludes that "the terms that express redemption in the New Testament refer only to the fact of redemption, and not to the formal principle or the redemptive mechanism."[5] In other words, the New Testament neither affirms, still less concentrates on the idea that because there was suffering there is redemption, and therefore neither a cult of suffering nor masochism find a justification in it, still less the idea that God had to pay someone a heavy ransom.

What the New Testament does emphasize—and here there is a point of contact with the logic of the theoretical model of sacrifice—is that Jesus was pleasing to God, and was therefore accepted by God, just as sacrifices, to be effective, have to be accepted by God. Now in the New Testament what was pleasing to God was the whole of Jesus' life—in the words of the Letter to the Hebrews, a life in faithfulness and mercy—and what Jesus' cross highlights, beyond any doubt, is that this is how Jesus' life was.

Given the human condition and the realities of history, faithfulness and mercy are phenomena that depend for their existence on being tested. Initial generic faithfulness and mercy face the test and in the test either cease to be faithfulness and mercy or emerge triumphant from the test and become real. In simple words, the New Testament says that what is pleasing to God has appeared on earth because a life of love to the end has appeared.

It is a conviction derived from accumulated historical experience that love has to go through suffering. We may wonder—or protest at the fact—why things are like this, but they are like this and therefore anyone who tries to perform mercy toward others and save them has to be prepared for suffering. This insight may be phrased in ways bordering on cruelty—"There is no salvation without the shedding of blood," as the church Fathers said—or be processed through an explanatory theoretical model, without being explained, as I have insisted. But however it is formulated, the insight retains its force. It is therefore understandable up to a point that human beings should have associated salvation with bloodshed, and so with sacrifice. Salvation always presupposes the recomposition of something that has been destroyed, and this recomposition is always historically costly. "Blood" is the symbol of the burden involved in any salvation that really constructs what has been destroyed. Or, in different terms, sin has a negative power that shatters this completely, and to check this power Jesus accepted it on the cross.

What we must not do is theoretically to equate love and sacrifice, still less assert that God was pleased by or even demanded Jesus' cross. The cross, as a historically necessary component of love, is part of its historical fullness, and what God was pleased by was this fullness of love. This means that what is pleasing to God is not just one event, the incarnation in theology of Greek stamp, the cross in the Latin tradition. All these specific instances say something important, but they are guided by an interest, conscious or unconscious, in trying to understand how Jesus brings salvation through a specific act or event.

The incarnation, then, is "drawing near," something that can be interpreted through the fundamental experience that "closeness," "welcome," is already salvation; or, in the Greek philosophical outlook, the incarnation can be understood as a "participation" in human nature, from which we get its famous maxim: "What has not been accepted cannot be redeemed." In this way the cross is sacrifice, death, the supreme expression of negativity, acceptance of which, in Latin theology, is the condition that alone makes it possible to overcome the negativity, though the specific models used to explain this have an excessively legalistic and formal ring to them. Both explanations contain an important insight, but they maintain their validity only if they are taken together to express the whole of Jesus' life: real incarnation in a world of sin is what leads to the cross, and the cross is the product of a real incarnation.

Jesus' life as a whole, not one of its elements, is what is pleasing to God. This is what the Gospels tell us descriptively and the Letter to the Hebrews analytically. This principle should be used as the basis for a reinterpretation of the Servant Songs as a whole—not just the last song—if they are to be used as theoretical models for understanding the salvation Jesus brings. We then see that the Servant who comes to establish justice and law (first songs) becomes in the end the Suffering Servant (last song); and, vice versa, the Suffering Servant is no other than the Servant who establishes justice and law. It is this whole Servant whom we must proclaim as "light" and "salvation."

The question may now arise of what importance for our salvation there is in the fact that Jesus is "what is pleasing to God." Well, if this is what is pleasing to God, it is not something arbitrary, much less cruel, so its importance for salvation consists in the fact that what God wants human beings to be has appeared on earth: "He has told you, O mortal, what is good; and what does the LORD require of you but to do justice, and to love kindness and to walk humbly with your God" (Mic. 6:8).

The Jesus who is faithful even to the cross is salvation, then, at least in this sense: he is the revelation of the *homo verus*, the true and complete human being, not only of the *vere homo*, that is of a human being in whom, as a matter of fact, all the characteristics of true human nature are present. This *homo verus* is depicted by the New Testament as one who "went about doing good," who was "faithful and merciful," who came "not to be served but to serve."

The very fact that true humanity has been revealed, contrary to all expectations, is in itself good news and therefore is already in itself salvation: we human beings now know what we are, because the truth about ourselves, which we sinfully kept captive, has been liberated. And since the central core of this true humanity is Jesus' great love for human beings, we can assert that love exists and that not only does evil makes its presence felt on this earth, but we are also enfolded in love. How powerful this love is, is another matter, but at least—and this least is a most—human beings have been able to see love on earth, to know what they are, and what they can and should be.

As often occurs in Latin America, in the presence of the martyrs, when human beings understand that there has been love, they understand it as good news, as something deeply humanizing. "It is good for human beings that Archbishop Romero spent time on earth." They also understand it as an invitation to continue it—remember the "testamentary formula" of the Last Supper: Jesus leaves us the legacy of being Servants like him. On this principle, Jesus' cross as the culmination of his whole life can be understood as bringing salvation. This saving efficacy is shown more in the form of an exemplary cause than of an efficient cause. But this does not mean that it is not effective: there stands Jesus, faithful and merciful to the end, inviting and inspiring human beings to reproduce in their turn the *homo verus*, true humanity.

4. The Credibility of God's Love

Everything that has been said so far is still not the last word about the saving efficacy of Jesus' cross, nor the most characteristic element of the New Testament's interpretation of the cross. For the New Testament, salvation comes from God himself, and so we have to ask what is the definitive message of Jesus' cross about the God who saves.

First of all, the New Testament does not say that Jesus' life and cross were necessary to change God's attitude to human beings, to make him change from being a justly angry God to a duly appeased God. Neither could the shedding of blood require this, nor did even the appearance of Jesus, the one pleasing to God, have to compel this. The New Testament's assertion is bold and unprecedented: God himself took the initiative to make himself present to save in Jesus, and Jesus' cross is not, therefore, only what is pleasing to God, but that in which God expresses himself as pleasing to human beings. It is not efficient causality, but symbolic causality. Jesus' life and cross are that in which God's love for human beings is expressed and becomes as real as possible.

This is a fact. There is no doubt that the New Testament interprets the life and cross of Jesus in this way. Jesus is God's initiative, and so is—scandalously—the cross: "God did not withhold his own Son ... for all of us" (Rom. 8:32), "God gave his only Son" (John 3:16). Whatever the impact, the fear, unease or protest these words may cause, there is no room for doubt that the initiative came from God himself. Jesus did not make God change; Jesus is the historical sacrament in which God expresses his irrevocable saving change toward us. And if, despite the dizziness these words produce, we continue reading the New Testament, we discover why God's initiative took this form: "God so loved the world that he gave his only Son" (John 3:16); "God's love was revealed among us in this way: God sent his only Son" (1 John 4:9).

The New Testament's final word about Jesus' cross is that in it God's love was expressed. This language of love includes more than the language of "redemption," "salvation from sins." It includes these, but it goes beyond them and, above all, it offers—without explaining it or trying to explain it—the great theoretical explanatory model: love saves, and the cross is the expression of God's love. That is why Paul says, "He who did not withhold his own Son..., will he not with him also give us everything else?" (Rom. 8:32). And that is why John says, "God did not send the Son into the world to condemn the world, but in order that the world might be saved through him" (John 3:17).

Jesus' cross is the expression of God's love, and the novel and unexpected nature of this affirmation makes it a better confirmation than anything else of the initiative and credibility of God's love. "In this is love, not that we loved God but that he loved us and sent his Son to be the atoning sacrifice for our sins" (1 John 4:10). "While we still were sinners Christ died for us" (Rom. 5:8). And this is where we find the credibility of God's love, the proof of God's love for us (Rom. 5:8). Christ did not die for a just person—something that is rare, but does happen—but "died for the ungodly" (Rom. 5:6ff).

This is the New Testament's fundamental affirmation. This affirmation does not "explain" anything, but it says everything. In Jesus' life and cross God's love has been displayed. And God chose this way of showing himself, because he could not find any clearer way of telling us human beings that he really wills our salvation. The New Testament's language is powerful: not even what was dearest to God, his own Son, placed a limit on God's showing his love for human beings. Not sparing the Son is the way of saying that there is no restraint on God's love for human beings.

I have already said that these words are not a theoretical explanation of the "how" of salvation, but no others can express better what God's love is. And if human beings do not understand that, by preferring us to his own Son, God wanted to show us his love, nothing will convince them of it. Their reason may continue to ask why God chose this way, may protest and rebel against this God, but what it cannot do is deny the force of the argument: nothing, absolutely nothing was an obstacle to God's indicating his definitive, saving, welcoming, irrevocable yes to this world.

Something of this can be sensed in history. Loves appear that have no limits, and the clearest way of showing this is that nothing becomes an obstacle for the love. If a mother freely lets her son go—although she foresees that she will lose him— to defend a people's cause, one may think many things of her, but there can be no doubt that that mother loves that people. "Do to us what you will and we will still love you. Bomb our homes and threaten our children; send your hooded perpetrators of violence... and drag us out on some wayside road, beating us and leaving us half-dead, and we will still love you" (Martin Luther King).

What does Jesus' cross really say? It says that God has irrevocably drawn near to this world, that he is a God "with us" and a God "for us." And to say this with the maximum clarity he lets himself be a God "at our mercy." This is what the New Testament writers saw. There can be no logic here, only faith. Understandably, they tried logic, and put forward the theoretical models I have analyzed, but end with faith: Jesus' cross saves because in it the love of God for human beings has appeared with maximum clarity.

In the next chapter I shall examine who this God of Jesus' cross is. Now I want to say simply that he is a God of love. And if the question still presses, what type of love is this, what capacity does it have to save, the answer on this point is extremely ambivalent. The cross says nothing directly about the power of God's love, but says with the greatest clarity that it is a credible love because of its absolute closeness. Again, reason will continue to ask what use a credible but impotent love is, and the answer is anything but easy. Only the resurrection of Jesus—if one believes in it—will break the ambivalence, but there is something in a credible love that may be impotent, but attracts human beings by being good and saving, and has its own efficacy. Years ago Dietrich Bonhoeffer said it: "Only a suffering God can save us."[6] And history repeats itself. "Not any life is an occasion for hope, but this life of Jesus' is, since he took upon himself, in love, the cross and death."[7] "How well Christ identifies himself with the sufferings of our peoples!"[8]

There is something in a pure and credible love, even if it is impotent, that—paradoxically—generates hope in the power of love as such. "The day will come when we win freedom, and not just for ourselves: we will defeat you, we will conquer your hearts and your consciences, and in this way our victory will be doubled" (Martin Luther King). In this way God wishes to show us his love on the cross and so save us.

Chapter 9

The Death of Jesus (3)
The Crucified God

In this chapter and the next, "The Crucified People," we really come to a fundamental issue. The historical reason for Jesus' death may be clear, but the questions remain why things are like this and why there are innocent victims in history. The New Testament may interpret the meaning of this death as the greatest expression of God's love, but the question always remains why God did not find a different way than this of showing his love. In essence, we are left with the question why sin has power and why not even God—if he wishes to be faithful to the condition of human beings—can escape this law of history.

If my task is to formulate dilemmas that force thinking to advance, I do not think a more radical problem can be imagined than "Why does sin have power?" In comparison with this all the other problems that preoccupy the human mind—reconciling creator and creature, the one and the many, subject and object—pale into insignificance. Maybe this supreme paradox of the power of sin cannot be thought about in absolute terms, nor even in the way the others are thought about. Nevertheless it is good to think about it, because this thinking, which is not the product of admiration, but of perplexity and protest, introduces us better than anything else to what is specifically Christian, a risen one who was first crucified.

From the outset we have to remember that the cross in itself is a scandal for reason. It is a scandal for the death it embodies, though reason can soften this by seeing it as a natural phenomenon, given the human condition. It is a scandal in a higher degree in that it involves death unjustly inflicted on a just and innocent person by human beings. And it is a scandal in the highest degree because the one who died on the cross was Jesus, the person who is recognized in faith as the Son of God and as God. It is true that the resurrection can bring some relief to reason, since in this case at least "the executioner has not triumphed over the victim," but we are still left with the question why even the Son of God became a victim of the sin of this world. In this precise sense Jesus' resurrection further deepens the scandal of the cross. As Leonardo Boff asks, "How do we reconcile the paradox of

233

the death-curse of Jesus (cf. Deut. 21:23) and the glorious resurrection when both have the same divine origin?"[1] In other words, it is necessary to dwell on the scandal of the cross in itself and not to rush to dissolve it through the "solution" of the resurrection.

It is necessary because history goes on producing crosses—in El Salvador it has produced 75,000—and there is nothing good in getting used to this tragedy or coming to terms with it, or trying to find a quick answer to it. Let us hope that these crosses do some good; in fact, they do produce many positive results: hope, commitment, solidarity . . . , and let us hope that they help liberation. But they exist, and the possible and actual service they do to life and liberation should not conjure away the horror that history is like this and that not even God changes things. Bishop Pedro Casaldáliga says:

> For some time—since, in fact, I have come into everyday contact with the native populations—I have felt the disappearance of whole peoples as an absurd mystery of historical iniquity which reduces me to the most abject state of faith. "Lord, why have you abandoned them?" How can the Father of Life, the Spirit who creates all culture, allow these annihilations?[2]

This is the question about the ultimate meaning of history and the question of theodicy: how can a good and powerful God be reconciled with the horrors of history? And, once more, it is not appropriate to rush in with the well-known theoretical answers to these questions: God puts things right in another life, God brings good out of evil, God respects human freedom, because otherwise the metaphysical monstrousness would be even greater. It is good to try and find relief for a scandalized reason, but it is bad if this relief should eliminate the scandal.

To dwell on the scandal of the cross is necessary, but it is also salutary, not to encourage any cult of suffering or provide a basis for some conceptual Platonic or Hegelian dialectic—if the abyss of the negative (the cross) was so deep, how lofty will the positive (the resurrection) be!—but simply to be honest about the world, the first step in any humanization. It is salutary for theoretical reasons, because the cross makes all theological themes—God, Christ, sin, grace, hope, love,—radically Christian. As has been said, Jesus' cross is either the end of all theology or it is the beginning of a new and radically Christian theology, in a different realm from the atheism and theism that always envisage God in correspondence and continuity with humanity.[3] It is so also in fact. It is true, if surprising, that those who accept historical crosses in the most radical way and make the least attempt to glorify them, those who least get used to them and least accept "cheap" answers to the question of theodicy,[4] are the ones who most seriously commit themselves to suppressing historical crosses—even if this brings them too to the cross—and they are the ones who most commit themselves to this mysterious God who was on the cross.

For all these reasons I regard this chapter as extremely important in any christology, and also as extremely personal, whether one admits it or not, because in reflecting on God and the cross, whether one knows it or not, one is saying which God one believes in, one is setting out one's own vision of history and human beings. For these reasons, I think that, in this chapter above all, it is not enough to use and interpret biblical and patristic texts and quotations from the countless theologies that deal with the subject, as if one could find a text or a set of texts that would silence the question with an explanation. Of course one may decide that one exegesis, one theological interpretation, is more reasonable than another, but not in the last resort because they explain the issue conceptually once and for all, but because in particular texts one can see most clearly reflected what the writer thinks his or her own faith is in the presence of the ultimate question of the cross.

Since this is a very personal chapter, I hope I shall be allowed to add a final reflection. What moves me to go deeply into the scandal of the cross is not that I am proposing a cult of suffering or masochism, or that I want to diminish the resurrection—some critics say I insist too much on what Paul says about the crucified Jesus and not enough on what he says about the risen Christ. Nor am I led by fidelity to a particular Christian tradition—some critics suggest that I am very influenced by the Lutheran tradition, on the assumption, which sometimes becomes a real obsession, that no one can have an idea that isn't connected to some earlier idea.

No doubt, this, like any other christology, is influenced more by some traditions than others, but the fundamental influence comes from the real crucified world. I do not think one has to have read a word of Paul or Luther or Urs von Balthasar or Moltmann—although undoubtedly their writings help us to conceptualize the cross in a particular way—to understand this scandal if one lives in the world where historical crosses are everyday events. The only thing one has to do is not to ignore them. "Woe to the people who forget their martyrs!" Don Pedro Casaldáliga keeps saying. My version is: "Woe to human beings and believers if they forget the crucifixion!"

If we do not forget those who are being crucified today, it will be more difficult to forget the crucified Jesus. But if we keep him in mind, of necessity we must ask about God. And, although the formulation, like all formulations, is limited, and is open to questioning, I think there is no substitute for calling this God "the crucified God." Allow me to say this with a very personal experience. On 16 November 1989, when the Jesuits of the Central American University were murdered outside their house, the body of Juan Ramón Moreno was dragged inside the residence into one of the rooms, mine. In the movement one book from the bookcase in the room fell on to the floor and became soaked in Juan Ramón's blood. That book was *The Crucified God*. It is a symbol, of course, but it expresses the themes of this chapter, God's real participation in the passion of the world.

1. The Silence of God on the Cross of Jesus

The very fact that Jesus, the Son of God, died on the cross is in itself scandalous, but the description the Gospels give of this death does nothing to reduce the scandal, but increases it. Jesus' death is described, in the traditions taken as a whole, as something frightening. They do not present his death as a pleasant death, still less as a beautiful death. In their accounts, Jesus does not die with the wisdom of Socrates or the Stoic calm of Seneca. He does not die like many other religious and political martyrs before or since, who gave themselves up enthusiastically to death. He does not go to his death singing like many Christian martyrs since him or like the "red martyr" described by Ernst Bloch. Whatever Jesus' state of mind between the garden and the end of his life, his death is not described in any of these ways.

(a) Jesus' Words on the Cross

(i) It is well known that the evangelists quote various sayings of Jesus on the cross. What we might call his penultimate words are certainly heavily shaped by later theology: the word of forgiveness for his executioners (Luke 23:34), the promise to the good thief (Luke 23:43), the words to his mother and the beloved disciple (John 19:25-7), the "I am thirsty" (John 19:28). More important, however, are what we may call the last words, his theologal words, those which indicate the reality of God on the cross. In these words Jesus addresses his God in his last moment.

According to Mark 15:34, followed by Matthew 27:46, Jesus cries out, "My God, my God, why have you forsaken me?" which is the beginning of Psalm 22. According to Luke 23:46, Jesus says, "Father, into your hands I commend my spirit," which is verse 5 of Psalm 31, a psalm of trust. According to John 19:30, Jesus says, "It is finished." All these sayings have been composed in the context of various traditions which Léon-Dufour sums up as follows:

> *Mark*, situating the crucified man's cry in an apocalyptic context, shows Jesus as a person dying alone, abandoned by God to the violence of his enemies, the cowardice of his disciples, without any extraordinary help. Jesus shows his tragic state in a "Why?".... *Luke* presents Jesus as the model of the just martyr placing himself in God's hands.... *John* again finds a meaning in Jesus' last cry, "You are my God," though without disguising the tragic situation.[5]

How Jesus really died is not easy to determine. It was most probably from asphyxiation, which might have meant that it was impossible for these last words to be spoken and heard clearly. What is therefore historically most likely is the "loud cry" Jesus utters (Mark 15:37; Matt. 27:50; Luke 23:46),[6] and the evangelists' versions are probably "the result of the primitive community's elaborations of a cry without words."[7] What is clear is that there are various interpretations in the Gospels—none of them pleasant—of this death. The tragedy reaches a climax in Mark and Matthew with the abandonment by God, while in Luke the death has a meaning and in John it is the crowning of Jesus' triumphal progress to Jerusalem.

A crucial point is which interpretation of Jesus' death is primary, and according to exegetes of various schools (Boismard, Benoît, Bultmann, Schrage) it is Mark's.

It is certainly the most consistent with the data of his life and certainly could not have been invented by later communities in view of the scandal presupposed by the picture of the risen one, the Son of God, dying abandoned by the Father. The bare fact of presenting Jesus dying abandoned by the Father must have been very difficult to accept, and I think that it is extraordinary that these passages of Mark, and more generally his whole anti-triumphalist Gospel,[8] were written down and accepted into the New Testament canon.

(ii) A negative proof of this is that the radical tone of Mark's description was gradually softened in various ways, even in the New Testament. As we have seen, in Luke, Jesus dies as the trusting martyr, although he does not give any reason for that confidence, and, in John, Jesus dies as he lived, in a unity of will with the Father. At the level of narratives there is, then a process of softening, although it should be remembered that in other places where the New Testament attempts a systematic account the tragedy of Jesus' death is restored and so, in Pauline theology, Jesus dies as a man accursed, made into sin, given up by the Father, and in the Letter to the Hebrews, Jesus offers up great groans and tears to the one who could save him from death. Both systematic interpretations reflect Mark's description more than Luke's and John's.

This attempt to soften Jesus' end can also be seen in the search at all costs for explanations of Mark 15:34 that will remove the idea of abandonment by God. The commonest has been to mention the fact that in Psalm 22 the just person who suffers certainly complains to God, but also places total trust in God and emerges triumphant (vv. 5ff.). This line of argument, however, is speculative and inevitably invites the question why Mark did not mention these verses but does mention the one that expresses abandonment by God.

The attempt to soften the image of God abandoning Jesus is much more clearly visible down through the centuries, and it should be noted that the various attempts were not prompted by fidelity to textual exegesis but, in general, by theological assumptions, which shows how difficult it is to accept even the possibility of this abandonment. If we take only the church Fathers,[9] many interpret Jesus' abandonment metaphorically. When reciting Psalm 22, Jesus was not speaking in his own name, they argue, but in the name of sinful humanity: in his person sinners are abandoned by God (see Origen, Cyril of Alexandria, Augustine). Among the Latin Fathers this interpretation was reinforced by a bad translation of the text of Psalm 22:2b. Instead of translating correctly "the voices of my groaning," the translation had "the voices of my sins." As Jesus could not have spoken of himself as a sinner, he must have been speaking in the name of others, and so he did not complain of himself being abandoned by God, but did so in the name of others. Other Fathers, such as Epiphanius and Eusebius, interpreted the words as a dialogue between Christ's human and divine nature: the man Jesus complains to the Word of the Word's abandonment of human nature in the tomb. In this subtle way they avoid the impression that the Father is abandoning Jesus. Finally, others, such as Tertullian, Ambrose (and Thomas Aquinas), admit that Jesus suffered abandonment by God in his human psychology, but say this did not cause him anguish or despair.

I shall not try here to analyze how correct or incorrect the Fathers' exegesis was, nor the philosophical and theological presuppositions that operated to prevent acceptance of Jesus' words as quoted by Mark. All I want to show is how difficult it is to maintain a (possible) abandonment by God on Jesus' cross. The difficulty has very good reasons: if it had taken place, this abandonment transforms and questions our ideas of God.[10]

(b) God's Absence on Jesus' Cross

Let us now return to the death of Jesus. Although we cannot determine exactly either his words or his mental state at the moment of death,[11] Mark's account seems to me, objectively and systematically, the most adequate because it conveys better than the others the really tragic aspect of Jesus' death, its radical discontinuity with his life. This radical discontinuity—whether expressed in terms of abandonment by the Father or in other terms—is real and constitutes the *objective* and specific tragedy of Jesus' death. In general, Jesus on the cross is not presented as one more martyr, in the sense that the martyrs (or many of them) interpreted their own deaths in continuity with their lives and as their last service to their cause.[12] They will disappear, but the cause will go on, and their death will help the cause to go on. In the presence of this continuity between their own lives and their cause and their own death, their physical and mental sufferings are, up to a certain point, secondary. The Christian martyrs, in addition, interpreted their deaths as the greatest grace and as the gift of God by antonomasia, that which finally brings them close to God, that which consummates and completes their continuity with God. But Jesus' death was not reported like that.

Even if Jesus' cry on the cross were to be interpreted as a cry of fidelity—"You are my God"—it is impossible to ignore the theologal discontinuity between Jesus' death and his life, and this is what the Markan tradition asserts very clearly, and the other traditions do not allow us to draw the opposite conclusion. In the Lukan tradition, according to Léon-Dufour, we have to take seriously "the profound isolation in which Jesus finds himself."[13] And the Johannine tradition "might be misunderstood if it led us to ignore the older interpretations of Mark and Matthew."[14] Let us, then, examine the elements of this discontinuity, the objective tragedy of Jesus' death, whatever may have been his mental state at the moment of death.

Essential to Jesus' life and mission was the conviction that the Kingdom "has come near." In the accounts of the cross, however, there is no sense of this nearness, or any real signs of its coming. On the cross Jesus is not presented as thinking that now at last the blind will see, the lame walk, and the poor have the good news preached to them.... Not only is there no sign of this, but, on the contrary, we see the immense power of the anti-Kingdom triumphing over the Kingdom. True, Jesus had been getting used to this in the last phase of his life, to the idea that maybe the Kingdom would come in a different way than he expected, that maybe his own death would hasten it (see the earlier discussion about his hope at the Last Supper). Nonetheless, nowhere, not in the garden, nor at the trials, nor on the way of the cross, nor on the cross, is Jesus presented as thinking of the coming Kingdom, or showing that what is happening to him is a service to the Kingdom. No doubt it can be argued that the psychological context was not the most auspicious for this, but that is the fact: the traditions of Jesus' death do not present it in relation to and as a service to what was fundamental in his life and mission, the coming of the Kingdom of God. There is an important objective discontinuity here, which in strong language can be called "failure."

The words on the cross, however, disclose an even more dramatic discontinuity, the radical discontinuity in Jesus' relationship with his Father, God. It is true that during his life Jesus had to learn that in this close Father there was an element of mystery, of a novel and demanding will; Jesus even had to accept that doing the will of this God would lead him to Jerusalem, where he would be delivered up. But on the cross this mystery becomes doubly a mystery, because there all that remains is the naked mystery of God without the personal closeness of the Father. This is what constitutes the radical discontinuity. Whereas, for Jesus, the "infinite distance" of God as mystery was always accompanied by the "absolute closeness" of God as Father, this vanishes on the cross: there is no closeness of God, there is no experience of God as a kind Father. The accounts give no sign that Jesus heard any word from the Father in answer to his questions.

In conclusion, if the passion narratives describe the gradual desertion of Jesus' disciples, including the betrayal of one and the cowardice of another, so that Jesus' death is presented in historical isolation, the end of Jesus' life in Mark's account ends with the silence of God or, at all events, without the active presence of God the Father. And in this there is a great objective discontinuity with Jesus' life.

This new form of God's relationship with Jesus, whether it be called abandonment, silence, or simply distancing or inaction on the part of God, is the most wounding element of Jesus' death. In the language of systematic theology, on the cross sin appears with greater power than the Father, God. Jesus, like Job and Jeremiah,[15] turns to God, but in Mark's account he hears no answer.

To conclude this section I want to say that it is difficult, if not impossible, to know what Jesus' real relationship to his God was as he died. But if all the evidence is taken as a whole, I think that his death shows much more theologal desolation than consolation, that what is to be heard from God is much more his silence than a word of closeness. Theologians have attempted in numerous ways to put into words this theologal desolation of Jesus, and I have nothing new to offer. I therefore end this section with two quotations, the first, more circumspect, from Eduard Schillebeeckx, and the second, bolder, from Jürgen Moltmann:

> Jesus was indeed condemned because he remained true to his prophetic mission "from God," a mission which he refused to justify to any other authority than God

himself. In all this Jesus continued to rely on the Father who had sent him. The Father, however, did not intervene. Nowhere, indeed, did Jesus see any visible aid come from him whose cause he had so much at heart. As a fact of history, it can hardly be denied that Jesus was subject to an inner conflict between his consciousness of his mission and the utter silence of the One he was accustomed to call his Father.[16]

Like no one before him in Israel, Jesus had proclaimed the imminence of the Kingdom of God and demonstrated amongst the incurable, the rejected and the hated that it was a gracious imminence, not to judge but to save.... Anyone who lived and preached so close to God... could not regard his being handed over to death on the cross as one accursed as a mere mishap, a human misunderstanding or a final trial, but was bound to experience it as rejection by the very God whom he had dared to call, "My Father."[17]

2. God's Suffering

If the person who died in this way was the Son of God, we cannot avoid the question of what God does about suffering, what Jesus' cross says about God, who God is. And the answer is not at all easy. It is not easy because of the scandal of the cross, but it is not easy also because, according to scripture, we know God through what God *does* and *says* in history: the liberation of a people shows us God the liberator, defender of orphans and widows, in other words the God of the victims. But on the cross—objectively—God does not act or speak, does not intervene, lets things— this terrible thing which is the death of his Son—simply be. The cross therefore raises the most serious problem, whether and how not acting, not speaking, how silence, withdrawal, inaction can reveal anything of God.

This problem is independent of what Jesus' words and thoughts on the cross were, because the fundamental objective fact is death inflicted unjustly on the just man, Jesus—and the countless unjust deaths throughout history—which God did nothing to prevent.

(a) God's Response to Suffering

Whether or not Jesus uttered them, the words "Why have you forsaken me?" have rightly become the *locus classicus* for discussing the problem of the relationship between God and suffering and God and negativity in general. I want to look first at how this problem is dealt with in current theology, and especially at the underlying prejudices that influence the treatment. I shall do so by following and commenting on Leonardo Boff's discussion.[18]

(i) Suffering remains the supreme enigma for human reason. Reason can understand the fact and, up to a point, the meaning of suffering and pain, which are necessary for growth; it can also understand that there is suffering, the product of natural limitations and disasters, which is necessary because it is part of the nature of things. However, if these evils can be accepted in some way, even if not totally, there is historical evil, the evil inflicted deliberately and unjustly on some human beings by others, which has no meaning in itself. "What meaning is there in the murder of so many anonymous people, peasants and workers, who fought for a more decent and more human life for themselves and others, and were exterminated by the arrogance of the powerful?"[19] I would add, what meaning is there in the deaths of anonymous victims who were not even able to fight and died slowly or in massacres simply through the fact of being poor?

In the face of this problem, present-day theology in general reacts without naivety. "There is evil which cannot be turned into good. The history of those who have been unjustly murdered and condemned cannot be reversed.... There is a negativity that cannot be reformed because it has no meaning. But it may have a future" (Metz). Suffering in itself has no meaning; the only suffering that has any meaning is the suffering we accept in the fight against suffering (Sölle). Suffering cannot be accepted, only fought (Hedinger).

These quotations show how difficult it is for reason to deal with human suffering. Reason can find ways of coming to terms with the suffering that results from the natural human condition and even that that results from love (although the question always remains why those who love others generously and selflessly have to suffer). But what seems impossible is to come to terms with innocent suffering: nothing can confer meaning on the fact of the death of innocent victims, who, moreover, are not exceptions or curiosities, but frequent in the history of humanity.

(ii) For faith, too, suffering remains an enigma, and before it the religious, Christian person contemplates God on Jesus' cross, at the highest symbolic moment of suffering. What does God do about the suffering of the cross? Can the cross give meaning to suffering? These are the questions to which we seek answers.

One theological view rejects any attempt at finding meaning in suffering and protests against the very attempt to find such a meaning, even in God. Attempts to justify suffering on the ground that God himself was present in the suffering of the cross are, in this view, useless and even dangerous because this approach in the past has proved alienating. Worse still, sublimating this suffering, if only in God, is cruel because God has to be seen as the stronghold of pure positivity. We therefore have to reject, it is argued, any attempt to reconcile God and distress and we have to reject, of course, any attempt to understand God as the person who sends suffering as a punishment (Sölle). "Any justification of suffering which includes God makes the problem worse rather than solving it" (Hedinger).

Another trend in theology, represented by Urs von Balthasar on the Catholic side and Moltmann on the Protestant side, approaches the issue from a different perspective, which in my opinion has not always been correctly understood. This approach does not, or not necessarily, try to contemplate God in the presence of suffering in order to look for a possible meaning, but first and foremost to see God as he is and see if suffering affects God himself or not, with the proviso that God cannot become any sort of solution because the question not only returns despite God's involvement, but even becomes worse. This, then, is not, or not necessarily, an attempt to explain, justify or sublimate human suffering, or to find an ultimate meaning for it beyond the world, because this radical "beyond" the human sphere, which is God, is also affected by suffering. It is simply an attempt to be honest with revelation and to allow its revelation to offer a new perspective, wherever it leads. In the face of suffering God "doesn't do anything" of the sort that human beings would like him to do. What is unexpected and novel for us is that God too participates in suffering. God, in other words, neither provides a meaning for suffering nor deprives it of a meaning. The only thing the cross says is that God himself bears suffering and—for those who in faith accept his presence on Jesus' cross—that it has to be borne.

(b) Suffering in God

(i) So let us go to the heart of the matter. What can it mean to say that suffering affects God? From a dogmatic point of view, we have to say, without any reservation, that the Son (the second person of the Trinity) took on the whole reality of Jesus and, although the dogmatic formula never explains the manner of this being affected by the human dimension, the thesis is radical. The Son experienced Jesus' humanity, existence in history, life, destiny and death. However this statement may be used or manipulated, whether to promote resignation or to inspire action for liberation, whether to try and explain suffering or, on the contrary, to raise it to the status of an ultimate mystery—that is, of what cannot be explained— it still holds good. And this, undoubtedly, was the first great difficulty in the way of accepting the divinity of Christ at Nicea, the first council of the universal church, because it presents a Son—who is divine—taking on unreservedly every dimension of humanity.

But the problem becomes more radical if we ask whether and how the suffering of the cross affects "God," the Father, the ultimate origin and future of everything, who appears to be beyond everything. At this point all we can have are speculations and reflections in which all theologians in fact offer their own ideas and their own faith, and rely on their own ultimate premises in the presence of suffering and God. Nevertheless I think the question is inevitable, though the answer leads us into unknown territory.

As a way into a possible answer, I want to make a preliminary remark. We saw before that it is only possible to talk about God "in himself" doxologically, on the basis of something accessible to experience, although linking the data of experience to God is a matter of faith, and in this way faith operates with positive data. If, for example, an oppressed people is liberated or Jesus is raised, by attributing these events to God in faith we can say something about God-in-himself: God is a liberator, God raises the dead. While these statements belong to faith, and so are unintelligible, they can be accepted in faith and usually are accepted by theology "without much difficulty," because they introduce into God something positive, though new, but without introducing into God any sort of limitation, in the sense that "limitation" has in Greek thought.

Christian faith, however, introduces a radical novelty in the way it makes doxological statements about God on the basis of the central datum of the incarnation. Accepting the incarnation is, of course, a matter of faith, but once it is accepted faith—and theology—finds itself forced into truly dizzying statements. If the Son is really flesh, then "becoming" has taken place in God who is not flesh. If Jesus has been raised as the firstborn, and only at the end will God be all in all, then "the future" applies to God and is one of God's modes of being. These two scandalous assertions about God becoming and having a future have already been accepted by theology, the first from ancient times, the second more recently (Pannenberg, Moltmann, Rahner, Metz).

In saying this I simply want to point out that the dynamic of a faith based on the incarnation shatters the normal premises of human thinking about God, including the believer's method of making doxological statements about God.

(ii) To return to God's suffering, if Jesus is neither only what "God has become," nor only "the firstborn" who points to God's future, but also the one who suffered on the cross and suffered specifically abandonment by God, the unavoidable question is what the reality of God on the cross was (although we all sense that there will be no adequate words to answer it), the question how suffering can be a possible mode of being for God.

Describing—which does not mean explaining—what suffering in God is, is clearly not easy, and in the New Testament there are no formulations about "God's suffering," not even in the way it refers to God's "becoming" and God's "future." Talking about God's suffering on the cross is, therefore, theological reflection, but I do not think it is arbitrary reflection. Paul says that God *was present* on Jesus' cross, and in Mark 15:39 the centurion makes his profession of faith: "Truly this man was *God's Son!*" after Jesus' death.

The important point about these exercises in theology is the statement that God *was present* on Jesus' cross. But this *being present on* cannot be separated from *the cross*, on which God was present, because it is a feature of the historical structure of revelation that the nature of the place in which God manifests himself is a mediation of God's own nature. We would know nothing of a good "God" if God had not *been present* in Jesus' good works. We would know nothing of a forgiving "God" if he had not *been present* in Jesus' welcome to sinners. We would know nothing of a "God" who calls into life that which does not exist, if he had not *been present* in the resurrection of Jesus.... In other words, God's revelation is sacramental in character, and not just deductive, when it becomes present in historical phenomena. If this is the case, it is at least plausible to proceed in the opposite direction: in every place where Jesus' nature is present, something of God is revealed. It is therefore likely that God's presence on the cross, insofar as it is a cross, reveals something of God.

What it reveals is a matter for reflection, and for that reason debatable, and much more so in this case because of the nature of the matter. The Lutheran tradition tends to press the formulation of this mystery to a magnificent extreme: *"Nemo contra Deum nisi Deus ipse,"* "No one against God but God himself." In this view,

God's presence on the cross shows that there is a split within God and a breach between the Father and the Son, which has led to the statement that the Father rejects the Son, and this is what constitutes his greatest suffering. In my view, such conceptual extremism to express God's suffering is exaggerated, but I also do not think it is honest to ignore completely the question of how God is affected by *being present* on Jesus' cross. If Jesus' God clearly contradicts *apatheia*, the indifference of the Greek gods, throughout Jesus' life, there is no reason to suppose that on the cross he became indifferent, opted out. It seems inconsistent to say that God on the cross is not affected, but indifferent.

To deal with this, I think it is sufficient to say, in anthropomorphic language, of course, that God suffered on Jesus' cross and on those of this world's victims by being their non-active and silent witness. God's non-action in the face of the death of his beloved Son is a fact, and if this fact is not interpreted as extreme cruelty, then this non-action and silence can be interpreted as the negative way in which the cross affects God himself.

I think it is a secondary matter how we describe God's suffering, and to describe it adequately is in the end impossible. What is important, I believe, is to insist that God is involved in the passion of Jesus and the passion of the world. If we want a doxological formula, perhaps these bold words of Jürgen Moltmann will do:

> In the Son's passion the Father himself suffers the pain of abandonment. In the Son's death death reaches God himself, and the Father suffers his Son's death for love of abandoned human beings.[20]

(iii) Is this cruelty? Is it impotence? Both are qualities that are repugnant to the idea of God. I have already said that the New Testament interprets God's handing over of his Son in the last resort as love: God is inactive on the cross so that we human beings can rely on his love. God does not speak to Jesus in order to be able to go on talking to human beings. God lets Jesus die to be able to communicate to us his plan for life. And in order to be able to say this as something so inherently positive and insist that the indifference of the Greek gods is totally foreign to the Christian God, we have to say it also in negative terms. God, too, is affected by suffering. God is crucified.

The core of this idea is that God himself has accepted, in a divine manner, to become consistently incarnate in history, to let himself be affected by it and to let himself be affected by the law of sin which brings death. The cross should not be seen as an arbitrary plan of God's or as a cruel punishment inflicted on Jesus, but as a consequence of God's original choice, incarnation, a radical drawing near for love and in love, wherever it leads, without escaping from history or manipulating it from outside. This, in human words, also means God's accepting suffering.

This should not be seen as either a sublimation or a justification of suffering. What God encourages is real incarnation in history, because only in this way will history be saved, *even though* this leads to the cross. The phrase "crucified God" is therefore no more than another term, provocative and shocking, with the same meaning as "God of solidarity." Again, the question remains why solidarity has to be shown in this way, why even God himself, to show solidarity, has to do so in the mode of crucifixion. But we human beings understand very well—without finding a logical explanation for it—that in history there is no such thing as love without solidarity and there is no solidarity without incarnation. Solidarity that was not prepared to share the lot of those with whom it wanted to show solidarity would be paternalism, to put it mildly, or would lead to despotism. Solidarity in a world of victims that was not prepared to become a victim would in the end not be solidarity.

God's suffering is, then, very "likely," if it is true that God wanted to reveal his solidarity with this world's victims. If from the beginning of the gospel God appears in Jesus as a God *with* us, if throughout the gospel God shows himself as a God *for* us, on the cross he appears as a God *at our mercy* and, above all, as a God *like* us.

Once again, reason may ask what is interesting about this God like us, when what we human beings want is something very different from us, which will save us from our limitations, and this is not what we will find on the cross. But we must not despise the hope generated by God's solidarity on the cross. Moltmann has put this in vigorous, perhaps extreme, language:

> Only if there is in God himself every form of perdition, abandonment by him, the infinite curse of condemnation and falling into nothingness, only then does communion with this God represent eternal salvation, infinite joy, indestructible election and divine life.[21]

Latin Americans understand very well that solidarity leads to incarnation. When the Salvadoran government offered Archbishop Romero personal protection, he replied, "The shepherd does not want protection when his flock is denied it,"[22] and the reaction of the poor in El Salvador was one of gratitude and enthusiasm. As pure speculation, we could discuss whether Archbishop Romero was or was not right to refuse the protection he was offered, on the assumption—not at all probable—that this would have spared him a premature death and he would now be still doing good and promoting liberation in this world. Nonetheless, there can be no doubt that Archbishop Romero's words were understood as words of genuine solidarity with his people and, therefore, as words of love.

What God's suffering on the cross says in the end is that the God who fights against human suffering wanted to show solidarity with human beings who suffer, and that God's fight against suffering is also waged in a human way. It may not be a philosophical truth, and I do not know if it is present in other religious traditions, but it is an essential element of the biblical, and certainly of the Christian, tradition that it is necessary to fight resolutely against sin in order to eradicate it, but that this fight means bearing sin. What God's suffering makes clear in a history of suffering is that between the alternatives of accepting suffering by sublimating it and eliminating it from outside we can and must introduce a new course, bearing it.

However, we must also add that in bearing this suffering God says what side he is on, what struggles he is in solidarity with. God's silence on the cross, as a silence that brings suffering to God himself, can be interpreted, very paradoxically, as solidarity with Jesus and with the crucified of history: it is God's portion of the necessary suffering involved in the historical struggle for liberation. In this sense, Leonardo Boff is quite right when he says:

> If God is silent in the face of suffering, it is because he himself is suffering and making his own the cause of the martyrs and those who suffer (cf. Matt. 25:31). Suffering is not foreign to him; but if he accepted it it was not to make it eternal and leave us without hope, but because he wants to put an end to all the crosses of history.[23]

History's victims are looking, of course, for an effective love, but they also welcome a credible love. The crucified peasants of El Salvador express this intuitively: "We meditate on the passion of Jesus and so maintain the hope of the resurrection." This credible love is also effective. That is how things are. A credible love has the effect in history that others carry on the cause that was expressed in that love. This does not have to come from an analysis of the concept, but springs up out of real life. That is why we can argue theoretically *ad infinitum* about whether the crucified God functions ultimately as a sublimation and justification of suffering or is the greatest possible protest against suffering and the greatest possible stimulus to fight against it. For me, the matter is simpler. The crucified God is not a phenomenon that can be approached through theoretical concepts, but through practical concepts; it is not a case for theo-logy but for theo-praxis: the question is, what process does the crucified God initiate? In Latin America it is a tangible fact that God's suffering has also been an idea that has encouraged liberation rather than resignation. And it is true that love, when it is credible, has its own efficacy. What this crucified God reminds us of constantly is that there can be no liberation from sin without bearing of sin, that injustice cannot be eradicated unless it is borne.

3. Knowing God on Jesus' Cross

What the cross directly reveals of God is his non-action and his suffering, and this statement raises the question what it means to know God, and by means of what we know him, given that knowing God always presupposes, in one way or another, relating God to something positive.

Given this situation, what usually happens is that either God's suffering is ignored, which means that the problem disappears, or this knowledge is raised to the level of pure scandal, beyond all reasoning. In my view, what we have to do is to situate the revelation of God on the cross as adequately as possible alongside other moments of revelation; that is, understand God's revelation and maintain it as the history of his revelation, made up of different elements, whatever the difficulty or the ease of relating them to each other and obtaining a synthesis. That is to say, we must hold together the element of revelation of the creation in Genesis, of liberation in Exodus, of justice in the prophets, of silence in Job, of the Kingdom in the evangelists and, especially, the moment of suffering on the cross and that of restoring life to an innocent victim in the resurrection.

In a reading of history based on faith, all these elements reveal God. The problem arises with the attempt to systematize them, which can be done by making one of them absolute, giving it priority, or really treating God's revelation as an open history of revelation that will reach a climax only at the end, allowing each element of revelation to be itself during history, without trying to reduce one to increase another. In the end, it means, as Micah said, walking "humbly" with God without trying to find a finished synthesis of the reality of God in history, accepting in faith—and with the greatest possible faith—that only at the end will God be all in all. Only at the end will God be revealed as pure positivity and as a whole, while in history his revelation is affected by fragmentariness and negativity.

I want to add, nonetheless, that the very fact of not being able adequately to hold together and synthesize the various elements of revelation is the practical—the most conclusive—proof that we are really in the presence of God, in the presence of the mystery of God. It is a proof for the *fides quae*, theoretical and orthodox, and above all for the *fides qua*, practical and existential. Only in surrender to this mystery and to the new and innovating dimension of this mystery do we respond to it.

Having said this, I want now to concentrate on the meaning of the element of negativity in the revelation of God: what does the phenomenon of a crucified God mean for the possibility of our knowing God? I repeat that I am not interested in conceptual extremism, but I want to take absolutely seriously the negative as well as the positive, so that finally we do not turn God into a God in our own image and likeness, which is always easier when, as is inevitable, we concentrate on the positive elements of the revelation of God.

(a) Redefining Transcendence: the "Greater" and the "Lesser" God

Religious men and women have always used comparatives, the idea of "more," to express the transcendence of God. God is further back (than creation), further outside (nature), further on (in eschatology). God is closer to us than we are to ourselves (Augustine), the ground of being (Paul Tillich). These different expressions are all attempts to express the radical discontinuity, the infinite distance between God and creatures. Corresponding to this distance is a God who is always "greater."

This discontinuity can, however, go beyond what human beings imagine to be truth and want as salvation; it may be in harmony with our best thoughts and desires, but it may also be a critique and contradiction of them. The revelation of God may be fulfillment, but it may also be scandal. This means that human beings must always allow for the active possibility that God may be radically different and scandalous. We must allow, in other words, for not only greatness, but also smallness, to be a mediation of God. This is what happens on the cross.

In the light of the cross, the language of "greater" must be complemented by the language of "less": God is also in what is small, in suffering, in negativity; all this also affects God and reveals him. To the "greater" God we must add the "lesser" God. God's transcendence is now expressed precisely in holding together God's greatness and God's smallness.

In the New Testament God's transcendence is expressed by a "greater," of course, but a "lesser" is also added: we have God's unfathomable wisdom and unheard-of love, but on Jesus' cross. "Greater" continues to be the mode of referring to God's transcendence, but now alongside a "less." And when the two are mentioned together, God becomes *more* transcendent, *more* unencompassable, *more* indescribable, *more* a mystery.

Specifically, in terms of the "less" of the cross two typically biblical ways of expressing God's transcendence are drastically redefined. The first is the prohibition of making images of God (Deut. 5:8), which the New Testament takes further: "No-one has ever seen God" (John 1:18). We saw earlier the particular reason for this prohibition: an image cannot speak.

The cross, however, adds that any image we might want to make of God would have no meaning, because the cross is the end of all images; it is the fulfillment in action of the second commandment. It reveals nothing of what is usually presented as divine. In addition, however, on the cross not only is there no image, there is not even speech: there is only God's silence. God does not show himself in a positive challenge, but in silence. On the cross his image and his word have a quality we had not imagined, and therefore we have to redefine his transcendence.

The second biblical formula is that—in contrast to what occurs in Greek thought—the future is an attribute of God, and by creating a future he shows his divine power and proves himself to be God. "You shall know that I am the LORD your God.... I will bring you into the land that I swore to give..." (Exod. 6:7-8). "Today... you shall know that I am the LORD" (1 Kings 20:13, 28; Ezek. 25:7). Only at the end will God be all in all (1 Cor. 15:28). The future is one of God's modes of being. God is the power that moves history from the future and will show his power at the end by renewing all things.

On the cross, however, there is neither power nor future. The cross is not directly the not-yet of the future, but the radical failure of all the past and present, and the closing off of any future. The cross reveals, not power, but impotence. God does not triumph on the cross over the power of evil, but succumbs to it. The faith-interpretation, as we have seen, sees in this the love of God in solidarity, to the end, with human beings, but what appears on the cross on the surface is the triumph of the idols of death over the God of life. The idea that in the battle of the gods the true God could lose and through that defeat prove himself the true God requires us to rethink his transcendence.

In the light of Jesus' cross, God's transcendence cannot be thought of in terms of the "greater" of the positive—in however purified a form the good things of creation may be conceptualized, as in the method of analogy and perfection—it must also be thought of in terms of the negative. Part of God's greatness is his making himself small. And, paradoxically, in this plan of his of taking on what is small God makes himself a greater mystery, a new and greater transcendence, than the stammered definitions of human beings.

(b) The Inadequacy of Any Natural Theology

(i) Since the time of the Greeks the fundamental premise of any attempt to know God has been the possibility of access to him through the positive elements of reality, that is, through some type of affinity: "Like is known by like" (Plato). In the created world, fragmentary though it is, we seek a positive access to God, whether through nature (the Greeks), in being (Thomas Aquinas), in history (Hegel) or in consciousness (the modern age). There is something in the world that allows (and demands) access to God. This is positive and in the last resort necessary, because without some type of affinity with God knowing him would be simply impossible.[24]

Here, however, I want to insist on the element of discontinuity in our knowledge of God, since the positive element does not appear directly on the cross. In itself, the cross is suffering, failure, death, silence. There there is no life, no beauty, no power, no reason, none of these things through which human beings seek access to God. If the cross can offer access to God, this has to happen *sub specie contrarii*, and this means learning to see power in impotence, speech in silence, life in death. In other words, natural theology—which objectively reaches God only through the positive elements of creation—shows itself inadequate to discover God on the cross.

(ii) It is also inadequate in the subjective dimension. Aristotle maintains that what sets the process of discovery in motion is wonder: there exists in the world something that not only can be known, but which also moves us to discover and seek coherence in the order of things, which then produces pleasure. On the cross, however, there is no positive wonder that moves us to discover or to move our knowledge forward until it reaches God. If God can be known in the presence of the cross, the principal motor of that knowing is not wonder, but suffering. Only through suffering can there be a *sumpatia*, a connaturality, with the object one seeks to know. "Suffering precedes thought" (Feuerbach). Subjective inner suffering, in the presence of objective external suffering, is what can enable us to know something of God on the cross; without it nothing of God will be revealed on the cross.

But coming to know something through suffering always means something more than knowing. External suffering, by its very nature, is not only something to be noted, registered in consciousness, analyzed, even explained, but something in relation to which we have to adopt a position. This position can be a stratagem for not seeing it, resignation or protest; but it can also be a decision to eradicate this suffering. Knowing through suffering is always committed knowledge, in various ways, by action or omission, but committed from beginning to end. If God is to be known on the cross, an involvement of some sort has to be accepted. And according to the nature of the involvement, it may be possible to understand God with the radicalness of events rather than that of pure concepts.

Wonder moves us to discover more and more until we reach what brings peace to reason. It starts off an infinite movement that seeks peace and rest. In Augustine's beautiful words, "Lord you made us for yourself, and our hearts are restless until they rest in you." The type of "wonder" caused by the cross, however, starts off a different type of movement. Whoever encounters God on the cross encounters a God who does not let us rest or have peace. The "more" knowledge God's nature demands, when he is seen through negativity, is not a purely intellectual "more," but a "more" that includes as main elements hope and action; it is a "more" that leaves hearts forever restless, questioned and questioning.

(iii) Finally, knowledge is always moved by some interest (Habermas), and so is knowledge of God. It is an understandable and necessary interest, but it can be spurious, when in seeking to know God we seek a reaffirmation of what we wanted to know. This is the charge that, in an extreme, though not totally unjust, form, dialectical theology, and especially Karl Barth, brings against all natural knowledge of God and all forms of religion. The criticism is that we look for a God who pleases us, one to give answers to what we think are the real questions. Taking this position to an extreme, Barth asserts that natural religion and theology are idolatry, the claim of human beings to justify themselves by their own resources.

This position requires harsh correction from the standpoint of this world's victims, since they have every right to imagine a God who is theirs, who rights their wrongs, who confers life on them, and they have that right because God is like that; that is how he has been revealed.[25] But this does not make Barth's criticism totally wrong. It continues to be true that we human beings want to dictate to God what he should be like, even though in that form God is not as he really is.

Our interest in looking for God may be, in principle, legitimate or illegitimate. On the cross illegitimate interests are unmasked, and legitimate interests are reformed, but what the cross shows in any case is that our interests are broken. In this sense the cross is not an answer to our question about God, but it is a radical question to us when we wonder about God. The way the cross breaks our interest in knowing God can be seen in these verses of Dietrich Bonhoeffer's, which are already classic:

> Men go to God when they are sore bestead,
> Pray to him for succour, for his peace, for bread,
> For mercy for them sick, sinning or dead;
> All men do so, Christian and unbelieving.

> Men go to God when he is sore bestead,
> Find him poor and scorned, without shelter or bread,

Whelmed under weight of the wicked, the weak, the dead;
Christians stand by God in his hour of grieving.[26]

These verses need to be carefully understood. They allow an extremely cruel interpretation and another which is Christian. The cruel interpretation would be to delete the first verse or interpret it only as an expression of human *hybris*, because the truth is that human beings, and certainly the poor, need all this. A Christian interpretation would be to see the crucified of this world coming to God, not from any illegitimate interest, but looking for bread, dignity, for God to help them to come down from the cross. (It is different with the crucifiers, those who want more wealth and more power, and therefore look for a god.)

The second verse, however, is more typically Christian. It is so polemically, because it unmasks the spurious interests that may be expressed in the first verse; and it is Christian above all because it asserts reality: God, too, is present in the passion. Whether finding God in this way is a questioning or a consolation, alienation or encouragement to commitment, curse or blessing, depends in the last resort on who comes to the cross. In Latin America the egoism of those who create poverty always makes them recite the first verse, endlessly, while they regard the second as utter nonsense, and, if they read it carefully, a total challenge. The poor, for their part, of necessity and in truth recite the first verse, and many of them also accept the second, without thereby becoming alienated. They accept it because on the cross they see "their" God and this God on the cross who is "theirs" gives them, paradoxically, hope and encouragement.

(c) The Victims as a Setting for God's Revelation

Bonhoeffer's poem ends with the words: "Christians stand by God in his hour of grieving." Knowledge of God always has a material setting, and the place where the crucified God is known is the crosses of this world, which function, not mechanically, but almost *ex opere operato*. This is what the New Testament maintains, when it specifies what sort of suffering makes the Christian God present: not any suffering, but the suffering of this world's victims. God is present on Jesus' cross, says Paul. God is present in the poor of this world, says Matthew 25.[27]

The victims of this world are the place where God is known, but sacramentally. They make God known because they make him present. As on Jesus' cross, in them "the Godhead hides," as Ignatius says in the meditations on the passion, but God is there. To stand at the foot of Jesus' cross and to stand at the foot of historical crosses is absolutely necessary if we want to know the crucified God.[28]

But if this is so, the knowledge we obtain of God on the cross is really "revelation." It is revelation not only because on the cross what was previously not known or imagined is revealed, but also because what is made manifest is really unthinkable. This is what Paul asserts when he recognizes that making an essential connection between God and the cross is madness for Gentiles and a scandal to Jews

(1 Cor. 1:23). You may or may not accept the presence of God on the cross, Paul seems to be saying. However, if you accept it, then you have not reached God by extrapolation—rational or believing—from hopes or aspirations, but God himself has shown himself without any base in human expectations, and God himself has given the power in which he can be recognized as God. Jesus' cross, then, functions strictly as revelation of God, in its double sense of unveiling of the unexpected and gracious power in which God can be recognized as God. This is the precise perspective in which the cross must be regarded as gospel.

There is no recipe for recognizing God on the cross, and initially there is nothing on the cross but silence and scandal. If in faith, however, we accept that God is there, then we have to be ready for the great surprise that God is not as we think. We have to be ready to find God not only through the positive, but also through the negative. We have to be ready to see God, not only as the greater God, but also as the lesser God. We have to be ready for this scandalous surprise to change and turn upside down our interest in knowing God. And we have to be ready, above all, for incarnation at the foot of the cross and to bring the crucified down from their crosses. This readiness does not guarantee automatically that we will find God on the cross, since human beings can carry on very reasonably thinking that there can be nothing of God there. But without this readiness, certainly, we will not find God on the cross.

I said at the beginning that this chapter on the crucified God is very personal. Certainly, there could be questions about why I have put so much stress on it—though I have insisted that I have interpreted the cross, not as the whole of God's revelation, but as "one moment" of it—and there can be theoretical discussion of my interpretation. The point I really want to stress, however, indefensibly from the point of view of argument, is that it is the situation of Latin America, and not a particular theological trend that moves me to speak in this way.

When Gustavo Gutiérrez asks the central question, "How can we talk about God in Ayacucho?"[29] his article begins with the same words with which I began, though in his case not on the lips of the crucified Jesus, but on those of Guamán Poma: "So, my God, where are you? Will you not hear me and relieve your poor?" And Gutiérrez ends with these words: "The people cry: Lord, how long? O God, why?,"[30] words identical to those of the first Christian martyrs: "Sovereign Lord, holy and true, how long will it be before you judge?" (Rev. 6:10).

What has to be added is that in Latin America there is an insistence on presence with the crucified, and in a particular way, to bring them down from the cross. In the language of Matthew 25, giving food to the hungry.... In Ignacio Ellacuría's terminology, "coming to terms with" God on the cross has to be accompanied by "carrying" the cross and taking responsibility for the crucified.

And the situation in Latin America is that we are not doing theology *after* Auschwitz, but *during* Auschwitz, and this is what has moved me to write this chapter on the crucified God and the following one on the crucified people. That is why I end with Pedro Casaldáliga's poem, "Inside Auschwitz":

"How do we talk about God after Auschwitz?,"
you ask yourselves,
over there, on the other side of the sea, in plenty.

"How do we talk about God inside Auschwitz?,"
ask my friends here,
laden with reason, weeping and blood,
immersed in the daily deaths of millions....[31]

Chapter 10

The Death of Jesus (4)
The Crucified People

This chapter is not usually included in christologies. Some analyze what the cross has to say about Jesus' Father and speak of "the crucified God," but it is unusual to analyze what this same cross has to say about Jesus' body in history. Of course it is traditional to relate the cross of Jesus to individual sufferings, but not to relate it to the sufferings of his body as a whole. Nevertheless, as is repeatedly stated in ecclesiology, Christ has a body that makes him present in history. So we need to ask whether this body is crucified, what element of this body is crucified, and if its crucifixion is the presence of the crucified Christ in history.

From the Third World viewpoint, there is no doubt that the cross exists, not just individual crosses, but collective crosses of whole peoples.[1] In speaking about the historical situation of the Third World, Ignacio Ellacuría used to say that it is right to speak about the "crucified God" but just as necessary or even more so to speak about the "crucified people."[2] This also gave the situation of Third-World peoples a theologal status.

It is obvious that the Third World represents a historical catastrophe and we have to give it some name. This is recognized in the official language of our world when it calls these peoples the "Third World," the "South," "developing countries." These names indicate that something is wrong but they do not convey how wrong. To express the gravity of this wrong here I am going to use the term "crucified peoples."

"Crucified peoples" is useful and necessary language on the *factual* level. "Cross" means not only poverty but death. And death is what the peoples of the Third World suffer in a thousand ways. It is a slow but real death, caused by poverty, so that the poor are those who die before their time, as Gustavo Gutiérrez repeatedly says. It is swift and violent death caused by repression and wars, when the poor decide simply to escape from their poverty and live. And it is indirect but effective death when poor peoples are deprived even of their own cultures, in order to subjugate them, weaken their identity and make them more vulnerable. "Crucified

254

peoples" is also useful and necessary language on the *historical-ethical* level, because "cross" makes it quite clear that we are not talking about just any death, but a death that is actively inflicted by unjust structures—called "institutionalized violence" by Medellín. To die crucified does not mean simply to die but to be put to death. So "cross" means that there are victims and there are executioners, that the crucified peoples have not fallen from heaven (if we followed the drift of the metaphor, we ought to say risen from hell). And however much we try to soften the fact and complicate its causes, it is true that the Third-World peoples' cross is a cross inflicted on them by the various powers that dominate the continent in connivance with local powers.

Last, "crucified peoples" is useful and necessary language on the *religious* level, because the cross is the death Jesus died. So for the believer it can evoke the fundamentals of the faith, sin and grace, damnation and salvation. We must not forget that this suffering world is "God's creation," and to create religious awareness of this primary tragedy of the Third World, it is right to use the terminology of the cross.

It is possible, therefore, to speak about crucified peoples, and, given our human and Christian language, it is a necessity. In this chapter I wish to add that the term "crucified peoples" is also useful and necessary language in christology. The crucified peoples are those who fill up in their flesh what is lacking in Christ's passion, as Paul says about himself. They are the actual presence of the crucified Christ in history, as Archbishop Romero said to some terrorized peasants who had survived a massacre: "You are the image of the pierced savior."[3] These words are not rhetorical, but strictly christological. They mean that in this crucified people Christ acquires a body in history and that the crucified people embody Christ in history as crucified.

1. The Crucified People as Yahweh's Suffering Servant

The christological interpretation of the crucified people developed in Latin America from the analysis of similarity between the crucified people and the figure of Yahweh's Suffering Servant. Two Salvadoran martyrs did this and they knew what they were talking about. Archbishop Romero said that Jesus Christ, the liberator, "is so closely identified with the people that interpreters of scripture cannot tell whether Yahweh's Servant proclaimed by Isaiah is the suffering people or Christ who comes to redeem us."[4] Ignacio Ellacuría said: "This crucified people is the historical continuation of Yahweh's Servant, whom the sin of the world continues to deprive of his human face. The powerful of this world continue to strip them of everything, to snatch everything from them, even their lives, especially their lives."[5] This theological interpretation of the crucified people as Yahweh's Suffering Servant has taken root in Latin America, while in other places it may still seem too bold or simply to be unscholarly pious talk. This interpretation has taken root through insight rather than through exegetical analysis, but it is possible to show that the insight is sure and not arbitrary. To do this we have to look at two fundamental facts about the Servant: that he is a historical victim and that he is a saving mystery. Both these ideas are very new in christology, especially the second one. Hence Ellacuría insisted on a "historical soteriology,"[6] specific to the crucified people. Let us begin with the facts. To mention only one example among many, from El Salvador:

> There we were when we were attacked by the soldiers. They were about 300 yards away. When I say "we" I mean almost 5000 people. We were crossing the River Sumpul. It was horrendous. Everyone tried to get away. The children ran downstream, the old people did not fight back either, they drowned. Children, old people, women all drowned there trying to cross the river."

These are the words of a woman survivor of the massacre at the River Sumpul, between El Salvador and Honduras. It happened in 1981. On that occasion thousands of peasants were trapped between the Salvadoran army pursuing them and the Honduran army waiting for them on the other bank. Hundreds died that day. Some were killed by the armies with incredible cruelty—children thrown in the air and bayoneted as they fell—others drowned in the river. Sumpul, Huehuetenango in Guatemala, where hundreds of indigenous people were massacred, and many other places are the new name for Golgotha today and their peoples are the Suffering Servant. In order to grasp this, all we need to do is read the Servant Songs, with Isaiah's text in hand and our eyes fixed on the peoples. So let us look firstly at the likeness between the crucified people and Yahweh's Servant, at them both as victims. We shall do this first by way of a meditation and narrative theology. Then we shall look more systematically at the way in which they both bring salvation.

(a) Meditation on the Crucified People

The first thing we are told about Yahweh's Suffering Servant is that he is "a man of suffering and acquainted with infirmity" (53:3). That is the normal condition of the crucified people: hunger, sickness, slums, illiteracy, frustration through lack of education and employment, pain and suffering of all kinds. Even though there is no end to their sufferings in "normal" times, they become much worse when, like the Servant, they and others with them decide to "establish justice" (42:4-7). Then they are greeted with violence and the verdict that they are "guilty of death." Repression and death follow and they become even more like the Servant: "so marred was his appearance, beyond human semblance, and his form beyond that of mortals... he had no form or majesty, that we should look at him, nothing in his appearance that we should desire him" (52:14; 53:2). To the ugliness of daily poverty is added the horror of torture, when some are beheaded, some burned with acid.... Then like the Servant, they arouse fear and disgust: "many were astonished at him" (52:14). He became "as one from whom others hide their faces" (53:3), and so do the crucified people, because they are disgusting to look at, and also because they might disturb the false happiness of those who have produced the Servant, unmask the truth covered up by the euphemisms we invent every day: developing countries, new democracies....

Like the Servant, the crucified people are "despised and rejected by others" (53:3). Everything has been taken from them, even their dignity. And really, what can the world see in them? What can it learn from them? What do they offer the world apart from their raw materials, their beaches and volcanoes, their peoples' folklore for the tourist industry? They are not respected but despised. They are despised most when ideology takes a religious tone to condemn them in God's name. It is said of the Servant: "we accounted him stricken, struck down by God, and afflicted," "numbered with the transgressors" (53:4, 12). And what is said about the crucified peoples? If they bear their sufferings patiently, we acknowledge they have a certain goodness, simplicity and above all, religious sense—unenlightened and superstitious in first-world terms—but nevertheless religious. But when they decide to live, when they become aware of their crucifixion, protest against it and struggle to escape from it, then they are not even recognized as God's people and the well-known litany is intoned against them: they are subversives, criminals, Marxists, terrorists, even atheists, they who invoke the God of life.... Despised in life, they are also despised in death. It is said of the Servant: "They made his grave with the wicked" (53:9). This is also the crucified people's epitaph. Sometimes they have no epitaph at all. For whereas ancient piety denied nobody a grave, now the crucified people lack even that. They are "disappeared," corpses thrown on to rubbish tips, buried in clandestine cemeteries. It is said of the Servant: "He was oppressed, and he was afflicted, yet he did not open his mouth; like a lamb that is led to the slaughter" (53:7). Today not all the crucified die like that. Archbishop Romero spoke out while he was alive and his death itself was a cry that shook many consciences, as are the murders of priests, nuns and well-known leaders of the people. But what word has been spoken by the great majority of the 75,000 murdered in El Salvador or the 100,000 in Guatemala or the starving children in Ethiopia? They are thousands and millions and they do not say a word. We do not know how they live or how they die. We do not know their names—Julia Elba and Celina are known because they were murdered with the Jesuits—and we do not even know exactly how many they are. It is said of the Servant: "By a perversion of justice he was taken away" (53:8), totally powerless to resist arbitrary injustice. Again this does not apply precisely to the crucified people today. Many struggle for their lives and they do not lack prophets to defend them. But the repression against their struggle is brutal. As for the prophets, first they try to discredit them, then to co-opt them into a society that will present them as an example of freedom and democracy—a well-calculated risk—until they become really dangerous. Then they kill them too. Is there really a court to defend the cause of the poor, or at least hear them? Is there a court that will take any notice of them and give them justice? During their lives they are not seriously listened to and when they are murdered their deaths are not investigated. Finally it is said of the Servant that he is innocent: "he had done no violence, and there was no deceit in his mouth" (53:9). And truly, what crimes were committed by the Guatemalan Indians who were burned alive inside the church of San Francisco, in Huehuetenango, or by the peasants murdered at the River Sumpul or the children dying of hunger in Ethiopia, Somalia or Sudan? What guilt do they have for the greed of those who rob their lands or the geopolitical interests of the great powers?

This is the crucified people's reality. It is the reality of "peoples," not just individuals. They are suffering peoples and they suffer in a way that is like the horrors we are told are inflicted on the Servant. In their poverty and death they are like the Servant and at least in this—but this least is a maximum—they are also like Jesus crucified. In the way they die, there can be no doubt that these peoples are the ones who go on filling up in their flesh what is lacking in Christ's passion. But it is also true that the crucified people point us to Jesus and help us to understand that the crucified Jesus is the Servant and why faith has proclaimed him as the Servant.

(b) Reflection on the Mystery of the Crucified People

I have used the language of simile and meditation to show how the crucified people are like the Servant. Technical language is not sufficient to communicate the likeness, and especially not the horror of it. But Isaiah's songs not only describe the reality and fate of the Servant but also reflect on him as a mystery, on the causes and consequences of his fate. And here too there is a likeness to the crucified people, although this time it is by analogy. That is why we shall explore it more analytically.

(i) The Servant is killed for establishing right and justice. Unlike the Synoptics telling the story of Jesus, Isaiah does not report the cause of the Servant's fate. But by collating the Servant's beginning and end into the same collection of songs, he does something similar. Originally the Servant was chosen by God to "bring forth justice to the nations" (42: 1, 4). He has been called "in righteousness" (42:6). In language that will later be taken up by Luke, he is to "open the eyes that are blind, to bring out the prisoners from the dungeon, from the prison those who sit in darkness" (42:7). This is the Servant's origin and the object of his mission, in which he becomes actively involved: "He will not grow faint or be crushed until he has established justice in the earth" (42:4).

In this way the Servant shares both Jesus' mission and his fate. This is also true of the crucified people, although here the reason for their death is tragically extended. In fact today too many die formally like the Servant for trying actively to establish justice: all kinds of prophets, priests and bishops, nuns and catechists, peasants and workers, students and lecturers. They try to establish right and justice and end up like the Servant. Their death is formally like the death of Jesus. But among the crucified people there are also many—the majority—who end up like the Suffering Servant but not directly for what they actively do, simply for what they are. They are killed *passively*, for just being what they are; even when they say nothing, they are the greatest proof of injustice and the greatest protest against it.

They are children, women and old people who die in massacres, simply because they live in conflict zones or because their deaths will terrorize and paralyze the poor even more.

Today the crucified people share analogously in the Servant's fate, but both groups have in common the fact that death is unjustly inflicted (nearly always), when they are completely helpless and in order to eradicate any attempt to establish justice. Some are more openly prophets, they denounce injustice and try to establish justice, whereas others are silent witnesses and their word is the most powerful there is, the irrepressible cry of reality itself. Some are more explicitly preachers of the gospel, proclaimers and initiators of the good news of justice, whereas others display in their lives the urgent need that the good news should come true. We may discuss where the *analogatum princeps* of the Servant lies. This is an important problem. But without the active Servant, the passive Servant would have no voice and unless the passive Servant existed, the active Servant would have no reason to exist.

(ii) The Servant is chosen by God for salvation. This Servant is mysteriously and paradoxically chosen by God (42:1; 49:3-7). In the earlier songs he is chosen to establish justice. This is the Servant's election as active prophet. But in the song of the Suffering Servant, even though the term "election" is not used, we hear of God's unfathomable plan that salvation should come from this Servant's pain and humiliation. This is not just another example of what we find in many places in the Old and New Testaments, a statement of God's partiality toward defending the poor and the victims. Here God chooses them and makes them the principal means of salvation, just as Jesus is, in his double character of proclaimer of the Kingdom and victim on the cross. In the language of today, here we have the mystery of salvation "from below." What is weak and little in this world has been chosen to save it. The song does not analyze this scandalous paradox any further, but we must stress how extreme it is. "Only through a difficult act of faith is the Servant poet capable of discovering what appears to be directly contrary to historical evidence."[7] Throughout history, philosophies, ideologies and theologies have not usually expected the chosen saviour to come from below, although of course Karl Marx also saw in the oppressed the positive possibility of emancipation "in the formation of a class of civil society which is not a class of civil society; of a class which is the dissolution of all classes; of a sphere which has a universal character because of its universal sufferings and which does not claim any special right for itself because no special wrong is done to it, just wrong pure and simple. . . ."[8] Here we have an attempt to formulate theoretically the role of the weak (of a social class, the proletariat, which nevertheless excludes the even more dispossessed) in historical salvation. But the Servant Song goes further. The election of the Servant is primarily a matter of faith, scandalous faith, in God's unfathomable plan. After this act of faith, we can seek some a priori reason for it, and we may say that internalized oppression generates (or may generate) awareness and this generates organization

for liberation, which can unite the masses—the passive Suffering Servant, from whom no one expects salvation—with their leaders and defenders, equivalent to the active Suffering Servant, who are usually considered as bringers of salvation. In language that has been official in the church, we can also state that the oppressed are their own agents of liberation. But the fundamental statement continues to be a matter of theologal faith. We cannot go beyond it, just as we cannot go beyond the statement that the one crucified is the one chosen to bring salvation. This is because accepting "election" is always of its nature a matter of faith.

It is not easy to determine very clearly who the one elected is today. But this does not mean that we cannot particularize at all and that this is not required by faith. In our world today "the First World is not the elect, and if the Third World is, the rich and oppressing classes are not. And if the oppressed classes are, those who serve oppression are not, however much they suffer in this service. But those who struggle for justice and liberation are."[9] Those who bring salvation to the world today, or at least those who are the principle of salvation, are the crucified poor peoples. And this, in historical language, is as scandalous as accepting God's choice of the Servant and the crucified Christ to bring salvation.

(iii) The Servant bears the sin of the world. The Servant is presented as innocent and without sin: "he had done no violence, and there was no deceit in his mouth" (53:9). Nevertheless he is the greatest proof of the real existence of sin. "He was wounded for our transgressions, crushed for our iniquities" (53:5), "the LORD has laid on him the iniquity of us all" (53:6), "he was ... stricken for the transgression of my people" (53:8), "he shall bear their iniquities" (53:11), "he bore the sin of many" (53:12).

The song tells us that the Servant bears the sin of others and thus he saves sinners from their sins. Thus we are told both what sin is and what is to be done with it. Sin is above all what causes death, what produces victims as real and visible as the Servant. Sin is what caused the death of Jesus and sin is what continues to cause the death of the crucified people. The invisible wrong done to God becomes historical in the visible wrong done to the victims. "Died for our sins," a fundamental statement in the New Testament, means really to be crushed on a particular historical occasion—by sinners. On the other hand, as to what should be done about sin, another fundamental question in the New Testament, the answer is clear, eradicate it, but with one essential condition: by bearing it. And rather than taking on the guilt of sin, bearing the sin of others means bearing the sin's historical effects: being ground down, crushed, put to death.

In this the crucified people certainly resemble the Suffering Servant. The crucified people bear the sins of their oppressors on their shoulders. There is nothing rhetorical about saying that the peasants and indigenous peoples carry on their shoulders what the powerful and the oligarchies have laid on them, that the Third World carries what the other worlds have laid on it. This load destroys them and they die like the Servant. The disfiguring of the Third World's face is the price for the other worlds' make-up. Third-World poverty is the price of their abundance; Third-World death the price of their life. In the words of Ellacuría, which I am not sure can be translated into other languages, the successive oppressors and exploiters of Latin America have "left it like a Christ."[10]

Nevertheless by really taking on the sin historically, the Servant can eradicate it. It becomes light and salvation and the scandalous paradox is resolved. Then the crucified people become the bearers of "historical soteriology." This is the main point and originality of the Latin American theological analysis of the Servant, and what distinguishes it from theology elsewhere.

(iv) The Servant is a Light to the Nations. In the songs about his mission we hear that the Servant is a "light" (42:6; 49:6). They add that he is a light not just for Israel but for all nations. When he is formally presented as the Suffering Servant, the term "light" is not used (although the term "salvation" is). Nevertheless the song stresses the visible appearance of the Servant, which is not shining but "shocking" and disgusting. And in this capacity to "shock" the Servant continues to be a light, unmasks the nations' lies and offers them humanizing truth.

The mere existence of the crucified people is what can—and in the last resort the only thing that can—unmask the lie by which this world's reality is concealed. Imprisoning truth with injustice is the fundamental sin of human beings and also of nations. From it very grave evils arise, as Paul tells us, among them the darkening of hearts. A light that has the power to unmask the lie is beneficial and very necessary. This is the light offered by the crucified people.

Confronted with the crucified people, Ellacuría said, the other worlds can know their own truth from what they produce, as in an inverted mirror. Using a metaphor taken from medicine, he said that to test the First World's health, we needed to do a "coproanalysis," that is, an examination of faeces. For what appears in this analysis is the reality of the crucified peoples and this is what gives the measure of the producers' health. The discovery is tragic, but necessary and healthy, because only in this way can the nations base themselves on the truth.

But the crucified people also offer positive light. They offer it as an instrument for a complete diagnosis of our world:

> From my point of view—and this can be both prophetic and paradoxical at the same time—the United States is much worse off than Latin America. Because the United States has a solution, but in my opinion it is a bad solution, both for it and for the world in general. On the other hand, in Latin America there are no solutions, only problems, but however painful this may be, it is better to have problems than to have a bad solution for the future of history.[11]

The crucified people show with blinding clarity that the solution offered by the First World today is bad in fact, because it is unreal since it cannot be universalized. It is bad ethically, because it is dehumanizing for all, for them and for the Third

World. Last, the crucified people throw light upon what utopia can and should be today. Utopia in the world today cannot be other than a "civilization of poverty,"[12] with all austerely sharing the earth's resources, and a "civilization of work" taking precedence over capital. Defining utopia in this way, apparently so simple but really so difficult to bring about, is possible through the light offered by the crucified people and not that coming from other worlds.

"They shall look on him whom they have pierced," says the Gospel of John about the crucified Christ. A powerful light also shines from the crucified people and it lights up the darkness of our world. It brings this world's evil to light. The temptation will always be not to look at the crucified people so as not to be dazzled by such a strong light. But what we cannot say is that there is no light in this world to guide our steps in the right direction.

(v) The Servant brings salvation. It is said of the Servant that he "shall make many righteous" (53:11), "through him the will of the LORD shall prosper" (53:10), that he "made intercession for the transgressors" (53:12). I have already analyzed the conceptual model that explains salvation (expiation) and its content (forgiveness of sins) in a previous chapter. To bring these reflections on the crucified people to a close, let us see whether they bring salvation to the world and if so what salvation. I want to stress that I mean historical salvation, because their crucifixion is historical and so is their carrying the sin of the world. [13]

There is much that is mysterious in this question, because we are still speaking about the salvation that the crucified people bring to "others." And of course there is much that is scandalous. But however scandalous, if we do not accept the possibility that the crucified people bring salvation, it is pointless to repeat that the Servant and the crucified Christ bring salvation. If we do not make salvation historical in some way, it is pointless to repeat that the Servant and the crucified Christ bring real concrete salvation.[14] Otherwise we would be reducing this to God's arbitrary will, which would be completely invisible and only known by him and quite unverifiable. But let us recall Ellacuría's remark: "There is no history of salvation without salvation in history."[15]

Above all, the crucified people demonstrate the existence of enormous sin and demand conversion because of it. But they also offer the possibility of conversion as nothing else in the world can. If the crucified people are not able to turn hearts of stone into hearts of flesh, nothing can. Once again Ellacuría expressed this vigorously:

> I only want—I am trying not to be too demanding—two things. I want you to set your eyes and your hearts on these peoples who are suffering so much —some from poverty and hunger, others from oppression and repression. Then (since I am a Jesuit), standing before this people thus crucified you must repeat St Ignatius' examination from the first week of the Exercises. Ask yourselves: what

have I done to crucify them? What do I do to uncrucify them? What must I do for this people to rise again?[16]

The crucified peoples also offer values that are not offered elsewhere. We may discuss whether they generate these values because they have nothing else to hang on to, and whether these values will disappear when their present economic and social context disappears and is swallowed up by the Western world and its "civilization." But the values are there and they offer them to all. Puebla said it in plain words, of which very little notice is taken in Western countries and churches. Speaking of the poor, those we have called the crucified people here, it says that they offer an evangelizing potential. It describes this potential as "gospel values of solidarity, service, simplicity and openness to accepting the gift of God" (1147). Put into historical language, the poor have a humanizing potential because they offer community against individualism, service against selfishness, simplicity against opulence, creativity against an imposed copycat culture, openness to transcendence against bleak positivism and crass pragmatism. Of course, it is true that not all the poor offer these things. Many of them internalize opposite values and fall victim to them. But it is also true that the poor as a whole do offer them and, structurally speaking, they offer them in a way not offered by other worlds. "Poor with spirit" was Ellacuría's phrase to stress the saving power of the poor; but he added that the material conditions of poverty and not others produce a connaturality with this spirit, which enables them to live as people who are saved and saving.

The crucified people offer hope, senseless and absurd, it may be said, "because it's all they have left," others may argue. But there it is and it should not be trivialized by other worlds. Of course it is hope against hope, but it is also active hope that has been demonstrated in work and struggle for liberation. What success this has is another matter. The oppressors' world appears to be emerging triumphantly and suffocating these struggles, although they should not trumpet this as a triumph but mourn it as a disaster. By their triumph they crush the crucified people's hope and deprive themselves of these people's humanizing potential. In any case, the very fact that hope rises again and again in the crucified people shows that there is a hopeful current in history available to all. As the main source of this hopeful current is the crucified people, they are able to give hope to others.

The crucified people offer great love. It is not that they are masochists or suicidal, or that they are forced to make a virtue of necessity. It is simply that the crucified people's countless martyrs show that love is possible, because it is real and great love is possible because many have shown it. In a structurally selfish world, certainly based on egocentrism, which mocks this, this love is a great humanizing gift.

The crucified people are prepared to forgive their oppressors. They do not want to triumph over them, but to share with them, [17] and offer them a future. To those who draw near to help them, they open their arms and accept them and thus, even without their knowing it, forgive them. At the same time the miracle described in Karl Rahner's phrase, "Only the forgiven know they are sinners," now takes place. When the crucified people allow the oppressors' world to approach them, they make it possible for this world to recognize itself for what it is, sinful, but also to know that it is forgiven. In this way they introduce into the oppressors' world the humanizing reality so absent from it, grace: becoming something not only through what you achieve, but also through what is given to you, unhoped for, undeserved and gratuitously. The crucified people generate solidarity,[18] mutual support between human beings and believers, openness to one another, giving the best of oneself to others and receiving their best in return. This solidarity—small in quantitative terms—is nevertheless real and new. It offers a small-scale model of human and Christian relationships between peoples and churches.

Last, the crucified people offer a faith, a way of being church and a holiness that are more authentic, more Christian and more relevant to the present-day world, and that recapture more of Jesus. Again, this is still at the seed stage rather than a tree in full leaf, but it is there. And there is no other form of faith, no other way of being church or of holiness that seems to make humanity more human or be a better way to God.

(c) The crucified people as the presence of christ crucified in history. I have analyzed the crucified people's situation in relation to the Suffering Servant through its historical similarity to what the Servant Songs say. But the crucified people also make Christ present in history through the fact that they are a people and not just an individual. They make Christ present first and foremost through the bare fact of being massively on the cross. But they also make him present because, like the lamb of God, they carry the sin of the world and by carrying it they offer light and salvation to all. This insight does not come from pure biblical textual analysis, but nevertheless I think it is true.

Of course, my presentation of the crucified people here may be open to question. But we must be aware of the fundamental issue, which is much more important: it would be idle to say that Christ crucified has a body in history and not identify it in some way.

From the viewpoint of christology we must ask what this body is. I believe the christology of the cross described above helps us to find it in the crucified people and to see the saving mystery of the cross in them. Therefore we can say that the crucified people are Christ's crucified body in history. But the opposite is also true: the present-day crucified people allow us to know the crucified Christ better. He is the head of the body and in him we can see Yahweh's Suffering Servant and understand his mystery of light and salvation.

2. The Crucified People as a "Martyred People"

To call the peoples of the Third World "crucified people," "Yahweh's Suffering Servant," "the presence of the crucified Christ in history," is the most important theological statement we can make about them. Nevertheless, I also want to call them a "martyred people," not because this adds anything new, but for immediate pastoral reasons and broader theological reasons.

For pastoral reasons, we should remember that Latin America is the continent where, since Vatican II, more Christians have suffered violent death than any other. A theoretical argument has arisen about whether to call them martyrs or not. What is important is not so much the name but the fact that if this problem is not solved we fall into the anomalous situation in which, on the one hand, martyrdom is the supremely Christian death, and on the other, those who today are killed in a way that most resembles Jesus' death are not held to share in this supreme death because they do not fulfill the canonical and dogmatic conditions for martyrdom. It is an important subject for theological reasons, because in order to clarify it we have to look to Jesus: to his death, but also to his life; that is, what he was killed for. This radically shifts the focus of the question and it now becomes: was Jesus himself a martyr or not? So let us look briefly at what is understood by martyrdom and what, in our view, should be understood by the term.

(a) The Traditional Understanding of Martyrdom

The New Testament realized very early that persecution is inherent in the new faith. In its earliest text it says: "You yourselves know that this is what we are destined for. In fact, when we were with you, we told you beforehand that we were to suffer persecution" (1 Thess. 3: 3-4). It was realized very early that this persecution could reach the point of violent death. Out of this situation a theology of martyrdom developed, understood as bearing "witness"—*martyrion*—to the truth of the faith to the point of laying down one's life [19]. On the other hand, John's theology developed another tradition on the virtue of laying down one's life for love of others (John 15:13; 1 John 3:16).

The persecutions of the early centuries forced Christians to deepen their theological reflection on martyrdom and it gradually became more complex. Briefly, martyrdom was considered to be the necessary result of the specific conflict inherent in Christian faith and not as something unexpected or arbitrary. Positively speaking, it was thought of as a way of sharing in the death and resurrection of Christ; as God's greatest grace; as the highest form of love for God and neighbor; and as death with saving power for those who survived the martyrs.[20]

In the course of history, the theological notion of martyrdom became more precise and even canonical. In our days there is an official definition of martyrdom in force, according to which it is the "free and patient acceptance of death for the cause of the faith (including its moral teaching) in its totality or with respect to a particular doctrine (but with the totality of the faith always in view)."[21] Two elements of this definition are important in order to understand the point of current debate: martyrdom is caused by *odium fidei* and death should not be a response to previous violence on the martyr's part.

Here, then, is a theological definition of martyrdom, but it is undoubtedly the case that the various formulations throughout history have always arisen from the actual violent deaths that Christians died. To give an example from this century: Maria Goretti, murdered in 1902 for defending her virginity, was declared a martyr. Thus witness borne through moral conduct was added to the earlier criteria for martyrdom: death bearing witness to the faith and the related *odium fidei*. We are in a similar situation in Latin America today. The historical novelty lies in the fact that Christians are violently killed, not for publicly professing the faith or a doctrine of the church against other religious faiths (or atheist ideologies) or against other churches, as was the norm in the past. The most dramatic illustration of this is the fact that today those who murder Christians are also nominally Christians and sometimes they even justify their murders as defending the Christian faith.

This new reason for the murders of Christians and their huge number have forced us to rethink the definition of martyrdom. Otherwise we would have the paradoxical situation in which many Christians were violently put to death but could not be called martyrs. And whatever the official definition of martyrdom, common sense and the sense of faith say that this cannot be. Karl Rahner, in one of his last writings, which was specifically about Latin American martyrs, defended the need for a wider concept of martyrdom: "But, for example, why should not someone like Bishop Romero, who died while fighting for justice in society, a struggle he waged out of the depths of his concern as a Christian—why should he not be a martyr?" [22] Above all, this requires the reformulation of *odium fidei* as *odium iustitiae* (which accords so well with God's biblical revelation). And it presupposes that the condition "without violence" can allow for prophetic violence (which is in perfect accord with the prophets of Israel and Jesus).

(b) The "Christian" Understanding of Martyrdom

The Latin American martyrs have forced us to rethink the traditional notion of martyrdom. In our opinion they have done something even more important: they have obliged theology to rethink its methodological approach to Christian martyrdom. Should it be through the current official definition (according to which they probably would not be martyrs) or through the death of Jesus (for which we have to change the official notion of martyrdom)? In Latin America we have in fact followed the latter course, both in popular Christian awareness and in theology. Leonardo Boff, for example, begins his analysis of martyrdom starting from "Jesus Christ the basic sacrament of martyrdom," [23] so the martyrs are considered to be "martyrs of the kingdom of God" [24] and are recognized in terms of the Kingdom to be built or the anti-Kingdom to be destroyed. [25]

To approach martyrdom like this, however, is not just the result of an undeniable Christian insight, but the fundamental methodological choice running right through Latin American christology: to go back to Jesus in order to rethink all theological realities in terms of him. It means that analysis of Christian death and martyrdom must also begin with Jesus. The most "Christian" death will be that of Jesus, and throughout history the deaths that most resemble that of Jesus will be the "Christian" ones, whether they are called martyrdom or not. But if we continue to use the term "martyrdom" to describe the supremely Christian death, we must change our standpoint when we analyze it. We must not start from a definition of martyrdom according to which even Jesus might not have been a martyr, but from Jesus' cross.

Those who defend the official definition as a way of understanding martyrdom can say that the New Testament itself did not describe Jesus' death as martyrdom and did not give Jesus the title of martyr. But this argument is not conclusive. It is well known that after the resurrection Christians concentrated on titles that explained his unique divine status, whereas the more human and humiliating titles were few in number and less to the fore. Some titles related to the term "martyr" were maintained (the "lamb that was slain" in Revelation) and we should not forget the Synoptic revival of the title "Servant," although in narrative form. As for the specific term "martyr" (witness), it is understandable that it was used more for Christians who bore witness to Christ than for Christ himself who was witnessed to (although the Letter to the Hebrews also speaks of Christ, by implication, as a witness). In New Testament logic the same thing may have occurred with the concept of martyr as with the concept of faith: it speaks about faith in Christ but not about Jesus' faith, although, as we have seen, the Synoptics also revived this.

Nevertheless even in the official definition there is obviously a relation between the martyrdom of Christians and Christ: bearing witness to Christ. What happens is that it is not essential to this relation that the martyr's death and its causes should reproduce the specific type of death that Jesus died on the cross. In the official definition a person is a martyr for being faithful to something demanded by Christ, but the way of being a martyr does not have to reproduce historically either Jesus' death or its historical causes.

If we follow the other approach, the main addition to the concept of martyrdom is affinity with what Christ was: a martyr is defined not only, or principally, as someone who dies *for* Christ, but someone who dies *like* Christ; a martyr is defined as not only or principally someone who dies *for Christ*, but someone who dies *for Jesus' cause*. Martyrdom, in this definition, is not only death in fidelity to a demand of Christ's—which, for the sake of argument, could be imagined as being arbitrary—but the faithful reproduction of Jesus' death. The essence of martyrdom is affinity with the death of Jesus.

I think the Latin American martyrs have forced a rethinking of martyrdom and brought out the basic limitation of the official definition: martyrdom is not thought of in terms of Jesus' life and death. The Latin American martyrs did die to defend the same cause as Jesus, God's Kingdom for the poor, and they were threatened, persecuted and put to death by the anti-Kingdom. Whatever the subjective holiness of these martyrs in comparison with others, there can be no doubt that objectively they are more "like" Jesus. They are not martyrs, strictly speaking, because they defended something central to the church, any more than Jesus could have been, but because they defended something central to God's Kingdom. They are not martyrs *for* the church, even though they lived and died *in* it, but martyrs for God's Kingdom, humanity. To put it graphically, when Archbishop Romero was murdered, at the altar, we had to go back to the twelfth century to find a precedent, in Thomas à Beckett, archbishop of Canterbury. But there was one essential difference, brought out in the following lines by José María Valverde:

> The story tells how long ago
> by a king's command
> a certain archbishop died
> his blood splashed into the chalice
> for defending the Church's liberty
> against the royal power.
> All very well
> but when have we ever heard
> of an archbishop murdered at the altar
> not for preaching the Church's independence
> but simply because he stood
> on the side of the poor
> and voiced their thirst for justice
> crying aloud to heaven?
> Perhaps we must go back to the original
> one they put to death
> as a subversive criminal. [26]

These present-day deaths for God's Kingdom are like Jesus' death, and they also illuminate the aspect of martyrdom and witness in the death of Jesus. We saw this before but we may recall it here. Jesus did not preach himself and did not come to bear witness to himself. He preached God's Kingdom and the God of the Kingdom, and bore witness to it with his life. So Jesus is also a witness and martyr for the Kingdom of God. And therefore, theologically, those who today bear witness with their lives to God's Kingdom, like Jesus, are martyrs and in them we find the *analogatum princeps* of martyrdom.

With these thoughts I am not simply trying to reconcile the traditional notion of martyrdom as witness with the death of Jesus. I am also trying to understand martyrdom today from the standpoint of Jesus and "his" fundamental witness, in order to be able to speak of the Latin American martyrs properly and precisely. All martyrdom bears witness to ultimate values, and Christian martyrdom is not concerned with just any reality held to be the ultimate, but with what is in fact the ultimate reality, and with how to bear witness to this ultimate reality.

Jesus did not bear witness to just any God but to the God of the Kingdom, the God of the poor, the God of life, mercy and justice. He bore witness to "that" God directly by carrying out works of life, mercy and justice for those who are the true God's preferred ones, and by fighting against the idols who put them to death. The fundamental witness that Jesus bore to his God is therefore expressed primarily in his works of love rather than in a confession of faith. It is expressed primarily in a sacramental way by making the true God present, rather than by defending true definitions about this God. When such witness requires Jesus to give his life, then remaining faithful to this love is his final witness to a God who is love.

Therefore I believe that we should understand Christian martyrdom formally and directly above all in the Johannine terms of death for the sake of love, as Thomas Aquinas also states: love is the formal element that gives excellence to martyrdom.[27] Of course, bearing witness to love and bearing witness to truth are not mutually exclusive, but we have to see where Christian faith puts the priority. Both things can be united if we say that in martyrdom for the cause of justice the martyr is bearing witness to the truth of the God of justice, the truth of the God of the poor; and the practice that leads to martyrdom is often explicitly, or sometimes implicitly, accompanied by a faith in this God. Vice versa, the evident *odium justitiae* contains an implicit but very real *odium fidei*. So it is not a question of opposing one to the other, but of priority. In practice, this is obvious in Latin America, because at present people are not assassinated for purely external confessions of faith, but they are being assassinated for witness to the faith operating through charity (justice). Theologically, it also seems obvious because the most complete way of bearing witness to the God of love, mercy and justice is to make God present through loving activity in history, through works of mercy and justice. In conclusion, this "new" way of seeing means only that we are returning to the "older" way, thinking of Jesus' cross as the ultimate witness to God's love, particularly for victims and against their oppressors. And this is how Archbishop Romero saw it: "For me, who are the true martyrs in the popular sense?... They are people who have preached this embracing of poverty. They are real people who have gone to the dangerous limits, where the White Warrior Union threatens them, where warnings can be sent to people and they end up being killed, as Christ was killed.[28]

(c) Martyrdom by Analogy: the "Martyred People"

Understanding martyrdom in terms of Jesus' death clarifies what is fundamental about it. This also means we must speak of martyrdom by analogy. The analogy is necessary, because today many people are dying in a context similar to that of Jesus, whereas others are dying in different contexts. To illustrate the analogy, let us describe three typical situations, although they cannot always be adequately distinguished.

(i) At present there are many martyrs who structurally reproduce the martyrdom of Jesus. Examples are the martyrdom of Archbishop Romero and many other priests, nuns, catechists, delegates of the word, students, trade unionists, peasants, workers, teachers, journalists, doctors, lawyers....[29] Subjectively, some may have been holier than others, of course, but in their lives they defended the Kingdom and attacked the anti-Kingdom, they exercized prophetic violence and were put to death. So they are like Jesus; and in them we see clearly what I have called the Christian notion of martyrdom. Nevertheless, there are other kinds of death that are not exactly the same as the above. In them the "vulnerability" or "freedom," which are characteristics of true martyrdom according to the official definition, and appear in the death of Jesus, are not as obviously present. So we have to ask whether they can also be called martyrs by analogy.

(ii) There are many Christians in the popular organizations, who defend the Kingdom by open struggle and make use of some sort of violence—beyond the prophetic word—social, political and even armed violence. Many of them are put to death, but not all of them are defenceless. In order to tell whether they can be called martyrs, we have to take into account—supposing the ethical legitimacy of the various kinds of struggle—the central criterion for martyrdom: that it should be unjustly inflicted death for love's sake. From this viewpoint Aquinas saw no difficulty in considering a soldier's death as a possible martyrdom, since "the good of the republic is the highest of goods" and "any human good can be a cause of martyrdom insofar as it is referred to God."[30]

Whether these deaths are martyrdom or not may be considered a *quaestio disputata*, and in the end only God can judge where great love has been shown. But it is worth reflecting on the question because we cannot ignore the countless Christians who struggle politically, socially and even by taking up arms for love of the people, and who are ready to lay down their lives generously for love. Only God knows how great their love is and whether and how they overcome the dehumanizing dangers, the mystique of violence condemned by Archbishop Romero, and the negative by-products generated by struggle, especially armed struggle. However, they can reproduce a central element of martyrdom: laying down one's life for love, and so they can share in martyrdom by analogy. In any case, it is very important that in death their dignity is maintained, whether they are called "fallen" or "martyrs" and that their mothers at least have this comfort.

(iii) Finally, there are the masses who are innocently and anonymously murdered, even though they have not used any explicit form of violence, even verbal. They do not actively lay down their lives to defend the faith, or even, directly, to defend God's Kingdom. They are the peasants, children, women and old people, above all, who die slowly day after day and die violently with incredible cruelty and totally unprotected, as we saw in the meditation on the crucified people. They are simply killed and massacred. And they die without freedom, if not through necessity.

I have called these crucified people Yahweh's Servant, but there is no word in church language to express what, if any, excellence there is in their death, and they are not called martyrs because they lack the requisite of having given their lives "freely." This is because the poor do not have freedom (just as they often do not have the material conditions to possess the kind of virtues required for canonization).[31] We must find some solution to this paradox so that we do not fall into the absurd position of saying that the faith has nothing to say to these passively crucified people and they have nothing important to say to the faith. In order to be able to call them martyrs we must understand martyrdom analogically, and we also must give deep thought to what is martyrdom's *analogatum princeps*, and think about it looking at the cross of Jesus.

In comparison with Jesus' death, the deaths of these murdered masses, descriptively and historically speaking, do not so much illustrate the active character of the struggle against the anti-Kingdom or the freedom with which this is undertaken. But they do illustrate their historical innocence—because they have done nothing to deserve death except to be poor—and vulnerability—because they are not even physically capable of avoiding it. Above all, their deaths make clear that it is these masses who are unjustly burdened with a sin which has been annihilating them little by little throughout their lives and annihilates them finally in their death. Whether they are called martyrs or not, these masses who are oppressed during their lives and die in massacres are the ones who illustrate best the vast suffering of the world.

If we consider martyrdom in terms of the anti-Kingdom's response to those who struggle actively for the Kingdom, the *analogatum princeps* of the martyr is that exemplified by Archbishop Romero. If we consider it in terms of really bearing the sin of the anti-Kingdom, the *analogatum princeps* becomes the unprotected masses, who are put to death in huge numbers innocently and anonymously. Earlier we called them Yahweh's Suffering Servant, now we call them the "martyred people." They are the ones who most abundantly and cruelly "fill up in their flesh what is lacking in Christ's passion". They are the Suffering Servant and they are the crucified Christ today.

Epilogue

This volume ends with the cross of Jesus and with the cross of his body in history. The reason for this is not theoretical but purely practical: to divide between two volumes material that would be excessively long for one. I hope, God willing, to continue with the history of Jesus in a second volume tracing this history from the faith unleashed by his resurrection down to the faith of our own time. Even allowing for this, the fact of a book on Jesus the liberator ending with a crucified Christ and a crucified people may seem excessively abrupt and disconcerting, and readers may well feel inclined to look for a way beyond the resultant uncertainty, normally provided by speaking of Jesus' resurrection. So I should like to say a final word about this.

The history of Jesus does not end with the cross, since God raised him from among the dead. The cross is not, therefore, the last word on Jesus, nor is the cross of the crucified peoples God's final word to them. But I do not think that we should thereby make the liberative aspects of Jesus' life depend only on his resurrection. This, in effect, cannot be understood simply as a happy ending, but must be seen as the intrinsic consummation of his life. It is not just an exaltation of Jesus, but also a confirmation of the truth of his life.

This Jesus who concentrated his life on proclaiming and building the Kingdom of God for the poor, who showed ultimate mercy to them, who for defending the victims of this world faced up to his executioners and ended up as a victim himself, who through all this placed himself face to face with God and placed God before us—this Jesus is liberation and good news for the poor and for all those who seek to be human in this world.

The divine confirmation that this life is the true life is the resurrection, but the historical confirmation that Jesus' life is liberating and good news is—paradoxically—the cross. Because of this, not only in spite of, but also through the cross, Jesus' life is liberation and good news today. Leonardo Boff, at the end of his book on the passion and cross of Jesus, asks "how do we preach the cross of Christ today?" and, hesitantly and tortuously—since there is no other way of speaking about the cross—concludes in the language of good news: "Living the cross of our Lord Jesus Christ implies a mysticism of life."[1] And Juan Luis Segundo, at the start of his own book of christology, quotes these words of Boff's, calling them "gospel," "the gospel of the cross."[2]

This is what I have tried to set out and examine in this book. The omnipresent cross of Latin America questions, but also—miraculously—empowers the liberative element of those who take up their cross out of love and with love, and so the Jesus who devoted his life to the crucified of history and at the end bore his cross himself goes on being liberator and good news for the poor of this world and those who seek solidarity with them.

Our reason can, undoubtedly, formulate many questions about this way of ending a book on Jesus the liberator, and can, quite rightly, look to the resurrection to shed light on the cross. But such an abrupt ending can also have its advantages. The scripture scholar Xavier Alegre, who was kind and patient enough to read through the manuscript, commented that this ending reminded him of that other ending, the shorter ending of Mark's Gospel. This has no appearances of the risen Christ, but simply the commandment: "Go . . . to Galilee; there you will see him . . ." (16:7).

Galilee is the setting of Jesus' historical life, the place of the poor and the little ones. The poor of this world—the Galilee of today—are where we encounter the historical Jesus and where he is encountered as liberator. And this Galilee is also where the risen Christ who appears to his disciples will show himself as he really is, as the Jesus we have to follow and keep present in history: the historical Jesus, the man from Nazareth, the person who was merciful and faithful to his death on the cross, the perennial sacrament in this world of a liberator God.

Notes

Introduction

1. Recently, J. I. González Faus has compiled a list of thirty works, which he classifies as showing the "revolution in christology": "La revolución de las cristologías," *El Ciervo* 433 (1987), pp. 4-13. See also J. A. Fitzmeyer, "The Biblical Commission and Christology," *Theological Studies* 3 (1985), pp. 407-79.

2. These christologies show a radical approach to the specificity and uniqueness of Christ's salvific mediation and this needs to be compared to that of other religious mediators.

3. In my view, the foremost question for christology produced by these theologies is what really mediates God. Christ reveals God through being "human" in masculine form, but this does not exhaust being human, and therefore does not exhaust God's mediation.

4. From a pastoral point of view, popular images of Christ should obviously be taken into account. But the reflections of the communities on Christ also need to be taken into account theologically, since, though one can argue about whether or not the communites are "doing theology" properly so-called (see the different views of J. L. Segundo and L. Boff), their actual faith at least provides "light" for theoretical christology, and a sort of light that does not usually come from anywhere else.

5. González Faus, *La humanidad nueva. Ensayo de cristología* (Santander, 7th ed., 1986), p. 9.

6. This is also the title given to a two-volume collective work setting out the basic concepts of liberation theology. I. Ellacuría and J. Sobrino (eds) *Mysterium liberationis. Conceptos fundamentales de la Teología de la Liberación* (Madrid, 1990). Eng. trans. (abbreviated, one volume) *Mysterium Liberationis. Basic Concepts of Liberation Theology* (Maryknoll, N.Y.: Orbis Books, 1993).

7. L. Boff, *Jesucristo y la liberación del hombre* (Madrid, 2d ed., 1987), p. 41.

8. C. Duquoc, *Mesianismo de Jesús y discreción de Dios. Ensayo sobre los límites de la cristología* (Madrid, 1985), p. 11. Sp. trans. of *Christologie: Essai dogmatique, t. 2, Le Messie* (Paris, 1972).

9. J. L. Segundo, *El hombre de hoy ante Jesús de Nazaret* II/1 (Madrid, 1982), p. 29. Eng. trans. *Jesus of Nazareth Yesterday and Today. Vol. III, The Humanist Christology of Paul* (Maryknoll, N.Y.: Orbis Books; London: Sheed & Ward, 1986).

10. *"Con los pobres de la tierra." La justicia social en los profetas de Israel* (Madrid, 1984), p. 13

11. Segundo has insisted on this point in *El dogma que libera* (Santander, 1989), pp. 188-90, quoting Augustine's fine words: "The Lord himself, in deigning to be our way, did not wish to hold on to us, but to pass on." Eng. trans. *The Liberation of Dogma* (Maryknoll, N.Y.: Orbis Books, 1992). See also Duquoc, *Mesianismo*: from another point of view he

stresses the danger that christologies can end up by presenting Christ as a pure and simple substitute for God.

12. W. Pannenberg, *Fundamentos de cristología* (Salamanca, 1974), p. 22: "The succession of interpretations belongs to the historical essence of the very material to be interpreted, insofar as this, thanks to its universally significant intent, constantly encourages the inclusion of new points of departure and so produces new interpretations." Sp. trans. of *Grundzüge der Christologie* (Gütersloh, 3d ed., 1969). Eng. trans. *Jesus—God and Man* (London: SCM Press; Philadelphia, PA: Westminster Press, 1968).

13. Boff, *Jesucristo y la liberación*, p. 196.

14. The present work is a more systematic development, with additions and corrections, of what I have written in *Cristología desde América Latina* (Mexico City, 1977). Eng. trans. *Christology at the Crossroads* (Maryknoll, N.Y.: Orbis Books, 1978); *Jesús en América Latina* (San Salvador, 1982). Eng. trans. *Jesus in Latin America* (Maryknoll, N.Y.: Orbis Books, 1987); "Jesús de Nazaret," C. Floristán and J. Tamayo (eds) *Conceptos fundamentales de pastoral* (Madrid, 1983), pp. 480-513.

15. In this work, I am concentrating on liberation from injustice, this being the most comprehensive expression of oppression, as it denies life and community, and not dealing explicitly with other forms of oppression.

16. On the concept of liberation, see I. Ellacuría, "En torno al concepto y a la idea de liberación," I. Ellacuría and others (eds), *Implicaciones sociales y políticas de la teología de la liberación* (Madrid, 1989), pp. 91ff.

17. J. Sobrino, "Jesús como buena noticia. Repercusiones para un talante evangélico," *Sal Terrae* (1988), pp. 715-26.

18. González Faus, *La humanidad nueva*, p. 579.

19. I. Ellacuría, "Historicidad de la salvación cristiana," *Mysterium liberationis* I, pp. 323-73. Eng. trans, "The Historicity of Christian Salvation," *Mysterium Liberationis*, pp. 251-89.

20. What I mean by "spiritual," "spirituality," "living with spirit" is explained in my *Liberación con espíritu* (San Salvador, 1986). Eng. trans. *Spirituality of Liberation* (Maryknoll, N.Y.: Orbis Books, 1988).

PART I: THE METHOD OF LATIN AMERICAN CHRISTOLOGY

1. A New Image and a New Faith in Christ

1. Years ago, Juán Luís Segundo said, "Leftwing, rightwing and centrist Christians will all agree that Jesus Christ is truly human and truly God, that God is one in three persons, that Jesus Christ, by his death and resurrection, redeemed the human race," "Las 'élites' latinoamericanas: problemática humana y cristiana ante el cambio social," Varios, *Fe cristiana y cambio social* (Salamanca, 1973), p. 209.

2. Quoted in G. Gutiérrez, *Dios y el oro en las Indias*, (Salamanca, 2d ed. 1990), p. 157.

3. Gutiérrez, *Dios y el oro*, p. 156.

4. Centuries later Medellín and Puebla were to take up again this christology of the body of Christ. Archbishop Romero was to speak of the poor people as the "servant of Yahweh" today, and Ignacio Ellacuría called them the "crucified people."

5. S. Trinidad, "Christology, conquista, colonización," J. Míguez Bonino (ed.), *Faces of Jesus* (New York, 1977), pp. 58-62.

6. L. Boff, "Salvation in Jesus Christ and the Process of Liberation," *Concilium* 96 (vol. 6, no. 10) (1974), pp. 78-91.

7. Walter Kasper, *Jesus the Christ* (London: Burns & Oates; New York: Herder and Herder, 1976), p. 15.

8. The conflict and threat inherent in the new faith has been very well understood by the powerful, from the Rockefeller report after Medellín to the Santa Fe document produced by Reagan's advisers.

9. When Archbishop Romero commented on the tragedy that the Salvadorean peasants fought each other, some being in popular organiszations and others in pro-government organizations, he said with great insight: "The worst thing is that our rural people are being disunited by what most profoundly unites them, shared poverty, the shared need to survive, to be able to give something to their children, to be able to bring bread, education and health to their homes," J. Sobrino, I. Martín-Baró, R. Cardenal, *La voz de los sin voz* (San Salvador, 1980), p. 100. Eng. trans. *Voice of the Voiceless* (Maryknoll, N.Y.: Orbis Books; London: CIIR, 1985), p. 92.

10. F. Damen, "Sectas," I. Ellacuría & J. Sobrino (eds), *Mysterium liberationis. Conceptos fundamentales de la teología de la liberación*, II (Madrid, 1990) makes a detailed analysis of the meaning of the sects and also of their salvific significance. He identifies the principal cause of the proliferation of the sects as "the permanent and developing social crisis" (p. 431). This is the origin, as regards the ecclesiological aspects, of new communal forms for living religious experience which differ from the traditional institutional ones, but what underlies all this is the Christological question, the need for "salvation." (Eng. trans.: see n. 6 to Intro. above.)

11. We may query how widespread were R. Bultmann's existentialist image of Christ or Teilhard de Chardin's evolutionary image or Rahner's transcendental image without diminishing the value of their christologies. Those who claim that liberation christology is a failure or merely elitist, because the image of Christ it encourages and from which it starts is a minority one, should be reminded that the importance of a christology is not measured in this way, but by its influence on the collective consciousness of the majority, whatever explicit familiarity they have with it.

12. In my view, the importance of this fact goes beyond Latin America. The image of "Christ the liberator" restores the essence of the title "Messiah," which though maintained down the centuries, has by now lost any sense of historical or popular messianism. The title "Christ the liberator" picks up a history which was more or less broken off after the first generations of Christians.

13. *Instruction on Some Aspects of the "Theology of Liberation"* (1984), Introduction.

14. *Christian Freedom and Liberation* (1986), Introduction, 1.

15. To this there should be added other ways of making Christ absolute, this time based on the universalization of what in Jesus is only particular: Jesus as white, male, Asian (although the underlying presentation of him has been as "European"), absolutes which justify, or at least facilitate, oppression by race, gender or religion.

16. It is very important to emphasize this fact. Medellín and Puebla are the best and most original expression of the Latin American church tradition. They express what is new about this church in relation to its own past and in relation to other churches in the present. And since the situation of the Latin American continent has not substantially changed from the time of Medellín and Puebla, both must continue to be an obligatory reference point. They are our basic tradition.

17. In another passage it says that "all growth in humanity brings us close to reproducing the image of the Son" ("Education," 9).

18. "Opening Address," I, 14.

2. The Ecclesial and Social Setting of Christology

1. I. Ellacuría, "Estudio teológico-pastoral de la Instrucción sobre algunos aspectos de la teología de la liberación," *RLT* 2 (1984), pp. 148-9.

2. "Estudio teológico-pastoral," p. 150.

3. *Ibid.*, p. 150.

4. I. Ellacuría, *Conversión de la Iglesia al reino de Dios* (San Salvador, 1985), p. 168.

5. J. Ratzinger, in his commentary on section 11 of *Gaudium et spes* in *Das Zweite Vatikanische Konzil* III, in *Lexikon für Theologie und Kirche* (Freiburg, 1968), pp. 313-4, says that the Zurich text used "signs of the times" in the sense of "the voice of God in the present," which was not accepted in this radical form on the basis of exegetical, christological and ecumenical arguments. But, though the formulation was modified, the intention of the text remains, according to Ratzinger, to complement the past by the present, and stress the presence here and now of Christ and his Spirit.

6. Normally the "signs of the times" are understood in the historical-pastoral sense, but people are very suspicious of attempts to use them in the historical-theolagal sense. This is the view of A. Tornos, quoting a remark by the council observer Lukas Vischer, "We have no criterion for distinguishing the voice of God from any other deceptive voice in the great phenomena of our age," "Los signos de los tiempos como lugar teológico," *Estudios Eclesiásticos* 207 (1978), pp. 527-8.

7. J. L. Segundo, "Revelación, fe, signos de los tiempos," *RLT* 14 (1988), pp. 123-44; J. Sobrino, "Los 'signos de los tiempos' en la teología de la liberación," Various, *Fides quae per caritatem operatur* (Bilbao, 1989), pp. 249-69.

8. I. Ellacuría, "Discernir el 'signo' de los tiempos," *Diakonía* 17 (1981), p. 58.

9. J. Sobrino and others, *La voz de los sin voz* (San Salvador, 1980), p. 208. (See n. 9 to ch. 1 above.)

10. Some might think that these words are important pastorally and spiritually, but that they are not "scientific," although it would be difficult to accuse Ignacio Ellacuría's theology of lack of intellectual discipline.

11. Ellacuría, "Discernir el 'signo' de los tiempos," p. 58.

12. K. Rahner, *Ich glaube an Jesus Christus* (Einsiedeln, 1968), pp. 11-15.

13. K. Rahner, "Líneas fundamentales de una cristología sistemática," K. Rahner and W. Thüsing, *Cristología. Estudio teológico y exegético* (Madrid, 1975), p. 21. Sp. trans. of "Grundlinien einer systematischer Christologie," *Christologie—systematisch und exegetische Arbeitsgrundlagen für eine interdisziplinäre Vorlesung*, QD 55 (Freiburg, 1972). Eng. trans. *A New Christology* (London: Burns & Oates; New York: Crossroad, 1980). The author bases his argument on the reality of the object of faith, Christ: "the original unity of his 'being in itself' and his 'meaning for us,' a unity which cannot be adequately dissolved" (*ibid*).

14 Traditionally, since the time of Melchior Cano, the *loci theologici* have been scripture, tradition, the magisterium, theological opinions: that is, texts given to us that enjoy greater or lesser authority.

15. The particular places also have their importance. So, in ideal terms, a university may encourage intellectual discipline and debate with other academic disciplines, a seminary a pastoral, everyday perspective, a base community the grassroots perspective of the people of God, a bishop's office fidelity to the magisterium. Their dangers are also easily imagined: irrelevant, sterile academicism, clericalism, immediate responses, submission without freedom. . . .

16. J. Miranda, *Marx y la Biblia* (Salamanca, 1972), p. 82. Eng. trans. *Marx and the Bible* (Maryknoll, N.Y.: Orbis Books, 1974), p. 57.

17. J. L. Segundo, "La opción por los pobres como clave hermenéutica para entender el evangelio," *Sal Terrae* 6 (1986), pp. 473-82.

18. Speaking of God's revelation, Segundo says that "it is necessary for difference to produce a difference" ("Revelación, fe, signos de los tiempos," p. 125). The entry of the poor on to the scene (the causal difference) in fact produced a difference in faith (resulting difference) that was felt as good and positive, more human and more Christian. This is the ultimate basis for our ability to present the causal difference as a sign of the times and identify it as the situation in which christology should be done.

19. Ellacuría, "Discernir el 'signo' de los tiempos," p. 58.

20. J. Lois, "Cristología en la teología de la liberación," *Mysterium liberationis* 1 (Madrid, 1990), pp. 224-30. Eng. trans., pp. 168-94. (See n. 6 to Intro. above.)

21. Ellacuría, *Conversión de la Iglesia al reino de Dios*, p. 183.

22. I have analyzed the tension between the personal and community aspects of faith in J. Sobrino, *La resurreción de la verdadera Iglesia* (San Salvador, 1986), pp. 143-76. Eng. trans. *The True Church and the Poor* (Maryknoll, N.Y.: Orbis Books, 1984; London: CIIR, 1985), pp. 129-38.

23. Segundo, "Revelación, fe, signos de los tiempos," p. 134.

24. The church of the poor is "a church in which the poor are its principal motor and its internal structural principle," Ellacuría, *Conversión de la Iglesia al reino de Dios*, pp. 207-8.

25. Of Jesus himself, C. Duquoc asserts that "it is in action that Jesus decides that invocation of the Father will reach a new form," "El Dios de Jesús y la crisis de Dios en nuestro tiempo," Various, *Jesucristo en la historia y en la fe* (Salamanca, 1977), p. 49.

26. W. Kasper, *Jesus the Christ* (London: Burns & Oates; New York: Herder & Herder, 1976), p. 27.

27. L. Boff, *Jesucristo y la liberación del hombre* (Madrid, 2d ed., 1987), pp. 14-25; "Jesucristo liberador. Una visión cristológica desde Latinoamérica oprimida," Various, *Jesucristo en la historia y en la fe*, pp. 175-8. Eng. trans. "A Christological View from the Periphery," *Jesus Christ Liberator* (Maryknoll, N.Y.: Orbis Books; London: SPCK, 1974), pp. 264-8.

28. Boff, "A Christological View," pp. 265-6.

29. Christology that attempts to become conscious of its social context must pay attention as far as possible to the findings of the social sciences, as is required by the principles of liberation theology. In my view, however, more important than any accumulation of sociological knowledge that theologians may possess—more or less in different instances—is that they should really make the epistemological break, that their intellect should begin to function in a different way, as we shall see later.

30. According to recent findings of CEPAL, seventy-one million people lived in poverty in Latin America in 1971, and in 1990 the number had risen to 183 million. Ninety

thousand million dollars would be needed for Latin America in 1995 to reach the economic (poverty) level of 1980.

31. H. Assmann, *Teología desde la praxis de liberación* (Salamanca, 2d ed., 1975), p. 40. Eng. trans. *A Practical Theology of Liberation* (London: Search Press; New York: Crossroad, 1975), p. 57 (translation adapted).

32. *Ibid.*

33. H. Assmann, "Tecnología y poder en la perspectiva de la teología de la liberación," Various, *Tecnología y necesidades básicas* (San José, 1979), pp. 31-2.

34. The quotation comes from I. Ellacuría, "Teología de la liberación y marxismo," *RLT* 20 (1990), p. 126. Ellacuría uses the distinction between *medium quo* and *medium in quo* to analyze Marxism's contribution to liberation theology, but the same can be said, and more truly, of the situation of the poor.

35. See the article by J. L. Segundo cited in n. 17 above.

36. I have explained what I mean by mercy in "Iglesia samaritana: el principio-misericordia," *Sal Terrae* 10 (1990), pp. 665-78, and "Iglesias ricas y Iglesias pobres, y el principio-misericordia," *RLT* 21 (1990), pp. 307-23.

37. J. Sobrino, "Teología en un mundo sufriente. La teología de la liberación como *intellectus amoris*," *RLT* 15 (1988), pp. 243-66.

38. I. Ellacuría, "La teología como momento ideológico de la praxis eclesial," *Estudios Eclesiásticos* 207 (1978), pp. 457-76.

39. "Hacia una fundamentación filosófica del método teológico latinoamericano," *ECA* 322-3 (1975), p. 419; see also I. Ellacuría, *Filosofía de la realidad histórica* (Madrid, 1991).

40. I should like to say, speaking personally, that this way of envisaging the functioning of understanding is one of the aspects of Ellacuría's thought that made the greatest impact on me. This point is stressed in the articles by J. Hernández Pico, J. I. González Faus and V. Codina in *RLT* 21 (1990), an issue dedicated to the memory of the UCA martyrs.

41. A. González, in an excellent analysis of Ellacuría's philosophical work, says that "what is characteristic of Ignacio Ellacuría's intellectual work does not consist so much in having put the practice of liberation at the heart of his philosophical reflections, but in having made philosophy a constituent element of an existence devoted to liberation," "Aproximación a la obra filosófica de I. Ellacuría," *ECA* 505-6 (1990), p. 980. This can be said as much, if not more so, of his theology and in general of all liberation theology.

42. See Sobrino, "Theological Understanding in European and Latin American Theology," *The True Church and the Poor*, pp. 7-38.

43. Boff, "A Christological View," p. 279.

3. The "Historical Jesus," the Starting Point for Christology

1. See W. Pannenberg, *Jesus—God and Man* (London: SCM Press; Philadelphia, PA: Westminster Press, 1968), pp. 183-7; *Basic Concepts in Systematic Theology* I (Edinburgh: T. & T. Clark; Grand Rapids, MI: Eerdmans, 1970), pp. 211-38. I have used here the more intelligible terms "limit-statements" and "historical statements" for what Pannenberg calls "doxological statements" and "kerygmatic statements." The basic point is that in these doxological or limit-statements there is a surrender of reason, an *obsequium* in traditional terminology. For this surrender to be rational, however, *obsequium rationabile*, it must have some foothold in something known to reason.

2. W. Kasper, *Jesus the Christ* (London: Burns & Oates; New York: Herder & Herder, 1976), p. 198.

3. "The predicate of all christological statements is Jesus, so that, strictly speaking, we ought to say Messiah, Lord, Son of God mean Jesus," F. J. Schierse, "La revelación de la trinidad en el Nuevo Testamento," *Mysterium salutis* II-I (Madrid, 1969), pp. 136-7.

4. P. van Buren is speaking ironically, but he is nonetheless right when he says, "Even when on the one hand Christ was professed to be 'truly human,' the humanity was defined in such a way that it seemed to threaten Jesus' position in the world of human beings. The problem can be seen as early as the writings of Justin Martyr, where the writer insists that Jesus was human, with a body, soul and spirit, and yet with no historical relationship with the rest of humanity. . . . He was someone like us, but he was not one of us," *The Secular Meaning of the Gospel* (London, 1966), p. 38.

5. W. Künneth, *Glauben an Jesus?* (Hamburg, 1962), p. 286.

6. "Current Problems in Christology," *Theological Investigations* 1 (London: Darton, Longman & Todd; Baltimore: Helicon Press, 1961), pp.149-200; "On the Theology of the Incarnation," *Theological Investigations* 4 (London: Darton, Longman & Todd; Baltimore: Helicon Press, 1966), pp. 105-20.

7. "The Eternal Significance of the Humanity of Jesus for Our Relationship with God," *Theological Investigations* 3 (London: Darton, Longman & Todd; Baltimore: Helicon Press, 1963), pp. 47-59.

8. "Thoughts on the Possibility of Belief Today," *Theological Investigations* 5 (London: Darton, Longman & Todd; Baltimore: Helicon Press, 1966), pp. 3-22.

9. "Líneas fundamentales de una teología sistemática," K. Rahner and W. Thüsing, *Cristologia. Estudio teológico y exegético* (Madrid, 1975), pp. 31-9. (Eng. trans. see n. 13 to ch. 2 above); K. Rahner and K. H. Weger, *¿Qué debemos creer todavía?* (Santander, 1980), pp. 97-115.

10. It is generally recognized today in christology that Jesus did not preach himself, but the Kingdom of God, and this point brings together theologians who differ on others: K. Rahner, W. Pannenberg, J. Moltmann, W. Kasper, H. Küng, J. I. González Faus, etc.

11. E. Schillebeeckx, *Jesús. La historia de un viviente* (Madrid, 2d ed. 1983), pp. 41-9. Sp. trans. of *Jesus, het verhaal van een levende* (Bloemendal, 1974). Eng. trans. *Jesus. An Experiment in Christology* (London: Collins; New York: Harper & Row, 1979), pp. 44-8; W. Kasper, *Jesus the Christ*, pp. 26-8.

12. H. Assmann, *A Practical Theology of Liberation* (London: Search Press; New York: Crossroad, 1975), p. 103.

13. *Ibid.*

14. G. Gutiérrez, *Teología de la liberación. Perspectivas* (Salamanca, 1971), p. 285. Eng. trans. *A Theology of Liberation: History, Politics and Salvation* (Maryknoll, N.Y.: Orbis Books, 1973; London: SCM Press, 1974), p. 226 (adapted).

15. L. Boff, *Jesus Christ Liberator* (Maryknoll, N.Y.: Orbis Books; London: SPCK, 1978). The Brazilian original appeared in 1972.

16. *Teología política* (San Salvador, 1973), p. 11. Eng trans. *Freedom Made Flesh* (Maryknoll, N.Y.: Orbis Books, 1976), p. 18.

17. *Freedom Made Flesh*, p. 25.

18. *Ibid.*, p. 26.

19. *Ibid.*, p. 27.

20. *Ibid.*

21. J. Comblin, *Teología de la revolución* (Bilbao, 1973), p. 306.

22. P. Miranda, *El ser y el Mesías* (Salamanca, 1973), p. 9. Eng. trans. *Being and the Messiah* (Maryknoll, N.Y.: Orbis Books, 1976).

23. See H. Echegaray, *La práctica de Jesús* (Lima, 1981). Eng. trans. *The Practice of Jesus* (Maryknoll, N.Y.: Orbis Books, 1984); C. Bravo, *Jesús, hombre en conflicto* (Mexico City, 1986); and the monumental three volumes of J. L. Segundo, *El hombre de hoy ante Jesús de Nazaret* (Madrid, 1982-). Eng. trans. *Jesus of Nazareth Yesterday and Today* (Maryknoll, N.Y.: Orbis Books; London: Sheed & Ward, 1984-).

24. *Jesus Christ Liberator*, p. 279 (Epilogue added to the English edition).

25. J. Jiménez Limón, "Una cristología para la conversión en la lucha por la justicia," *Christus* 511 (1978), p. 47.

26. A. Schweitzer, *Geschichte der Leben-Jesu Forschung* (Munich, latest ed. 1966), p. 47. Eng. trans. *The Quest of the Historical Jesus* (London, 1910). See C. Palacio, *Jesucristo. Historia y interpretación* (Madrid, 1978), pp. 51-2.

27. In our time a notable attempt to defend Christianity by meeting this Enlightenment criterion has been made by Pannenberg, *Basic Concepts in Systematic Theology*, esp. vol. I, pp. 38-50, 80-94, 137-81.

28. See the analysis by Palacio, *Jesucristo. Historia y interpretación*, pp. 36-51.

29. This is the fundamental thesis of Pannenberg's *Jesus—God and Man* (London: SCM Press; Philadelphia, PA: Westminster Press, 1968), esp. pp. 53-114.

30. Kasper, *Jesus the Christ*, p. 20.

31. Schillebeeckx, *Jesus*, p. 28

32. *Ibid.*, p. 30

33. Segundo, *El hombre de hoy ante Jesús de Nazaret*, p. 30.

34. See J. Sobrino, *The True Church and the Poor*, (see n. 22 to ch. 2 above), pp. 10-21.

35. J. I. González Faus, "Hacer teología y hacerse teología," Various, *Vida y reflexión. Aportes de la teología de la reflexión al pensamiento teológico actual* (Lima, 1983), p. 79.

36. E. Schillebeeckx, "Befreiungstheologie zwischen Medellín und Puebla," *Orientierung* 43 (1979), pp. 6-10, 17-21.

37. J. I. González Faus, *La humanidad nueva* (Santander, 7th ed., 1986), p. 15.

38. This is Jürgen Moltmann's claim when he analyzes in what sense Jesus' resurrection is historical, *Teología de la esperanza* (Salamanca, 1960,) p. 237. Eng. trans. *Theology of Hope* (London: SCM Press; New York: Harper & Row, 1967).

39. In this respect the modern studies on the sociology of the "Jesus movement" are very important. What Jesus directly started was a "movement" to keep his cause alive. See R. Aguirre, *Del movimiento de Jesús a la Iglesia cristiana* (Bilbao, 1987).

40. For myself I have found great illumination in Ignacio Ellacuría's formula "poor with spirit," for relating material reality with the reality of spirit. To define the poor theologically, Ellacuría insisted on the materiality of the poor and on coherent action to combat poverty, but added the need to be and do all this "with spirit."

41. Boff, *Jesus Christ Liberator*, p. 279. This structural similarity does not need to be worked out in every detail or through comparative explanations of social situations, as some writers sometimes demand; the general parallel suffices. I think it is enough to point—at least for an understanding of Jesus' activity—to the situation of oppression in which the life and death of the masses are in the balance.

42. *Ibid.*

43. F. Belo, *Lectura materialista del evangelio de Marcos* (Estella, 1975). Eng. trans. *A Materialist reading of the Gospel of Mark* (Maryknoll, N.Y.: Orbis Books, 1981); M. Clévenot, *Lectura materialista de la Biblia* (Salamanca, 1978), pp. 109-12. Eng. trans. *Materialist Approaches to the Bible* (Maryknoll, N.Y.: Orbis Books, 1985). What Latin American christology values in these studies is that they present Jesus' life as the story of words and deeds, but, going beyond them, this christology insists in not bracketing off the "practitioner" Jesus, who might then disappear behind his practice.

44. Boff, *Jesucristo y la liberación del hombre*, pp. 539-40.

45. *El precio de la gracia* (Salamanca, 1968), pp. 20-21.

46. As ever, spirituality went ahead of theology, something that also happens in our own day. It is notable, for example, that the encyclopedias produced in Germany since the Second Vatican Council, *Mysterium salutis, Sacramentum mundi, Lexikon Theologischer Grundbegriffe*, very valuable in other respects, do not take discipleship of Jesus seriously in their christologies.

47. J. O. Tuñí, "Jesús de Nazaret, criterio de identidad cristiana en el Nuevo Testamento," *Todos Uno* 82 (1985), p. 12. My remarks here are based on what the author says programmatically in this article and in his others on the same subject on the Letter to the Hebrews and the Johannine and Pauline writings.

48. Tuñí, p. 13.

49. J. O. Tuñí, "'Jesús' en la carta a los Hebreos," *RLT* 9 (1986), pp. 283-302.

50. Tuñí, "Jesús de Nazaret," pp. 16-17.

51. According to A. Vanhoye, *Le Christ est notre prêtre* (Paris, 1969), there may be an echo of this in Col. 2:18: "Let no one disqualify you, insisting on self-abasement and worship of angels," worship that consisted in the keeping of feasts, new moons and sabbaths (Col. 2:16), and in the ritual use of food and drink (Col 2:18), which could be attractive as a "seductive mixture of false mysticism and religious formalism" (Vanhoye, p. 19).

52. Tuñí, "Jesús de Nazaret," p. 16.

53. Tuñí, "La vida de Jesús en el evangelio de Juan," *RLT* 7 (1986), pp. 3-43. See also the appendix, "La vida de Jesús en 1 Jn," pp. 31-4.

54. Tuñí, "Pablo y Jesús. La vida de Jesús y la vida de Pablo," *RLT* 15 (1988), pp. 285-305.

55. Tuñí, "Pablo y Jesús," p. 297.

56. Tuñí, "Jesús de Nazaret," pp. 17-18.

57. E. Schweizer, "Die theologische Leistung des Markus," *Evangelische Theologie* 24 (1964), pp. 337-55, abridged in *Selecciones de Teología* 33 (1970), pp. 50-61.

58. González Faus, *Acceso a Jesús* (Salamanca, 6th ed., 1967), pp. 45-6.

59. Schillebeeckx, *Jesús*, pp. 85-102.

PART II: THE MISSION AND FAITH OF JESUS

4. Jesus and the Kingdom of God

1. J. I. González Faus, *La humanidad nueva. Ensayo de cristología* (Santander, 7th ed., 1986), p. 46.

2. K. Rahner, "Líneas fundamentales de una cristología sistemática," K. Rahner and W.

Thüsing, *Cristología. Estudio teológico y exegético* (Madrid, 1975), p. 35. (See n. 13 to ch. 2 above.)

3. J. Jeremias, *Teología del Nuevo Testamento* (Salamanca, 5th ed., 1986), p. 119. Sp. trans. of *Neuetestamentliche Theologie* vol. I, *Die Verkundigung Jesu* (1971). Eng. trans. *New Testament Theology*, Part I *The Proclamation of Jesus* (London: SCM Press; New York: Harper & Row, 1971); W. Kasper, *Jesus der Christus* (Mainz, 1974): Eng. trans. *Jesus the Christ* (London: Burns & Oates; New York: Herder & Herder, 1976), p. 72: "The centre and framework of Jesus' preaching and mission was the approaching Kingdom of God."

4. Not only from what Jesus preached to his listeners, but on the level of his own self-understanding, there is no evidence that he wished to preach himself, which means that any christology must, on principle, be an indirect christology. And much the same can be said if Jesus is approached from the resurrection: there too Jesus has to be presented in relational form: cf. W. Thüsing, "La imagen de Dios en el Nuevo Testamento," J. Ratzinger (ed.), *Dios como problema* (Madrid, 1973), pp. 80-120.

5. Matthew's expression is a common circumlocution to avoid using the name of God out of respect. It means exactly the same as "Kingdom of God" and has no connotation of being beyond time and history.

6. Jesus clearly did not think in terms of a church, as it developed, though he did promote a movement that led to a church, which referred back in belief and practice to Jesus (and his Spirit). Cf. R. Aguirre, *Del movimiento de Jesús a la Iglesia cristiana* (Bilbao, 1987).

7. On this theme, which runs through the whole of theology and is a major concern of liberation theology, see I. Ellacuría, "Historicidad de la salvación cristiana," *Mysterium liberationis*, I (Madrid, 1990), pp. 323-73. Eng. trans. "The Historicity of Christian Salvation," *Mysterium Liberationis* (Maryknoll, N.Y.: Orbis Books, 1993), pp. 251-89.

8. Kasper, *Jesus the Christ*, p. 72.

9. E. Schillebeeckx, *Jesus, het verhaal van een levende* (Bloemendal, 1974). Eng. trans. *Jesus: An Experiment in Christology* (London: Collins; New York: Harper & Row, 1979). Sp. trans. *Jesús. La historia de un viviente*, p. 130.

10. The classic work by R. Schnackenburg, *God's Rule and Kingdom* (London: Burns & Oates; New York: Herder & Herder, 1968), provides a good methodological example of how the meaning of the Kingdom of God for Jesus, compared to its meaning in the Old Testament and the later church, is being clarified.

11. W. Pannenberg, "Die Offenbarung Gottes in Jesus von Nazareth," *Theologie als Geschichte* (Zurich, 1967), p. 143.

12. Aguirre, *Del movimiento de Jesús*, p. 47. Jesus does not use the more precise apocalyptic terminology, the "future aeon," nor does he express utopia in the more usual form used by rabbis and Pharisees, the "coming of the Messiah."

13. This obvious consideration has not been so obvious in theology, which has tended precipitately to universalize the recipients of salvation. Liberation theology, though, is very conscious of the need to historicize the recipients of salvation in order to know, in turn, what salvation and what liberation is meant.

14. Schillebeeckx, *Jesús*, p. 130.

15. This is one example, among many, of the consequences of making the option for the poor in theological undertakings. If theology is done for and from the poor, at least one realizes that good news is not so for all equally; hence the need to determine its addressee as carefully as possible so as to be able to know what good news is involved.

16. The expression as such was not central in late Judaism nor even in the apocalyptic from which it came. Schillebeeckx, *Jesús*, p. 135.

17. L. Armendáriz, "El 'Reino de Dios,' centro y mensaje de la vida de Jesús," *Sal Terrae* 756 (1976), p. 364.

18. Like any major reality, including that of God, understanding of the "Kingdom of God" can be falsified, either reducing it individualistically—"so that Christ may reign in our hearts"—or, above all, going to the other extreme of making it into a theocracy, in the name of which one can oppress and kill all who simply do not share in this kingdom. All the terrible "holy wars," so common in history, use this as their final justification.

19. Jeremias, *Teología del Nuevo Testamento*, p. 122.

20. G. Bornkamm, *Jesús de Nazaret* (Salamanca, 3d ed., 1982), pp. 68ff. Sp. trans. of *Jesus von Nazareth* (Stuttgart, 9th ed., 1971). Eng. trans. *Jesus of Nazareth* (London: Hodder & Stoughton, 1960, new ed. 1980).

21. This popular and active type of hope—not any hope—is also real and new in Latin America, and because of this the Kingdom of God has been understood in a specific way: popular, historical and liberating. The main reason for this is the analogy between the two situations, that of Israel and ours, with their common history of disasters and oppression.

22. The theses of Cullmann (*Jesus and the Revolutionaries of His Time*) and Hengel (*The Zealots*) on the existence of the Zealots at the time of Jesus are now generally questioned. Their rise seems to have been later, though this did not prevent Jesus and the first Christians from being seen as political agitators (Acts 5:35-9). On this point, see R. A. Horsley and J. S. Hanson, *Bandits, Prophets, and Messiahs: Popular Movements at the Time of Jesus* (San Francisco: Harper; Edinburgh: T. & T. Clark, 1985); H. Guevara, *Ambiente político del pueblo judío en tiempo de Jesús* (Madrid, 1985); J. P. Meier, "The Bible as a Source of Theology," *CTSA Proceedings* 43 (1988), pp. 1-14. (See also Horsley, "Palestininan Jewish Groups and their Messiahs in Late Second Temple Times," *Concilium* 1993/1, pp.14-29. TRANS.)

23. On John the Baptist and his relation to Jesus, see J. Becker, *Johannes der Taufer und Jesus von Nazaret* (Neukirchen-Vluyn, 1972).

24. The specific nature of the figure of John the Baptist is brought out in Q: "But when he saw many [people] coming for baptism, he said to them, 'You brood of vipers! Who warned you to flee from the wrath to come? Bear fruit worthy of repentance . . .'" (Matt. 3:7-8; Luke 3:7-8).

25. "The Baptist, through baptizing by immersion, brought penitents together to gather them into the eschatological people so as to save them from the verdict of condemnation at the last judgment." Jeremias, *Teología*, p. 62.

26. Jeremias, p. 63; Becker, *Johannes der Taufer*, p. 15; K. Niederwimmer, *Jesus* (Göttingen, 1968); J. Moltmann, *Der Weg Jesu Christi. Christologie in messianischen Dimension* (Munich, 1989), pp. 107ff. Eng. trans. *The Way of Jesus Christ. Christianity in Messianic Dimensions* (London: SCM Press; New York: Harper & Row, 1990).

27. The biblical scholar Xavier Alegre commented during his visit to El Salvador that the way the Synoptics narrated the beginning of Jesus' mission suggested this to him: "After Rutilio Grande was assassinated, Mgr Romero began to preach. . . ." There is of course no need to look for precise analogies, but the example of Archbishop Romero might be of some help in understanding Jesus' existential decision.

28. A. Pérez, "El reino de Dios como nombre de un deseo. Ensayo de exégesis ética,"

Sal Terrae 780 (1978), pp. 392ff, has expressed this problem well, though he exaggerates in saying that theology has taken virtually no notice of it.

29. Jeremias, *Teología*, p. 126.

30. In his parables, Jesus also stresses that this coming of the Kingdom is humble, through hardly detectable little signs, but certain and sure. Jeremias, *Las Parábolas de Jesús* (Estella, 1970), pp. 179-96. Sp. trans. of *Die Gleichnisse Jesus* (Zurich, 1954). Eng. trans. *The Parables of Jesus* (London: SCM Press; New York: Macmillan, 1972).

31. See O. Cullmann, *Jesus und die Revolutionären seiner Zeit* (Tübingen, 1970). Eng. trans. *Jesus and the Revolutionaries of his Time* (London: SCM Press; New York: Harper & Row, 1970).

32. W. Schrage, *Etica del Nuevo Testamento* (Salamanca, 1986), pp. 27-146. Eng. trans. *The Ethics of the New Testament* (Edinburgh: T. & T. Clark; Philadelphia, PA: Fortress Press, 1988).

33. *Ibid.*, p. 53. This is what Jesus himself makes possible. "Jesus is God's mercy coming in person to this world, approaching us concretely, physically, touching us in his temporality and in his flesh, so that we can surrender trustingly and unconditionally to this same action of God's and become what God is, mercy. Forgiven, we in turn are capable of mercy." G. Baena, "El sacerdocio de Cristo," *Diakonia* 26 (1983), p. 133.

34. In Paul it appears forty-eight times in his authentic letters, of which twenty-two in its absolute sense. Its meaning is more restricted referring directly to the suffering, cross and resurrection of Christ.

35. Schillebeeckx, *Jesús*, p. 98.

36. "Salvation in Jesus Christ and the Process of Liberation," *Concilium* 96 (vol. 6, no. 10) (1974), p. 81.

37. Aguirre, *Del movimiento de Jesús*, p. 51.

38. The old theology naturally affirmed the universal saving will of God, but added *voluntate tamen inequali*, "but with unequal will." It should therefore not surprise us to find God taking sides. What happens is that those who are for the poor still cause disquiet and scandal.

39. Schillebeeckx, *Jesús*, p. 131.

40. Jeremias, *Teología*, pp. 132, 142, my italics.

41. Cf. Jeremias, *Teología*, pp. 134-138; J. Pixley and C. Boff, *The Bible, the Church and the Poor* (Tunbridge Wells: Burns & Oates; Maryknoll, N.Y.: Orbis Books, 1989); G. M. Soares-Prabhu, "Clase en la Biblia: los pobres, ¿una clase social?," *RLT* 12 (1987), pp. 217-39.

42. Jeremias, *Teología*, p. 137.

43. What should be understood by "poor" historically and theologically will be examined in the *Excursus* following this chapter.

44. Social segregation is a perennial temptation for the religious mentality and was so at the time of Jesus. Schillebeeckx, *Jesús*, pp. 131-2: "Such circles tend to uphold the principle of loving those whom God loves (and chooses) and hating those whom God rejects. . . . Above all, 'publicans and sinners' are avoided like the plague; dealing with them means making oneself into a sinner."

45. My analysis follows the article by Soares-Prabhu (n. 41). This does not contradict, but rather complements, that of Jeremias, less socio-politically oriented.

46. Soares-Prabhu, "Clase en la Biblia," p. 223.

47. *Ibid.*, p. 225.

48. *Ibid.*, p. 228.

49. *Ibid.*

50. R. Sivatte, "La práctica de la justicia, criterio de discernimiento de la verdadera experiencia de la fe, según el Antiguo Testamento," Various, *La justicia que brota de la fe* (Santander, 1982).

51. J. L. Sicre, *"Con los pobres de la tierra." La justicia social en los profetas de Israel* (Madrid, 1984), p. 448.

52. G. Gutiérrez, *El Dios de la vida* (Lima, 1982, revised and expanded ed., 1989). Eng. trans. *The God of Life* (Maryknoll, N.Y.: Orbis Books, 1991).

53. *Dodekaprofeten*, I, p. 304.

54. Jeremias, *Teología*, p. 122.

55. J. P. Miranda, *Marx y la Biblia* (Salamanca, 1972), pp. 140ff: Eng. trans. *Marx and the Bible* (Maryknoll, N.Y.: Orbis Books, 1974).

56. Jeremias, *Teología*, p. 145.

57. *Ibid.*, p. 128.

58. *Ibid.*

59. Bornkamm, *Jesús de Nazaret*, p. 103.

60. Jeremias, *Teología*, p. 235.

61. Soares-Prabhu, "Clase en la Biblia," p. 224.

62. E. Käsemann, *La llamada de la libertad* (Salamanca, 2d ed., 1985), p. 35.

63. C. Escudero Freire, *Devolver el evangelio a los pobres* (Salamanca, 1978), p. 226.

64. *Ibid.*, p. 273.

65. *Ibid.*, p. 270. See also J. Dupont, "Jésus annonce la bonne nouvelle aux pauvres," Various, *Evangelizare pauperibus* (Brescia, 1978), p. 183: "The good news proclaimed to the poor cannot be anything other than the news that they will cease to be poor and undergo poverty. Just as the blind see, the deaf hear and the dead live, so their needs will be met, they will cease to be victims of an unjust distribution of goods."

66. González Faus, *Clamor del reino. Estudio sobre los milagros de Jesús* (Salamanca, 1982).

67. Jeremias, *Teología*, p. 115. He considers that the cures are mostly of psychogenic sicknesses, but also of lepers (in the wide sense used at the time), paralytics and blind people: "These are sufferings of the sort to which medicine applies a 'therapy of overcoming.'"

68. González Faus, *Clamor*, p. 157.

69. Schillebeeckx, *Jesús*, p. 168. The exegetical reason he gives is that the miracle stories stem from Jesus' activity in Galilee, where he was surrounded by crowds of simple people. Based on this original nucleus of healing miracles among the people, tradition proceeded to elaborate more spectacular miracles.

70. B. Lauret, "Cristología dogmática," B. Lauret and F. Refoulé (eds), *Iniciación a la práctica de la teología* I (Madrid, 1984), p. 309. Sp. trans of *Initiation à la pratique de la théologie*, five vols (Paris, 1967-87).

71. See the fine pages by A. Nolan, *Jesus Before Christianity* (London: Darton, Longman & Todd; Maryknoll, N.Y.: Orbis Books, 1977), pp. 49ff.

72. J. Blank, *Jesús de Nazaret* (Madrid, 1982), p. 88: Sp. trans. of *Jesus von Nazareth. Geschichte und Relevanz* (Freiburg, 1972).

73. Nolan, *Jesus Before Christianity*, p. 56.

74. Schillebeeckx, *Jesús*, pp. 180ff.

75. See González Faus, "Jesús y los demonios. Introducción cristológica a la lucha por la justicia," *Estudios Eclesiásticos* 52 (1977), pp. 487-519. Much of the following section is taken from this article.

76. Jeremias, *Teología*, p. 115.

77. *Ibid.*, p. 117.

78. *Ibid.*, p. 187.

79. Jeremias, *Las parábolas de Jesús*, pp. 29-142.

80 Lauret, "Cristología dogmática," pp. 302-6.

81. *Ibid.*, p. 303.

82. J. L. Segundo, *El hombre de hoy ante Jesús de Nazaret* II/I (Madrid, 1982), pp. 303-20. Eng. trans. *Jesus Christ Yesterday and Today. Vol III, The Humanist Christology of Paul* (Maryknoll, N.Y.: Orbis Books; London: Sheed & Ward, 1986).

83. *Ibid.*, p. 186.

84. Jeremias, *Jesús*, p. 171.

85. *Ibid.*, p. 196.

86. *Ibid.*, p. 244.

87. "Homilía con motivo de la expulsión del P. Mario Bernal," *ECA* 348/347 (1977), p. 859.

Excursus 1: The Kingdom of God in Present-Day Christologies

1. I. Ellacuría, "Aporte de la teología de la liberación a las religiones abrahámicas en la superación del individualismo y del positivismo," *RLT* 10 (1987), p. 9; J. Sobrino, "La centralidad del 'reino de Dios' en la teología de la liberación," *RLT* 9 (1986), pp. 247-81; also *Mysterium Liberationis* I (Madrid, 1990), pp. 467-511. Eng. trans. "The Central Position of the Reign of God in Liberation Theology," *Mysterium Liberationis* (Maryknoll, N.Y.: Orbis Books, 1993), pp. 289-328.

2. A. Schweitzer, *Geschichte der Lebens-Jesu-Forschung* (Munich, 1966), pp. 402-50.

3. C. H. Dodd, *The Parables of the Kingdom* (London and New York: Cambridge University Press, 1961), pp. 146ff.

4. O. Cullmann, *La historia de salvación* (Barcelona, 1967), pp. 217-26. Eng. trans. *Salvation in History* (London: SCM Press; New York: Harper & Row, 1967).

5. R. Bultmann, *Theology of the New Testament* (London: SCM Press; New York: Macmillan, 1968).

6. Bultmann, *Jesus* (Munich, 1967), pp. 38ff; *Geschichte und Eschatologie* (Tübingen, 1964), p. 180.

7. Bultmann, *Glauben und Verstehen* II (Tübingen, 1958), p. 119.

8. *Ibid.*, p. 101.

9. W. Pannenberg, *Cuestiones fundamentales de teología sistemática* (Salamanca, 1976), p. 27. Sp. trans. of *Grundfragen systematischer Theologie* (Göttingen, 1966). Eng. trans. *Basic Concepts in Systematic Theology* (Edinburgh: T. & T. Clark; Grand Rapids, MI: Eerdmans, 1971).

10. Pannenberg, *Fundamentos de cristología* (Salamanca, 1974), p. 280. Sp. trans. of *Grundzüge der Christologie* (Gütersloh, 3d ed., 1969). Eng. trans. *Jesus—God and Man* (London: SCM Press; Philadelphia, PA: Westminster Press, 1968).

11. *Ibid.*, p. 281.

12. *Ibid.*

13. *Ibid.*, p. 283.

14. *Ibid.*, pp. 283ff.

15. Pannenberg, "Zur Theologie des Reiches," *ZEE* 7 (1963), 29.

16. Pannenberg, *Fundamentos*, p. 288.

17. *Ibid.*, pp. 288ff.

18. *Ibid.*, p. 280.

19. Pannenberg, *Teología y reino de Dios* (Salamanca, 1974), pp. 41-84. Sp. trans. of *Theologie und Reich Gottes*. Eng. trans. *Theology and the Kingdom of God* (London: SCM Press; Philadelphia, PA: Fortress Press, 1969).

20. Pannenberg, "Die politischer Dimension des Evangeliums," *Die Politik und das Heil* (Mainz, 1968), p. 19.

21. Pannenberg, *Teología y reino*, p. 68.

22. J. Moltmann, *Teología de la esperanza* (Salamanca, 4th ed., 1980), p. 21. Sp. trans. of *Theologie der Hoffnung* (Munich, 7th ed., 1968). Eng. trans. *Theology of Hope* (London: SCM Press; New York: Harper & Row, 1967). I follow here his basic theses expressed in the above work and in *Der gekreuzigte Gott* (Munich, 1972). Eng. trans. *The Crucified God* (London: SCM Press; New York: Harper & Row, 1974); also *Trinität und Reich Gottes* (Paderborn, 1978). Eng. trans. *The Trinity and the Kingdom of God* (London: SCM Press; San Francisco: Harper, 1981).

23. Moltmann, *Esperanza*, p. 244.

24. Moltmann, *El Hombre*, p. 152.

25. Moltmann, *Umkehr zur Zukunft* (Hamburg, 1970), p. 76. Eng. trans. *Creating a Just Future* (London: SCM Press; Philadelphia, PA: Trinity Press International, 1989).

26. The vicissitudes of the situation in El Salvador have not allowed me to locate the citation.

27. Moltmann, *La Iglesia fuerza del Espíritu* (Salamanca, 1978). Sp. trans. of *Kirche in der Kraft des Geistes* (Munich, 1975). Eng. trans. *The Church in the Power of the Spirit* (London: SCM Press; New York: Harper & Row, 1977). Citations in the rest of this section are from this.

28. This shows in his recent book, *Der Weg Jesu Christi. Christologie in messianischen Dimensionen* (Munich, 1989), see pp. 59, 70, 119, 187, 190, 224ff. Eng. trans. *The Way of Jesus Christ* (London: SCM Press; New York: Macmillan, 1990).

29. W. Kasper, *Jesus der Christus* (Mainz, 1974). Eng. trans. *Jesus the Christ* (London: Burns & Oates; New York: Herder & Herder, 1976).

30. I. Ellacuría, "Aporte de la teología," p. 9.

31. This reflection is similar in form to that of Vatican II: ". . . there exists an order or 'hierarchy' of truths, since they vary in their relationship to the foundation of the Christian faith," UR 11, Abbott, p. 354.

32. Ellacuría, "Aporte," p. 9.

33. Miranda, *Marx y la Biblia*, p. 315. Eng. trans. *Marx and the Bible* (Maryknoll, N.Y.: Orbis Books, 1974).

34. L. Boff, "Salvation in Jesus Christ and the Process of Liberation," *Concilium* 96 (vol. 6 no. 10) (1974), p. 90.

35. Ellacuría, *Conversión de la Iglesia al reino de Dios* (San Salvador, 1985) p. 181.

36. J. L. Segundo, *El hombre de hoy ante Jesús de Nazaret* II/I (Madrid, 1982), p. 132.

Eng. trans. *Jesus of Nazareth Yesterday and Today. Vol III, The Humanist Christology of Paul* Maryknoll, N.Y.: Orbis Books; London: Sheed & Ward, 1986).

37. Ellacuría, *Conversion de la Iglesia*, pp. 25-178, from which the citations in the text are taken; *idem*, "Pobres," C. Floristán and J. J. Tamayo (eds), *Conceptos fundamentales de pastoral* (Madrid, 1983), pp. 786-802. For a systematic view of the poor at the present time, see J. Pixley and C. Boff, *The Bible, the Church and the Poor* (Tunbridge Wells: Burns & Oates; Maryknoll, N.Y.: Orbis Books, 1989), pp. 108-56; G. Gutiérrez, "Pobres," *Mysterium liberationis* I (Madrid, 1990), pp. 303-21. Eng. trans. "The Poor: Object of a Basic Option," *Mysterium Liberationis*, pp. 235-51.

38. Ellacuría, "Teología de la liberación y marxismo," 133ff.

39. See G. M. Soares-Prabhu and his analysis of the poor as a "dynamic class," "Clase en la Biblia: los pobres, ¿una clase social?" *RLT* 12 (1987), pp. 229-33.

40. Boff, "Salvation in Jesus Christ," pp. 90-91.

41. Ellacuría, *Conversión de la Iglesia*, pp. 178-216.

42. R. Schnackenburg, *God's Rule and Kingdom* (London: Burns & Oates; New York: Herder & Herder, 1968).

43. *Ibid.*

44. A modern example of this can be found in Archbishop Romero's speech at the University of Louvain, 2 Feb. 1980: "La dimensión política de la fe desde la opción por los pobres," *La voz de los sin voz*, pp. 183-93. Eng. trans. *Voice of the Voiceless* (Maryknoll, N.Y.: Orbis Books; London: CIIR, 1985).

45. Segundo, *El hombre de hoy.* p. 129.

46. Ellacuría, "Pueblo de Dios," *Conceptos fundmentales*, p. 843.

47. *Ibid.*, p. 846.

48. This phenomenology is based on innumerable experiences in El Salvador. See, e.g., *La fe de un pueblo. Historia de una comunidad cristiana en El Salvador* (San Salvador, 1983).

49. Ellacuría, "Utopía y profetismo desde América Latina. Un ensayo concreto de soteriología histórica," *RLT* 17 (1989), p. 160; cf. *Mysterium liberationis* I, pp. 393-443.

50. Ellacuría, "Pobres," p. 790.

5. Jesus and God (1). Jesus and a God-Father

1. H. Kessler, *Erlösung als Befreiung* (Düsseldorf, 1972), pp. 77ff.

2. G. Gutiérrez, *El Dios de la vida* (Lima. 1982), pp. 6ff. Eng. trans. *The God of Life* (Maryknoll, N.Y.: Orbis Books, 1991).

3. W. Pannenberg, *Fundamentos de cristología* (Salamanca, 1974), pp. 285ff follows this line, citing U. Wilckens, *Offenbarung als Geschichte* (Göttingen, 1961), p. 56 as exegetical grounding.

4. H. Conzelmann, *RGG* III, 641, cited by Pannenberg, p. 285.

5. J. Jeremias, *Teología del Nuevo Testamento* I (Salamanca, 5th ed., 1986), p. 211; see also pp. 21ff, 120. See note 3 to ch. 4 above.

6. H. Braun, *Jesús, el hombre de Nazaret y su tiempo* (Salamanca, 1975), p. 166.

7. Jeremias, *Teología*, p. 222.

8. *Ibid.*, pp. 220-24; P. Benoît and M. E. Boismard, *Sinopsis de los cuatro evangelios* II (Bilbao, 1976), p. 157. Sp. trans. of *Synopse des quatre évangiles* II (Paris, 1975).

9. J. Gnilka, "Jesus und das Gebet," *Bibel und Leben* 2 (1965), 82ff.

10. Jeremias, *Teología*, p. 166.

11. For a more detailed study, see Benoît and Boismard, *Sinopsis*, pp. 367-70; Jeremias, *Teología*, pp. 166ff; G. Schneider, *Die Passion Jesu nach den drei ältesten Evangelien* (1972), pp. 43-54; L. Schenke, *Der gekreuzigte Christus* (1974), pp. 11-34.

12. Jeremias, *Teología*, p. 167.

13. *Ibid.*, pp. 294-6.

14. E. Schillebeeckx, *Jesús. La historia de un viviente* (Madrid, 2d ed., 1983), pp. 209-32. He devotes these pages to the liberation worked by Jesus in our vision of God. (See n. 9 to ch. 4 above.)

15. See the fine pages by J. I. González Faus on "El ser como ternura," *Acceso a Jesús*, pp. 173-7. In the words of Bartolomé de las Casas, taken up by G. Gutiérrez: "God has the most vivid memory of the littlest."

16. González Faus, "La autoridad en Jesús," *RLT* 20 (1990), pp. 189-206.

17. *Ibid.*, p. 197.

18. *Ibid.*, p. 200. For exegetical analysis, see pp. 197-200.

19. J. Blank, *Jesús de Nazaret* (Madrid, 1982), p. 126.

20. *Ibid.*, p. 132.

21. See C. Duquoc, *Jésus, homme libre* (Paris, 1974); A. Salas (ed.), *Jesús significa libertad* (Madrid, 1987).

22. G. Gutiérrez, *Beber en su propio pozo* (Salamanca, 5th ed., 1989), pp. 120ff. Eng. trans. *We Drink from Our Own Wells* (Maryknoll, N.Y.: Orbis Books; London: SCM Press, 1984).

23. See the classic works by J. Jeremias, *Teología*, pp. 80-87, 210-38; "Abba," *Abba, Studien zur neutestamentlichen Theologie und Geistesgeschichte* (Göttingen, 1966), pp. 15-67. Sp. trans. *Abba. El mensaje central del Nuevo Testamento* (Salamanca, 3d ed., 1989), pp. 17-37 cited in this section. Eng. trans. *The Prayers of Jesus* (Naperville, Ill: A. R. Allenson, 1967).

24. *Ibid.*, p. 29.

25. See González Faus, "La 'filosofía de la vida' de Jesús de Nazaret," *RLT* 13 (1988), pp. 34-7.

26. *Ibid.*, p. 37.

27. Jeremias, *Abba*, p. 37.

28. K. Rahner, "Líneas fundamentales de una cristología sistemática," (see n. 13 to ch. 2 above), p. 34.

29. L. Boff, "Salvation in Jesus Christ and the Process of Liberation," *Concilium* 96 (vol. 6, no. 10) (1974), p. 82.

30. I. Ellacuría, *Teología política* (San Salvador, 1973), p. 30.

31. *Ibid.*, p. 32. The citation continues: "(Jesus) overcame it, but as the great temptation of his life. But he did not go to the other extreme of taking the bite out of his message of salvation. If he had taken this out, what finally happened to him would not have done."

32. "Los misterios de la vida y actividad pública de Jesús," *Mysterium salutis* III/II (Madrid, 1971), p. 94; Boff, "Salvation," p. 82.

33. C. H. Dodd, *The Founder of Christianity* (London and New York: Cambridge University Press, 1971). The crisis is expressed most strongly in Mark.

34. F. Mussner, "Gab es eine galiläische Krise?," *Festschrift für Josef Schmidt* (Freiburg, 1973), pp. 238-52.

35. R. Aguirre, "Jesús y la multitud a la luz de los sinópticos," R. Aguirre and F. García,

Escritos de Biblia y Oriente (Salamanca, 1981), pp. 259-82; *idem*, "Jesús y la multitud a la luz del evangelio de Juan," *Estudios Eclesiásticos* 218-9 (1980), pp. 1055-73.

36. Aguirre, "Jesús y la multitud . . . Juan," p. 1086. With regard to v. 15: "When Jesus realized that they were about to come and take him by force to make him king, he withdrew again to the mountain by himself," Aguirre does not see this as the reason for the crowd's disillusion and later abandonment of him. From his exegetical analysis (pp. 1068ff) he concludes rather that "the historical fact that may be present in this verse could reflect Jesus' caution about the consequences that the crowd's reaction could bring from Herod's part" (p. 1069).

37. Aguirre, *Del movimiento de Jesús a la Iglesia cristiana* (Bilbao, 1987), p. 51.

38. Dodd, *The Founder*, p. 162.

39. Aguirre, "Jesús y la multitud . . . Juan," p. 1071.

40. X. Alegre, "Marcos o la corrección de una ideología triunfalista," *RLT* 6 (1985), p. 239.

41. See Rahner, "Ponderaciones dogmáticas sobre el saber de Cristo y su conciencia de sí mismo, *Escritos de teología* V (Madrid, 1964), pp. 221-43. Sp. trans. of *Schriften* V. Eng. trans. *Theological Investigations* 5 (London: Darton, Longman & Todd; Baltimore: Helicon Press, 1966).

42. Rahner, "Líneas fundamentales" (n. 26 above), p. 34.

43. *Ibid.*

44. Pannenberg, *Fundamentos*, p. 414, n. 24.

45. Rahner, *Escritos* V, p. 14.

46. Boff, *Jesucristo y la liberación del hombre* (Madrid, 2d ed., 1987), p. 137.

47. ST III, q. 7 a. 3.

48. See Rahner's critique, "Ponderaciones" (n. 41 above); Pannenberg, *Fundamentos*, pp. 405-15; H. Riedlinger, *Geschichtlichkeit und Vollendung des Wissens Christi* (Freiburg, 1966).

49. H. Urs von Balthasar, "Fides Christi," *Ensayos teológicos* II, *Sponsa Verbi* (Madrid, 1964), p. 67. Sp. trans. of *Sponsa Verbi. Skizzen zur Theologie* II (Einsiedeln, 1965); P. Schoonenberg, *Un Dios de los hombres* (Barcelona, 1973), pp. 168-74. Sp. trans. of *Hij is een God van mensen* (Den Bosch, 1969). Eng. trans. *The Christ: A Study of the God-Man Relationship in the Whole Creation and in Jesus Christ* (New York: Herder & Herder, 1971); C. Duquoc, "Jesus' Hope," *Concilium* 59 (vol. 9, no. 6) (1970); D. Wiederker, "Esbozo de cristología sistemática," *Mysterium salutis* III/I (Madrid, 1969), pp. 649-52; E. Fuchs, "Jesus und der Glaube," *Wort und Glaube* (Tübingen, 1962), pp. 203-54; Pannenberg, *Teología*, pp. 403-33.

50. W. Thüsing, "Neuetestamentliche Zugangswege zu einer transzendental-dialogischen Christologie," *Christologie*, pp. 211-26.

51. *Ibid.*, p. 220. For his exegetical analysis, pp. 218ff. He also translates v. 26 as "the faith *of* Jesus," as a parallel to 4:16: "the faith of Abraham."

52. J. O. Tuñí, "Pablo y Jesús. La vida de Jesús y la vida de Pablo," *RLT* 15 (1988), p. 296.

53. Thüsing, *Christologie*, pp. 212ff.

54. Tuñí, "'Jesús' en la carta a los Hebreos," *RLT* 9 (1986), pp. 283-302.

55. G. Baena, "El sacerdocio de Cristo," *Diakonia* 26 (19830, 128-34.

56. Boff, *Jesucristo y la liberación*, p. 122.

6. Jesus and God (2). Jesus' Prophetic Practice as Defense of the True God

1. H. Echegaray, *La práctica de Jesús* (Lima, 1981), pp. 52-3. Eng. trans. *The Practice of Jesus* (Maryknoll, N.Y.: Orbis Books, 1984). See also the classic work by J. Jeremias, *Jerusalem in the Time of Jesus* (London: SCM Press; New York: Harper & Row, 1969); J. I. González Faus, *Jesús y los ricos de su tiempo* (Mexico City, 1987).

2. Five more controversies appear at the end of his life, after the entrance to Jerusalem: the expulsion of the traders from the Temple (Matt. 21:12-17; Mark 11:11, 15-17; Luke 19:45-6), the controversy over Jesus' authority (Matt. 21:23-7; Mark 11:27-33; Luke 20:1-8), the tribute payable to Caesar (Matt. 22:15-22; Mark 12:13-17; Luke 20:20-26), the resurrection of the dead (Matt. 22:23-33; Mark 12:18-27; Luke 20:27-40) and the greatest commandment (Matt. 22:34-40; Mark 12:28-31. Luke moves this forward: 19:25-8). This chapter also deals with the greatest commandment.

3. P. Benoît and M. Boismard, *Sinopsis de los cuatro evangelios* II (Bilbao, 1976), pp. 96-110. (See n. 8 to ch. 5 above.)

4. *Ibid.*, p. 107.

5. H. Braun, *Jesús, el hombre de Nazaret y su tiempo* (Salamanca, 1974), p. 161.

6. *Ibid.*

7. *Ibid.*

8. X. Alegre, "La Iglesia que Jesús quería," *Diakonía* 51 (1989), p. 243.

9. I. Ellacuría, "Fe y justicia," *Christus* (Oct. 1977), pp. 23ff.

10. G. Bornkamm, *Jesús de Nazaret* (Salamanca, 3d ed., 1982), p. 105. Eng. trans. *Jesus of Nazareth* (London: Hodder & Stoughton, 1960, revised ed. 1980).

11. Benoît and Boismard, *Sinopsis*, pp. 328-31.

12. *Ibid*, p. 329.

13. Braun, *Jesús*, p. 163.

14. See J. L. Segundo, *The Liberation of Theology* (Maryknoll, N.Y.: Orbis Books; Dublin: Gill & Macmillan, 1977).

15. Braun, *Jesús*, p. 86.

16. E. Käsemann, *Exegetische Versuche und Besinnungen* (Göttingen, 1959), p. 207.

17. Bornkamm, *Jesús de Nazaret*, p. 11.

18. Käsemann, *La llamada de la libertad* (Salamanca, 2d ed., 1985), p. 35.

19. I. Ellacuría, *Conversión de la Iglesia al reino de Dios* (San Salvador, 1985), pp. 140ff.

20. J. L. McKenzie, "The Gospel according to St Matthew," *Jerome Biblical Commentary* III (Englewood Cliffs, N.J.: Prentice-Hall; London: Geoffrey Chapman, 1969).

21. Ellacuría, *Conversión*, p. 142.

22. G. M. Soares-Prabhu, "Clase en la Biblia," *RLT* 12 (1987), p. 228.

23. Clement of Alexandria, *Quis dives salvetur* 31, cited in González Faus, *Jesús y los ricos*, p. 69, nn. 40ff.

24. Letters, PL 22, 984. González Faus, *Vicarios de Cristo. Los pobres en la teología y espiritualidad cristianas* (Madrid, 1991), provides an anthology of texts on rich and poor throughout the history of the church.

25. C. Escudero Freire, *Devolver el evangelio a los pobres* (Salamanca, 1978), pp. 273, 315.

26. J. L. Sicre, *Los dioses olvidados* (Madrid, 1979), p. 107.

27. *Ibid.*, p. 116. He continues: "Because 'Mammon' is a secular god' it does not need

a sacred space or special ceremonies. Any site is good for its cult . . . any daily activity can be dedicated to it. . . . Amos did not confine himself to listing a series of actions; he also qualified them: of oppression . . . and vexation."

28. *Ibid.*, p. 164.

29. González Faus tackles the theme in this way: *La humanidad nueva*, pp. 57-71. On Jesus' attitude to the law, see J. Ernst, *Anfänge der Christologie* (Stuttgart, 1972), pp. 145ff; Käsemann, *La llamada*, pp. 22-54; C. Duquoc, *Cristología*, pp. 109ff; Jeremias, *Jerusalem*, pp. 240-47; Bornkamm, *Jesús*, pp. 101-5; L. Boff, *Jesucristo y la liberación del hombre* (Madrid, 3d ed., 1967), pp. 95ff.

30. Benoît and Boismard, *Sinopsis*, pp. 355ff.

31. E. Schillebeeckx, *Jesús. La historia de un viviente* (Madrid, 2d ed., 1963), pp. 220-26; González Faus, *Jesús y los ricos*, pp. 72-82. These show differing interpretations of the difficult incident of the expulsion of the traders from the Temple.

32. For Boismard, the nucleus of the tradition is to be found in Mark 11:15-16: *Sinopsis*, pp. 314ff.

33. Jeremias, *Jerusalem*, p. 175.

34. Ellacuría, "Carácter político de la misión de Jesús," *Teología política* (San Salvador, 1973), pp. 11-43.

Excursus 2. The Question of God: God of Life and Idols of Death

1. J. L. Segundo, *Nuestra idea de Dios* (Buenos Aires, 1970); idem, *Faith and Ideologies* (Maryknoll, N.Y.: Orbis Books, 1984); G. Gutiérrez, *The God of Life* (Maryknoll, N.Y.: Orbis Books; London: SCM Press, 1991); idem, *On Job: God-talk and the Suffering of the Innocent* (Maryknoll, N.Y.: Orbis Books, 1987); idem., *Dios o el oro en las Indias* (Salamanca, 2d ed., 1990); R. Muñoz, *The God of Christians* (Tunbridge Wells: Burns & Oates; Maryknoll, N.Y.: Orbis Books, 1991); P. Richard (ed.) *The Idols of Death and the God of Life* (Maryknoll, N.Y.: Orbis Books, 1983); V. Araya, *El Dios de los pobres* (San José, 1980); I. Ellacuría, "Voluntad de fundamentalidad y voluntad de verdad: conocimiento-fe y su configuración histórica," *RLT 8* (1986), pp. 113-31.

2. The conclusion could be the following: "God? Nothing other than a human projection (Feuerbach), the opium of the people (Marx), the resentment of the frustrated (Nietzsche), an infantile illusion (Freud)." Intro., "Dios de vida, ídolos de muerte," *Misión Abierta 5/6* (1985), p. 5.

3. M. Horkheimer, "The Longing for What is Wholly Other," *A la búsqueda del sentido* (Salamanca, 1976). Horkheimer opts for theology as "the expression of a wish, of a nostalgia for the executioner not to triumph over his innocent victim. . . . I am ever more convinced that one should speak not of the longing but of the fear that God may not exist."

4. I have analyzed this in "Reflexiones del significado del ateísmo y de la idolatría para la teología," *RLT 7* (1986), 45-81.

5. Frei Betto, "God is born from the experience of Life," Richard, (ed.) *The Idols of Death and the God of Life*, pp. 159-64.

6. Segundo, *Nuestra idea de Dios*, p. 18.

7. *Ibid.*

8. J. L. Sicre, *Los dioses olvidados*, p. 16. He excepts a few Old Testament experts, including G. von Rad.

9. *Ibid.*

10. W. Kasper, *Der Gott Jesu Christi* (Mainz, 1982).

11. O. Romero, "Unmasking the Idolatries of Our Society," *Voice of the Voiceless* (Maryknoll, N.Y.: Orbis Books; London: CIIR, 1985).

12. *Ibid.*

13. *Ibid.*

14. *Ibid.*

15. Ellacuría, "Historicidad de la salvación cristiana," *Mysterium liberationis* I (Madrid, 1990), pp. 323-72. Eng. trans. *Mysterium Liberationis* (Maryknoll, N.Y.: Orbis Books, 1993), pp. 251-89.

16. Analyzed in J. Sobrino, *Spirituality of Liberation* (Maryknoll, N.Y.: Orbis Books, 1988). For the spirituality needed to, on the one hand, fight against the basic idol, and, on the other, overcome the negative by-products of this struggle, see pp. 23-45.

17. S. Trinidad, J. Míguez Bonino (eds) *Faces of Jesus* (Maryknoll, N.Y.: Orbis Books, 1977), p. 57. For greater detail, see E. Dussel, *Fe cristiana y cambio social* (Salamanca, 1973), p. 67.

18. "Libertad y liberación," *RLT* 14 (1988), p. 190.

19. L. Boff, "Quinto centenario de América Latina: ¿Descubrimiento o encubrimiento?," *RLT* 21 (1990), p. 271.

20. "Perdona nuestras deudas como nosotros perdamos a nuestros deudores," *Mensaje de la diócesis de Colón y del viciarato del Darién*, 22 Jan. 1991.

21. G. von Rad, *Teología del Antiguo Testamento* (Salamanca, 1972), p. 269: Sp. trans. of *Theologie des Alten Testaments* (Munich, 4th ed., 1965): Eng. trans. *Old Testament Theology* (London: SCM Press; New York: Harper & Row, from 3d ed., 1965).

22. J. L. Sicre, *Con los pobres de la tierra* (Madrid, 1984), p. 448.

23. *Ibid.*, p. 457.

24. J. P. Miranda, *Marx y la Biblia* (Salamanca, 2d ed., 1972), pp. 62ff: Eng. trans. *Marx and the Bible* (Maryknoll, N.Y.: Orbis Books, 1974).

25. *Ibid.*, p. 63.

26. *Ibid.*

27. W. Schrage, *Etica del Nuevo Testamento* (Salamanca, 1986), p. 98. See n. 32 to ch. 4 above.

28. *Ibid.*, p. 97.

29. For exegesis and various interpretations, see *ibid.*, pp. 105-9; X. Pikaza, "Mateo 25:31-36: cristología y liberación," *Jesucristo en la historia y en la fe*, pp. 220-28.

30. Schrage, *Etica*, p. 107.

PART III: THE CROSS OF JESUS

7. The Death of Jesus (I): Why Jesus was Killed

1. I. Ellacuría, "Por qué muere Jesús y por qué le matan," *Diakonía* 8 (1978), pp. 65-75.

2. See the previously mentioned book by C. Bravo, *Jesús, hombre en conflicto* (Santander, 1986), in which the author analyzes the conflicts Jesus provoked according to Mark's account. I should like to add only that the very title embodies an essential fact about Jesus which is not usually reflected in other christologies, and that—in addition to the

exegetical analysis that justifies it—the author has been able to see that Mark's Gospel is "a small product of defeated people," because he writes among crucified peoples.

3. G. Bornkamm, *Jesús de Nazaret* (Salamanca, 2d ed. 1982), p. 161. Eng. trans. *Jesus of Nazareth* (London: Hodder & Stoughton, 1960; new ed. 1980), p. 153.

4. C. H. Dodd, *The Founder of Christianity* (New York, 1970 and London, 1971: Cambridge University Press), p. 128.

5. R. Aguirre, "Jesús y la multitud a la luz del evangelio de Juan," *Estudios Eclesiásticos* 218-9 (1980), pp. 1058-9.

6. E. Schillebeeckx, *Jesus. An Experiment in Christology* (London: Collins; New York: Harper & Row, 1979), pp. 294-8, tends to the view that Jesus also failed in some way with the people. However this may be, it should be stressed that it is one thing for the people not to have understood and to have been left with their hopes disappointed—although the acclamation at the entry to Jerusalem does not support this—and another for them to have taken part in the persecution, which is not historically plausible.

7. Bravo, Jesús, *hombre en conflicto*, p. 237.

8. *Ibid.*, pp. 237, 239.

9. X. Léon-Dufour, *Jesús y Pablo ante la muerte* (Madrid, 1982), p. 81. On Jesus' attitude to his death, see pp. 73-89. Eng. trans. *Life and Death in the New Testament. The Teaching of Jesus and Paul* (San Francisco: Harper, 1986).

10. Schillebeeckx, *Jesus*, p. 311

11. K. Rahner, "Líneas fundamentales de una cristología sistemática," *Cristología* (Madrid, 1975), pp. 32 and 38-9. (Eng. trans. see n. 13 to ch. 2 above.)

12. To take an example from the present, Archbishop Romero's words a few days before his murder are well-known: "If they kill me, I will rise again in the people of El Salvador. . . . May my blood be a seed of liberty and a sign that hope will soon become a reality. . . . May my death, if it is accepted by God, be for the liberation of my people and as a witness of hope in what is to come," *Romero: Martyr for Liberation* (London: CIIR, 1982), p. 76; *Voice of the Voiceless* (Maryknoll, N.Y.: Orbis Books; London: CIIR, 1985), pp. 50-51.

13. Léon-Dufour, *Jesús y Pablo*, p. 96.

14. X. Léon-Dufour, *La fracción del pan* (Madrid, 1983). Eng. trans. *Sharing the Eucharistic Bread* (Mahwah, N.J.: Paulist Press, 1987); R. Aguirre, *La cena de Jesús: historia y sentido* (Madrid, 1986).

15. Léon-Dufour, *La fracción del pan*, p. 117.

16. Aguirre, *La cena de Jesús*, p. 21.

17. *Ibid.*, pp. 42-6

18. Ellacuría, "Por qué muere Jesús," p. 71.

19. Schillebeeckx, *Jesus*, p. 303.

20. H. Schürmann, *¿Cómo entendió y vivió Jesús su muerte?* (Salamanca, 1982).

21. P. Benoît and M. E. Boismard, *Sinopsis de los cuatro evangelios* II (Bilbao, 1976), pp. 382-3. (See n. 8 to ch. 5 above.)

22. Benoît and Boismard, *Sinopsis* II, p. 382.

23. Schillebeeckx, *Jesus*, pp. 312-8.

24. *Ibid.*, p. 316.

25. J. I. González Faus, *La humanidad nueva. Ensayo de cristología* (Santander, 7th ed., 1987), pp. 20, 26.

26. Benoît and Boismard, p. 383.

27. J. Moltmann, *El Dios crucificado* (Salamanca, 1977), pp. 181-3. Eng. trans. *The Crucified God* (London: SCM Press; New York: Harper & Row, 1974), pp. 128-36.

28. X. Alegre, "Marcos o la corrección de una ideología triunfalista," *RLT* 6 (1985), p. 233.

29. Benoît and Boismard, *Sinopsis* II, p. 392; Bornkamm, *Jesús de Nazaret*, p. 173.

30. Benoît and Boismard, *Sinopsis* II, p. 391.

31. Bornkamm, *ibid.*, p. 172.

32. Benoît and Boismard, p. 392.

33. H. Braun, *Jesús, el hombre de Nazaret y su tiempo* (Salamanca, 1974), p. 65.

34. To give one notorious example among many, Archbishop Romero was not only regarded as "subversive," but in the files of one department of police intelligence he was listed—amazingly—as a top leader of a politico-military movement.

35. Ellacuría, *Freedom Made Flesh* (Maryknoll, N.Y.: Orbis Books, 1976), pp. 71-2.

36. X. Alegre, "Mi reino no es de este mundo," *Diakonia* 21 (1982), pp. 68-82, whom I follow on this point.

37. Alegre comments: "Jesus' remark exposes the elements of sin and untruth which may exist in the way the 'world' is and acts (and political authorities, when they possess the power of coercion, can easily fall into the temptation of not being guided by the principles of love and service or, at least, 'the world' will want to manipulate them), and 'force' 'the world' to take stands against Jesus," "Mi reino," p. 80.

38. Ellacuría, *Freedom Made Flesh*, p. 74.

39. Alegre, "Mi reino no es de este mundo," p. 73.

40. J. Moltmann, *The Crucified God*, p. 136. On the achievements and failures of the *pax romana*, see the critical analysis by K. Wengst, *Pax Romana. Anspruch und Wirklichkeit* (Munich, 1986), pp. 19-71; X. Alegre, "Violencia y Nuevo Testamento," *RLT* 23, analyzes the attitude of Christians to it: open criticism in Revelation, adaptation in Luke and mediation in Paul.

41. Ellacuría, *Freedom Made Flesh*, p. 75.

42. Ellacuría, "Por qué muere Jesús," p. 66.

43. C. Duquoc, "El Dios de Jesús y la crisis de Dios en nuestro tiempo," *Jesucristo en la historia y en la fe*, p. 49.

44. E. Käsemann, *La llamada de la libertad* (Salamanca, 2d ed. 1985, p.38).

45. R. Bultmann, *Die urchristliche Christusbotschaft* (Tübingen, 1970), p. 12.

Excursus 3: Jesus and Violence

1. J. Hernández-Pico, "Revolución, violencia y paz," *Mysterium liberationis* II (Madrid, 1991), pp. 614-15.

2. I. Ellacuría, "Violence and Non-Violence in the Struggle for Peace and Liberation," *Concilium* 215 (1988), pp. 69-97.

3. Medellín here quotes Paul VI, *Populorum Progressio*, 31.

4. J. Sobrino and others, *Voice of the Voiceless* (Maryknoll, N.Y.: Orbis Books; London: CIIR, 1985), pp. 85-161. The third pastoral letter is also available separately: *Christians, Political Organizations and Violence* (London: CIIR, 1985).

5. From a pastoral point of view, he stressed the need for pastoral accompaniment for

Christians involved in these struggles. His successor, Archbishop Rivera, has insisted on the need to "humanize the conflict."

6. As early as 1973 he published "Violencia y la cruz" in his book *Teologia politica* (San Salvador, 1973), pp. 95-127. Eng. trans. "Violence and the Cross", *Freedom Made Flesh* (Maryknoll, N.Y.: Orbis Books, 1976, pp. 165-231.

7. Ellacuría, "Violence and Non-Violence."

8. In note 22 to chapter 4, I mentioned authors who question the existence of a Zealot movement in Jesus' time, which would undercut the classic studies such as those of M. Hengel, *The Zealots*; O. Cullmann, *The State in the New Testament* and *Jesus and the Revolutionaries of His Time* (cf Ellacuría, *Freedom Made Flesh*, pp. 60-69), and certainly the thesis of S. G. F. Brandon, *Jesus and the Zealots* (Manchester: Manchester University Press, 1967). I cannot go into the area of critical exegesis, but with other exegetes I assume the existence of some armed groups and armed activity.

9. At least this is the impression the original readers of the Gospels would get, since when they were published Zealot movements certainly existed.

10. O. Cullmann, *El Estado en el Nuevo Testamento* (Madrid, 1966), p. 64. Eng. trans. *The State in the New Testament* (London: SCM Press; New York: Macmillan, 1957).

11. In the article by X. Alegre quoted in n. 40 to ch. 7, the author finds that none of the New Testament communities chose armed struggle to solve the problems created for them by the Roman Empire—which would anyway have been a historical impossibility—but their attitudes were very diverse, which shows that they did not see Jesus as providing an absolutely clear rule on how to deal with the issues between the emerging church and the repressive state.

12. J. I. González Faus, "La buena noticia de Jesús ante la mala noticia de un mundo violento," *Cristianos en una sociedad violenta* (Santander, 1980), pp. 185-98.

13. Ellacuría, "Violence and the Cross," pp. 172-85.

14. González Faus, "La buena noticia de Jesús," p. 189.

15. González Faus, *ibid.*, p. 187.

16. In my *Liberación con espíritu* (San Salvador, 1966), pp. 40ff., Eng. trans. *Spirituality of Liberation* (Maryknoll, N.Y.: Orbis Books, 1988), pp. 27ff., I have collected Archbishop Romero's criticisms of popular liberation movements, which today he would have extended to include the armed popular movements.

17. Ellacuría, in "Violence and the Cross," pp. 217-26, analyzes three Christian ways of redeeming violence, typified in Charles de Foucauld, Martin Luther King, Jr. and Camilo Torres. He analyzes them as Christian, different, and possibly complementary, and concludes with what is common to all three: "All three approaches recognize the reality of the sin of violence, of the mystery of iniquity which dominates so many political and socio-economic structures and which represents the very negation of a Christian order. All three feel that it is imperative for the Christian conscience to respond to this situation, and that this response involves a personal commitment of one's own life even to the extreme demanded by Christian love, that is death" (p. 123).

18. Ellacuría, "Violence and Non-Violence," pp. 86-8.

8. The Death of Jesus (2): Why Jesus Died

1. The New Testament analysis I use in this chapter is based on L. Boff, *Jesucristo y la liberación del hombre* (Madrid, 2d ed. 1987), pp. 367-404; E. Schillebeeckx, *Jesús. La*

historia de un viviente (Madrid, 2d ed. 1983), pp. 249-68. Eng. trans. *Jesus, An Experiment in Christology* (London, 1979), pp. 273-94; X. Léon-Dufour, *Jesús y Pablo ante la muerte* (Madrid, 1982), pp. 173-205. Eng. trans. *Life and Death in the New Testament. The teaching of Jesus and Paul* (San Francisco: Harper, 1986); J. I.González Faus, *Acceso a Jesús* (Salamanca, 6th ed. 1987), pp.128-36. I shall refer to them without giving specific references.

2. On the theological problem of the reality of sacrifice and priesthood, see J. Sobrino, "Hacia una determinación de la realidad sacerdotal," *RLT* 1 (1984), pp. 47-81.

3. "The expiatory sacrifices of the Temple, in which animals were offered and their blood shed, prevented such an explanation," Boff, *Jesucristo y la liberación del hombre*, p. 374.

4. A model with a greater impact on the imagination is that of the ransom Christ paid for our transgressions (1 Pet. 1:18; Mark 10:45; Gal. 3:13, etc.). The model is taken from the price that had to be paid for the freeing of a slave—in Latin *redemptio*, from where the word "redemption" comes. Related to this model is that of *purchase* (1 Cor. 6:20; 7:23): God acquires a people for himself by paying the price of the cross for it.

5. González Faus, *Acceso a Jesús*, p. 505.

6. *El precio de la gracia* (Salamanca, 3d ed., 1986), p. 211.

7. J. Moltmann, *Umkehr zur Zukunft* (Hamburg, 1970), p. 76.

8. J. Sobrino and others, *La voz de los sin voz*, p. 367.

9. The Death of Jesus (3): The Crucified God

1. L. Boff, *Jesucristo y la liberación del hombre* (Madrid, 2d ed., 1987), p. 367.

2. P. Casaldáliga, "The 'Crucified' Indians.   A Case of Anonymous Collective Martyrdom," *Concilium* 163 (1983), p. 51.

3. J. Moltmann, *The Crucified God* (London: SCM Press; New York: Harper & Row, 1974), pp. 200-07.

4. "Cheap grace is the deadly enemy of our church," Bonhoeffer said, *The Cost of Discipleship* (London: SCM Press: New York: Macmillan) p. 35. In the same way, we have to be on our guard against "cheap revelation," as though we had been told who God is without any objective or subjective scandal.

5. X. Léon-Dufour, *Jesús y Pablo ante la muerte* (Madrid, 1982), pp. 159-60. Eng. trans. *Life and Death in the New Testament. The Teaching of Jesus and Paul* (San Francisco: Harper, 1986).

6. In John the cry is replaced by "then he bowed his head and gave up his spirit" (19:30).

7. Léon-Dufour, *Jesús y Pablo*, p. 155. It is difficult to determine what Jesus' last words were, and various hypotheses have been proposed. Léon-Dufour, pp. 155ff., based on H. Salin and T. Boman, mentions the following one. What might really have been heard by the listeners was words mentioning the prophet Elijah. In Mark 15:34 Jesus utters his cry of abandonment in Aramaic: "*Eloi, Eloi, lema sabacthani,*" and the evangelist adds that the bystanders misunderstood the words as: "He is calling for Elijah" (v. 34). What therefore may have occurred is that the listeners heard the following words in Aramaic: *alia ta* ("Elijah, come"). But in Aramaic these words sound very similar to *eli atta*, "You are my God." The cry of complaint at abandonment by God may really have been a cry of commitment to God.

8. See X. Alegre, "Marcos o la correción de una ideología triunfalista," *RLT* 6 (1985), pp. 229-63.

9. P. Benoît, *Pasión y resurrección del Señor* (Madrid, 1971), pp. 220ff. Eng. trans. *The Passion and Resurrection of Jesus Christ* (New York: Herder & Herder, 1969), pp. 193ff.

10. What I have been describing is no more than an example of something much more serious, the constant attempt to tame Jesus' cross. It can be turned—with difficulty—into an ascetic and meritorious ideal, into something positive, in the end. Or it can be made the basis for the existence in Christianity of a sacrificial "cult" in which there is an unbloody commemoration—and taming of what in reality was very bloody. See Moltmann, *The Crucified God*, pp. 32-44.

11. We should remember Bultmann's famous comment: "It is impossible for us to know whether death had any meaning for Jesus. . . . We cannot exclude the possibility that it shattered him as a person," "Das Verhältnis der urchristlichen Christusbotschaft zum historischen Jesus," *Exegetica* (Tübingen, 1967), p. 453. The first sentence is usually criticized with reference to Jesus' words at the Last Supper, but the second has the advantage of reminding us provocatively of the danger of trivializing the death of Jesus in advance.

12. We do not know with what attitude and what explicit words Archbishop Romero died, but we have the words he spoke shortly before his death in which he thinks of his death in continuity with his mission: "If God accepts the sacrifice of my life, then may my blood be the seed of liberty, and a sign that hope will soon become a reality. . . . But I wish that they could realize that they are wasting their time. A bishop may die, but the church of God, which is the people, will never die," quoted in *Voice of the Voiceless*, p. 51.

13. Léon-Dufour, *Jesús y Pablo*, p. 159.

14. *Ibid.*, p. 160.

15. Let us remember their dialogues with God about their misfortunes. In the first account (Jer. 11:18—12:5), these misfortunes are a threat to Jeremiah's life: "You shall not prophesy in the name of the Lord, or you will die by our hand" (11:21). Jeremiah then turns to God, because he has entrusted his cause to him, and asks him to take vengeance on his enemies, and Yahweh replies that he will come to the aid of his prophet. In a second account (Jer. 15:10-21), Jeremiah complains again. He has borne the insults of the people for preaching Yahweh's word and his situation is desperate: "Woe is me, my mother, that you ever bore me, a man of strife and contention to the whole land!" (v. 10). And Yahweh replies: "They will fight against you, but they shall not prevail over you, for I am with you to save you and deliver you" (v. 19). Here Yahweh does not say that he will take full vengeance on his enemies, but continues to talk to Jeremiah and promise him his closeness. Jeremiah speaks to Yahweh twice more (17:14-18 and 18:18-23), and again complains, but now, in both accounts, there is no word of Yahweh: he neither promises to take vengeance on his enemies, nor even that he will be with him; there is only silence. In the last conversation (20:7-18), Jeremiah explodes: "Cursed be the day on which I was born!" (v. 14), at the climax of affliction of the prophet abandoned by God in his mission. Nevertheless Jeremiah surrenders to God: "O Lord, you have enticed me, and I was enticed. . . . Within me there is something like a burning fire, shut up in my bones. I am weary with holding it in, and I cannot" (vv. 7, 9).

16. Schillebeeckx, *Jesus*, p. 317.

17. Moltmann, *El Dios Crucificado*, p. 210. (See n. 3 above.)

18. In the chapter "The cross and death in current theology," *Jesucristo y la liberación del hombre*, pp. 405-36, Boff looks at the different theological positions on the question of God and suffering, and I shall summarize his discussion. The page references given in the text are to Boff's book.

19. Boff, p. 406.

20. Moltmann, *El Dios crucificado*, p. 269.

21. *Ibid.*, pp. 348-9.

22. *La voz de los sin voz*, p. 460.

23. Boff, *Jesucristo*, p. 419.

24. In this sense, J. I. González Faus and J. Jiménez Limón are correct in their critical remarks on what I wrote in *Christology at the Crossroads*. See *Christus* 511 (1978), pp. 3ff, 58ff.

25. This, in my view, could be the most appropriate place to consider popular religion. Again the critical remarks made about me by J. I. González Faus and J. Jiménez Limón in the article mentioned in the last note on not exaggerating the distinction between faith and religion are correct. In my view, the central element of popular religion is the need to dominate life at primary levels and an understanding of God from that standpoint, which seems to me completely legitimate, whatever subsequent dangers there may be. On popular religion, see D. Irarazaval,"Religión popular," *Mysterium liberationis* II (Madrid, 1990), pp. 345-75.

26. D. Bonhoeffer, *Letters and Papers from Prison*, 3d revised edition (London: SCM Press; New York: Macmillan, 1971), pp. 348-9.

27. W. Schrage, *Etica del Nuevo Testamento* (Salamanca, 1986), p. 107: "God has identified himself with the poor, with the hungry, with the sick and with prisoners." Eng. trans, *Ethics of the New Testament* (Edinburgh: T. & T. Clark; Philadelphia, PA: Fortress Press, 1988).

28. J. I. González Faus, "Los pobres como lugar teológico," *RLT* 3 (1984), pp. 275-308.

29. G. Gutiérrez *RLT* 15 (1988), pp. 233-41.

30. *Ibid.*, pp. 233-41.

31. P. Casaldáliga, *Todavía estas palabras*, (Estella, 1989), p. 45.

10. The Death of Jesus (4): The Crucified People

1. For recent data, see n. 29 to ch. 2 above.

2. In this chapter I frequently quote Ignacio Ellacuría, not only because his martyrdom has made him forever a member of the crucified people, but because he was always deeply aware of it in everything he did, and because as a theologian he was, in my opinion, a pioneer in developing the theology of Third World peoples as crucified peoples.

3. J. Sobrino and others, *La voz de los sin voz* (San Salvador, 1980), p. 208. Eng. trans. *Voice of the Voiceless* (Maryknoll, N.Y.: Orbis Books; London: CIIR, 1985).

4. *Ibid.*, p. 366.

5. I. Ellacuría, "Discernir el signo de los tiempos," *Diakonia* 17 (1981), p. 58.

6. Ellacuría, "El pueblo crucificado. Ensayo de soteriología histórica," *RLT* 18 (1989), pp. 305-333, first published, Various, *Cruz y resurrección* (Mexico, 1978), pp. 49-82 and later in *Mysterium liberationis* II (Madrid 1990), pp. 189-217. Eng. trans. "The Crucified People," *Mysterium Liberationis* (Maryknoll, N.Y.: Orbis Books, 1993), pp. 580-604.

7. Ellacuría, "El pueblo crucificado," p. 326
8. Quoted in *ibid.*, p. 308.
9. *Ibid.*, p. 331.
10. "Quinto Centenario. América Latina, ¿descubrimiento o encubrimiento?," *RLT* 21 (1990), p. 278.
11. *Ibid.*, p.277.
12. Ellacuría, "The Kingdom of God and Unemployment in the Third World," *Concilium* 160 (1982), pp. 91-6.
13. Ellacuría, "El desafío de las mayorías pobres," *ECA* 493-4 (1989), pp. 1075-80.
14. In my first essay I analyzed how the poor originate liberation movements for themselves. Here I concentrate on the salvation they bring "the nations" through their formal likeness to the Servant.
15. Ellacuría, *Teología política* (San Salvador 1973), pp. 1-10. Eng. trans. *Freedom Made Flesh* (Maryknoll, N.Y.: Orbis Books, 1976), pp. 3-19.
16. "Las Iglesias latinoamericanas interpelan a la Iglesia de España," *Sal Terrae* 826 (1982), p. 230.
17. These reflections are based on my particular experience of El Salvador. J. Sobrino, "Pecado personal, perdón y liberación," *RLT* 13 (1988) pp. 26-9.
18. J. Sobrino, "Conllevaos mutuamente. Análisis teológico de la solidaridad," *ECA* 401 (1982), pp. 157-78; "La comunión eclesial alrededor del pueblo crucificado," *RLT* 20 (1990), pp. 157-60.
19. J. M. Castillo, "El martirio en la Iglesia," *ECA* 505-506 (1990), pp. 959-65.
20 D. E. López, *Análisis histórico y teológico de la persecución y el martirio de los cristianos en los tres primeros siglos,* (San Salvador, 1989), thesis presented to the José Simeón Cañas Central American University.
21. This is how K. Rahner presents the usual concept of martyrdom from the viewpoint of dogmatics and fundamental theology, *LThK* VII, p. 136.
22. "Dimensions of Martyrdom: A Plea for the Broadening of the Classical Concept," *Concilium* 163 (1983), p. 10.
23. "Martyrdom: An Attempt at Systematic Reflection," *Concilium* 163 (1983), p. 12.
24. *Ibid.*, p. 15.
25. J. Hernández Pico, "Martyrdom Today in Latin America: Stumbling-Block, Folly and Power of God," *Concilium* 163 (1983), pp. 37-42; J. Sobrino, *Spirituality of Liberation* (Maryknoll, N.Y.: Orbis Books, 1985), pp. 80-102, 153-6; *The True Church and the Poor* (Maryknoll, N.Y.: Orbis Books; London: CIIR, 1988), pp. 160-93, 228-52; "Persecución a la Iglesia en Centroamérica," *ECA* 393 (1981) pp. 645-64.
26. J. M. Valverde, *Carta a las Iglesias* 136 (1987), p. 1.
27. ST II-II. q. 124, a 2, ad 2.
28. Romero, *La voz de los sin voz*, p. 330.
29. This is the place to mention the "anonymous martyrs," following the logic of the "anonymous Christians," and I think it is necessary to consider them today. To put it succinctly, during our lives we human beings have names and surnames. At death, we lose our names (Christians, Buddhists, Moslems, Hindus, agnostics, atheists . . .) but when we die for love we recover forever the name of "human" which God has given us all.
30. ST II-II, q.124, a 4, ad 3. He also states that those who die "defending the country from attack by enemies who were plotting the corruption of the Christian faith" can be

called martyrs, in *IV Sent. dis.* XLIX, q. V, a 3, *quaest.* 2, ad 11. The fundamental reason for these statements is that "not only one who suffers for faith in Christ, but also one who suffers for any work of justice, suffers for Christ" (*In Ep. ad Rom.*, c. VIII, *lect.* 7).

31. Sometimes I think that in order to possess the virtues usually required by the canonization processes, you have to belong to a socio-economic group that makes them possible. Structurally speaking, the poor cannot be quantitatively generous, they cannot humbly abase themselves, and they cannot offer professional talents for the service of others. Nor, in the absence of any other source of gratification, can they shine in virtues like purity. . . . So we must rethink the very idea of sainthood. Besides the real virtues the poor can possess, we believe they share in a primary holiness of a special kind, quasi-metaphysical we might call it, in their elemental work and hope simply to get by in life.

Epilogue

1. L. Boff, *Jesucristo y la liberación del hombre* (Madrid, 2d ed., 1987), pp. 437-41, 442.

2. J. L. Segundo, *El hombre de hoy ante Jesús de Nazaret* (Madrid, 1982), p. 11. See n. 9 to Intro. above.

Index